UML FOR REAL

UML for Real

Design of Embedded Real-Time Systems

Edited by

Luciano Lavagno
Politecnico di Torino, Torino, Italy and
Cadence Berkeley Labs, Berkeley, California, U.S.A.

Grant Martin
Cadence Berkeley Labs, Berkeley, California, U.S.A.

and

Bran Selic
Rational Software Canada and
Carleton University, Ottawa, Canada

KLUWER ACADEMIC PUBLISHERS
BOSTON / DORDRECHT / LONDON

A C.I.P. Catalogue record for this book is available from the Library of Congress.

ISBN 978-1-4419-5368-1   e-ISBN 978-0-306-48738-5

Published by Kluwer Academic Publishers,
P.O. Box 17, 3300 AA Dordrecht, The Netherlands.

Sold and distributed in North, Central and South America
by Kluwer Academic Publishers,
101 Philip Drive, Norwell, MA 02061, U.S.A.

In all other countries, sold and distributed
by Kluwer Academic Publishers,
P.O. Box 322, 3300 AH Dordrecht, The Netherlands.

Printed on acid-free paper

Contents

About the Editors

Bran Selic is Principal Engineer at the Rational Software division of IBM. In addition, he is an adjunct professor of computer science at Carleton University. He has over 30 years of experience in industry in the design and development of large real-time systems. He is the principal author of the book "Real-Time Object-Oriented Modelling," (1994), which pioneered the application of both object technology and model-driven development methods in the real-time domain. Bran has been involved with the definition and standardization of the Unified Modelling Language (UML) standard since 1996 including its first standard real-time profile. He received his Bachelor's degree in electrical engineering and a Master's degree in systems theory from the University of Belgrade in 1972 and 1974 respectively. He has been living and working in Canada since 1977.

Luciano Lavagno is a researcher at Cadence Berkeley Labs and an associate professor in the Department of Electronics of Politecnico di Torino. Before that, he worked for the research lab of Telecom Italia. He received his PhD in EECS from U.C. Berkeley in 1992 and from Politecnico di Torino in 1993.

Luciano is a co-author of two books on asynchronous circuit design and testing, and of a book on embedded system design. He was the architect of the POLIS project, which defined and implemented a complete hardware/software co-design environment for reactive embedded systems. He has been involved as technical program committee member and chair in several conferences and symposia, such as DAC, DATE, ICCAD, ICCD, CODES, and ASYNC. His main research interests are system-level modeling, design and synthesis, hardware/software co-design, dynamically reconfigurable hardware, and asynchronous circuit synthesis and testing.

Grant Martin is a Fellow in the Labs of Cadence Design Systems. He joined Cadence in late 1994. Before that, Grant worked for Burroughs in Scotland for 6 years and Nortel/BNR in Canada for 10 years. He received his Bachelor's and Master's degrees in Mathematics (Combinatorics and Optimisation) from the University of Waterloo, Canada, in 1977 and 1978.

Grant is a co-author of the books *Surviving the SOC Revolution: A Guide to Platform-Based Design*, published by Kluwer Academic Publishers, in November of 1999, and *System Design with SystemC*, published by Kluwer in May of 2002, and an editor of the book *Winning the SoC Revolution: Experiences in Real Design*, to be published by Kluwer in June of 2003. He co-chaired the VSI Alliance Embedded Systems study group in the summer of 2001. His particular areas of interest include system-level design, System-on-Chip, Platform-Based design, and embedded software.

Acknowledgements

Bran Selic would like to acknowledge all those people who have not yet given up on him—assuming that this is not an empty set, of course.

Luciano Lavagno would like to acknowledge his wife Paola and his newborn daughter Alessandra.

Grant Martin would like to acknowledge, as always, his wife Margaret Steele, and his daughters Jennifer and Fiona. He would also like to acknowledge the encouragement of his father and mother, John (Ted) and Mary Martin.

The three of us would like to acknowledge all the hard work by the contributors of the chapters in this edited volume. Any mistakes found should be regarded as the responsibility of the editors.

Preface

The complexity of most real-time and embedded systems often exceeds that of other types of systems since, in addition to the usual spectrum of problems inherent in software, they need to deal with the complexities of the physical world. That world—as the proverbial Mr. Murphy tells us—is an unpredictable and often unfriendly place. Consequently, there is a very strong motivation to investigate and apply advanced design methods and technologies that could simplify and improve the reliability of real-time software design and implementation.

As a result, from the first versions of UML issued in the mid 1990's, designers of embedded and real-time systems have taken to UML with vigour and enthusiasm. However, the dream of a complete, model-driven design flow from specification through automated, optimised code generation, has been difficult to realise without some key improvements in UML semantics and syntax, specifically targeted to the real-time systems problem.

With the enhancements in UML that have been proposed and are near standardisation with UML 2.0, many of these improvements have been made. In the Spring of 2003, adoption of a formalised UML 2.0 specification by the members of the Object Management Group (OMG) seems very close. It is therefore very appropriate to review the status of UML as a set of notations for embedded real-time systems - both the state of the art and best practices achieved up to this time with UML of previous generations - and where the changes embodied in the 2.0 specification are taking us.

This book, *UML for Real: Design of Embedded Real-Time Systems*, was created to provide that survey of UML theory and practice when applied to the real-time systems problem. The book aims to show the reality of UML as a medium for specification and implementation of real-time systems, illustrating both the current capabilities and limits of UML for this task, and future directions that will improve its usefulness for real-time and embedded product design. It also covers selected applications examples. The book is constructed as an edited volume of contributed chapters written by the real experts in this field. Each chapter has extensive references for those readers interested in follow-up reading.

The first chapter, *Models, Software Models and UML,* is a short discussion of the role and position of UML in software development in general. This includes a description of how UML is being used in specific application domains - the definition and use of profiles, within an overall model-driven architecture approach. Chapter 2, *UML for Real Time*, is an objective critique of UML as a tool for developing real-time software; the advantages that it brings and, more importantly, the difficulties encountered and approaches used to overcome those difficulties.

The next set of chapters cover how essential real-time concepts and patterns can be represented with UML. Chapter 3, *Structural Modeling with UML 2.0*, deals with how UML can be used to model the complex software structures that are typically encountered in large real-time software systems, including structural decomposition and identification of basic logical entities. It is followed by an extensive chapter dealing with the modeling of the dynamics of real-time systems using UML, including the necessary extensions to Sequence Diagrams and other notations. The chapter, *Message Sequence Charts*, presents the current state of the art concerning MSCs and related notions, such as HMSCs (Hierarchical Message Sequence Charts) and LSCs (Live Sequence Charts), including some proposals for adding object features (in particular classes) and timing constraints.

We then consider the modeling of common real-time mechanisms and target platforms. Chapter 5, *UML and Platform-based Design*, covers stereotypes and extensions to notations to represent platform services and their attributes and characteristics as a target for embedded software development. It also presents a design methodology for embedded systems that is fully in accordance with platform-based design principles. The next chapter, *UML for Hardware and Software Object Modeling*, is based on the HASoC design method for the lifecycle modeling of embedded systems. The object-oriented development technique supports a lifecycle that explicitly separates the behaviour of a system from its hardware and software implementation technologies. The methodology emphasizes the reuse of pre-existing hardware and software models to ease the development process.

Chapter 7, *Fine-Grained Patterns for Real-time Systems,* applies the theory of pattern-based design to the real time world with basic dynamic and static patterns. Chapter 8 then follows with high-level or architectural patterns for modeling real-time software systems, in *Architectural Patterns for Real-time systems*.

The next two chapters deal with quantitative modeling concepts. *Modeling Quality of Service with UML* describes how quantitative aspects can be introduced into UML models; in particular, how quality of service parameters are rendered in the standard real-time UML profile. *Modeling Metric Time* covers some of the abstract concepts of time modeling and how they are reflected in UML.

Chapter 11, *Performance Analysis with UML*, covers methods for applying traditional performance analysis techniques to UML models with special focus on the standard real-time UML profile. The next chapter, *Schedulability Analysis with UML*, applies schedulability theory for real-time systems in the UML context.

In the last part of the book we start looking at specific applications. Chapter 13 deals with the application of UML in the automotive domain. *Automotive UML* includes the structuring of requirements and presents the AML, a modeling language tailored to the development of embedded automotive systems based on the UML. Chapters 14 and 15, *Specifying Telecommunications Systems with UML*, and *Leveraging UML to Deliver Correct Telecom Applications*, deal specifically with the specification, design, implementation and verification of telecom systems using UML 2.0.

The last chapter, 16, *Software Performance Engineering*, illustrates the process of developing real-time systems based on the use of UML and quantitative analysis methods.

This comprehensive look at the status and applicability of UML to the real-time systems world, on the eve of the UML 2.0 adoption, will be useful to all who wish to find out more about UML, and apply it to the design and development of real products. The authors hope that this collection is one small step on the way to making UML a reality for all software and system designers.

Bran Selic
Luciano Lavagno
Grant Martin
Ottawa, Torino and Berkeley
April 2003

Chapter 1

Models, Software Models and UML

Bran Selic
Rational Software Canada Co.

Abstract: The use of models in the design of complex engineering systems is a long-standing tradition that is almost as old as engineering. Yet, its applicability to software has often been questioned. In this chapter, we explain why modeling and model-based techniques are, in fact, the only viable way of coping with the kind of complexity that is encountered in modern software systems (and, in particular, in embedded and real-time systems). The essentials of model-driven development methods are explained and the role that the Unified Modeling Language plays in them is described. The ability to customize UML for such purposes is also covered.

Key words: engineering models, software modeling, Unified Modeling Language, UML

1.   ON MODELS

1.1   The Role of Models in Engineering

In 1418 A.D., the guild of wool merchants of Florence announced a competition for a method of constructing the dome that was to cap the magnificent Santa Maria del Fiore cathedral. This presented a unique and very difficult engineering problem. First, the design called for a dome that was bigger than any built up to that time. Second, and even more challenging, this enormous dome was to have no external lateral supports, since the architect had deemed them "inelegant". Such supports, usually in the form of so-called "flying buttresses", served to counter the effects of the significant lateral forces generated by large vertical edifices.

The specifications for the cathedral and its dome were in the form of a scale model, which served to convey design intent to the construction team and also as a feasibility proof (the non-linear effects of scaling up were not

L. Lavagno, G. Martin and B. Selic (eds.), UML for Real, 1-16.
© 2003 *Kluwer Academic Publishers.*

fully understood at the time). Accordingly, submitters were asked to provide scale models that would demonstrate the proposed construction method.

Perhaps surprisingly, the winning entry did not come from a master mason but from a goldsmith, Philippo Brunelleschi. His model was made out of wood, brick, and mortar and was large enough to allow members of the jury to walk inside and inspect its interior. The most distinguishing and innovative aspect of this proposal was the claim that this dome of unprecedented dimensions was to be constructed *without* the use of expensive wooden scaffolding to support the vaulted ceiling during construction—even though at its apex the ceiling leaned as much as 30 degrees away from the vertical! Nothing similar had ever been attempted previously on such a scale and it is no understatement to say that the proposal carried a great deal of uncertainty [1].

Nonetheless, based on the insight and experience gained during the construction of his model, Brunelleschi felt confident and, despite dire warnings from numerous skeptics, he was able to convince the jury that the project was technically feasible. So, the model served not only to demonstrate the proposal to the clients, but also as a testbed for validating a new method of construction. Today, the magnificent dome of Santa Maria del Fiore, still the largest dome ever constructed with bricks and mortar, stands as much a testament to Brunelleschi's ingenuity as to the effectiveness of models in engineering.

The use of models for specifying systems is a long-standing engineering tradition that reaches into antiquity. There is evidence that it was a standard practice in Ancient Greece. Vitruvius, a Roman architect who lived in the first century B.C., discusses the use of models in the design of buildings and machinery of various kinds [2]. In the 15th century, Galileo introduced the notion of formal mathematical models that significantly increased the reliability of engineering design.

The main purpose of engineering models is to help us understand the interesting aspects of a complex system *before* going through the expense and effort of actually constructing it[1]. A good model can help shed light on features of a system where there is uncertainty either about requirements or about the adequacy of a proposed solution particularly where the complexity is such that unaided human reasoning is insufficient.

Besides risk mitigation, another fundamental purpose of engineering models is to communicate design ideas to the various parties interested in the system. This includes the many diverse members of the design and

---

[1] Engineering models are also used to analyze existing systems; for example, in situations where it might be too expensive or impractical to experiment with the actual system or because a model better isolates the phenomenon of interest.

construction teams including the patrons for whom the system is being built, as well as the intended users of the system. Of course, different stakeholders may require a different model emphasizing those aspects that are of interest to them. For example, in case of an airplane, the model used by an aerodynamicist is completely different than the one used by the designer of the cabin interior.

1.2   Characteristics of Good Engineering Models

There are a number of key requirements that any good engineering model must fulfill: first, it must support abstraction, that is, it must avoid or hide detail that is irrelevant to the domain of concern. This helps us focus on the important aspects of the problem. Second, it must be expressed in a form (notation, shape) that is close to our intuition, so that we can most easily comprehend it. For example, it is a lot easier to appreciate the esthetic aspects of a proposed building design from a three-dimensional scale model than a corresponding textual description or even a technical drawing. Similarly, a high-level functional block diagram of an electronic circuit is usually much easier to absorb than a corresponding fully-detailed electrical schematic. Third, a good model must be accurate, which means that it must faithfully represent the interesting aspects of the modeled system. Fourth, it should be possible to make accurate predictions about interesting properties of the modeled system from the information provided by the model. Last but not least, a good model must be significantly cheaper to construct or cheaper to experiment with than the actual system. Models that are lacking in any one of these characteristics are likely not to be very suitable as engineering models.

1.3   Models of Software

While the use of models in traditional engineering disciplines is generally accepted as a useful and effective technique, there is still an ongoing debate as to whether it is applicable in the case of software engineering[2]. There are numerous technical and social reasons for this. Regardless of the fact that we know so much about science and engineering in general, software development is an emerging and quite unique discipline that is often applied to systems of unprecedented complexity. Consequently, it still has much of the flavor of a craft about it, reminiscent of the uncertain and mysterious

---

[2] To avoid distracting discussions on whether software is "engineering" or not—at least for now—we use the term "engineering" here merely for convenience, referring to the general practice of designing and constructing artifacts for some human purpose.

nature characterizing medieval architecture. We still do not know how to construct software systems reliably – at least on the basis of industry statistics to date, which indicate an extremely high rate of failures for software-intensive projects [3][3].

Perhaps the primary reason for this is that—in contrast to traditional forms of engineering where models invariably capture relatively well-understood *physical* phenomena—a dominant element of all software is applied logic. Unfortunately for us, it is in the nature of logic that even the smallest flaw can render a complex logical construction completely useless. For example, an error in a single statement of a many-thousand-line program resulted in a catastrophic failure of a major part of the North American long-distance telephone network for close to 24 hours [4]. The financial cost of this error from lost business alone was tallied in the hundreds of millions of dollars. If the smallest detail can make a difference, and we have no clear idea which details are crucial in this way, it becomes very difficult to produce trustworthy models of software. And, as we noted earlier, abstraction is a key to successful modeling.

Furthermore, much of the initial experience with software modeling has not been encouraging. Software models based on early modeling techniques, such as structured analysis and structured design, often proved to be horribly inaccurate and led to faulty conclusions and a false sense of security. In essence, they failed to meet some of the essential criteria for good models described earlier. The skepticism and even disdain with which many practitioners view software modeling is succinctly expressed by that oft-cited quip by Bertrand Meyer that "bubbles don't crash" [5].

However, the situation is not as bleak as such opinions might indicate and models *do* have an important role to play in the development of software. Moreover, as we shall explain later, it is precisely because software is primarily spun out of non-physical "stuff" that gives software models a unique advantage compared to models in other engineering disciplines.

First, if we genuinely want to construct the kinds of complex systems that we are demanding of our software engineers, we really have no alternative. Most individuals quickly get lost when trying to contemplate too much interlocking detail at once. To quote Dijkstra, "I have a very small head and I had better learn to live with it and respect my limitations" [6]. Our only fundamental solution to dealing with complex problems is to think

---

[3] Actually, the situation may be even worse: no matter which statistics we believe, it is still true that *most* (> 50%) software projects are never completed. We have no statistics of the failure rate of, say, medieval cathedrals, but it does not seem as if it came anywhere close to that number.

hierarchically—which is really abstraction. Second, and most fortunate for us, even the most complex logical problems are amenable to this type of approach. Consider, for instance, one of the most complex and most elegant structures in mathematical logic, Gödel's proof of the incompleteness theorem [7]. There are numerous examples of high-level outlines (i.e., abstract models) of the extremely complicated proof that describe its essence without going into all the details (see, for example, [7, 8, 9])[4].

What does a software model look like? We shall illustrate this using the C++ code fragment in Figure 1-1.

```
int xs = 0;
do {
    receiveEvent(ev);
    switch (xs) {
        case 0:  printf ("starting");
                 break;
        case 1:  switch (ev) {
                     case e1: send(oa,5);
                              xs = 2;
                              break;
                     case e2: xs = 1;
                              break;
                 }
        case 2:  switch (ev) {
                     case e1: xs = 1;
                              break;
                     case e2: xs = 999;
                              break;
                 }
} while (xs < 999);
```

Figure 1-1. A C++ code fragment

Note that to understand what this code fragment is doing requires close and thorough inspection and interpretation of practically every token in the text, since the type and placement of syntactic details such as semi-colons, commas, brackets, and braces are all crucial to this understanding.

Next, let us look at the following simple state machine:

---

[4] Interestingly, the structure of this proof itself relies on hierarchies of logic. This was a key insight of Gödel's that made the proof possible.

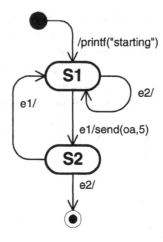

Figure 1-2. A state machine model

The observant reader may have spotted that this is, in fact, a state-machine representation of the code fragment in Figure 1-2. This representation eliminates much of the syntactical detail of the textual form and, moreover, makes it clear that the example program represents an event-driven application in which the response to an event may depend on previously received events. Finite state machines are a compact, well understood, and widely used graphical formalism for specifying this type of behavior. They are particularly common in real-time systems.

Therefore, the model in Figure 1-2 fulfills the two primary criteria of successful models: it abstracts out irrelevant detail[5], and it is expressed in a form that is easily understood. From this we can conclude that a software model is no different in its essentials and its purpose from any other type of engineering model.

Nonetheless, there is one quite remarkable difference that the software medium provides that is practically unattainable in any other engineering medium. To understand this, consider Figure 1-3, which represents an evolved version of the same state-machine model after a number of iterations and refinements have been added to the original. These include expanding the simple state, S2, into a composite state with an internal state machine and, possibly, adding more detail on some transition actions (these need not

---

[5] A suitable computer-based tool can be used to hide even the details of the transition actions if desired. Note that it is not necessary to omit or remove detail from a model—it is sufficient to hide it from view when it is deemed irrelevant. This is something that is easily achieved with computer-based models but much more difficult with other kinds of models.

be shown in the high-level model; they are only included here for illustration purposes). Such refinements are typical of the kind of evolution that takes place in an incremental software development process.

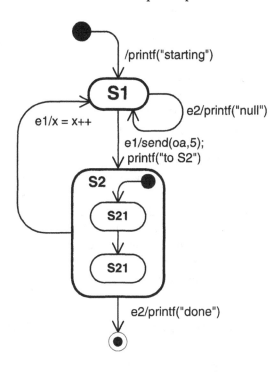

Figure 1-3. An evolved version of the model from Figure 1-2

Clearly, this type of refinement can be carried on until a complete behavioral specification is obtained—one that includes all the necessary detail required in the final product. This means that *we are able to move incrementally from a simplified and highly abstract model of the software to its final fully-specified form without having to change the notation, the implementation medium, the tools, or the method of work*! In other words, when it comes to software, it is possible to *evolve* our models directly into implementations (of course, this presumes that we can automatically generate programs from our models—we shall say more on this later in this chapter). The key advantage of this amazing capability is that it eliminates major error-prone discontinuities—so common in other forms of engineering—that occur when designs are translated into actual implementations. In this case, the design and its implementation are one.

This unique feature of software models has inspired an approach to software development that is sometimes referred to as *model-driven development*. Perhaps the aspect that most distinguishes model-driven development from traditional software development is that the focus and primary product of development is a model rather than a computer program. Of course, a program is still the ultimate output, but it is derived, usually automatically or semi-automatically, rather than being crafted explicitly.

Using models to automatically generate programs has long been an objective of many software developers and computer scientists. In effect, this represents a leap to the next generation of computer languages[6]. The technology required to realize this objective has taken a long time to develop[7], but it has now reached maturity with numerous successful examples of application in large industrial projects [10].

This maturity has progressed to the stage where the technologies for supporting model-driven development are now being standardized. In particular, this is the objective of the recent initiative announced by the Object Management Group (OMG)[8] called *Model-Driven Architecture* (MDA) [11]. This is a long-term plan for a series of technology "standards" in support of model-driven development. One of the cornerstones of MDA is the Unified Modeling Language (UML).

2.   THE UNIFIED MODELING LANGUAGE

The Unified Modeling Language is a modeling language based on the object paradigm [12, 13, 14]. It was devised as a consolidation of proven concepts that evolved and were refined during the dramatic surge of interest in object-oriented technologies in the late 1980's and throughout the 1990's. During this period, numerous competing object-oriented languages and

---

[6] I tend to think of such modeling languages as "fourth-generation" languages, except that this term has been appropriated for other things (not to mention "fifth-generation" languages). Regardless of which generation number we ascribe to them, these languages are clearly a step up in terms of the level of abstraction they provide compared to the current batch of "modern" languages such as C++, Java, or C#, whose lineage and conceptual foundations can be traced directly to languages invented in the 1950's (e.g., Fortran).

[7] Probably, too long. This is likely the result of the enormous investment in third-generation languages. As the example of COBOL demonstrates, it is almost impossible to displace these languages, even after they are technically obsolete. This will continue to be a major impediment to advanced methods such as model-driven development.

[8] The Object Management Group is an industry-based consortium of software tool users and vendors whose primary objective is to standardize software technologies that support interworking of software applications. More information on the OMG can be found at: http://www.omg.org/.

modeling approaches were proposed. While this created a lot of confusion and diversity—much of it gratuitous—it also provided a fertile base from which to garner the foundations for a common modeling language.

The idea for a unified language that would capture the state of the art in object-oriented technology in a common semantic base and single notation originated in 1995 at Rational Software. The work was first entrusted to the primary authors of two of the most widely-adopted object-oriented methods of the time: Grady Booch, author of "the Booch method" and Jim Rumbaugh, the lead author of the "Object Modeling Technique" method. Another noted methodologist, Ivar Jacobson, soon joined them and the three produced the initial draft versions of UML. These and subsequent drafts were circulated publicly and an invitation was sent out to other noted methodologists to participate in the work. When the OMG issued its request for proposal for a modeling language that could be used for the analysis and design of distributed object-oriented applications, the UML was proposed and, following further refinements by an expanded body of contributors, it was formally adopted as an OMG technology specification in 1997.

Over the next several years, UML underwent several revisions. The primary purpose of these revisions was to clarify certain aspects and to fix shortcomings and inconsistencies detected through practical experience. In addition, some lesser features were added and some existing ones expanded. The most significant addition came with the definition of the UML action language semantics [12]. This is a specification that describes the semantics of certain detail-level actions, such as the creation and destruction of objects, the sending and receiving of signals and the invocation of operations. In addition, several UML profiles have been defined and standardized within the OMG. We will discuss this in a bit more detail below.

As this text is being written, the first major new revision of UML, UML 2.0 is in the process of being defined with an anticipated adoption date some time in 2003. This version of UML will be adding some major new modeling capabilities including modeling support for describing software architectures.

Since its adoption, UML has been adopted quite rapidly by both industry and academia, indicating a genuine need for such a "lingua franca". It is being taught widely in professional and university courses, there are numerous published textbooks and dissertations on it, and it is supported by modeling and related tools from many different vendors. This, of course, minimizes training and support costs and provides a strong incentive for its use in industrial projects.

2.1   Customizing UML

A fundamental challenge of any "unified" computer language is dealing with the diversity that exists across the spectrum of different application domains. Although there may be consensus across multiple domains about the *general* (high-level) meaning of shared abstractions, in most cases different domains and technologies will have subtly different interpretations. These differences may become significant when increased modeling precision is sought. For example, in concurrent systems (and most real-time systems involve concurrency), there are many different models of scheduling of concurrent activities. The choice of a scheduling discipline is an important design decision that is usually based on the specific requirements of the problem at hand. Clearly, it is inappropriate to select one form of scheduling for all of UML since that would severely limit its applicability.

For this reason, standard UML was defined with built-in genericity and provided with mechanisms for specializing it for specific domains and purposes. Namely, the general definition of UML has built-in semantic variation points—relatively detailed aspects, which are defined in a way that leaves open multiple possibilities. For high-level modeling, where these details are of little or no concerns, standard UML may be sufficient. However, when the appropriate level of detail is reached, the specialization mechanisms are often required to provide a domain-specific interpretation of the general concepts.

These mechanisms are knows as *extensibility mechanisms* and comprise a means by which additional semantics can be ascribed to certain general concepts. A crucial constraint imposed on such specializations is that they cannot contradict, in any way, the semantics of the general concepts from which they are derived. (Note that rather than calling these "extensibility" mechanisms, it would have been more appropriate to call them "specialization" mechanisms.)

To illustrate how specialization works in UML, let us consider the example of representing a domain-specific concept such as a real-time clock.

It is common practice to represent clock values by integers, with each integer value corresponding to a point in time or distance in time relative to some reference event. A real-time clock is one whose value keeps increasing with the passing of physical time[9]. Each clock "tick" the value of the clock is incremented by some fixed amount. A relatively trivial and direct approach

---

[9] To keep this example simple, we are intentionally ignoring the numerous subtleties involved with physical time and time measurement. See Chapter 10 for more on time.

might be to define a special subclass of the general Integer class[10] as depicted in Figure 1-4.

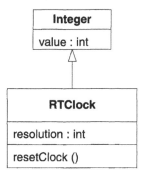

Figure 1-4. Using specialization to define a domain concept

Although this seems to do the job, it has some drawbacks. The most serious is that this model does not actually specify the semantics of real-time clocks. In fact, except for the additional features, the class RTClock seems to have exactly the same general semantics as Integer or, more generally, as any other class defined using standard UML. There is no mention of the fundamental semantic connection between the values of instances of this class and the progression of physical time. We could associate these special semantics through naming conventions (e.g., "any class name that has the keyword 'clock' embedded in it implies a clock"), but this is informal and, hence, unreliable and difficult to enforce.

Furthermore, such conventions are necessarily of a local nature and would not be understood outside the project or organization in which they were defined. Although they are not general, concepts such as real-time clocks are encountered in many different applications and development environments. Hence, it would be useful to define them in a way that is independent of such applications or environments but still confined only to those domains where they are useful. In other words, we must be able to *selectively* add new specialized modeling concepts to UML.

So, we need a mechanism that allows us to capture a model element that has all the properties of UML classes in general *plus* the idiosyncratic properties of real-time clocks. Clearly, something like this can be achieved if

---

[10] Assuming such a class exists, of course. If it does not, then we could define a class that has an integer attribute. Such details are irrelevant here.

we defined a real-time clock class concept (RTClock) as a subclass of the standard UML "class" concept, as shown in Figure 1-5 below:

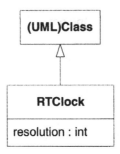

Figure 1-5. Specializing a basic UML modeling concept

This is precisely the effect that is achieved through the *stereotype* extensibility mechanism of UML. In essence, a stereotype is used when a new modeling concept is required that is a refinement of a standard UML concept (e.g., "class", "association") or another stereotype. The additional special semantics can be provided using any combination of different mechanisms including formal constraints, tagged values, informal text, etc., whichever is appropriate for the situation on hand. In the case of real-time clocks, we may define their special semantics either using a mathematical model or an informal natural language description.

A stereotype definition may also include one or more *tags* representing specific additional attributes associated with instances of the stereotype. When a stereotype is used in a model, its tags can be assigned suitable values (hence, the name *tagged value* for this type of extensibility mechanism). In Figure 1-5, the tag resolution, which has to have an integer value, is used to describe the granularity of a specific real-time clock.

The use of a stereotype in a UML model is usually denoted by a graphical symbol corresponding to the default notation for its base UML concept with an additional label bearing the name of the stereotype between special quotation marks called *guillemots*. Alternatively, stereotype-specific icons may be used. Tagged values are usually shown by an expression in which the appropriate value is "assigned" to the tag name. These notational conventions are illustrated in the collaboration diagram in Figure 1-6.

The example depicts three collaborating instances, two of which (watchdogTimer and systemClock) are branded with the «RTClock» stereotype. This means that, in addition to the usual semantics shared by all UML objects, these two objects also incorporate the semantics of real-time clocks. In this specific case, those semantics might mean that some internal value changes synchronously with the progress of physical time and that this happens with a specific resolution. Note that the classes from which these two objects originate (WD and SC respectively) do not necessarily have a common superclass. This means that the semantics imparted by stereotyping can be independent of any application class hierarchy.

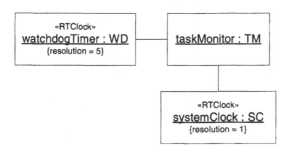

Figure 1-6. A stereotype in use

Because stereotypes inherit the semantics of their base UML concepts and cannot change them, all the semantic and syntactic rules of general UML also apply to models involving stereotypes. This means that, despite the flexibility of UML to be customized for a given domain or purpose, the essential advantages of a standard are preserved. Thus, tools that work with standard UML can be used for models based on stereotypes and also, knowledge of the general standard is fully applicable in such cases.

Note that, if stereotypes are standardized, models using those stereotypes can be exchanged and understood by tools from different vendors. This not only eliminates the dependency on specific vendors, but, even more importantly, it supports interworking of complementary specialized tools through a standardized interoperability format. For instance, a UML model created using a model-editing tool could be passed to a specialized timing-analysis tool for formal analysis.

2.2 UML Profiles

Specializations like the real-time clock stereotype described above typically represent concepts that are specific to a given domain or viewpoint. Since most domains involve multiple related concepts, it is convenient to group their corresponding extensions so that they can be applied jointly. This also allows specializations for different domains to be clearly distinguished from each other. In UML, this is achieved through *profiles* – packages of domain specific UML extensions.

The utility of profiles has been recognized within the OMG and a number of standard UML profiles have been adopted. Among these are a profile for modeling OMG's Common Object Request Broker (CORBA) technology [15], a profile for modeling software development processes [16], and a profile for accessing enterprise software [17].

For the purposes of this volume, the most interesting profile in this series is the so-called "real-time" UML profile, officially called the *UML Profile for Schedulability, Performance, and Time* [18]. It provides the conceptual foundations needed for *quantitative* modeling of the time-related characteristics of systems. It also defines two specialized profiles based on those foundations that support two of the categories of quantitative analysis most commonly used in real-time systems: schedulability analysis and performance analysis. A description of this profile can be found in chapter 8.

The significance of UML profiles such as the real-time profile is that they enable UML models to be used to evaluate not only the logical soundness of proposed designs but also their quantitative correctness. Moreover, this can be done early in the development process, when crucial design decisions are being made. This provides a systematic means for avoiding catastrophic design failures, all too common when it comes to large real-time and embedded systems, in which these systems badly fail to meet critical non-functional requirements such as response time, throughput, or load.

3.   SUMMARY

Models and model-based techniques seem to be almost as old as engineering. They are the fundamental means by which engineers are able to cope with otherwise unmanageable complexity and reduce design risk. Due to the relative ease with which software-based systems can be constructed (there is no metal to bend or heavy material to be moved) and to the increasing demands for more sophisticated functionality, many of them are among the most complex human-designed artifacts ever attempted. This is particularly sensitive in case of real-time and embedded systems, where much of the complexity emanates from the unpredictable physical world with which the software has to contend. Hence, the use of models and model-based techniques appears to be absolutely crucial to the success of software design and its maturation from craft to a true engineering discipline – a discipline that can be trusted to reliably produce reliable systems.

In this regard, software models have the distinct advantage that they can be *evolved* from high-level views of possible designs into actual implementations, ensuring a relatively smooth and potentially much more reliable process compared to traditional forms of engineering. This unique opportunity is now starting to be exploited with the advent of model-driven software development methods. Although this advanced vision has long been forecast, it is only recently that the technology has finally matured to the point where it has become feasible. Full-fledged model-driven development, using models and automatic code generation has been used with success on large-scale industrial projects.

The Unified Modeling Language—a widely adopted, widely supported and customizable industry standard—plays a key role in this new style of software development. With the addition of standardized UML profiles, such as the real-time UML profile, it provides the fundamentals for a true engineering-oriented approach to the construction of software. That is, system models can be used to understand and assess designs and predict design risks in meaningful (e.g., quantifiable) ways. Full automatic code generation from UML models facilitates preservation of proven model properties in the final implementation.

Undoubtedly, a great deal of technical work still remains to be done, concerning UML itself, its profiles, and its accompanying tools, before the full potential of model-driven development is reached. But, as noted, all the technical essentials of this vision are in place and being used to good effect.

REFERENCES

[1]   R. King, *Brunelleschi's Dome*, Penguin Books, New York NY, 2000.
[2]   M. Vitruvius, *The Ten Books on Architecture*, (M.H. Morgan transl.), Dover Publications Inc., New York NY, 1960.
[3]   Standish Group International Inc., *The CHAOS Report (1994)*, http://www.standishgroup.com/sample_research/chaos_1994_1.php, West Yarmouth MA, 1994.
[4]   L. Lee, *The Day the Phones Stopped*, Donald I. Fine, New York NY, 1991.
[5]   B. Meyer, "UML: The Positive Spin," http://archive.eiffel.com/doc/manuals/technology/bmarticles/uml/page.html, 1997.
[6]   E.W. Dijkstra, "Notes on Structured Programming," http://www.cs.utexas.edu/EWD/ewd02xx/EWD249.PDF, 1969.
[7]   J.L. Casti, J.L. and W. DePauli, *Gödel – A Life of Logic*, Perseus Publishing, Cambridge MA, 2000.
[8]   R. Hofstadter, *Gödel, Escher, Bach – an Eternal Golden Braid*, Basic Books Inc., New York NY, 1979.
[9]   M. Davis, *The Universal Computer*, W. W. Norton & Company, New York NY, 2000.
[10] K. Smith, "Object Behavior Modeling in Large Software Systems", Practitioner's report in pre-addendum to *Proceedings of ACM OOPSLA'98 Conference*, New York NY, Oct. 1998.

[11]   Object Management Group, *Model Driven Architecture (MDA)*, OMG document
       ormsc/2001-07-01, Needham MA, 2001.
[12]   Object Management Group, *Unified Modeling Language (UML) – Version 1.5*, OMG
       document formal/2003-03-01, Needham MA, 2003.
[13]   G. Booch , J. Rumbaugh, and I. Jacobson, *The Unified Modeling Language User Guide*,
       Addison Wesley Longman Inc., Reading MA, 1999.
[14]   J. Rumbaugh, I. Jacobson, and G. Booch, *The Unified Modeling Language Reference
       Manual*, Addison Wesley Longman Inc., Reading MA, 1999.
[15]   Object Management Group, *UML Profile for CORBA, V 1.0*, OMG document
       formal/02-04-01, Needham MA, 2002.
[16]   Object Management Group, *Software Process Engineering Metamodel (SPEM)*, OMG
       document formal/02-11-14, Needham MA, 2002.
[17]   Object Management Group, *UML Profile for Enterprise Application Integration (EAI)*,
       OMG document ptc/02-02-02, Needham MA, 2002.
[18]   Object Management Group, *UML Profile for Schedulability, Performance, and Time*,
       OMG document ptc/02-03-02, Needham MA, 2002.

Chapter 2

UML for Real-Time
Which native concepts to use?

Sébastien Gérard and Francois Terrier
CEA-LIST ("Commisariat à l'Energie Atomique - Laboratoire d'Intégration des Systèmes et des Technologies" is the Systems and Technologies Integration Laboratory of the French Agency for Atomic Energy)

Abstract: Engineers are increasingly facing the hard problem of developing more sophisticated real-time systems while time to market and cost constraints are constantly growing. The necessity of adopting object oriented modeling in the real-time domain appears to be essential in order to face the rapidly changing market conditions. The main obstacles are the lack of standards and the mismatch with real-time needs. With the standardization of UML, the first main drawback is being reduced. Current work performed at the OMG on UML standards evolution to better integrate real-time issues shows both that there is a strong interest in the subject and that current proposals are neither completely satisfying, nor completely compatible. This chapter aims to describe in minute detail what UML proposes as support for parallelism, behavior and communication modeling, and how it is also possible to express quantitative real-time features (such as deadlines, periods, priorities...). Apart from UML, OMG has specified two additional profiles well-suited for real-time, the Scheduling, Performance and Time profile and the Action Semantics profile. Due to size limitations, the goal of this chapter is not to describe precisely their content. It aims at skimming through both profiles to outline their purpose and content. Finally after having detailed the native possibilities of the UML in terms of notations for real-time, this chapter outlines a prospective approach showing how to use such notations to build real-time applications.

Key words: UML, real-time, concurrency, communication, behavior

1. INTRODUCTION

Several years ago the real time and embedded systems market was considered as a very specific and "confidential" sector (about 5% of the

L. Lavagno, G. Martin and B. Selic (eds.), UML for Real, 17-51.
© 2003 *Kluwer Academic Publishers.*

global market of software based systems). Now several studies of the evolution of the software market consider that embedded systems may represent by the year 2003 and beyond more than 50% of the global market (including personal computers, client-server and information system applications).

This explosion of the market for real time systems and the constant increase of embedded services force engineers to face more and more the hard problem of developing sophisticated real-time systems while competition through time to market and cost constraints increases day after day. Classical real-time development of software systems is reaching its limits in a world where on the one hand hardware targets cannot be known in advance and where on the other hand version evolution becomes increasingly fast and time to market must be shortened drastically in order to meet economic requirements. Reusability and evolvability become mandatory requirements for modeling methods and development techniques. In such a context, real-time systems development cannot be achieved efficiently without a strong methodological support and accompanying tools. In parallel, object oriented techniques have reached a sufficient level of maturity to successfully provide the flexibility required by new applications. Up to now however, the real-time community has been long reluctant to cross this Rubicon; mainly for both of the following reasons:

– The state of object-oriented approaches was not mature enough to provide stability in their solutions (methods, tools,...);
– The real-time specifics were generally not well covered by existing methods.

During the last few years *UML* has become the lingua franca among system modelers all over the world. With the arrival of the *UML* standard in 1997, the signal that many editors were waiting for has appeared, and a first step is being achieved that will permit the spread of a new tool generation. Indeed, object oriented modeling with a standard formalism such as *UML* brings significant solutions to the issues mentioned previously. At least, *UML* is becoming a "de facto" widespread standard for software engineering, and also object oriented approaches now fit quite well both of the following needs: (i) to have a fine level of modularity for component based development; and (ii) to improve reusability and maintainability properties of subsystems.

For UML and real-time, the OMG Platform Technology Committee is concerned with both task forces, the Analysis and Design PTF[11] (AD PTF - http://adtf.omg.org/) and the Realtime, Embedded, and Specialized Systems

---

[11] Platform Task Forces are groups dedicated to a domain that may initiate Requests For Proposals (RFP) in order to later produce new standards.

PTF (RTESS PTF - http://realtime.omg.org/). The first task force is in charge of the UML standard and also of standards directly connected to the UML such as the SPEM[12] and EDOC[13]. The latter task force, the RTESS PTF, works within the OMG to augment already standardized technologies for the requirements of real-time, embedded and fault tolerant systems, and to promote CORBA[14] technology in the real-time market place.

UML being a language and not a method, the purpose of this chapter is not to introduce a way to use the UML to model real-time embedded systems but what are the native concepts available in the UML to describe real-time features of your applications. The rest of this chapter is then organized around four main sections. Section 2 is dedicated to tackling real-time qualitative aspects of a system, whereas section 3 will introduce how it is possible in the UML standard to model real-time quantitative features of an application. Section 4 will outline a methodology called ACCORD/UML that, based on all these concepts, allows engineers to build safe real-time embedded systems. Finally, section 5 gives to the readers some perspective related to real-time work at the OMG through the incoming UML revolution with UML 2.0 and also the MDA paradigm.

2. QUALITATIVE REAL-TIME FEATURES

This section focuses on UML notations for modeling qualitative real-time aspects of systems. This family of features relates to every real-time property of an application that may not be measured. For our purpose, it concerns concurrency (also called parallelism), communication, behavior and actions.

2.1 Concurrency Modeling

The concurrency specification is an important issue to tackle when modeling real-time applications because these ones are intrinsically concurrent. Indeed, according for example to [1] and [2] definitions, "real-time" implies that such systems are coupled with the real world which is fundamentally concurrent. The focus of this section is to describe the native concepts of UML supporting concurrency modeling. As described in minute detail in the rest of this section, one will see that it is natively possible to model concurrency with UML at different levels of granularity: at the class

---

[12] Software Process Engineering Meta-model
[13] UML Profile for Enterprise Distributed Object Computing
[14] Common Object Request Broker Architecture

level via the active object paradigm; or at the operation level via a specific concurrency attribute.

2.1.1   Concurrency and Active Object

The active object concept is the usual way for OO programming languages to integrate concurrency issues within their object view [3], [4] and [5]. Examples of such works are [6], Act++ [7], Hybrid [8], ABCL [9], Argus [10] and, when integrating real-time concerns, PRAL-RT [11], DROL [12], RTC++ [13], RTGOL [14], TOM [15], etc.

In UML, classes may be either *active* or *passive*. The meta-model class ***Class*** has the attribute ***Class::isActive***, whose explanation is:

*"**Class::isActive** specifies whether an **Object** of the **Class** maintains its own thread of control and runs concurrently with other active **Objects**. If false, then the **Operations** run in the address space and under the control of the active **Object** that controls the caller."*

UML active objects are instances of active classes. They own their execution resource and have mechanisms for *controlling the incoming invocations* that protect the object's integrity against concurrent invocations.

From the above excerpt one could infer that an active object has only one concurrency resource. However, if we take into account the state machine definition, with the possible presence of concurrent states and do-activities, and the fact that UML aims to be as general as possible, it is reasonable to consider that an active object has at least one (involving possibly many) concurrent resource.

From the notation point of view, the active property of a class or an object (instance of a class) is shown either with a heavy border on the rectangular symbol that models it, or directly with the keyword (Figure 2-1). In the other case, one assumes that it is a passive class (or object).

Figure 2-1. Notation for active classes and objects

In addition, UML defines two other stereotypes to specify the type of flow of control owned by an active class: *« process »* and *« thread »*. The first one specifies that the active object owns a resource which is of type "heavy-weight flow of control" and runs in its own address space that it doesn't share with another active object. The second one specifies that the active object may run with some other active objects in the same address space. It is a thread in the sense of POSIX [16, 17].

2.1.2 Concurrency and State Machine

In the *UML*, concurrency modeling may also be achieved within state machines through two ways: concurrent composite state and do-activity.

CompositeState meta-class owns a meta-attribute called *isConcurrency*. If true, this means that the composite states are directly decomposed in orthogonal regions, so-called AND-States. The *ModelElement* whose behavior is described by AND-states executes them concurrently. Therefore concurrent states offer a means to express parallel execution.

Figure 2-2 illustrates the use of a concurrent composite state in a state machine. In this case, the state S_1 owns both orthogonal regions, S_{11} and S_{12}. If the transition t_0 is fired the model element owning this state-machine will be in the state S_{11} AND S_{12} in parallel.

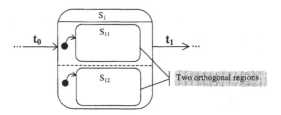

Figure 2-2. Example of concurrent composite states

It is not the purpose of this section to describe in minute detail the semantics of state-machines. Nevertheless, let's just say a few words about it relative to concurrency. The *UML* state-machine semantics relies on the Run-To-Completion (RTC) assumption. In short, this latter involves a state-machine managing only one event at a time. But relative to concurrent states, these semantics needs to be clarified. In *UML*, it is said in fact that in the case of concurrent regions, two cases are possible: either RTC is applied to the whole state-machine; or this constraint may be relaxed and applied then on each orthogonal region.

Possible concurrency with the do-activity concept is also possible within state-machines. When entering a state, a specific action, called do-activity, is forked after entry actions are finished execution. In this case, two concurrency sources are then possible: (i) if entering a series of nested states, a series of do-activities is then forked concurrently; (ii) or if internal transitions are fired because such specific transitions, as opposed to "normal" transitions, do not involve any state exit that should abort ongoing do-activities. In the example depicted in Figure 2-3, if *State11* is entered, both do-activities, respectively the do-activity of *State1* and the do-activity of *State11* will be forked concurrently executing actions specified respectively in both procedures *proc1* and *proc2*.

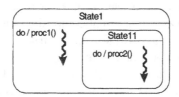

Figure 2-3. Concurrency resulting from multiple do-activities launching

2.1.3   Concurrency and Operation

The meta-class *Operation* has an attribute *concurrency* that specifies the semantics of concurrent calls to the same object. This attribute is typed *CallConcurrencyKind* and it can have one of the values: *sequential, guarded,* or *concurrent.* The operations of a class are divided into three categories, according to the following values of the *concurrency* attribute:

- from the Sequential category, only one operation may be active at a time (for a certain object), but the system does not protect them by default. If two calls are made simultaneously to two such operations, the integrity of the object cannot be guaranteed. However, specifying such a property may be useful when designing the system rather than when implementing it, because it may be not easy and safe to achieve it in practice;
- from the *Guarded* operations, only one is allowed to execute at a time (for a certain object), but this constraint is guaranteed by the object itself. This means that when an operation from the Guarded category is executed, the object will block all the other calls for Guarded operations. How this is done, and whether blocking other operations means that their calling threads are locked or that they return an unavailability response, is not mentioned in the *UML* semantics. Guarded operations in UML should not be confused with methods with guard conditions that exist in many other concurrent object models;
- any number of operations from the *Concurrent* category may be active at a time and the object designer must guarantee that the object's integrity is not destroyed by this.

Usually, this feature concerns passive objects, i.e. objects instantiated from classes with the property *isActive=false*. Active objects used to be linked to a state machine specifying their behavior. In this case, active objects can then handle concurrent calls due to their associated execution semantics. Section 2.3.1 will discuss this point in minute details.

2.1.4   Concurrency and Procedure

Another mean of specifying parallelism is offered in procedures. These latter may be used to specify behavior of an operation, or on state machine transitions, or as entry/exit/do actions in states. The *UML* tenet about actions focuses on allowing the highest level of parallelism possible. By virtue of this principle, all the actions in a procedure are assumed to run in parallel by default unless specified otherwise. Actions are then sequenced implicitly via the data flow specification. The data flow concept means that two actions exchanging data are sequenced by construction. A consumer action needs an input data supplied by a producer action in order to be executed.

2.1.5   Summary

UML is then a well-suited language to support concurrency modeling in various forms and at different levels of specification. Parallelism may be introduced either at the system level ensured by the concurrency between objects (several objects may run concurrently at a time), or also at the object level where an object may perform various things at a time. The main difficulty in using the previous described concurrency mechanisms is to use them together without contradictions. To solve such issues, each methodology dedicated to the real-time domain has to make a choice between them and to clarify some semantic rules in order that their choices may be applied coherently. Finally, the active object concept needs also to be clarified in order to fix the status of its concurrency capacities, i.e. does it have one or multiple flows of control. Our point on this issue, is that the model should keep open as much as possible. And as concurrency is possible in state-machines, it follows that active objects whose behavior is described by a state diagram may run concurrent activities internally and then must possess several flows of control.

2.2   Communication Modeling

Whatever the object-oriented methodology an engineer uses to work, the developed applications consist of various objects interacting together in order to collaborate in the realization of a task (also called Interaction). The generic concept of communication proposed by UML is based on the usual message passing paradigm. UML messages may take different forms depending on the action type that generates them. They can be *signal sending, operation call* or *creation and destruction* of other objects of the application.

A message (*Message*) may be synchronous or asynchronous and it may convey in, out and inout parameters. A message owns a sender and a receiver. The sender is a class instance that after executing a specific action (*Action*) generates the sending of the message. UML proposes two specific types of action whose execution involves communication between objects:
- *CallAction*, whose execution involves message exchanges relying on operation calls;
- *SignalAction*, whose execution involves sending signals.

2.2.1   Operation-based messaging

The UML definition of the *Operation* concept is:

"An operation is a service that can be requested from an object to effect behavior. An operation has a signature, which describes the actual parameters that are possible (including possible return values)."

From the modeling point of view, the structural specification of a class has a specific compartment containing the declaration of its operations. For example, the class *Regulator* in Figure 2-4 specifies that it has two operations: *starRegulating* owning a parameter *sp* typed integer and *endRegulating*.

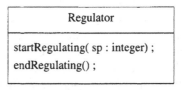

Figure 2-4. Operation specification

In addition to its concurrency feature modeled with the following constraint {*concurrency* = *'sequential, guarded or concurrent'*} an operation may also have an attribute called *isQuery*. This feature deals with the impact of the execution of an operation on the state of the object. If true, an execution of the operation leaves the object state unchanged. In the other, false, case, it may have side-effects on the object state.

To model the side-effect possibility of an operation, the user has to put the tagged value {*isQuery* = *'true or false'*} after the name of the operation in the class specification. For example, the operation *endRegulating* of

Regulator class in Figure 2-5 has no side-effects on its related object features when executed.

Regulator
startRegulating(sp : integer) ; {**concurrency = sequential**} endRegulating() ; {**isQuery = true**}

Figure 2-5. Operation concurrency specification

After detailing the **Operation** concept itself, let's answer the question: *how to generate an operation call?*

To generate an operation-based message, one needs to execute a specific action typed **CallAction**. This involves the sending of an operation call to a given instance, the target of the communication. Such a call action may be either asynchronous or synchronous. In the first case, the caller waits for the end of the execution of the invoked operation. In the second case, the caller does not wait and immediately continues its own activity.

Some operation calls have a particular status:
- the one involving an object creation resulting from the execution of an action typed **CreateAction**;
- the one involving an object destruction resulting from the execution of an action typed **DestroyAction**.

Concerning the synchronization pattern of previous operation calls, nothing is specified in UML. So, they can be synchronous or asynchronous depending on the underlying approach used.

Now one knows how to generate an operation call, what does the receipt of this call imply?

The concepts directly involved on the communication receipt side are *Operation, CallEvent* and *Method*.

When an object receives a message in the form of an operation call it may interpret it in two ways:
- a call event (*CallEvent*) characterizes the receipt of an operation call on the receiver instance side. Consequently, the receiver object affects behavior by performing a sequence of actions which characterizes the operation behavior at a particular state. A call event is also linked to the operation that triggers the execution. As a call action, there exist two specific types of call events corresponding to the two specific call actions, *CreateAction* and *DestroyAction*. As with all events, a call event may have a list of parameters that matches those of the called operation. The UML specification does not define any formal rules of consistency between parameters of the received call event and the operation it

triggers. Thereby, it is necessary for each approach to clarify some consistency rules in order to have no ambiguities concerning parameter passing between the event and its associated operation. Besides, the sequence of actions performed following a call event receipt may be ended by a specific primitive action called *ReturnAction* (e.g. *return('return-value')*). If an operation returns values and the caller does not receive any or if there is an inconsistency with the declared types of the return value, the model is also considered to be ill-formed.

– a method (*Method*) is a particular implementation of an operation. It specifies the algorithms or procedure that affects the results of an operation. The signature of a method has to be similar to that of the operation that describes the behavior. In the UML meta-model, the Method inherits from the same attributes as the operation that implements the behavior. It also has the same properties, *concurrency* and *isQuery*. The value of the two features has to be either equal to those of the underlying operation, or to be more restrictive. For example, if the concurrency attribute of an operation is set to *guarded*, the method implementing its behavior has to set its *concurrency* attribute either to *guarded*, or to *concurrent*.

The reaction of an instance to operation calls is then an ambiguous point of the behavioral semantics of UML. The receipt of an operation call may also be interpreted in the form of a call event triggering a transition of a state machine. In this case, the receiver performs a sequence of actions specified on the transition possibly triggered. Alternatively, the receipt is perceived as a <u>classical</u> Object-Oriented operation call, i.e. triggering the execution of a given method describing the behavior of the called operation.

2.2.2   Signal-based messaging

In UML, messages may take two forms. Either they are operation-based messages as detailed just above, or they may convey signals.

A signal always models an asynchronous communication. The *Signal* meta-class inherits from the *Classifier* meta-class. Then, it can have some attributes that, in fact, represent <u>eventually</u> <u>some</u> parameters of the signal-based communication. Indeed, unlike signals in Harel's initial statecharts concept [18], the UML signal concept can convey parameters. Moreover, a signal may be specialized or generalized in an inheritance tree. A signal is a specific classifier that cannot have any operations and association relationships with any other classifiers as classes, actors, or even other signals.

A signal is on the one hand linked to the set of behavioral features (e.g. *Operation*) that generates it and, on the other hand, linked to the classes prepared to handle it through a reception declaration (***Reception***). A reception is a structural specification that specifies that a given class may receive a signal. It does not describe the reaction of the class at the receipt of a signal. This will be done in the behavioral description of the class via a state machine. A reception is similar to an operation for two reasons. First, it has a signature that is the declaration of the parameters of the received signals; and, secondly, it is involved in the structural specification of a class in the same capacity as operations.

From the modeling point of view, the structural specification of a class may have as many compartments as needed. In particular, it is possible to introduce a specific compartment dedicated to the reception specification. Thereby, each class requiring the specification of some signal reception will have an additional compartment stereotyped « ***Signals*** » where it will specify each receivable signal (Figure 2-6).

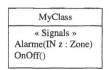

Figure 2-6. Notation for signal Receptions

After detailing the ***Signal*** concept itself, let's answer the question: *how to generate a signal?*

Sending a signal is generated using a particular primitive action typed ***SendAction***. A signal-based message may be directed either explicitly towards a set of targets, or implicitly towards an undefined set of targets. This feature is also specified via an attribute called ***target*** and typed ***ObjectSetExpression*** (a UML predefined type). This predefined type defines a statement that will return a set of instances when evaluated. When used to specify the targets of a send action, such a statement may be the keyword ***all***. In this case, it evaluates to all instances that can receive the signal, as determined by the underlying runtime system. For example, exceptions are specific kinds of signal whose receivers are determined by the underlying operating system.

SendAction is above all an action. It can also have arguments that have to match with the parameters conveyed by the signal-based communication resulting from its execution and that are specified on the side of the Signal itself through its possible attributes.

What does the receipt of a signal imply?

The receipt of a signal is seen by an instance as an event typed ***SignalEvent***. As an event, an instance of ***SignalEvent*** may have parameters and is stored in a dedicated queue handled by the state machine describing the behavior of the class.

But what happens once a signal is sent?

The affected behavior of a class following the receipt of a signal is also to trigger a transition of its state machine and then to perform a set of actions specified on the possibly triggered transition.

As with the communication via operation calls, signal-based communication raises some questions about its specific semantics:

- May a passive object receive signals?
- Is there a formal link between attributes of the signal declaration and the parameters of a signal event?
- Is there a formal link between attributes of the signal declaration and the parameters of a send action?
- What kind of parameters may a signal convey? In, Out, InOut?
- et cetera

These questions do not get a clear answer in the UML documents. Moreover, positions may be different regarding the answers. For example, concerning the first question about the possibility for a passive object to receive signals, we could have a variety of points of view: when one uses or defines a way to use UML, i.e. a UML-based methodology, one must be concerned with such semantics issues *a fortiori* for real-time systems where no ambiguities are supported.

2.2.3   Summary

As in usual OO languages, communication is based in the UML on the message paradigm. This one may take both forms: either it is the classical operation call involving possible synchronous or asynchronous communication with in and out parameters; or it a signal-based communication. In this latter case, communication are asynchronous and may be point-to-point as for operation calls or even multicasting or broadcasting-based.

2.3   Behavior Modeling

One will focus now on behavior modeling of an application. This aspect is mainly introduced by UML through following concepts: *StateMachine, Interaction and Action*:

- *StateMachine* describes dynamic behavior of one element model using state-based diagrams. It is more suitable to describe local behavior (e.g. behavior of classes, use cases, etc.). There are two versions of this kind of diagrams: *State Diagrams* and *Activity Diagrams*;

- *Interaction* consists of a set of messages that various objects exchange in order to perform a given activity or task. This concept ensures the system behavior to be globally described. Interaction diagrams come in two forms: *Collaboration Diagrams* and *Sequence Diagrams*;
- *Action* defines the lowest level of behavior it is possible to model with UML. Thanks to the action semantics defined in the standard it is then possible to build executable UML models.

2.3.1   State Diagrams

State-transition machines are constituted of states connected to each other through transitions. The states can be simple or composite. A composite state can contain some other composite states and/or some simple states. The composite states can also be concurrent. In that case, they own two or more orthogonal components called regions that are often linked to a concurrent execution.

A state-transition machine has a principal state called the ***root state***. This state is a composite state that contains all the possible states of the state-transition machine. It cannot be the resource state of a transition and must own at least an initial state from which only one specific transition is initiated when an instance of the state-transition machine is created.

Transitions can be simple or composed. A composed transition contains several simple transitions and the firing of a composed transition can be executed according to different paths depending on the context. Indeed, the different simple transitions which are part of a composite transition are connected to each other through pseudo-states that can be from different origins: ***Choice***, ***Fork***, ***Join***, ***DeepHistory***, ***ShallowHistory***, ***Initial*** and ***Junction***. With these pseudo-states, it is then possible to build transitions that give different routes depending on their firing context.

Finally, a simple transition is adorned with a label made up of two distinct parts:

- The left side specifies the triggering condition of the transition. It may contain one event type specification that on receipt triggers the transition. There are four kinds of event in the UML[15]: receipt of operation call (***CallEvent***), receipt of a signal (***SignalEvent***), timing event (***TimeEvent***) or boolean statement becoming true (***ChangeEvent***). Moreover, events may have parameters (object values, references, etc.). In addition to the event receipt specification, this triggering part may also have a boolean expression, the guard;

---

[15] Both ***CallEvent*** and ***SignalEvent*** related to communication issues have been detailed earlier in section 2.2. The ***TimeEvent*** concept is explained in minute detail in section 3.1.

– The right side specifies the behavior resulting to the transition firing. It takes the form of a procedure that is a set of actions to execute.

The label syntax of a transition is then as following: *EventSignature '['guard']' '/' ProcedureSignature*

Figure 2-7 depicts a state diagram illustrating the various concepts that a state machine may contain.

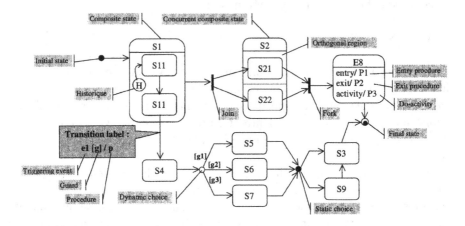

Figure 2-7. Notation elements for UML state diagram modeling

UML state machine semantics have been specified above following an operational style. They are then described in terms of the mechanisms of a hypothetical machine that implements a state machine specification. There are three key components of this hypothetical machine: (i) an *event queue* that holds incoming event instances until they are dispatched; (ii) an *event dispatcher* that selects and dequeues event instances[16]; (iii) and an *event processor* that processes the current event according to *UML* semantics. This component is simply referred to as the "state machine".

---

[16] The UML standard does not define the order in which events are dequeued. This point is a so-called open variation semantics point that any UML-based approach should explicitly describe.

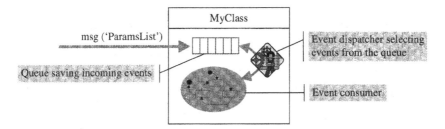

Figure 2-8. An operational semantics for state-machines

In *UML*, the order of dequeuing is not defined, leaving to the user the possibility of modeling different priority-based dequeuing schemes. The event processing semantics are based on the "run-to-completion" assumption (in short RTC), meaning that an event can only be dequeued and dispatched if processing of the previous current event is fully completed.

The run-to-completion assumption simplifies the transition function of a *UML* state machine since, by serializing treatments triggered by various events, it precludes conflicts between them.

Once an event instance is generated, it may:
- involve one or several transitions to be enabled. If several transitions are enabled a sub-set is selected to be triggered (following the algorithm described below), procedures specified on the right side of every transition are executed and when execution is finished the transitions are then said to be "fired";
- be saved if it does not trigger any outgoing transitions of the current active state configuration while it matches an event type specified in the set of deferred events attached to the current state. In this case, the event instance is not de-queued and it will be managed during the next step;
- be lost in other cases.

Whatever the situation is, the state-machine is said to have performed an "RTC step" once the method triggered by firing it has been fully executed.

If the current state is concurrent it is then possible to fire several transitions at the same time, that is to say, as many transitions as there are concurrent states in the active state configuration of the state-machine. In this case, the event instance is said to be fired once every orthogonal region reaches a stable state. The « RTC step » of the state machine is then considered to be finished and the next event in the queue may be handled.

The firing of a transition usually involve action execution. Among these ones, some may be synchronous actions. In this case, the end of the RTC step depends on the ending of every synchronous action. In some specific situations, it may create deadlock as for example in Figure 2-9.

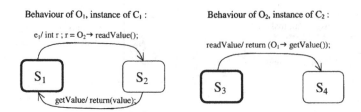

Figure 2-9. Example of Deadlock

In the previous example, the object O_1 receives the e_1 event instance whereas its current state is S_1. It fires then its outgoing transition and, by the way, sends the message ***readValue*** to the O_2 object. When receiving the message, if its current state is S_3, O_2 fires the transition originating from S_3 and send also the message ***getValue*** to O_1. But O_1 is still locked waiting for a response from O_2 to its previously sent message, ***readValue***. This case raises then a specific situation called deadlock. This is a very typical case arising from circular synchronous calls.

The model outlined in Figure 2-10 is a possible solution to overcome this deadlock issue. It is possible to avoid such a problem using orthogonal regions. If a state machine remains locked within one RTC step of one of its orthogonal regions because of a circular synchronous call, it may be possible to trigger a transition in another orthogonal region that is not still locked.

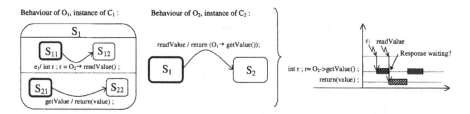

Figure 2-10. How to avoid deadlock arising from circular synchronous calls

Usually a UML-based methodology relies on a UML state-machine semantic related to the RTC assumption applied to a whole state-machine. However it still remains a possibility to restrict the scope of the hypothesis to the level of every orthogonal region of a state-machine. The serialization constraint may then be relaxed because in this case, it is applied at the concurrent states level instead of at a state-machine level. But if according to the standard it is possible, it is also said that this way to consider RTC assumptions is not described at all.

> Note : *it is important not to confuse Run-To-Completion with Pre-emption. As described in section 2.1.1, active objects own their flow of control and are then able to execute concurrently. In this way, they may pre-empt each other depending on their priority. If an active object is handling an event it cannot be pre-empted to manage a new incoming event even if this one has higher priority. However, if another active object is receiving an event and the flow of control of the active object has higher priority than the flow of control of the previous running active object, it will pre-empt this latter in order to manage the incoming event.*

In the *UML*, it is possible for more than one transition to fire at the same time. When this happens, such transitions may be in conflict with each other. Take the case of two transitions originating from the same state, triggered by the same event, but with different guards: if both guard conditions are true, then there is a conflict between the two outgoing transitions. Only one of them must be fired. But which one, and what criteria can be used to make the choice?

UML state machines afford also the possibility of specifying some kind of automatic behavior via very specific transitions known as ***completion-transitions***. This type of transition has no explicit trigger event, although it may have a guard defined. Completion transitions are triggered by a special internal event known as the "completion event". The state machine implicitly generates such an event each time it reaches a stable state, i.e. when all transition and entry actions and activities in the currently active state are completed. A completion event is processed as soon as it is generated. That is to say, this kind of event bypasses the event queue of the state machine and has to be consumed as soon as it has been sent or else it is lost. If the current state configuration of the state machine has an outgoing completion transition, firing of this transition takes priority over that of any other transitions emanating from that state!

Moreover, if a state has several outgoing completion transitions, because they are all triggered by the same type of event (completion event), all of them can potentially be activated and must therefore be mutually exclusive. The respective guard for each outgoing completion transition of the state must ensure this mutual exclusion condition. Any other solution would be a modeling error.

2.3.2   Activity Diagrams

Activity Diagrams have been introduced to ease the modeling of a computational process in terms of control-flow and object-flow among its constituent activities. They can be seen as a special case of State Diagrams providing shorthand forms for this kind of modeling:

> *"The purpose of this diagram is to focus on flows driven by internal processing (as opposed to external events). Use activity diagrams in situations where all or most of the events represent the completion of internally-generated actions (that is, procedural flow of control). Use ordinary state diagrams in situations where asynchronous events occur."* *(From "OMG Unified Modeling Language Specification", Version 1.5, September 2002).*

They are described in terms of states and transitions where a state is attached to a given action (**ActionState**) or a sub-activity (**SubactivityState**) representing nested activities that ultimately resolve to individual actions.

Action states are attached to atomic actions: it is left only when the action is completed. Action states have some duration corresponding to the processing of the action. As they are built from a set of state actions (or other sub-activity states), sub-activity states have also some duration.

Although there no particular formal restrictions, at this precise moment, on the use of the transitions in Activity Diagrams, it is generally considered that action states should not have internal transitions, outgoing transitions triggered by explicit events or exit actions. That means that the transitions are always triggered by the implicit completion event of the action state. However, as depicted in Figure 2-11 some elements can be added to specify under which conditions transitions can reach the target state:

– Usual guard conditions;
– Availability of an object in a certain state, defined in the diagram through definition of an object flow;
– Occurrence of a signal. In this case, a specific notation is attached to the target state where receipt of the signal is defined as the atomic action attached to the state.

In addition, Activity Diagrams allow one to model concurrent activities and provide for a notation to fork the control flow into several control flows or to synchronize (also called join) several control-flows at a given step.

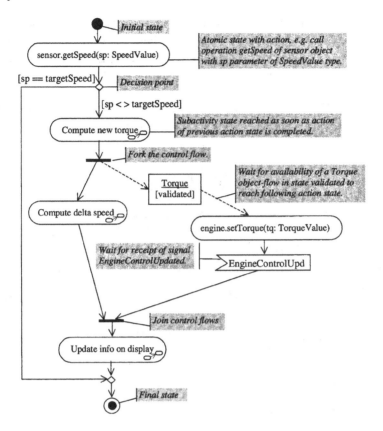

Figure 2-11. Example of Activity Diagram Notations

2.3.3 Sequence Diagrams

Sequence Diagrams are used to show the explicit sequence of communications among objects of the system (or more generally among Classifier roles defined in the model). In this way it has a strong link with the structural model of the system: communications are supposed to be supported by an association link defined between the two communicating entities (Figure 2-12). A Sequence Diagram represents an interaction, which is a set of messages between object instances to produce a desired operation or result.

Objects involved in the interaction are identified along the horizontal axis while the time sequence of the messages is shown by their relative order along the vertical axis. This time progress (vertical) axis represents only a partial order without implying any metric. Each object in the diagram has a lifeline (dashed vertical line) allowing the explicit display of a sequence of messages it receives during its lifetime. When we want to show that a message triggers some processing in the object (that can itself trigger sending of other messages), we use a small vertical rectangle along the lifeline to show this. They can be nested in order to show nested processing. Arrows between the object instances represent messages sent between the objects that can be identified through the corresponding signal or operation call names (see Figure 2-12).

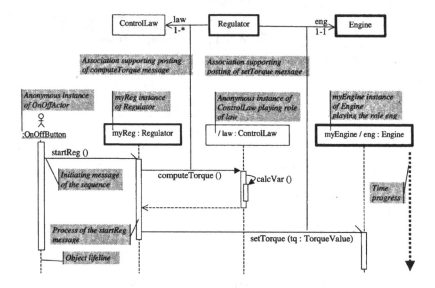

Figure 2-12. Example of Sequence Diagram and links with a Class Diagram

Concerning real time modeling, objects can be identified as instances of active classes by drawing thick borders around the rectangle representing them. In addition, synchronous or asynchronous communication modes can be specified by using, respectively, a filled solid arrowhead or stick arrowhead. When synchronous communication is indicated, the entire nested sequence is completed before the outer level sequence resumes. It can be associated with a dashed arrow with a stick arrowhead representing the return of an operation call. When asynchronous communications are specified, this means the sender dispatches the Stimulus and immediately continues with the next step in the execution (Figure 2-13).

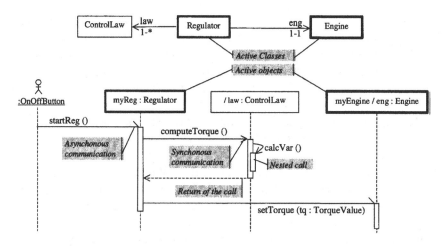

Figure 2-13. Example of communications protocol modeling among concurrent objects

Collaboration diagrams are another (and equivalent) way to represent object interactions. Their advantage is to show explicitly on the association links connecting the objects the messages that are sent. However, this figure loses the time dimension of the sequence diagrams and requires one to adorn messages with numbers in order to obtain an equivalent, but less intuitive, level of information. Consequently they are used less often than sequence diagrams to model concurrent or real-time systems.

2.3.4   Action Modeling

When dealing with real-time applications, it is very useful, for simulation or prototyping for example, to be able to model executable models with enough modeling details. For that purpose UML offer a particular action package that defines in minute detail how to model this aspect.

The higher-level entity of this package that is also the link with other model elements of the UML is the *Procedure* concept: "*A procedure is a group of actions caused to execute as a unit.*" Procedure is used either to specify a method body in a specific programming language, or within the context of state machine, to specify effects whenever a state is entered, exited, within a do-activity, or when a transition is fired.

The *Actions* Package consists then of the following sub-packages:

– *Foundation actions* package defines the basics for *Action* and *Procedure*. *Procedure* consists of *Actions* that exchange data flow via *InputPin* and *OutputPins*;

– *Composite actions* package defines recursive structures from which it is possible to define more complex actions from more primitive ones;

- *Read and write actions* package defines how to create/delete objects and to consult/modify their features, i.e. attributes, variables or links;
- *Computation actions* package defines how to transform data. It is used to model essentially mathematical functions;
- *Collection actions* package defines high-level actions that ensure a sub-action is applied on a set of elements;
- *Messaging actions* package defines how objects may communicate exchanging messages (synchronous, asynchronous, broadcasting, etc.);
- *Jump actions* package defines how to quit a main flow of control in order to continue in the context of a different flow of control.

Action semantics have been designed in order to support a very large variety of programming languages. This includes, obviously, the usual object languages such as Java or C++. But intrinsically it supports also parallel programming models at the instruction level, thus allowing them to ensure concurrent program modeling. However, time aspects are not taken into consideration and would require specific extensions.

Within all previous sub-packages, the standard focused on defining the abstract syntax and the semantics of the UML action language. It did not provide any concrete (or surface) language mapping with this proposed semantics! If one wants to build executable UML models it is then necessary to choose/create a notation (textual or graphical) and to define its mapping with elements of the abstract syntax defined in the various *Action* sub-packages outline in the previous section. Currently, there are a few proposals offering this possibility, for example *SDL2000, ACCORD/UML* [19-22].

2.3.5   Summary

State diagrams offer concepts that are traditionally available in such state machines and especially mix Mealy and Moore paradigms, i.e. actions are possible either on states or/and transitions. *UML* state machines are used to specify local behavior for any model elements and usually ensure modeling of discrete-time based systems. Although often criticized, state machines are not only a notation but also have a defined semantics and this latter is the subject of a lot of work aiming at formalizing its content [23-25].

Activity diagrams can be typically used for both purposes: modeling of computational or organizational aspects. On one hand, to model computational aspects, Activity Diagrams may specify detailed behavior of the operations of a class. In fact, in this case, they are used to describe the detailed specification of the method that implements an operation. On the other hand for organizational aspects, Activity Diagrams can be used at the global level of the system to describe chaining of activities of any classifier, such as use cases or packages [26]. But they are also often used for business process engineering or workflow modeling [27, 28].

Sequence diagrams are proposed to specify communication interactions among a set of objects. Strongly linked with the structural model of the system, sequence diagrams allow one to make explicit the messages exchanged along the association links between the objects. For concurrent models, they also ensure the description of communication protocols with synchronous or asynchronous communications among concurrent objects including the size effects on mainly passive objects. And finally sequence diagrams are, with their temporal dimension (i.e. the vertical axis), one of the most appropriate and intuitive diagrams in UML to model temporal interactions.

Action semantics support the lowest level of behavioral modeling, ensuring engineers can build executable UML models. Today, there are only a few implementations of this part of the UML standard, and this feature is thus not widespread in UML methodologies and tools. This is certainly due to the fact that it proposes no unified notation!

3. QUANTITATIVE REAL-TIME FEATURES

The previous sections were dedicated to qualitative aspects of real-time specification: concurrency, communication, behavior and actions. It is now time to focus our minds on quantitative aspects of real-time applications modeling.

For that purpose, UML defines first two data types dedicated to time specification, *Time* and *TimeExpression*:
- the *Time* type defines a value that refers to absolute or relative movement in time or space.;
- the *TimeExpression* type refers to statements that return a *Time* value when they are evaluated.

In the sequel of this section, we will see how to use these timing statements firstly in state diagrams and secondly in sequence diagrams.

3.1 RT modeling within state diagrams

For time specification in state machines, UML defines a specific event called *TimeEvent*. This event models the expiration of a specific deadline that may be either relative to a reference time, or absolute:
- a relative time event is modeled in a state machine via the keyword *after* followed by an expression typed *TimeExpression* and specifying its relative deadline;

– an absolute time event is modeled in a state machine via the keyword *when* followed by an expression typed ***Time*** and specifying its absolute deadline.

Tabel 2-1 illustrates different possible uses of the time event in UML state machines.

Table 2-1. Time Event specification in UML

Time event modeling	Description
S — after (10 ms) / 'actions-list' ...	The time event is generated 10 ms after the entry time[17] in state *S*.
S — after (10 ms after the exit of S2) ... / 'actions-list'	The time event is generated 10 ms after the exit time[18] in state *S2*.
S — when (1st January 2000, 0h00) ... / 'actions-list'	The deadline specified by the time event is an absolute moment. Here it is generated the 1st January 2000 at 0h00.

For all preceding cases, when a timer expires it generates a time event which is saved every time in the queue of the state machine. If this one is in state *S* at the moment where the time event is selected from its queue, the time event is consumed and the transition associated with the time event is triggered. In the other case, if the state-machine fires another outgoing transition (i.e. different from this one associated to the time event), the time event is cancelled. By this way, contrary to other kinds of events, it is not possible to defer time events.

The occurrence time of a temporal event should then match with its reception time. **However, it is important to notice that there may exist some delay between the reception and the handling time of a time event!** Moreover this delay is variable and very difficult to measure - even to find a maximum. Indeed, this delay depends on the management policy adopted by each tool in terms of event handling [29-31].

---

[17] The entry time is considered to be the moment where the state-machine reaches a stable state, that is to say when finishing the execution of the entry actions specified in the target state and all nested states.

[18] The exit time is considered to be the moment where the state-machine has finished the execution of all exit actions specified in the original state of the triggered transition including also all exit actions of nested states.

3.2   RT modeling within sequence diagrams

The second type of UML diagram that is especially well-suited for real-time system specification is sequence diagrams. Indeed, as depicted previously a sequence diagram has two dimensions:
–   an horizontal axis with objects involved in the interaction described by the diagram;
–   a vertical axis modeling time progress.

Within a sequence diagram, *time progresses from top to bottom along the vertical axis but with no quantitative metrics system defined*. Therefore, real-time constraint modeling in a sequence diagram relies on this graphic feature.

In general, one assumes in sequence diagrams the transmission delay of a message is negligible compared with other activities of an application. This explains the fact that message modeling is done using a horizontal arrow. However, if needed, a user can specify that a transmission of message takes time. To do that, he/her has to tilt the arrow so its point (marking the sending-time of the message) is lower than its tail (marking the reception-time of the message)(Figure 2-14).

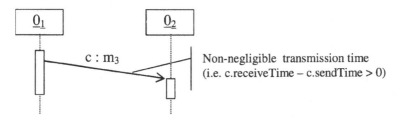

Figure 2-14. Propagation delay specification of a message

To make temporal constraint modeling easier, UML introduces some specific functions intended for time handling during message exchange realized in the sequence diagram. The functions *sendTime* and *receiveTime* specify respectively the sending and the receiving moments of a message. These functions serve to construct time expressions that may be attached to a particular set of messages of an interaction described within a sequence diagram. These timing functions are applied to the name of a message in order to characterize one of its timing features. For example, the expression *"aMessage.receiveTime"* denotes the sending moment of the message called *aMessage*. The set of timing functions is not limited to these two. The user can define other ones to satisfy her/his requirements (e.g. *elapsedTime*, *executionStartTime*, *queuedTime*, etc.).

To specify a real-time constraint in a sequence diagram, *UML* proposes also two ways: either via timing marks, or in terms of *UML Constraint* with a time expression.

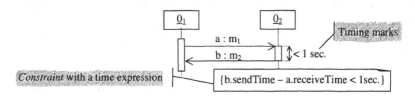

Figure 2-15. Time specification in a sequence diagram

The first technique consists of marking a time dimension on the vertical axis (representing time progress) of a sequence diagram by two dotted lines and connecting them by a double arrow labeled with a time constraint. In the example above, the time specification specifies that the execution-time of the O_2 activity triggered by m_1 receipt has to be lower than 1 second. This way of time modeling is visually appealing but it is not formally defined in the *UML*. It is just part of the notation section of the *UML* standard and has no equivalent concepts described in the semantics of the *UML*. So, a tool providing this possibility has to translate it in terms of time constraints (as explained below) before attaching it semantically to a model.

The second way to model time in a sequence diagram is also to use *UML Constraint* with time expressions as described above. In the example of Figure 2-15 the time constraint *"{b.sendTime – a.receiveTime < 1sec.}"* specifies also that the time between the send-time of m_2 and the receive-time of m_1 has to be lower than 1 second. This time constraint is equivalent to this one expressed with blueprints style.

Whatever UML-based method, it is important for each one wishing to be real-time oriented to formalize these time specification features because they are only notations. Indeed, it should be inadequate to content oneself with using them as is, without integrating them in a complete approach to modeling real-time applications.

3.3   UML Profile for Scheduling, Performance, and Time

The *UML* profile for Scheduling, Performance and Time *(SPT)* aims to define a minimal set of concepts needed for modeling real-time aspects of an application. All these concepts have to ensure application modeling with enough information in order to either produce implementations or frameworks from tagged *UML* models or to analyze the real-time behavior of an application (schedulability and performance). For that purpose, the

SPT is mainly organized around two parts: (i) the first one defines a set of generic concepts that are the basis for the definition of more elaborated concepts ensuring modeling of real-time features; (ii) the second one specified on the base of the previously defined concepts are high level concepts required to analyze real-time behavior of *UML*-based applications.

The first part of the SPT consists of three sub-packages:

- The General Resource Modeling (GRM) package defines in very generic terms both concepts of *Resource* and *QualityOfService*. It introduces also among others a causality model that clarifies the cause-effect chains in the application dynamics;
- The General Time Modeling package defines time and time-related mechanisms such as timer, clock, etc.;
- The General Concurrency Modeling package defines basic concepts to specify parallelism in applications. For that purpose it relies mainly on the *ConcurrentUnit* concept that is in fact an entity able to execute a sequence of actions concurrently with other concurrent entities.

The second part of the SPT is then focused on analysis techniques of real-time behavior of UML-based applications. The extensions proposed in the three sub-packages should ensure an ability to achieve on *UML* models classical schedulability analysis (RMA[19], EDF[20], etc. [32]), performance analysis and also schedulability analysis in the context of RT-CORBA.

Finally, the UML profile for SPT proposes in the first place a set of stereotypes, tagged values and constraints that may be very useful when dealing with modeling of real-time applications requiring a high level of detail. But this profile forms also a good framework to redefine more specialized concepts for solving real-time modeling issues if needed.

4. FROM NOTATIONS TO DEVELOPMENT PLATFORMS: THE ACCORD/UML APPROACH

Although its presence in the software domain has been successful, *UML* still lacks significant semantics that will allow its dominance in specific domains, like the one of real-time systems [33]. The description of the real-time behavior of such systems is not completely satisfying yet even in current *UML 2.0* proposals. This leads to a continuation of the debate on the adequacy of object-oriented methods for real-time specifications. In particular, this is the case for the real-time behavior specification of an

---

[19] Rate Monotonic Analysis
[20] Earliest Deadline First

application and its mapping onto the implementation level where in general the object concept has not been widely introduced until now.

At the least, current proposals are not yet completely satisfactory, from two points of view:

- First, there remain some deficiencies in expressing timing properties (deadlines, periods, priorities, execution time, etc.) and some points of semantics of the dynamic models have to be clarified;
- Second, users' needs are evolving quickly due to the market explosion. In particular, more and more non real-time specialists must be concerned with real-time system modeling, and need to specify, and even sometimes to develop, new embedded services or systems.

The first point can be tackled by enriching and clarifying the semantics of current UML concepts connected to real-time modeling, but the second point leads to the necessity of proposing new modeling concepts at a higher level, completely hiding the underlying implementation techniques and solutions. This consequently requires the provision of more elaborate procedures (and also tools) to automatically generate application implementations.

Several years ago studies were performed to extend the object oriented programming paradigm to concurrent programming. They have led to the definition of the active object concepts, better integrating both sets of paradigms in fully object oriented and unified models. They have been the basis for the definition of the real-time object paradigm supporting real-time developments with automatic real-time implementations keeping the low-level real-time implementation mechanisms transparent to the developers.

The *ACCORD/UML* approach is one such attempt [26, 34-36]. Its objective is to provide a framework for real-time development as close as possible to classic object oriented methods. Thanks to high level abstractions (namely the real-time active object concept [15]) real-time modeling can be achieved without mixing up implementation issues with domain specific ones. The main purpose of this new concept is to offer to engineers a rich and efficient abstraction that will allow them to very quickly model complex real-time applications. It aims to answer their need to describe real-time features of their applications. So within this approach, it is trying to keep the well-known advantages of object-oriented techniques yet with the idea of integrating real-time features in this model to provide sufficient abstractions of the real time field.

To achieve this objective, *ACCORD/UML* proposes an extension of *UML* supporting both aspects of a real-time behavior specification: quantitative and qualitative. For that, the main modeling features introduced by *ACCORD/UML* method are:

- Concurrency concerns of applications are specified and defined through identification of the real-time objects (extension of UML active objects).

The *ACCORD/UML* method proposes to define them on the basis of the following heuristic: real-time objects are either interface objects of the application managing events coming from the application external environment, or objects that need to perform automatic processing, in particular for periodic activities. Implementation of these real-time objects is taken in charge by a dedicated implementation framework supporting task allocation, object queue management and inter-object communications. In addition, the method allows the definition of a passive object shared by several real-time objects; they are called "protected objects". In this case, the ACCORD implementation framework automatically implements concurrency management of their parallel use by several objects [37].

- The specification of quantitative real time constraints on the model itself (deadlines, periods, priorities, etc.) can be set from the early stage of the development and are maintained during model enrichment until final implementation. Executing models of real-time objects and *ACCORD* implementation frameworks avoid requiring the developers to translate the real time constraints into low level mechanisms implementing their management (timer setting is not necessary anymore, and scheduling policies are automatically provided and implemented in the application through the implementation framework). Concurrency constraints are managed in the same way by this approach: these are declared at the operational level (because they rely on their implementation specification) and automatically managed in the final application. Scheduling policies integrate both these types of constraints (i.e.: the real-time and concurrency constraints) [38].

- Communication schemes among objects remains very close to that used in sequential object oriented programming: objects can exchange messages both through operation calls (with output parameters if needed) and also with signal sending (in this case, it also allows one to have broadcast and anonymous communications: the sender does not need to know the target objects and target objects do not need to know the senders of the signals). The execution model for operation calls and signal sending are the same: they are processed in the processing resources of the target if it is a real-time object and they are processed in the sender processing resource when the target is a passive object.

- The usual object-oriented structure of the model is preserved by specification of object behavior with two levels of state machines [26, 39, 40]. First, at the object level state machines only specify the logical control of chaining the operations performed by the object (it corresponds to the "protocol state machine" defined in *UML 1.x* and more formally defined in *UML 2.0*). In this state machine the transitions only trigger the processing of an operation defined in the object interface (actions are restricted to local invocations of an object method). Second, at the object operation level, state machines specify the detail of the actions performed to execute this operation (actions used at this level are chosen to be consistent with the action of the *UML* [41]).

Even if this approach is the result of laboratory studies, its operational feasibility has been demonstrated by its complete implementation on an industrial *UML* modeling case tool: Objecteering[21]. The available configuration involves a set of modules allowing the generation of the real-time behavior of an object from its state machine specification into C++ code. Moreover, a specialized C++ generator has also been developed in order to support the concepts of the extended active objects. Finally, with respect to the underlying real time operating system (RTOS), two layers have been defined between the application and the RTOS, namely *ACCORD/UML Kernel* and *ACCORD/UML Virtual Machine*. The first one implements mechanisms supporting active object semantics and above all the mechanisms allowing one to schedule application tasks respecting the main scheduling policies such as the Earliest Deadline First (EDF) policy or the Highest Priority First (HPF)[22] policy. The second one gives the application independence as far as the underlying RTOS is concerned. The latter exists for a *POSIX* compliant operating system and, namely, *Solaris*, *Linux* and *VxWorks*.

Integrating the active object paradigm within an object-oriented method permits a simple, complete and homogeneous modeling of requirements and needs for multitasking within an application. The use of the same object paradigm during the whole development cycle of an application reinforces the seamlessness of the model among the several modeling stages. The *ACCORD/UML* proposal for extending *UML* to real-time is based on this paradigm enriched for real-time concerns. On this basis we can obtain with very few specializations an enrichment of *UML*, the framework for methods supporting real-time development with intellectual approaches and concepts very close to those used in usual object-oriented modeling. Moreover, this proposal allows one to postpone all the parallelism, real-time and implementation choices very late in the design. Thus changing the parallelism granularity will not cause the redesign or re-analysis of the whole application, but will just require the tuning of implementation choices and of the last real-time design of the application. The approach maximizes

---

[21] Objecteering is a trademark of Softeam.

[22] In each case constraint inheritance mechanisms have been introduced to ensure the consistency between the global scheduling policy, operation concurrency constraints and real-time constraints put on the processing/messages.

reusability and designers may fully benefit from object-oriented experience acquired in other domains.

In addition to an obvious benefit in terms of quality due to the fact that constraints related to multitasking and real-time behavior of the application can be expressed in the model itself, the use of the *ACCORD/UML* approach prevents users from needing a deep knowledge of the fine synchronization mechanisms used in multitasking programming. Its similarity with the usual object-oriented programming model allows its use by non real-time specialists and the ability to automatically implement the real-time features specified in the model ensures that they do not need to have a deep knowledge of real-time development techniques.

This way they can concentrate on the modeling and on application specific code rather than wasting precious time in tuning low-level mechanisms. Development time is saved; it becomes possible to develop quite rapidly multitasking applications whose behavior can be as reliable and efficient as code obtained with the use of classical techniques using ad hoc system solutions for each application [42, 43].

Part of this work has been supported by the *AIT-WOODDES*[23] project. It has led to a *UML* profile dedicated to embedded system modeling for the automotive industry [44]. This profile will be presented at the OMG with eventually standard evolution proposals required to support it.

Further works consider the creation of formal *UML* models of a real-time application. On this point studies are currently under progress at the LSP Laboratory of the CEA-LIST to translate extended *UML* models into a model based on asynchronous communicating automata. It will then be possible to analyze these automata - that will be automatically built - with existing tools and methods for validation. In particular, *ACCORD/UML* models will be interfaced with the *AGATHA* tool [45-47]. This tool relies on proof and model checking techniques and helps the engineer to validate the behavior of his or her application, in particular by automatically extracting from the *UML* model all the possible execution paths of the application and by generating test cases of each of them [48].

[23] AIT- WOODDES project, n° IST-1999-10069, was partly funded by the European Commission and involves the following partners: Peugeot Citroën Automobiles – France, Mecel – Sweden, Commissariat à l'Energie Atomique – France, Softeam, I-Logix Ltd – Israel, Intracom S.A – Greece, Uppsala University – Sweden and Kuratorium OFFIS e.V. – Germany.

5.   OMG PERSPECTIVES

Among ongoing works at the OMG, four actions are particularly important for real-time domain: a UML profile for Quality-of-service and Fault Tolerance mechanism [49]; a UML profile for system engineering [50]; a standard for model transformation language in the context of the MDA technology space [51]; and finally the UML 2.0.

-   The UML profile for QoS and Fault Tolerance Mechanism aims at defining first a generic QoS framework and also individual concrete paradigms of quality of service. The proposal has to reuse the abstract concept of QoS defined in the UML profile for Scheduling, Performance and Time. Secondly, based on the generic QoS framework proposed, the standard should also have to define a generic framework for tolerance mechanism support.

-   The UML profile for Systems Engineering aims at providing all UML extensions to model of any kind of systems. This profile will have to encompass in the one hand all aspects to consider when dealing with systems, i.e. hardware, software, data, personnel, procedures, and facilities. And in the other hand, this profile will have also to provide support for every process activities such as analysis, design, implementation, etc.

-   In the heart of the current OMG concerns is the MDA. This acronym stands for Model-Driven Architecture [52-54]. The main idea related to MDA is to put the model paradigm in the centre of the development process and to then supply all the technologies required to build applications, refining models step after step until reaching executable implementations. One of the major issues related to MDA is the issue of transforming models. In order to tackle this problem, OMG initiated the MOF 2.0 Query/View/Transformation RFP (in short QVT). Based on the premise that every OMG model relies on a meta-model defined in the context of the Meta-Object Facility (in short MOF), the request of this RFP is to have a universal model transformation language ensuring mapping implementations between various models, possibly based on various meta-models.

-   Finally, the last but not least point is the new standard UML 2.0. Among others, one of the major novelties in this new standard is related to the component model. The idea is to propose a higher-level paradigm in order to support component based software engineering approaches. Moreover, UML 2.0 is improving/adding concepts that are more directly related to real-time issues, e.g.: behaviour aspects have been enriched via clarification of both protocol state-machines and activity diagrams; based on the experience of high-level message sequence charts of the

SDL, UML sequence diagrams have been largely modified allowing for example to factorise sequences and so on.

REFERENCES

[1] CNRS, "Le temps-réel", *TSI - Technique et Science Informatiques*, 1988. vol. 7 (5): p. 493-500.

[2] J.A. Stankovic, "Misconceptions about real-time : a serious problem for next-generation systems", *IEEE Computer*, 1988. vol. 21 (10): p. 10-19.

[3] C. Atkinson, *Object-oriented reuse, concurrency and distribution : an Ada-based approach*. 91: Addison-Wesley.

[4] R. Guerraoui, "Les langages concurrents à objets", *Technique et Science Informatiques (TSI)*, 1995. vol. 14 (8).

[5] A. Tripathi, J.V. Oosten, and R. Miller, "Object-Oriented Concurrent Programming Languages and Systems", *JOOP*, 1999. vol. november/december: p. 22-29.

[6] G. Agha, "Concurrent object-oriented programming", *Communication of the ACM (CACM)*, 90. vol. 33 (9).

[7] D. Kafura, M. Mukherji, and G. Lavender, "ACT++: a class library for concurrent programming in C++ using actors", *Journal of Object-Oriented Programming (JOOP)*, 1993. vol. (October): p. 47-55.

[8] O.M. Nierstratz. "Active Objects in Hybrid", in *OOPSLA'87*. 1987.

[9] A. Yonezawa, E. Shibayama, T. Takada, and Y. Honda, "Modelling and Programming in an Object-Oriented Concurrent Language ABCL/1", *Object-Oriented Concurrent programming*, 1987. vol.

[10] B. Liskov, "Distributed Programming in Argus", *Communication of ACM*, 1988. vol. 31 (3): p. 300-312.

[11] G. Fouquier and F. Terrier. "PRAL-RT : Un langage à objets concurrents temps réel pour machines multi-threads", in *Third Conference on Real-Time Systems (RTS'95)*. 1995. Paris, France.

[12] K. Takashio and M. Tokoro. "DROL: An object-oriented programming language for distributed real-time systems", in *The Object-Oriented Programming : Systems, Languages and Applications Conference (OOPSLA'92)*. 1992: ACM SIGPLAN Notices.

[13] Y. Ishikawa, H. Tokuda, and C.W. Mercer, "An object-oriented real-time programming language", *Computer*, 92. vol. (October): p. 66-73.

[14] J.L. Sourrouille and H. Lecoeuche. "Integrating States in an Object-Oriented Concurrent Model", in *TOOLS Europe '95*. 1995. Versailles, France.

[15] F. Terrier, G. Fouquier, D. Bras, L. Rioux, P. Vanuxeem, and A. Lanusse. "A Real Time Object Model", in *TOOLS Europe'96*. 1996. Paris, France: Prentice Hall.

[16] POSIX, "Realtime system API extension", IEEE: POSIX, POSIX 1003.4b/D4. 1992.

[17] POSIX, "Threads extension for Portable Operating Systems", IEEE: POSIX, POSIX 1003.4a/D6. 1992.

[18] D. Harel, A. Pnueli, J.P. Schmidt, and R. Sherman. "On the formal semantics of statecharts." in *Second IEEE Symposium on Logic in Computer Science*. 1987. New York: IEEE Press.

[19] S.J. Mellor. "Advanced Methods and Tools for Precise UML: Visions for the Future", in *OOPSLA, workshop pUML*. 2000. Denver.

[20] I. Wilkie, A. King, M. Clarke, C. Weaver, and C. Rastrick, "UML ASL Reference

Guide", Kennedy Carter. 2001. p. 90.

[21] C. Mraidha and S. Gérard, "ACCORD/UML Action Language", CEA/LIST: Internal report, DTSI/SLA/03-190/MC/ASG. 2003.

[22] ITU-T, "Recommendation Z.109 : Languages for telecommunications applications - SDL combined with UML", ITU-T. 1999.

[23] R. Wieringa, "Formalizing the UML in a Systems Engineering", *ECOOP98*, 1998. vol. (Workshop on Precise Behavioral semantics): p. 254-266.

[24] J. Lilius and I. Porres. "Formalizing UML state machines for model checking", in *UML'99*. 1999: Springer Verlag.

[25] G. Reggio, E. Astesiano, C. Choppy, and H. Hussmann. "Analysing UML active classes and associated state machines – a lightweight formal approach", in *FASE 2000*. 2000: Springer-Verlag.

[26] S. Gérard, *Modélisation UML exécutable pour les systèmes embarqués de l'automobile*, PhD Thesis, in *GLSP*. 2000, Evry: Paris.

[27] M. Dumas and A.H.M.t. Hofstede. "UML Activity Diagrams as a Workflow Specification Language", in *UML'2001*. 2001. Toronto, Canada: Springer.

[28] H. Eshuis, *Semantics and Verification of UML Activity Diagrams for Workflow Modelling*, PhD Thesis, in *Centre for Telematics and Information Technology*. 2002, University of Twente (The Netherlands): Enschede. p. 240.

[29] F. Bause and P. Buchholz, eds. *Protocol Analysis using a timed version of SDL*. Formal Description Techniques, ed. J. Quemada, J. Manas, and E. Vasquez. 1991: North Holland.

[30] S. Leue. "Specifying Real-Time Requirements for SDL Specifications - A Temporal Logic-Based Approach", in *PSTV*. 95: Chapmann & Hall.

[31] U. Hinkel. "SDL and Time - A mysterious Relationship", in *SDL Forum*. 97.

[32] A. Burns, "Scheduling hard real-time systems: a review", *Software Engineering Journal*, 1991. vol. May.

[33] F. Terrier and S. Gérard. "Real time system modeling with UML: current status and some prospects", in *2nd Workshop on SDL and MSC 2000*. 2000. Grenoble, France.

[34] F. Terrier, A. Lanusse, D. Bras, P. Roux, and P. Vanuxeem, "Concurrent objects for multitasking", *L'objet*, 1997. vol. 3 (2): p. 179-196.

[35] A. Lanusse, S. Gérard, and F. Terrier. "Real-Time Modeling with UML : The ACCORD Approach", in *"UML98" : Beyond the Notation*. 1998. Mulhouse, France: J. Bezivin et P.A. Muller.

[36] S. Gérard, "The ACCORD/UML profile", CEA-LIST: Internal report. 2002.

[37] G. Fouquier, *Programmation temps réel à objets : études et propositions*, PhD Thesis. 1996, Université d'Orsay, Paris XI.

[38] L. Rioux, *Développement à Objets Temps Réel : Etude et Proposition d'une Architecture d'Ordonnancement Parallèle*, PhD Thesis, in *LLSP*. 1998, UFR Scientifique d'Orsay: Saclay. p. 205.

[39] S. Gérard, N.S. Voros, C. Koulamas, and F. Terrier. "Efficient System Modeling of Complex Real-time Industrial Networks Using The *ACCORD/UML* Methodology", in *Architecture and Design of Distributed Embedded Systems (DIPES 2000)*. 2000. Paderborn University, Germany: Kluwer Academic Publishers.

[40] C. Mraidha, S. Gérard, F. Terrier, and J. Benzakki. "A Two-Aspect Approach for a Clearer Behavior Model", in *The 6th IEEE International Symposium on Object-oriented Real-time distributed Computing (ISORC'2003)*. 2003. Hakodate, Hokkaido, Japan: IEEE.

[41] OMG, "UML 1.5 with Action Semantics", OMG, ptc/02-09-02. 2002. p. 754.

[42] AIT-WOODDES, *Public Final Report*. 2003.

[43] P. Tessier, S. Gérard, C. Mraidha, F. Terrier, and J.-M. Geib. "A Component-Based Methodology for Embedded System Prototyping", in *14th IEEE International Workshop on Rapid System Prototyping (RSP'03)*. 2003. San Diego, USA: IEEE.

[44] D.A. S. Gérard, "UML profile for real time embedded systems development", AIT-WOODDES (IST-1999-10069): public document, 10069/D2/CEA/WP1/V1.0. 2003.

[45] J.P. Gallois and A. Lanusse, "Le test structurel pour la vérification de spécifications de systèmes industriels", *Génie Logiciel*, 1997. vol. 46: p. 145-150.

[46] J.P. Gallois and A. Lapitre. "Analyse de spécifications industrielles et génération automatique de tests", in *ICSEA*. 1999. Paris.

[47] D. Lugato, N. Rapin, and J.-P. Gallois. "Verification and tests generation for SDL industrial specifications with the AGATHA", in *Workshop on Real-Time Tools, CONCUR'01*. 2001.

[48] D. Lugato, C. Bigot, and Y. Valot. "Validation and automatic test generation on UML models: the AGATHA approach", in *FMICS'02, 7th International ERCIM Workshop in Formal Methods for Industrial Critical Systems*. 2002. University of Malaga, Spain: Elsevier Science Publishers - Electronic Notes in Theoretical Computer Science.

[49] OMG, "UML Profile for Modeling QoS and FT Characteristics and Mechanisms RFP", OMG, ad/02-01-07. 2002.

[50] OMG, "UML for Systems Engineering RFP", OMG: Request For Proposal, ad/03-03-41. 2003. p. 56.

[51] OMG, "MOF 2.0 Query / Views / Transformations RFP", OMG: Request For Proposal, ad/02-04-10. 2002.

[52] R. Soley and t.O.S.S. Group, "Model Driven Architecture (Draft 3.2)", OMG: White paper. 2000. p. 8.

[53] S. Gérard, F. Terrier, and Y. Tanguy. "Using the Model Paradigm for Real-Time Systems Develoment: ACCORD/UML", in *OOIS'02-MDSD*. 2002. Montpellier: Springer.

[54] J. Bézivin and S. Gérard, "A Preliminary Identification of MDA Components", OOPSLA 2002 Workshop: Generative Techniques in the context of Model Driven Architecture. 2002.

Chapter 3

Structural Modeling with UML 2.0
Classes, Interactions and State Machines

Øystein Haugen[1], Birger Møller-Pedersen[1], Thomas Weigert[2]
[1]Ericsson, [2]Motorola, Inc.

Abstract: This chapter will provide an overview of the structuring concepts that are proposed for the coming UML 2.0. This will be done through an example. We will illustrate that these concepts are designed such that structuring applied to classes may be reflected in the corresponding structuring of the interactions between the parts of a class.

Key words: UML 2.0, Structured classes, Interactions, State machines

1. STRUCTURAL CONCEPTS OF UML 2.0 – THE ORIGINS

The structuring of systems in terms of their constituents and the topology of connections between these constituents has been addressed by various communities, and a number of languages and notations have been designed in its support. While programming languages often merely provide the general mechanism of object references, specification and modeling languages typically support more advanced structuring mechanisms.

In the telecom industry, specifying systems as a set of interconnected (composite) blocks was common practice already in the seventies [1]. SDL was one of the first standardized notations for modeling and specification with support for such structuring mechanisms [2]. In the 1984 version, the notion of systems consisting of entities executing state machines that define their behavior and connected by communication links was introduced. Object-orientation was first proposed for SDL in 1987 [3]; in 1992 these concepts became part of the language, when types of entities and gates as connection points for communication links were introduced. In addition,

L. Lavagno, G. Martin and B. Selic (eds.), UML for Real, 53-76.

specialization was defined for types of entities with an internal structure of connected parts, and for state machines.

Proprietary variations of sequence diagrams (these were often referred to as "message flow graphs" or "bounce diagrams") had long been in use in the telecom industry. The standardization of Message Sequence Charts (MSC) was triggered by a paper by Rudolph and Grabowski [4], leading to the first MSC recommendation in 1992. MSC-2000 [5] refined earlier structuring mechanisms such as MSC references and inline expressions. UML chose a somewhat different dialect similar to, but not identical to MSC-92, as the foundation of sequence diagrams, and did not support reuse and hierarchy. With UML 2.0, the two dialects have reached more or less the same expressiveness.

In 1987, Harel introduced structuring mechanisms for state machines [6]. While then state machine-based languages relied on "flat" state machines (albeit SDL supported hierarchy through calls to procedures in turn specified by state machines), Harel's state machines were explicitly hierarchical, with composite states containing in turn states and transitions.

Work on Architecture Description Languages began in the early nineties (see, for example, [7]). This area has produced a number of modeling languages such as ACME [8] and Rapide [9] which aim at analyzing certain properties of a system based upon the description of its architecture, without considering the detailed specification of its behavior.

In 1994, ROOM [10] combined statecharts and structuring mechanisms like those of SDL, inspired by the Chorus distributed operating system. While SDL gates are just connection points, ROOM introduced more general ports, i.e., boundary objects mediating the communication between connected objects. ROOM further introduced the ability to associate protocol specifications to both ports and connectors.

From the world of data and object modeling came the notion of contextual composition, i.e. composition with contextual links between parts of the composite [11].

In 1997, Harel and Gery applied the same structuring mechanism that had been proposed for SDL [3] earlier to statecharts, especially the mechanisms for specializing behavior specified through state machines [12].

SDL-2000 [13] adopted the ROOM port concept, as well as the hierarchical state machines of statecharts. However, it extended the latter with connection points taken from its structuring mechanisms.

When UML 1.1 was adopted, only few of these structuring mechanisms became part of the language. Lessons learned with respect to the lack of structuring mechanisms for UML have been summarized in [14] and [15]. The structuring mechanisms of the coming UML 2.0 are based upon experiences with all these efforts.

These languages have formalized what engineers and system designers have been doing all along: making informal "block" or "structure" diagrams for various reasons. Interconnected blocks were used in order to specify the structures (in terms of instances) of the complete running systems, statecharts were introduced in order to specify structures of state machines, while message sequence charts pioneered the structuring of behavior in a declarative manner.

2. EXAMPLE – AN ACCESS CONTROL SYSTEM

This chapter will use one example – an access control system – to explain how UML 2.0 structural concepts can be used to model a system in a compact, but readable way. This example has earlier been elaborated in the TIMe method [16].

2.1 Introducing the Example – Domain Statement

In order to give the reader a first insight into our example system, we present the structured domain statement in natural English. At this stage many UML users would also apply use cases. We have chosen to omit the use cases to save space and since our focus is on the structuring mechanisms.

Area of Concern: Access control has to do with controlling the access of users to a set of access zones. Only a user with known identity and correct access rights shall be allowed to enter into an access zone. Other users shall be denied access.

Services
– <u>User Access</u>: The user will enter an access zone through an access point. The authentication of a user shall be established by some means for secret personal identification (PIN code). The authorization is based on the identity of the user and the access rights associated with that user.
– <u>New User</u>: A supervisor will have the ability to insert new users into the system.
– <u>PIN change</u>: Users shall be able to change their personal code.

As the reader now clearly understands, we will describe a system known to many from their daily life.

2.2   Domain Class Model

We begin by constructing a simple class model describing the domain of
the access control system (see Figure 3-1). While the domain model does not
yet describe the classes as they ultimately make up the system to be
developed, it captures the essence of the system as it applies to the domain
statement. We see a number of classes that we expect to appear in the final
system, based on the domain statement, as well as high-level relationships
between these classes: an *AccessPoint* controls access to one or two *Doors*,
through which the user enters the *AccessZone*. The *Authorizer* controls
access through an *AccessPoint*, and thus governs access to each *AccessZone*.
Users interact with a *Panel* of the *AccessPoint* or the *Console*. We use
multiplicities and role names on the relationship to document important
characteristics of the system.

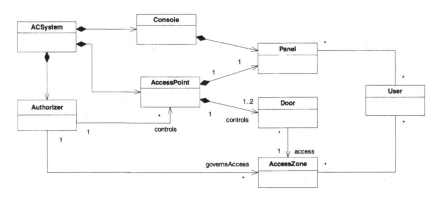

Figure 3-1. Domain model for the access control system.

As discussed in the domain statement, the system will interact with
various types of users: ordinary users try to gain authenticated access to the
access zones. A supervisor is a user who in addition has the ability to add
new users to the authentication system. A new user is not yet authorized to
enter any access zones. The hierarchy of users is shown in the class diagram
depicted in Figure 3-2.

Figure 3-3 shows the context of the access control system. The system
context is modeled as a collaboration. A UML collaboration describes a
structure of cooperating entities, each performing some specific function,
which jointly accomplishes the desired functionality. The behavior of the
system is the result of the cooperation of the entities that play a part in the
collaboration.

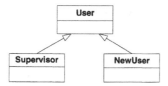

Figure 3-2. User class hierarchy.

The context in which the *ACSystem* operates is comprised of four sets of objects: the *ACSystem* proper, a set of *User* objects, a set of *NewUser* objects, and a set of *Supervisor* objects. These sets are shown as parts of the collaboration. The specified system will be made up of objects corresponding to each of these parts, as specified by the multiplicities of the parts.[24] The parts are linked by connectors, which specify communication paths between the objects playing these parts. Every one of these objects will be able to communicate along these paths with the linked objects.

A collaboration often specifies a view of the cooperating entities only. It specifies the required features of the parts as well as required communications between them. Any object that plays these parts must at least possess the properties specified by the classifiers that type the parts of the collaboration. The system specified by the collaboration may have additional parts not shown, and the objects playing the parts may possess additional properties.

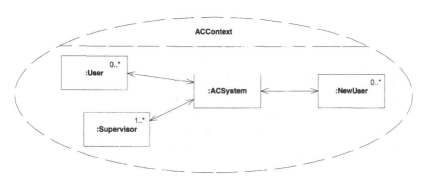

Figure 3-3. The context for the *ACSystem*.

---

[24] Multiplicities indicate lower and upper bounds on the number of objects that may play such part and are shown in the upper right-hand corner of the symbol representing a part, as shown in *Figure 3-3*. If no multiplicity is shown, it indicates that exactly one instance will be created for a part.

2.3   Behavior Modeling with Interactions (I)

In this section, we will describe the services of the access control system based on the domain statement in Section 2.1 and the concepts and structure outlined in Section 2.2.

Interactions are often described by Sequence Diagrams where horizontal arrows represent the messages between the lifelines represented by vertical lines.[25] Each lifeline represents a structural aspect of the system, such as its parts. In UML 1.x such sequence diagrams were quite simple, as illustrated by the utility service *GivePIN* in Figure 3-4: the *ACSystem* requests the personal identification number from the user and the user enters four digits. Each diagram has a frame with a name tag in the upper left corner.[26]

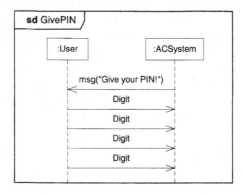

Figure 3-4. GivePIN - a very simple sequence diagram

We realize that *GivePIN* could be used within another interaction with the purpose of establishing access through the access control system. The sequence diagram *EstablishAccess* is shown in Figure 3-5.

We see in Figure 3-5 that *GivePIN* is referenced from within another sequence diagram with the obvious interpretation that the *GivePIN* reference (interaction occurrence) will be replaced by the full *GivePIN* interaction. The *EstablishAccess* interaction also shows a loop (depicted as a rectangle with a loop tag in the upper left corner) where the loop may iterate between 0 and 3 times, allowing for the user to try several times. Finally we show an

---

[25] The term "message" is used both for asynchronous signaling and procedure calls. The difference between these types of communication is indicated by the shape of the arrowhead. In our example we use asynchronous messages.

[26] The keyword "sd" is an abbreviation for "sequence diagram," but is used for all Interaction diagrams. There are four variants of interaction diagrams: sequence diagrams, communication diagrams, interaction overview diagrams and timing diagrams. This example uses only sequence diagrams.

alternative construct (depicted by a rectangle marked with the keyword "alt") distinguishing between the situation where the user is successful in getting access (ending in the continuation label *PIN OK*) and the situation where an error message (parameterized) is given (and ending in the continuation *PIN NOK*).[27] A dashed horizontal dividing line separates the different alternatives.

Loop and alternative are constructs introduced in UML 2.0 called combined fragments. This notation allows to concisely describe within one diagram a set of traces, which would otherwise require a number of diagrams.

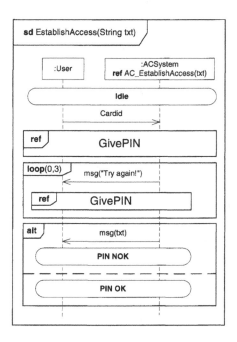

Figure 3-5. EstablishAccess

The interaction *EstablishAccess* is applied in the specifications of the three services *UserAccess* (see Figure 3-6), *PINChange* (see Figure 3-7), and *NewUser* (see Figure 3-8).[28]

---

[27] A "continuation" is a label such that scenarios starting on a continuation with a given label will continue where scenarios ending in the continuation with that label left off. Continuations are merely a syntactic device to break sequence diagrams into smaller units; no synchronization between lifelines is implied.

[28] The *ACSystem* lifelines have a ref-clause in their head. This notation refers to decomposition of the lifeline described in section 2.5.

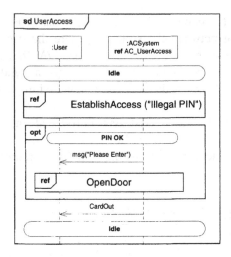

Figure 3-6. UserAccess

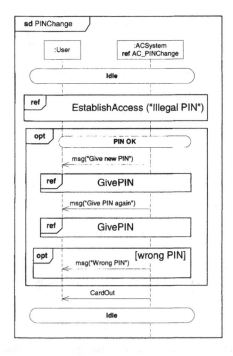

Figure 3-7. PINChange

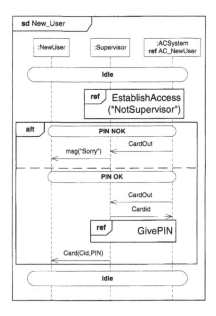

Figure 3-8. NewUser

In this section we have seen how the new structuring mechanisms of UML 2.0 contributes to making the description more compact and easier to overview.

2.4 Modeling with Internal Structures

As section 2.3 has shown, the behavior of the access control system is too complex to be captured by a simple class, and therefore we design *ACSystem* by decomposition: The *ACSystem* contains a number of access points, represented by parts specified by the class *AccessPoint*. The access points interact with the users who request access and are granted or denied access to the access zones. The access point does not make this decision; instead, it communicates with an *Authorizer* to verify the validity of an access request. The *ACSystem* may further have several *Consoles* that allow a supervisor to interact with the system, for example, to add new users.

The behavior of the *ACSystem* results from the cooperation of its parts, and the interaction of these parts with the context of the access control system. However, in contrast to the system shown in Figure 3-3, the *ACSystem* not merely emerges from its parts but there will indeed be a physical system object that can be identified as an instance of the *ACSystem*. Consequently, we use a class to model the *ACSystem*. The internal structure of the *ACSystem* is represented in a similar manner as shown earlier as a structure of connected parts.

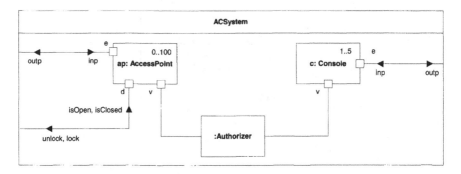

Figure 3-9. Internal structure of the access control system.

In addition to specifying which parts comprise the *ACSystem*, Figure 3-9 also specifies how many of these parts may be created when an instance of an *ACSystem* is created. As described by the multiplicities, the system will have at most one hundred access points and at most five consoles. When an *ACSystem* is created, it also will have an *Authorizer* object and one *Console* object (a non-zero lower multiplicity indicates the number of initial objects). Access points and additional consoles can be created up to the specified maximum and each will be linked as specified in the internal structure. The parts of the *ACSystem* can communicate amongst each other only as specified by the connectors; for example, it is not ordinarily possible for an *AccessPoint* object to communicate directly with a *Console* object.

Figure 3-9 shows the parts of the *ACSystem* linked in two manners: Connectors may directly attach to a part (as is the case with the *Authorizer*) or they may attach at ports. A port specifies a distinct interaction point between an object and its environment or between an object and its internal parts. It specifies the services a classifier provides to its environment as well as the services that a classifier requires of its environment. The provided and required interfaces of a port completely characterize any interaction that may occur between an object at the interaction point specified by the port and its environment. As such, a port fully isolates the object from its environment. This allows an object to be used in any context that satisfies the constraints specified by the ports on its classifier.

A port may forward any communicated information on attached connectors. Alternatively, a behavior port indicates that the instance directly handles the communication arriving at this port. Similarly, connectors attached to a part indicate that any arriving communication is handled by the corresponding instance rather than forwarded on a connector.

At times it will be of interest to highlight the information that is communicated along the connectors between parts of the internal structure. Information flows may be associated with connectors and describe the data that is communicated, as shown in Figure 3-9 for the information communicated from and to the environment of *ACSystem*.

Figure 3-10 shows the class definition for *Console*. With each of its ports we also show the interfaces that are provided and required by the respective ports. The services that are offered by the classifier at this port to its environment are indicated by the "ball" symbol. The services that this classifier expects from its environment are indicated by the "socket" symbol. (Alternatively, these interfaces can also be shown with the type of the port.)

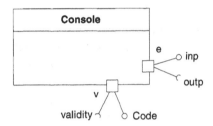

Figure 3-10. Class definition for *AccessPoint*.

2.5   Behavior Modeling with Interactions (II) – Decomposition

In section 2.3, we have shown how interactions are used to specify services between the system and its environment. Our next step towards designing the access control system would be to take advantage of the decomposition mechanisms of interactions and the internal structure of classes, as described in section 2.4. These mechanisms are closely related.

We shall have a closer look at the *PINChange* service (Figure 3-7) and see how this service is decomposed with respect to the *ACSystem*. Intuitively we apply magnifying glasses and look at the lifeline representing the *ACSystem* within *PINChange* following the ref-clause to *AC_PINChange*, shown in Figure 3-11. We see that the lifelines of *AC_PINChange* refer to the parts of the class *ACSystem*, as shown in Figure 3-9.

Furthermore, we observe that there are a number of messages going to and from the frame of the sequence diagram. The points on the diagram frame are called gates and represent the message interface between the decomposition and the environment of the lifeline being decomposed. Comparing with the service *PINChange* in Figure 3-7, we see that the gates and structuring concepts of the decomposition *AC_PINChange* correspond one to one with the event occurrences and structuring elements of *PINChange*. From the top we see that the interaction *EstablishAccess* has a counterpart in *AC_EstablishAccess*, the opt-fragment[29] has a counterpart and inside it we have *GivePIN* with its counterpart *AC_GivePIN*. A small difference is that in the decomposition the inner opt-fragment has an alt-fragment as its counterpart. This works since an opt-fragment is shorthand for an alt-fragment and the second operand of the alt-fragment in *AC_PINChange* has only a message that is between lifelines not visible on the upper level.

We also notice that the operands of the inner alt-fragment contain introductory constraints. These constraints are guards showing the assumptions that need to be true for the operand to be valid.[30]

A decomposition is an interaction occurrence; thus we may wonder about the interplay between plain interaction occurrences and decompositions. In Figure 3-7, we have decomposed *ACSystem*, which is covered by *EstablishAccess*. We can see the decomposition in Figure 3-11 and *EstablishAccess* in Figure 3-5. What would happen if we (as indicated in Figure 3-5) were to decompose the lifeline representing the *ACSystem* of *EstablishAccess*? As one can expect we must then obtain *AC_Establish-Access*, which is given in Figure 3-12. This interaction represents the intersection between the *ACSystem* lifeline in *ChangePIN* and the *EstablishAccess* interaction occurrence. The reader might want to verify that these sequence diagrams are consistent.

In doing so, the reader will notice that in *AC_EstablishAccess* (Figure 3-12) one of the lifelines represents an anonymous part of the class Entry, while no such part is present in the internal structure of *ACSystem* given in Figure 3-9. *Entry* represents the commonality between *AccessPoint* and *Console*, which we discovered through the decomposition process: in the services we have applied *EstablishAccess* between the *ACSystem* and the user. When we decomposed *ACSystem* into parts of type AccessPoint, *Console*, and *Authorizer*, we realized that in *AC_ChangePIN* (Figure 3-11) only the *Console* and the *Authorizer* were involved, since the user has to operate the *Console* when he wants to change the *PIN*. On the other hand, if we were to decompose *ACSystem* in the service *UserAccess*, we would see

---

[29] An "opt-fragment" is an "option" combined fragment. An option combined fragment is a shorthand for an alternative combined fragment ("alt-fragment" for short) where the second operand is empty.

[30] The keyword "else" represents the assumption that results from negating all other constraints of the same enclosing fragment.

that the *Console* is not involved at all while the *AccessPoint* was involved together with the *Authorizer*. Nevertheless, *Console* and *AccessPoint* are both be involved in establishing user access. This commonality is captured by the *Entry* class of the lifeline in *AC_EstablishAccess* (Figure 3-12).

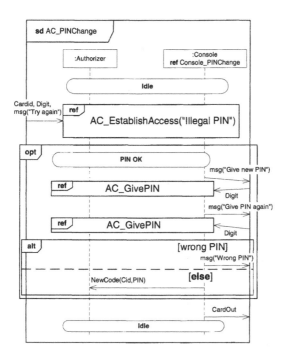

Figure 3-11. AC_PINChange

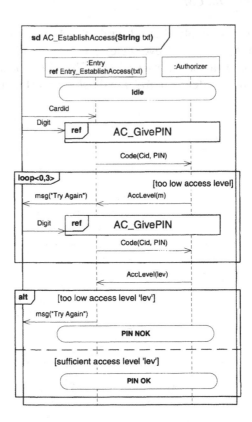

Figure 3-12. AC_EstablishAccess

2.6   Finalizing the Internal Structure

When studying the behavioral decomposition of *ACSystem*, we have learned that there are significant similarities between an access point and a console. This similarity was already hinted at in the internal structure shown in Figure 3-9: both *AccessPoint* and *Console* share a number of ports and are connected similarly. We introduce a common superclass, *Entry*, which abstracts these commonalities. *Entry* will not be able to stand alone; instead it is an abstract class, of which no objects will ever be created. Its concrete subclasses will add the necessary detail. This class hierarchy is shown in Figure 3-13.

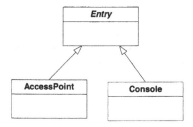

Figure 3-13. Class hierarchy for *Entry*, *AccessPoint*, and *Console*.

From examining the structure of *ACSystem*, we conclude that *Entry* will specify the interaction with the *Authorizer* as well as the user interactions. We decompose *Entry* further as shown in Figure 3-14. The *Entry* class also defines the classes for its *Panel* and *Controller* parts; these are shown as defined locally to *Entry* and are not visible outside of the context of *Entry*. We also see that *Entry* defines further interactions, *Entry_EstablishAccess* and *Entry_GivePIN*. Every instance of *Entry* will have the two interaction points represented by ports *e* and *v*.

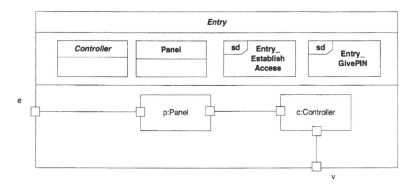

Figure 3-14. Internal structure of abstract class *Entry*.

We decide that the interaction with the user is mediated by a *Panel* where the user can enter the PIN. The interaction with the *Authorizer* will be mediated by the *Controller* class. It is clear that the *Controller* will provide different functionalities between access points and consoles. When specializing a class, all properties of the general class are inherited by the specialization but any redefinable element of the general class may be either replaced or extended. We make use of this capability and specify *Controller* as a redefinable class to indicate that subclasses of *Entry* will redefine its behavior.

Figure 3-15 and Figure 3-16 show the specification of *Console* and *AccessPoint*, respectively. From *Entry*, these classes inherit the structure comprised of *Controller* and *Panel*. As expected, both classes redefine the *Controller* to provide their specific behavior. For example, the *Console* will add the specifics of the interaction with the supervisor for adding a new user. While the *Console* is rather simple, the *AccessPoint* adds an additional part: a *Door*. The *Controller* in an access point also interacts with the door object; it senses the status of the door and sends lock and unlock commands. Class *AccessPoint* redefines the *Controller* inherited from *Entry*, extending it by adding a port to communicate with the associated door instance, in addition to augmenting its behavior. (Note that the inherited aspects are graphically represented by dashed lines to differentiate them from the extensions added in this class.)

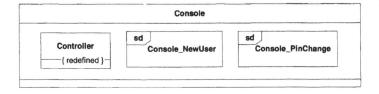

Figure 3-15. Internal structure of *Console*.

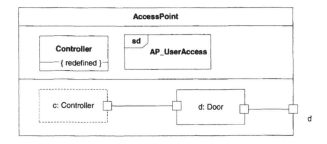

Figure 3-16. Internal structure of *AccessPoint*.

2.7   Behavioral Modeling with State machines

We have identified *Panel* as one of the parts of *Entry*. We could have synthesized the state machine behavior of *Panel* from the identified and specified interactions, but we choose to make it based upon an intuitive understanding of what the behavior is supposed to do.

This intuitive understanding takes as starting point the obvious states of the panel that a user will recognize: there is "no card" in the card reader or there is "one card" in the reader. The panel will behave differently in the two situations, and the user is supposed to do different things in the two situations.

In order to illustrate the different mechanisms of UML state machines, we give two versions of the *Panel* state machine. The *Panel* is not the intelligent part of our entry points: its only purpose is to accept cards with identifications and accept four digits of the PIN. In Figure 3-17, the behavior of *GivePIN* is defined by an operation, which is performed as part of two of the transitions. We have chosen to give the state machine behavior of class *Panel* the same name, but there is no such requirement.

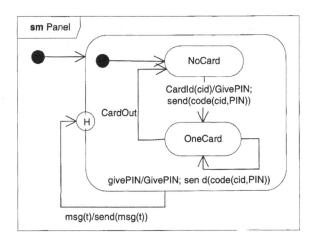

Figure 3-17. State machine *Panel* with *GivePIN* as an operation

In UML 1.x, the operation *GivePIN* would have to be defined as a private operation in the *class Panel*. With UML 2.0 it is also possible to define it more locally (and where it really belongs): as part of the state machine of *Panel*, as is illustrated in Figure 3-18: this symbol defines the properties (private attributes and operations) of the state machine *Panel*, while Figure 3-17 defines the states and transitions of *Panel*.

In the other version of the *Panel* state machine we have used a sub-state machine: *GivePIN* is defined as a separate state machine, and the *OneCard* state of the Panel state machine is a submachine state referring to the *GivePIN* state machine, see Figure 3-19 and Figure 3-20.

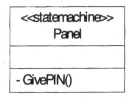

Figure 3-18. GivePIN defined as part of the Panel state machine

The effect of the submachine state *OneCard* is as if the *Panel* state machine had a composite state with the contents of *GivePIN*. The benefit of submachine states is that the referenced state machine can be defined independently of the containing state machine. Reading four digits and producing a PIN is a rather general behavior and can be (re)used in other parts of the same containing state machine, or even in other state machines, as we have already observed in the corresponding interactions.

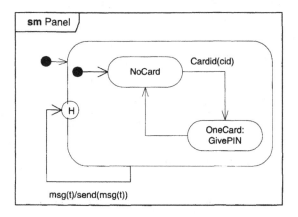

Figure 3-19. State machine *Panel* with submachine state according to *GivePIN*

The reusability of sub-state machines becomes more obvious when the independently defined state machine has a defined "interface" in terms of connection points for its transitions. Assume that the *GivePIN* state machine also has the ability to be triggered by a "golden" card instead of entering four digits. Entering a golden card will bypass the digit entering and send the code directly to the *Controller* and then wait for the card to be ejected from the panel. While the former *GivePIN* state machine only had an initial state as entry point, the gold card *GivePIN* state machine has a separate entry point called *goldenEntry*, see Figure 3-21. Entering the state machine through this entry point, the effect action of the transition leading to *waitCommand* will send the code to the controller. For illustration purposes, the former final state has been exchanged with an exit point called *exit*.

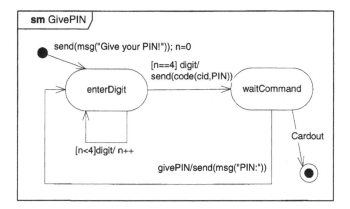

Figure 3-20. The state machine GivePIN

In Figure 3-22, the *Panel* state machine uses this new *GivePIN* sub-state machine by directing the transition triggered by the *goldcard* event to the entry point *goldenEntry* of the submachine state. It is also illustrated how an exit point is used as the source of a transition: a transition within *OneCard* leading to the exit point will imply that the transition in the containing state machine is triggered.

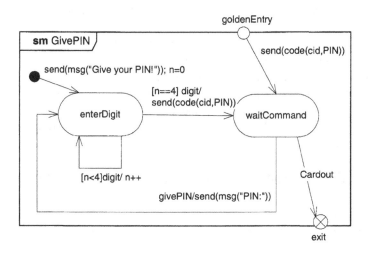

Figure 3-21. GivePIN state machine with *goldenEntry*

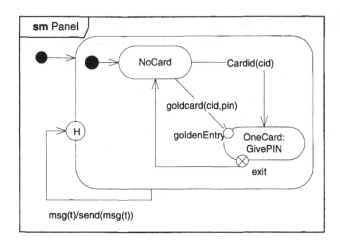

Figure 3-22. Panel with support for *goldcard* transition.

The benefit of entry/exit points is that the sub-state machine and the state machine referring to it may be defined independently. A referenced sub-state machine with entry/exit points can change internally without changing the referencing state machine.[31]

In addition to defining connection points for sub-state machines, the entry/exit points also split transitions. As an example, the transition triggered by the *goldcard* event is separated into one at the level of *Panel* and one at the level of *GivePIN*. Each of these partial transitions can have an effect action. In this example only the transition from the entry point and further to the waitCommand has an effect action.

This short introduction to state machine modeling with UML2.0 did not allow all structuring mechanisms to be covered in full detail. In addition, state machines can be specialized not only by behavioral subtyping, but also by structural subtyping [13]: similar to the inheritance of the internal structure of composite classes, a specialized state machine inherits the structure of the inherited state and transition graph and may redefine these states and transitions.

2.8   The Consistency of Interactions and State Machines

Having developed the UML model as a medley of creating class diagrams, interactions, composite structures and state machines, we may wonder whether our end result is internally consistent. Consistency is

---

[31] Stub states of UML 1.4 had a similar purpose, but stub states in the referring state machine had to be changed if the referenced sub-state machine was changed.

partially ensured by static requirements of the language, but there are behavioral aspects that we will not be able to establish from purely static rules.

Having established a number of behaviors defined through interactions on one hand and state machines on the other, we would like to assess whether the desired behavior of the interactions can be fulfilled by implementations derived from the state machines.

Our example here is the establishment of access, a utility applied in more than one of the services. We shall compare the definition of *Panel* given by state machines in Figure 3-19 and Figure 3-20 with the interaction given in Figure 3-12. In order to reach the necessary level of detail, Figure 3-23 shows the decomposition of *Entry* containing the *Panel* and the *Controller*.

The simple, partial check that we shall conduct is based on these principles:

1. Establish an initial alignment between the interaction and the state machine. What is the state of the state machine?
2. Assume that the messages into the state machine are determined by the interaction.
3. Check that the actions and especially output messages from the transition of the state machine correspond with the event occurrences on a lifeline.
4. Perform this test for all traces of the interaction.

The reader should appreciate that this procedure of consistency checking can be automated provided that the model is sufficiently precise. In our example there are a few places where informal text is used to simplify the illustrations, and this would obstruct automatic checking. It is, however, possible to define the interactions and the state machines such that automatic checking is feasible.

In our scenario, we will initially assume that the state *NoCard* corresponds to the continuation *Idle* in the interaction.

The interaction then describes that *Panel* will receive a *Cardid* message. In the *Panel* state machine this will trigger a transition leading to the state *OneCard* that is of sub-state machine *GivePIN*. There a message will be sent "Give your PIN!". We have not given the interaction *Entry_GivePIN* here, but looking in Figure 3-4 we can imagine what happens. The output from the state machine corresponds to that of the interaction. The interaction now specifies that there will be a number of digits entered. The corresponding behavior can easily be seen from the state *enterDigit* in *GivePIN*. The fourth digit will trigger a transition to state *waitCommand* and a code message with arguments is emitted. Again, the output message corresponds well with that specified in the interaction.

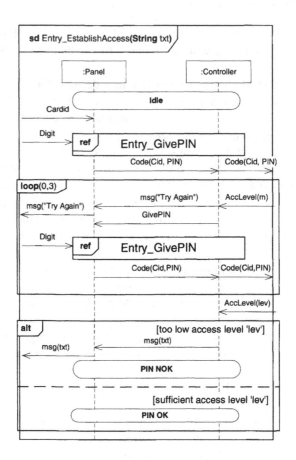

Figure 3-23. Entry_EstablishAccess

The loop of the interaction specifies a situation where the user has entered an incorrect PIN value and needs to reenter the PIN while the card is still in the card reader of the panel.

The interaction specifies the arrival of a message *msg* and that is handled from an outer composite state and returning to the same inner state *OneCard::waitCommand* through the history pseudo state. The output again corresponds to that of the interaction as *msg* is only forwarded to the user.

Then the interaction describes that the message *givePIN* arrives. The state machine then outputs a prompt and waits for digits again. The interaction indicates the same as pointed out above when first entering *Entry_GivePIN*.

Leaving the loop, the interaction specifies an alternative. One possibility is that a message is again relayed through the panel as we have considered before. Another variant is that nothing happens, but the interaction specifies a continuation label that indicates that the access has been successfully established. In either case, the panel is in state *OneCard::waitCommand* and depending on the services applying *Entry_EstablishAccess*, it will eventually get a *CardOut* message to eject the card.

We conclude that given our initial alignment assumption, the utility *Entry_EstablishAccess* is fulfilled by the state machine *Panel*, as defined.

3. CONCLUSIONS

In this chapter, we have introduced the structuring mechanisms of UML 2.0 showing that these new facilities will potentially make descriptions more concise, more precise, more detailed, more compact, and more easily reused.

The new structural concepts have made UML more expressive especially in domains where precise behavioral specifications and reuse of specifications are important.

The composite structure of classes makes it possible to define contextual structures. Interaction occurrences in interactions and sub-state machines in state machines have added to reusability of behavior. More widespread application of such mechanisms also makes the overall specification more compact and more maintainable.

In section 2.8, we showed that there is simple correspondence between concepts of declarative descriptions through interactions and the imperative descriptions through state machines. Formal or semi-formal validation techniques can be applied.

REFERENCES

[1] Jacobson, "Language Support for Changeable Large Real Time Systems", OOPSLA'86, *ACM Special Issue of Sigplan Notices*, Vol. 21, No. 11, 1986. pp. 377-384.

[2] Rockstrom, and R. Saracco, "SDL--CCITT specification and description language", *IEEE Trans. Communications*, Vol. 30, No. 6, 1982. pp. 1310-1318.

[3] Møller-Pedersen, D. Belsnes, and H.P. Dahle, "Rationale and Tutorial on OSDL: An Object-Oriented Extension of SDL", *Computer Networks*, Vol. 13, No. 2, 1987.

[4] J. Grabowski and E. Rudolph, "Putting Extended Sequence Charts to Practice", in *Proc. 4th SDL Forum*. North-Holland, Lisbon, 1989.

[5] International Telecommunications Union, *Message Sequence Charts (MSC)*, Recommendation Z.120, ITU-T, Geneva, 1999.

[6] Harel. "Statecharts: A visual formalism for complex systems", *Science of Computer Programming*, Vol. 8, No. 3, 1987.

[7] Garlan and M. Shaw, "An Introduction to Software Architecture", 1-39. *Advances in Software Engineering and Knowledge Engineering*, Vol. 2., World Scientific Press, New York, 1993.

[8]   Garlan, R. Monroe, and D. Wile: "ACME: An Architecture Description Interchange Language", *Proc. of CASCON*, 1997. pp. 169-183.

[9]   D. Luckham, et al., "Specification and Analysis of System Architecture Using Rapide", *IEEE Transactions on Software Engineering*, Vol. 21, No. 6, 1995.

[10] B. Selic, G. Gullekson, and P.T. Ward, *Real-Time Object-Oriented Modeling*, 1994.

[11] C. Bock and J. Odell, "A Foundation for Composition", *Journal Of Object-Oriented Programming*, Vol. 7, No 6, 1994.

[12] D. Harel and E. Gery, "Executable Object Modeling with Statecharts", *IEEE Computer*, July 1997.

[13] International Telecommunications Union, *Specification and Description Language (SDL)*, Recommendation Z.100, ITU-T, Geneva, 1999.

[14] B. Møller-Pedersen and T. Weigert, "Towards a Convergence of SDL and UML", *Proc. 2nd Intl. Conf. on the Unified Modeling Language*, Ft. Collins, 1999.

[15] D. Garlan, J. Knapman, B. Møller-Pedersen, B. Selic, and T. Weigert, "Modeling of Architectures with UML", *Proc. 3rd Intl. Conf. on the Unified Modeling Language*, York, 2000.

[16] R. Bræk, J. Gorman, Ø. Haugen, G. Melby, B. Møller-Pedersen, and R. Sanders, "Quality by construction exemplified by TIMe – The Integrated Methodology, *Telektronikk*, Vol. 95, No. 1, 1999. pp. 73-82. See also http://www.sintef.no/time, Sintef, Trondheim, 1997.

[17] International Telecommunications Union, *SDL Combined with UML*, Recommendation Z.109, ITU-T, Geneva. 1999.

Chapter 4

Message Sequence Charts

David Harel[1], and P.S. Thiagarajan[2]

[1]*Faculty of Mathematics and Computer Science, The Weizman Institute of Science.* [2]*School of Computing, National University of Singapore.*

Abstract: *Message sequence charts* (MSCs) constitute an attractive visual formalism that is widely used to capture system requirements during the early design stages in domains such as telecommunication software. A version of MSCs called *sequence diagrams* is one of the behavioral diagram types adopted in the UML. In this chapter we survey MSCs and their extensions. In particular, we discuss *high level* MSCs, which allow MSCs to be combined in various regular ways, and the more recent mechanism of *communicating transaction processes*, which can be used to structure sequence charts to capture system behaviors more directly. We also discuss in some detail *live sequence charts* (LSCs), a multi-modal extension of MSCs with considerably richer expressive power, and the *play-in/out* method that makes it possible to use LSCs directly as an executable specification.

Key words: Message Sequence Charts, scenarios, Live Sequence Charts, Communicating Transaction Processes, executable specification

The language of *message sequence charts* (MSCs) is a popular mechanism for specifying scenarios that describe patterns of interactions between processes or objects. MSCs are particularly useful in the early stages of system development. The language has found its way into many design methodologies, and a variant of it has been made part of the UML notational framework, where it is called *sequence diagrams*. There is also a standard syntax for MSCs that appears as a recommendation of the ITU (previously called the CCITT) [31].

In many object-oriented system development methodologies, the user first specifies the system's use cases and some specific instantiations of each use case are then described using sequence diagrams (MSCs). In a later modeling step, the behavior of a class is described by a state diagram (usually a statechart [8]) that prescribes a behavior for each of the instances

L. Lavagno, G. Martin and B. Selic (eds.), UML for Real, 77-105.
© 2003 *Kluwer Academic Publishers.*

of the class. Finally, the objects are implemented as code in a specific programming language. Parts of this design flow can be automated, such as the generation of code from object model diagrams and statecharts, as exemplified in ObjecTime [28] and Rhapsody [10,17].

In such design flows, the main role of MSCs is to capture system requirements in the form of "good" scenarios that the implemented system should exhibit. Sometimes an MSC is prepared for a "bad" scenario that the implementation should not allow. System requirements captured in this intuitive fashion can serve as a useful interface between the end-users of the system and the system designer. They can also serve as a test bench for validating some aspects of the implementation. A substantial portion of research on MSCs has been driven by this way of using MSCs, with the focus on mechanisms for describing collections of scenarios, techniques for analyzing such collections and relating them to a state-based executable specification.

However, there are several disadvantages to this way of using MSCs in a design methodology. First, MSCs possess a rather weak partial order semantics that makes it impossible to capture interesting behavioral requirements. For instance, one cannot say "if P sends the message M to Q then Q *must* pass on this message to R". In this sense, MSCs are far weaker than formalisms such as temporal logics for capturing requirements and constraints. A second disadvantage is that it is not obvious what the relationship between the MSC requirements and the executable specification (modeling the implementation) should be. Often, it is also very problematic to verify that the desired relationship between requirements and executable specification exists.

To address these concerns, a broad extension to MSCs called *live sequence charts* (LSCs) was proposed in [6]. LSCs can be viewed as a multi-modal version of MSCs, with various means for distinguishing between possible, necessary and forbidden behavior. The expressive power of LSCs is comparable to that of temporal logic and statecharts (except that for pragmatic reasons, LSCs have been limited in the allowed depth of nested alternation of modalities). Using LSCs, one can start to look more seriously at the relationships and possible automated transitions between requirements, as captured by use cases and LSCs, and executable specifications, as captured by, say, statecharts. In addition, the very recent *play-in/out* method and the corresponding Play-Engine tool, described in detail in [14], makes it possible to view the LSCs themselves as executable specifications.

In this chapter we present a brief survey of MSCs, covering both these themes. In Section 1, we focus on research related to the use of MSCs and their high-level extensions, HMSCs, to capture system requirements and test cases. As stated already, the main concerns here are the mechanisms for capturing a collection of MSCs and relating such collections to executable specifications. In Section 2, we turn to the use of LSCs to capture behavioral requirements, and in Section 3, we describe the play-in/play-out method and the Play-Engine. In Section 4, we present a related approach, in which a restricted kind of LSCs called *transaction schemes* are used, in conjunction with conventional control flow notations like Petri nets, to formulate executable specifications. Section 5 discusses some ideas about needed extensions.

1. MSCS AND HMSCS

Here we will focus on the most basic kind of MSCs; those that model communication through message-passing via reliable FIFOs. In what follows, we will often refer to MSCs as charts. We shall define MSCs as certain kinds of labeled partial orders. We shall use the visual representation shown in the MSC of Figure 4-1.

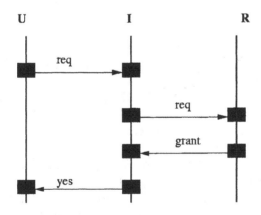

Figure 4-1. A simple MSC

This chart captures a scenario in which a user (U) send a request to an interface (I) to gain access to a resource R. The interface in turn sends a request to the resource, and receives "grant" as a response, after which it sends "yes" to U. The vertical lines represent the life-lines of the processes taking part in the scenario . As usual, time is assumed to flow downwards along each life-line. The directed arrows going across the life-lines represent the causal link from a send event (the source of the arrow) to the corresponding receive event (the target of the arrow), with the label on the arrow denoting the message being transmitted.

1.1   Basic MSCs

Throughout this section we assume a finite set of processes (agents, objects) P, a finite message alphabet M and a finite set of actions Act. We let p and q range over P, m and m' range over M, and a and b range over Act. The processes in P communicate with each other by sending and receiving messages taken from M via point-to-point, reliable FIFOs. The processes can also perform internal actions taken from Act, representing computational steps performed by the agents. We shall use Σ_p to denote the set of actions executed by the process p. These are actions of the form $< p!q,m >$, $< p?q,m >$ and $< p,a >$. The communication action $< p!q,m >$ stands for p sending the message m to q and $< p?q,m >$ stands for p receiving the message m from q. On the other hand, $< p,a >$ is an internal action of p, with a being the member of Act being executed. We set $\Sigma = \bigcup_{p \in P} \Sigma_p$.

Turning now to the definition of MSCs, we first define a Σ-labeled poset (partially ordered set) to be a structure $Ch = (E, \leq, \lambda)$, where $(E, \leq)$ is a partially ordered set and $\lambda : E \to \Sigma$ is a labeling function. For $X \subseteq E$ we define

$\downarrow X = \{e' \mid e' \leq e \text{ for some } e \in X\}$. When $X = \{e\}$ is a singleton we shall write $\downarrow (e)$ instead of $\downarrow (\{e\})$. We say that X is *downclosed*, whenever $X = \downarrow (X)$.

For $p \in P$, we set $E_p = \{e \mid \lambda(e) \in \Sigma_p\}$. These are the events in which p takes part. Further,

$$E_{p!q} = \{e \mid e \in E_p \text{ and } \lambda(e) = < p!q,m > \text{ for some } m \in M\}$$

Similarly,

$$E_{p?q} = \{e \mid e \in E_p \text{ and } \lambda(e) = < p?q,m > \text{ for some } m \in M\}$$

Finally, for each channel $c = (p,q)$, we define the communication relation R_c via $(e,e') \in R_c$ iff $|\downarrow (e) \cap E_{p!q}| = |\downarrow (e') \cap E_{q?p}|$ and $\lambda(e) = < p!q,m >$ and $\lambda(e') = < q?p,m >$ for some message m.

An MSC over (P,M,Act) is a Σ-labeled poset $Ch = (E, \leq, \lambda)$ that satisfies:

1. $\leq_p$ is a linear order for each p, where $\leq_p$ is $\leq$ restricted to $E_p \times E_p$.
2. Suppose $\lambda(e) = < p?q,m >$. Then $|\downarrow (e) \cap E_{p?q}| = |\downarrow (e) \cap E_{q!p}|$ and there exists $e' \in \downarrow (e)$ such that $\lambda(e') = < q!p,m >$ and $|\downarrow (e) \cap E_{q!p}| = |\downarrow (e') \cap E_{q!p}|$.
3. For every p,q with $p \neq q$, $|E_{p?q}| = |E_{q!p}|$.
4. $\leq = (\leq_p \cup R_p)^*$, where $\leq_p = \bigcup_{p \in P} \leq_p$ and $R_p = \bigcup_{p \in P} R_p$.

The first condition says that all the events that a process takes part in are linearly ordered; each process is a sequential agent. The second condition says that messages must be sent before they can be received. The third condition says that there are no dangling communication edges in an MSC; all sent messages have also been received. The final condition says that the causality relation between the events in an MSC is completely determined by the order in which the events occur within each process and communication relation relating a send-receive pairs. (Many other variants of MSCs with added features can be defined along similar lines.)

In the graphical presentation of the chart $Ch = (E, \leq, \lambda)$, the elements of E_p are arranged along a life-line with the earlier elements appearing above the later elements. Further, a directed arrow labeled with m is drawn from $e \in E_p$ to $e' \in E_q$ provided $\lambda(e) = < p!q, m >$ and $\lambda(e') = < q?p, m >$ and $|\!\downarrow (e) \cap E_{p!q}| = |\!\downarrow (e') \cap E_{q?p}|$.

1.2 Regular collections of MSCs

A collection of charts constitutes the requirements that an implementation should meet. One key issue involves the specific kinds of chart collections that should be considered as requirement sets, the point being that the requirements themselves could be subjected to analysis and thus help detect design errors at an early stage. Temporal logics, on which model checking is based, suggest that *regular* collections of behavioral objects are ideal candidates for logical analysis [29]. Hence a fruitful notion to look for is that of a regular collection of charts [16], in analogy with the standard notion of regular collections of strings (i.e., regular languages).

Let $Ch = (E, \leq, \lambda)$ be a chart. Each linearization of this Σ-labeled poset is a run of the scenario depicted by the chart and it is a member of Σ^*. Thus the runs of this chart are a subset of Σ^*, which we shall denote by $lin(Ch)$. For instance, the sequence $<U!I, req>$ $<I?U, req>$ $<I!R, req>$ $<R?I, req>$ $<R!I, grant>$ $<I?R, grant>$ $<R!U, yes>$ $<U?I, yes>$ is in $lin(Ch_1)$ for the chart Ch_1 shown in Figure 4-1. In fact, it is its only member.

Now let L be a collection of charts over (P, M, Act). Then L is said to be a *regular collection* if $lin(L)$ is a regular subset of Σ^*, where, as might be expected, $lin(L) = \bigcup \{ lin(Ch) \mid Ch \in L \}$. From now on we will use the term "language" instead of "collection".

Here now is a simple example of an MSC language that is *not* regular. Assume $P = \{P, C\}$, $M = \{O\}$ and $Act = \varnothing$. Then the language $\{Ch_1, Ch_2, \ldots, Ch_n \ldots\}$ is not regular, where for each n, the chart Ch_n is as shown in Figure 4-2. Intuitively the non-regularity follows from the fact that the FIFO size is not bounded in the set of scenarios described by this collection.

In the setting of strings and labeled trees there is a close connection between finite state automata, regular languages and Monadic Second Order (MSO) logics (which naturally contain temporal logics) [29]. A similar relationship exists also for regular chart languages. Here the corresponding automata are called *message passing automata* (MPAs), and they consist of a network of finite state sequential automata, one for each process, that communicate with each other through reliable FIFOs that are *bounded* in length. The component automata can perform three types of transitions; internal, send and receive. In general, these automata will need to use a "broader" alphabet than M. Thus, there will be a finite message alphabet Θ associated with each automaton. Consequently, messages that are sent and received by the component automata will be of the form (m, θ), with $m \in M$ and θ in Θ.

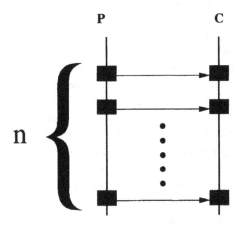

Figure 4-2. The producer-consumer example

Some of the global control states are designated to be initial and some are designated to be final ones. An initial configuration consists of an initial global control state and empty FIFOs. Similarly, a final configuration consists of a final control state and empty FIFOs. The notion of an accepting run over a string in Σ^* is defined in the usual way, and it is easy to show that any string accepted by an MPA is in $lin(Ch)$ for some chart Ch. Moreover, if one member of $lin(Ch)$ is accepted by the automaton, then all members of $lin(Ch)$ are accepted by it too. In this sense, an MPA accepts a language of charts.

The main result here is that a chart language is regular iff there is an MPA that accepts it. This result, as well as a number of other results concerning regular chart languages, including a logical characterization, can be found in [16].

1.3   High-level MSCs and message sequence graphs

Though MPAs characterize regular MSC languages, they are not an appropriate mechanism for presenting a collection of MSCs. Indeed, the visual appeal of MSCs is lost, especially in terms of capturing system requirements. Rather, it is the role of MPAs and related mechanisms to describe the implementation of a set of requirements. One popular and standard mechanism for directly presenting a collection of MSCs is called *high-level MSCs*, or HMSCs; see [31].

An HMSC is basically a finite state automaton whose states are labeled by MSCs. Consequently one can write out finite specifications involving choice, concatenation and iteration operations over a finite set of seed MSCs. In general, the specification can be hierarchical, in that a state of the automaton can be labeled by an HMSC instead of an MSC. In what follows we shall ignore this feature and instead consider flattened HMSCs, which will be called *message sequence graphs* (MSGs). An example of an MSG is shown in Figure 4-3.

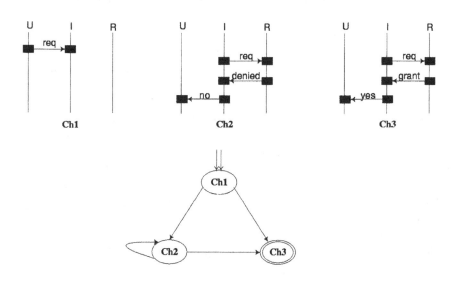

Figure 4-3. A simple MSG

Intuitively, this MSG captures a family of scenarios consisting of a user (U) sending a request to an interface (I) to access a resource (R). The interface queries the resource, and if it gets the response "denied", it sends a "no" to the user and tries again. It keeps trying until it gets the response "granted", at which point it send "yes" to U and the transaction ends.

The edges in an MSG represent the natural operation of chart concatenation. The collection of charts represented by an MSG consists of all those charts obtained by tracing a path in the MSG from an initial control state to a terminal control state and concatenating the MSCs that are encountered along the path. There are two intuitive ways of concatenating charts. In synchronous concatenation, $Ch.Ch'$ denotes a scenario in which *all* the events in Ch must finish before *any* event in Ch' can occur. This is the method that we will encounter in dealing with conditions and precharts in the setting of live sequence charts (LSCs) presented in the next section. The synchronous composition requires a protocol for all the concerned life-lines to synchronize. It rules out the parallelism that could arise had we let the second chart start its operation before the predecessor chart completely finished.

The second way of concatenating charts — which is the one we will consider in this section — is the asynchronous composition. Here the concatenation is carried out at the level of life-lines. More precisely, let $Ch^1 = (E^1, \leq^1, \lambda^1)$ and $Ch^2 = (E^2, \leq^2, \lambda^2)$ be a pair of MSCs. Assume that E^1 and E^2 are disjoint sets. Then $Ch^1 \circ Ch^2$ is the MSC $Ch = (E, \leq, \lambda)$, where:

- $E = E^1 \cup E^2$
- $\lambda(e) = \lambda^1(e)$ ($\lambda^2(e)$) if e is in E^1 (E^2).
- $\leq$ is the least partial ordering relation over E that contains $\leq^1$ and $\leq^2$ and satisfies: If $e \in E_p^1$ and $e' \in E_p^2$ for some p, then $e \leq e'$.

Clearly the asynchronous concatenation of two charts is also a chart. In contrast, the synchronous concatenation of two charts may not result in a chart. For instance, suppose the chart $PC0$ consists of two life-lines P and C, with P having a single send event $< P!C, m >$ and C having a single receiving event $< C?P, m >$. Consider the synchronous concatenation $PC0.PC1$, where $PC1$ is an isomorphic copy of $PC0$. In the resulting labeled poset, the first receive event of C will be earlier than the second send event of P with nothing in between. As a result, it is not an MSC.

Returning to MSGs, one traces a path from an initial state to a final state in the graph and concatenates *asynchronously* the sequence of MSCs encountered on the way. The resulting MSC is in the language defined by the MSG. Thus for the MSG shown in Figure 4-3, the chart $Ch1 \circ Ch2 \circ Ch2 \circ Ch3$ is in the language defined by the MSG, while $Ch1 \circ Ch2$ is not.

It turns out that MSGs have a surprising amount of expressive power in terms of the MSC languages they can define. For instance, they can easily define languages that are *not* regular. Both MSGs shown in Figure 4-4 define languages that are not regular. In these MSGs the one control state is both initial and final.

An interesting issue here is to figure out when an MSG specifies a regular chart language. In general, this is an undecidable problem [15]. However, there is a sufficient (though not necessary) condition for regularity, that can be checked syntactically, called com-boundedness [3,15]. To define this property, we need the following notion.

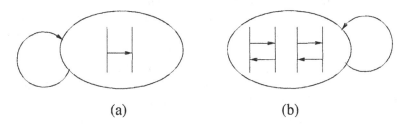

(a)   (b)

Figure 4-4. MSGs generating non-regular MSC languages

Let $Ch = (E, \leq, \lambda)$ be a chart. The *communication graph* of Ch, denoted by G_{Ch}, is the directed graph with node set P, in which there is an edge from p to q iff there is an event of the form $< p!q, m >$ in the chart. We say that Ch is *com-bounded* if G_{Ch} consists of precisely one strongly-connected component and possibly additional isolated nodes. An MSG is com-bounded if the chart obtained by concatenating all the charts encountered while traversing any one of its elementary circuits is com-bounded. For example, the MSG shown in Figure 4-4(a) is not com-bounded because the communication graph of the chart generated by the only elementary circuit does not have a strongly connected component. As for the MSG of Figure 4-4(b), it is not com-bounded because the chart generated by its only elementary circuit consists of *two* strongly connected components. A detailed characterization of the regular MSC languages definable by MSGs can be found in [15].

1.4   Other work on MSCs

A number of studies are available that are concerned with individual MSCs in terms of their semantics and properties [2,18]. Muscholl, Peled, and Su [24] investigate various *matching problems* for MSCs and MSGs, where matching denotes embedding one partial order in another. In [4] Ben-

Abdallah and Leue identify and characterize two properties of MSCs that are intuitively undesirable from an implementation point of view and give algorithms to detect such anomalies. The first of them is that of *process divergence*, signifying that the specification allows some process to have an unbounded number of unreceived messages in its buffer. Divergence-freeness is implied by regularity, but does not coincide with it. Figure 4-4(b) provides a simple counter-example, because the language of this MSG is divergence-free but not regular. The second under-specification detected by Ben-Abdallah and Leue is that of *nonlocal choice*. This denotes the existence of branching choices where different processes have the possibility of taking conflicting routes in the MSG specification.

Alur and Yannakakis [3] consider model checking problems (in a simple linear time framework) for systems modeled as MSGs with respect to various semantics. They show that for synchronous concatenation of MSCs on the paths of the MSG, the problem is co-NP-complete, while it is undecidable in general for asynchronous concatenation. They also define the notion of com-boundedness, which they term boundedness. They then show that the set of linearizations of the MSC language defined by a com-bounded MSG is a regular string language. Thus, in our terminology, com-bounded MSGs define regular chart languages. This notion has also been termed *locally synchronous* by Muscholl and Peled [23], who show that even for com-bounded MSGs two behavioral properties, race condition and confluence, are undecidable. Alur, Etiessami and Yannakaki [1] have also shown that one cannot effectively determine whether the MSC language specified by a bounded MSG is weakly realizable. Actually, weak realizability is a closure property; an MSC language L is deemed to be weakly realizable if for each MSC Ch, the following holds: Suppose for each p, there exists an MSC Ch_p in L such that both Ch and Ch_p have identical p-projections. Then Ch itself must be in L. The point is, if the chart languages specified by a bounded MSG has this property then it can be realized as message passing automata in a straightforward fashion whereas the corresponding problem for bounded MSGs in general is much more involved.

A detailed study about realizing HMSCs as Petri nets under different notions of approximation can be found in [5].

2.   LIVE SEQUENCE CHARTS

MSCs are excellent candidates for specifying *inter-object* behavior in the form of scenarios. However, the implementation of the system will have to be in terms of *intra-object* behavior, which describes — say, in the form of a statechart or an FSM — how an individual object behaves under all possible circumstances. A vital issue here is the relationship between the inter-object specifications given in terms of charts, which we have been referring to as *requirements* and the intra-object specifications that are state-based, and which we shall hence refer to as *executable specifications*. A number of possibilities are:

1. The scenarios generated by the executable specifications through all the possible runs should *be included* in the the set of scenarios constituting the requirements.

2. The scenarios generated by the executable specifications through all the possible runs should *include* the set of scenarios constituting the requirements.

3. The scenarios generated by the executable specifications through all the possible runs should *equal* the set of scenarios constituting the requirements.

Regardless of the choice made here, requirements given in MSCs still place only a weak *existential* constraint on the executable specifications. In possibility (1), for example, we require that for every scenario Ch in the requirements there *exists* a run of the executable specification that corresponds to Ch. Possibility (2) requires that if Ch is a scenario generated by the executable specification along *some* run, then Ch is in the set of requirements. Possibility (3) is just a conjunction of (1) and (2). Thus, there are no means for requiring that under certain conditions, a particular scenario *must* evolve, or that certain specific scenarios should *never* occur. The language of *live sequence charts* (LSCs; see [6]) has been designed to address this deficiency, yielding a far more powerful formalism for scenario-based behavioral specification. This formalism also helps to establish a tighter and more fruitful relationship between requirements and executable specifications. Indeed, later on we sketch a way to view the LSC requirements themselves as the executable specification.

2.1 The duality of possible and necessary

The basic feature of LSCs is its catering for the dual notions of possible and necessary, or existential and universal. This is done both on the level of an entire chart and on the level of its elements. There are thus two types of charts, *universal* and *existential*. The universal charts are used to specify requirements that *all* the possible system runs must satisfy. A universal chart typically contains a *prechart* followed by a main chart, to capture the requirement that if along any run the scenario depicted in the prechart occurs, the system *must* also execute the main chart. Existential charts specify sample interactions — typically between the system components and the environment — that at least one system run must satisfy. Existential charts can be used to specify system tests and illustrate typical unrestricted runs, whereas universal charts give the "hard" behavioral requirements of the system. So much for an entire chart.

As to elements in the charts, most of these can be *cold* or *hot*, corresponding to possible and necessary, respectively. Thus, LSCs have *cold* and *hot* conditions, which are provisional and mandatory guards. If a cold condition holds during an execution, control passes to the location immediately after the cold condition, and if it is false, the chart context in which this condition occurs is exited and execution may continue. A hot condition, on the other hand, must always be true. If an execution reaches a hot condition that evaluates to false this is a violation of the requirements, and the system should abort. For example, if we form an LSC from a prechart *Ch* and a main chart consisting of a single *false* hot condition, the semantics is that *Ch* can never occur. In other words, it is forbidden, an *anti-scenario*. On the other hand cold conditions can be used to program branches and if-then-else constructs. The LSC framework also allows bounded and unbounded loops which, when combined with cold conditions, can be used to construct *while* loops and *repeat-until* loops.

Other elements in an LSC can be cold or hot, such as events and locations along the life-lines, and we shall not dwell on the different semantics of these here. See [6] for details.

Figure 4-5 shows an example of an LSC that captures the following requirement: *Whenever the user dials '2' and then clicks the 'call' button on Phone1, the phone sends the message 'call(2)' to Chan1. If Chan1 is out of order the scenario ends. Otherwise it forwards the message to the switch, which then sends a message 'call(1)' to Chan2. If Chan2 is in order it forwards the message to Phone2. Otherwise, it sends an error message to Phone1.*

In the diagram, the if-like prechart (the top dashed hexagon) is placed at the beginning of the universal chart, and while the main chart contains the consequential part of the requirement. Cold elements are denoted by dashed lines and hot elements by solid lines.

The LSC shown in Figure 4-5 illustrates many features offered by the LSC formalism. It will be convenient to break these features down into simple units and present them individually.

A *basic universal LSC* (over (P, M, Act)) *with a prechart* is a structure $S = (E, \leq, Pch, \lambda)$ where :

1. $Pch = (E_{Pch}, \leq_{Pch}, \lambda_{Pch})$ is a chart with $E_{Pch} \cap E = \varnothing$.
2. $(E, \leq, \lambda)$ is a labeled partial order with $\lambda : E \rightarrow \Sigma \cup \{Pch\}$, where Σ is as defined in the previous section w.r.t. (P, M, Act).

3. There is a unique event e_0 which is the least under $\leq$ and $\lambda^{-1}(Pch) = \{e_0\}$.

4. $Ch = (E', \leq', \lambda')$ is a chart called the *main chart*, where $E' = E - \{e_0\}$ and $\leq'$ is $\leq$ restricted to $E' \times E'$ and λ' is λ restricted E'.

Pch is the prechart serving as the guard of the main chart. In this presentation, the prechart is specified as a refinement of the least event e_0, to capture the idea that the prechart must execute before the main chart can begin. The semantics of this basic LSC is that in any execution of the system, whenever *Pch* is executed, it must be followed by an execution of the main chart.

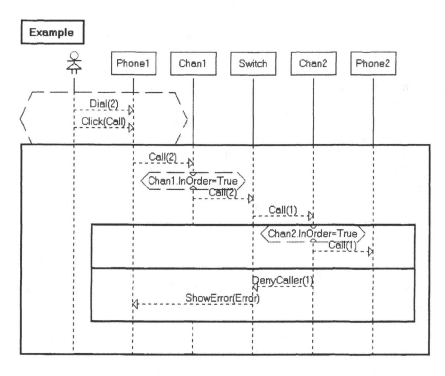

Figure 4-5. A sample LSC

We can also use conditions as guards. The conditions are predicates concerning the local states of the processes. In a basic setting, which is the one we will consider here, these predicates will be just propositional formulas constructed out of boolean assertions concerning the local states. We shall accordingly assume a family of pairwise-disjoint sets of atomic propositions $\{AP_p\}_{p \in P}$, and set $AP = \bigcup_{p \in P} AP_p$. We let A and B range over AP. Suppose φ is a propositional formula built out of AP. Then

$loc(\varphi)$ is the set of processes whose atomic propositions appear in φ. More precisely, $loc(A) = p$ if $A \in AP_p$, $loc(\Box\varphi) = loc(\varphi)$ and $loc(\varphi_1 \vee \varphi_2) = loc(\varphi_1) \cup loc(\varphi_2)$.

A *basic universal LSC* (over (P, M, Act)) *with a pre-condition* is a structure $S = (E, \leq, \varphi, \lambda)$, where :

1. φ is a boolean formula over AP.
2. $(E, \leq, \lambda)$ is a labeled partial order, with $\lambda : E \to \Sigma \cup \{\varphi\}$, where Σ is as before.
3. There is a unique event e_0, which is least under $\leq$ and $\lambda^{-1}(\varphi) = \{e_0\}$.
4. $Ch = (E', \leq', \lambda')$ is a chart called the *main chart*, where $E' = E - \{e_0\}$ and $\leq'$ is $\leq$ restricted to $E' \times E'$ and λ' is λ restricted E'.

Here again, the idea is that all the processes in $loc(\varphi)$ first synchronize and φ is evaluated. If true, the main chart is executed and if false it is skipped. The semantics of this basic LSC is that, along any execution, if φ holds it must be followed by an execution of the main chart, otherwise there is no constraint.

There are also corresponding versions of basic existential LSCs. For the version with the prechart, the semantics is that there exists an execution along which the prechart is executed followed by an execution of the main chart. This does not add much to the expressive power, except for the requirement that the prechart must finish executing before the main chart can execute. For the version with the pre-condition, the semantics is that there exists an execution along which the guard condition holds and this is then followed by an execution of the main chart.

Finally, we may define LSCs with post-conditions in a similar way. Here the event e_0 labeled with the condition is required to be the *greatest* event under the partial order associated with the LSC. The intended semantics is that along any execution, whenever the main chart of the LSC executes then at the end the post-condition must hold. This gives a different way to specify anti-scenarios: Ch would be taken to be the main chart and the post-condition would be taken to be false. One can also define basic existential LSCs with post-conditions with the obvious semantics.

Note that a "stand-alone" cold condition φ can be obtained by a basic universal LSC whose pre-condition is φ and whose main chart is empty. Similarly, a hot condition φ can be obtained by a universal LSC whose post-condition is φ and whose main chart is empty.

2.2 Control constructs

We can now compose the basic LSCs and the derived cold and hot conditions to construct more complex LSCs. One basic idea would be to allow the main chart of an LSC itself to be an LSC. The second idea would be to asynchronously concatenate LSCs. For instance, in Figure 4-5, at the outermost level, we have a universal LSC with a prechart. The prechart consists of the scenario where the user dials "2" and clicks "call". The main chart can be viewed as consisting of a simple chart concatenated with a universal chart with a pre-condition. This pre-condition consists of 'Chan1-in-Order' being true. The main chart of this universal chart can be viewed as consisting of a simple chart (Chan1 forwards the call to the switch which in turn forwards the call to Chan2) concatenated with a universal chart, etc. In [6] these combinatory operations were limited, so as not to overwhelm real-world users of LSCs. Thus, only one level of universal/existential alternation was allowed when nesting charts: you may have existential subcharts inside the main chart, but you cannot have universal charts inside those.

Yet another feature of LSCs is the looping construct, which comes in three flavors: The *unbounded* loop, in which a subchart is annotated with the * symbol, indicating that that the number of times it is executed is not known a priori. Typically, such a loop will contain a cold condition which is used to exit the loop upon becoming false. A *fixed* loop is annotated by a number or an integer variable name, and is executed a fixed number of times, according to the number or the variable's value. A third kind of loop, the *dynamic* loop, is annotated with a "?", and its semantics makes sense only in the context of play-out, described later, since the user determines the number of iterations at run time. In Figure 4-6, we show an LSC containing an unbounded loop.

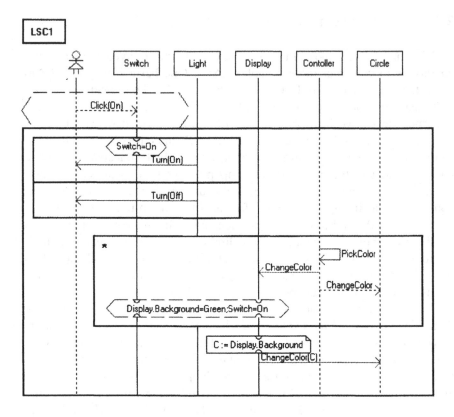

Figure 4-6. An LSC with a loop

3.   THE PLAY-IN/PLAY-OUT APPROACH

Given the expressive power of LSCs, it is tempting to consider using them to capture a *complete* set of requirements. Hence one could start looking seriously at the issue of going from the inter-object style specification, in terms of LSCs, to the intra-object style of description, say, along the lines of statecharts, that is needed for implementation. This is a difficult synthesis problem with a very bad worst case complexity, but efforts are under way to address it in ways that might be come useful in practice; see, e.g., [11]. In this section we discuss an alternative approach, which can be very useful for the design process, and for certain kinds of applications can serve as the final implementation itself. A full-fledged treatment of this approach (which also contains the syntax and operational semantics of LSCs, with several extensions), appears in [14].

3.1 Playing in Behavior

First we consider the following question: How should the LSC requirements themselves be specified in a practical context? Synthesizing LSCs or similar specifications from use cases is impractical since use cases are informal and abstract. Manually constructing LSCs is possible, but the user would still have to learn how to work with a formal (albeit visual) language, like LSCs, with its syntax and semantics. To make this task easier, the *play-in* approach has been developed [9,14].

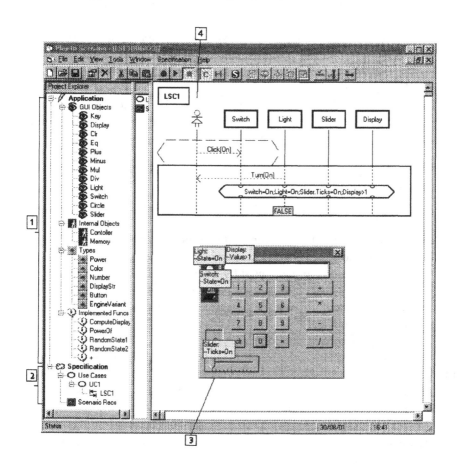

Figure 4-7. The Play-Engine environment

What "play-in" means is that the system developer first builds the GUI of the system with *no* behavior built into it. In systems in which hidden objects plays a role (e.g., a board of an electrical system), the user may build graphical representations of these objects as well. Often one can just use object model diagrams for representing the hidden objects. The user, usually the system developer, "plays" the GUI by clicking on buttons, rotating knobs and sending messages to hidden objects in an intuitive drag-and-drop manner. With the object model diagrams, the developer plays by manipulating the (GUI) of the objects, methods and parameters.

By playing with the GUI, the developer also describes the desired reactions of the system and the conditions that may or must hold. As this is being done, the Play-Engine (the underlying tool built to support the play-in approach; see [14]) continuously constructs LSCs. It queries the application GUI built by the developer for its structure and interacts with it. In the process, it automatically builds and exhibits the appropriate LSCs. An example of a Play-Engine development environment is shown in Figure 4-7.

The main elements of the environment are numbered in the diagram:

1. The Application Section

This section contains the items defined in the GUI application. The Play-Engine queries the application for this information and displays it in a tree format. The information consists of:

- The GUI objects defined in the application, such as Key, Display, Switch etc. Properties such as value, color, state may be defined for each object.
- The internal objects defined in the application, such as Controller and Memory.
- The types used for capturing the properties of the objects (Colors, Number, etc.).
- The functions implemented by the application that are external to the Engine and are used in the play-in process (e.g., ComputeDisplay updates the value of the display in response to a digit being clicked).

2. The Specification Section

This is the main part of the requirements specification and it consists of the use cases defined by the developer and the LSCs implementing them, which are constructed by the Play-Engine as the behavior is played in.

3. The GUI Application

The GUI application (for example, the calculator) created by the user. It can be constructed by any means as long as it supports the interface required by the Play-Engine. (The Engine actually comes with a GUIEdit package that helps with this.)

4. The LSCs

The LSC that is currently being constructed by the Play-Engine as a part of the play-in process, or the LSC that is currently being executed as a part of the play-out process, as discussed below.

3.2   Play-out

After playing in the specification (or a part of it), it is natural to try and verify that it reflects the user's intention. One way to achieve this would be to construct a prototype implementation and to test it. Instead, in the play-out approach, the power of the interface-based play-in methodology is extended to also validate the requirements. In play-out, the developer simply plays the GUI as he/she would have done when executing the system model but limiting himself/herself to the "end-user" and environment actions only. During this process, the Play-Engine keeps track of the actions and causes other events and actions to occur as dictated by the universal charts in the specification. To achieve this, the Play-Engine interacts with the GUI application and uses it to reflect the system state at any given moment.

This process of the developer operating the GUI application and the Play-Engine reacting according to the specification has the effect of working with a conventional executable model. No code needs to be written in order to play out the requirements, nor is any code generated. One does not have to prepare any kind of intra-object model, as is required in most system development methodologies, like statecharts or some other artifacts that describe the full behavior of each object. It is important to note that the behavior played out is up to the user and need not resemble the behavior as it was played in. Thus the user is not merely tracing the scenarios capturing the requirements. Rather, he/she is freely executing the system that incorporates all the requirements that have been captured. This minimalist system works like a perfect citizen, who does everything by the book; indeed does nothing unless it is called for by the grand "book of rules", but provided it does not contradict anything else written in the book. It is up to the requirements engineers to build the desired liveness properties into the requirements.

Play-out is an iterative process (see [14] for detailed explanations) where each step taken by the user is followed by the Play-Engine computing a sequence of steps called a *superstep*. This superstep is then carried out by the system as the system's response to the step input by the user/developer. The computation of the superstep is nontrivial for several reasons, one of which is that fact that in general more than one superstep may be possible. This is due to the fact at the requirement stage, each scenario just partially orders the events of the scenario. Moreover, the way different charts compose could also be under-specified. In the current implementation, the "naïve" play-out process simply picks one way to go, with no backtracking, but a more powerful process has been worked out too, called *smart play-out* (see [12]). This approach, which has been implemented in the Play-Engine for a subset of the LSCs, uses heavy-duty model checking methods to compute a "correct" super step or to declare that none exists (and hence there is a requirements violation).

We conclude this section by pointing to some related pieces of work. First, Magee et. al. [21,30] present a methodology supported by a tool called LTSA for specifying and analyzing labeled transition systems (LTSs). This tool works with a framework called SceneBeans, yielding a nicely animated executable model. An interesting idea would be to use SceneBeans as an animation engine to describe the behavior of internal (non-GUI) objects in the Play-Engine. Second, Lettrai and Klose [19] present a methodology supported by a tool called TestConductor, which is integrated into I-Logix's tool Rhapsody [17]. The TestConductor is used for monitoring and testing a model using a subset of LSCs. The charts can be monitored in a way that is similar to the way the Play-Engine traces existential charts. In order to be monitored, their charts are transformed into Büchi automata. Their work also briefly mentions the ability to test an implementation using these sequence charts, by generating messages on behalf of the environment (or other un-implemented classes).

4.   COMMUNICATING TRANSACTION PROCESSES

We now present another to approach to specifying system behavior using sequence charts. It is related to LSC-based executable specifications in the following way: We use simple universal LSCs with pre-conditions and post-conditions. However, the evaluation of the pre-conditions is carried out in an asynchronous manner. Further, the *control flow* between the different LSCs is specified explicitly. This leads to an execution model that is asynchronous and distributed. We shall present the resulting model, called *communicating transaction processes* (CTPs) in an informal fashion. The full details can be found in [27].

Consider a network of communicating sequential processes that synchronize by performing common actions together. The main idea underlying the CTP model is to refine each common action into a transaction scheme. A transaction scheme consists of a set of (universal) charts, each with a pre-condition and a post-condition. Figure 4-8 shows an example of a CTP, using the familiar Petri net notation to describe the control flow between three processes, I1, B, and I2.

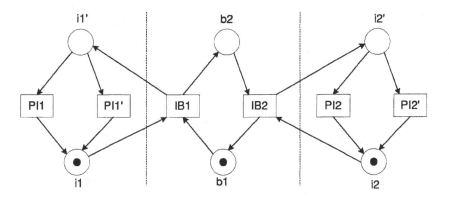

Figure 4-8. The control flow of a CTP

The figure captures a simplified and high level protocol that enables the two processors P1 and P2, via their interfaces I1 and I2, to transfer data to a shared memory via the bus B. The transitions of the Petri net are labeled with the names of the transaction schemes, and the schemes are shown separately in Figure 4-9.

The scheme IB1 captures the interaction between I1 and B. If I1 does not have data to transfer ($\Box$ *data.present*) then the transaction IB11 takes place: I1 informs B that it has no data to transfer (*nd*) and they both proceed to their respective next interactions. If I1 does have data to transfer but B is not free, the transaction IB12 takes place (*data.present* $\wedge \Box$ *bus.free*): I1 sends a request, B sends back a "no" and increments wc1, its wait-count corresponding to I1. Finally, if B is free and I1 has data to transfer (*data.present* $\wedge$ *bus.free*), the transaction IB13 takes place.

The transaction scheme IB2 is identical to IB1, except the I1 is replaced by I2 and can be read off in a similar fashion. We shall return to this example later to explain the pre-conditions and post-conditions associated with the individual transactions.

The schemes PI1 and PI1' are really degenerate schemes, where each transaction consists of a single internal action. They represent simple local choices. For example, in PI1, which takes place if I1 is "free" ($\Box$ *data.present*), there are two transactions with identical guards. Each of these transactions consists of a single internal action. The choice between the two internal actions is an external one, that depends on whether or not the processor P1 has data to transfer via the interface. The action *tr* (i.e., the associated transaction) has as a post-condition the I1-valuation V_1, of which *data.present* will be a member. Thus, *tr* represents I1 dequeuing a data-address pair. On the other hand, *ntr* ("no transfer") has the post-condition V_2 which is a I1-valuation of which *data.present* will not be a member. If I1 is not free, it engages in the scheme PI1'. This scheme's transaction consists of a single internal "no-op" action.

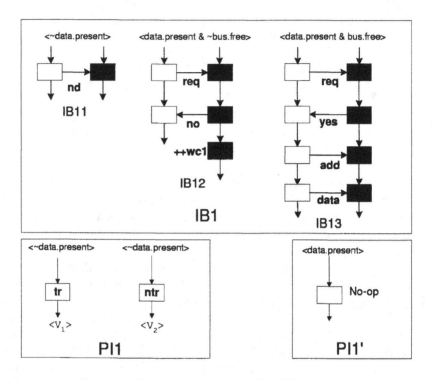

Figure 4-9. The transaction schemes of the CTP example

In this simple example, when we view PI1 and PI1' as transitions of a Petri net, their sets of output places are identical; it is the set $\{i1\}$. In general, these two sets of output places will be neither singletons nor equal. We could have merged PI1 and PI1' into a single, more complex transaction scheme. Instead, we have decided to remain with two transaction schemes in order to illustrate the possibility of locally branching control flow.

Continuing with the example shown in Figure 4-8 and elaborated in Figure 4-9, for most of the transactions we have not shown the post-condition. By convention, it is assumed that in such cases, the post-condition is the same as the condition that held when transaction began to execute. For more precise details, the reader is referred to [27].

The key feature of the CTP model is that it too yields an executable specification. The inter-object interactions are given in terms of the transactions schemes and the control flow is captured via standard notations, such as a Petri net, as illustrated in Figure 4-8. One can now extract, in a systematic manner, the intra-object behaviors. The main step is to combine the different guarded transactions within a transaction scheme into a single structure consisting of a parallel composition of computation trees: one tree for each process participating in the transaction scheme. The tree will glue together the individual behaviors from the different transactions. Finite labeled *event structures*, again a standard operational model [25], can be conveniently used for representing such a parallel composition of computation trees. For example, in our operational semantics the transaction scheme IB1 will be converted into the labeled event structure shown in Figure 4-10. In this diagram, in order to avoid clutter, we have not shown the labels of all the events. The labels incorporate information about the guards. As usual, the directed arrows represent the immediate causality relation and the squiggly undirected edges represent the immediate conflict relation [26].

We shall not present here the formal extraction of a labeled event structure from a transaction scheme; the details can be found in [27]. The transition system associated with the event structure captures the execution of the body charts and the setting of the post-conditions, all done in an asynchronous manner. The particular transaction that is chosen for execution will be determined by the valuation holding when control reaches the input places of the transaction scheme. The full operational semantics can now be obtained with the help of the top level Petri net, its initial marking and the initial valuation of the atomic propositions. Again, the details can be found in [27].

To conclude this section, let us briefly compare the CTP formalism with HMSCs. The main difference is that HMSCs are a mechanism for specifying a *collection* of charts, whereas CTPs constitute a system model in which component interactions are non-atomic and are specified as a guarded choice of charts. Admittedly, one must extract from such transaction schemes an executable thread for each of the participating processes (we achieve this via the event structure semantics of transaction schemes), but this appears to be easier than extracting an executable specification from an HMSC.

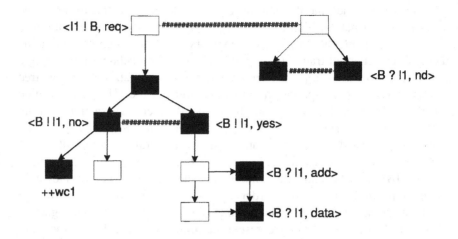

Figure 4-10. Event structure representation of a scheme

5.   SOME EXTENSIONS

As the preceding sections suggest, MSCs can form the basis of powerful requirements and executable specification languages. However, as presented, these languages are still at a low level of abstraction for describing reactive real time embedded systems. A minor limitation, especially following from Section 2, is the rigid nature of the partial order associated with MSCs and the implicit assumption that the interaction between the life-lines is solely in terms of sending and receiving messages via reliable FIFOs. These limitations can be easily removed by adding additional syntactic features, to model synchronization, for example, as is already done in LSCs. One can also relax the definition of the partial order to allow messages to "overtake" each other along the life-line of a receiving agent, etc.

In addition, given the intended domain of applications, we also need major extensions along (at least) two dimensions: object features and timing constraints.

5.1   Object Features

In MSCs, only specific objects have been associated with the life-lines and only fixed and limited information is exchanged between them. As a result, in systems of realistic size, an unacceptably large number of scenarios would have to be specified in order to get a complete description. This problem is yet to be addressed in any serious way for HMSCs and the CTP formalism. However, the LSC language, together with its Play-Engine tool, has been extended in a number of ways to deal with symbolic instances (see [22] and Chapters 7 and 15 of [14]).

One of these extensions is to use *symbolic messages*. In other words, the messages are viewed as variables rather than concrete values. These variables are local to an LSC and an occurrence of the variable may take any value from its type. By using the same variable in the chart, one can specify that the same value will occur in different places in the chart for each specific run (but of course not necessarily the same value for all runs). Thus, for example, we can use a variable "op" with type {*open, closed*} to specify: whenever the user opens or closes the cover of a cell phone (cover(op)) , the antenna also opens or closes (antenna(op)) correspondingly.

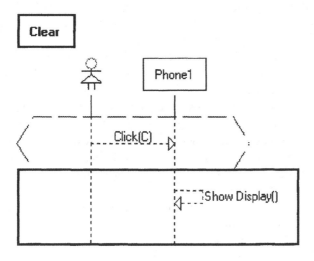

Figure 4-11. A generalised scenario

The more complex extension described in [22] is to allow for a life-line to be a *symbolic instance* of a class rather than a concrete object in the specification. Figure 4-11 illustrates the main idea with a very simple example.

The life-line denoted by Phone:: represents the *class* Phone rather than a concrete phone. The chart says that its scenario should hold for every concrete phone in the Phone class regardless of the number of phones and whether they were statically declared or created dynamically during the system run. The scenario itself just says that whenever the "C" button is clicked, the display should be cleared.

This extension throws up a host of problems related to the use of variables and expressions to specify symbolic instances, how to bind a symbolic instance to a concrete object (and possibly even to a *set* of objects) during run time. A detailed discussion here will take us too far afield, and the interested reader is referred to [22] and Chapter 15 of [14].

5.2   Timing Constraints

Many reactive systems must explicitly refer to and react to the passage of time. Hence a second type of extension to MSCs is to add timing features. Recommendation Z.120 [31] provides timers for expressing timing constraints within an MSC along a single life-line. The timer can be set to a value, can be reset to 0 and observed for a timeout. Thus, timers can be used to express a minimal delay between two consecutive events or a maximal delay between a sequence of events. Since timers cannot be shared by different life-lines, timing constraints between events lying on different life-lines can not be captured using these timers. A survey of HMSC-related timing issues can be found in [4] and a result relating timed HMSCs to timed automata can be found in [20].

In the UML, timing constraints in sequence diagrams can be represented by drawing rules and timing markers. Horizontally drawn arrows indicate synchronous messages while downward slanted arrows indicate a required delay between the send and receive events of the message. Timing markers are used to specify quantitative timing constraints. They are boolean expressions placed in braces that can constrain particular events or the entire chart. However, neither the syntax nor the semantics of timing markers are precisely defined in the UML.

The LSC formalism has been augmented with an expressive and natural mechanism for specifying timing constraints and this extension is implemented in the Play-Engine [13]; see also Chapter 16 of [14]. The basic idea is to introduce a single clock object (called *Time*) and to use constructs already existing in LSCs, namely assignments and conditions. These, together with their hot and cold variants, allow one to define a rich set of timing constraints. The clock variable Time is assumed to evolve inexorably and its value is readily available to the other life-instances. The *Time* object has one method *Tick*, and *Time* is linked to the host machine's internal clock. For convenience, the standard synchrony hypothesis [7] is assumed in the execution of the Play-Engine.

Suppose we wish to specify the minimum and maximum delay between two consecutive events $e1$ and $e2$ along a life-line. The current time (provided by the clock variable Time) is stored immediately after $e1$, using the variable $T1$. The minimum delay is specified by placing a hot condition of the form $Time > T1 + min\_delay$ just before the second event $e2$. Under the Play-Engine semantics, hot conditions are evaluated "continuously" until they become true. Hence this condition will be advanced only after the required amount of time has passed. If the condition is reached after min_delay units of time, then run will be advanced past this condition immediately. The maximal delay, on the other hand, is specified by placing a hot condition of the form $Time < T1 + max\_delay$ just after $e2$. If the condition is reached before the maximal delay has elapsed, it will evaluate to true and will be advanced immediately. If the condition is reached after the maximal delay has elapsed, then it evaluates to false and since Time can not decrease, this is treated as a constant *false* condition and will be reported as a violation of the requirements. This is illustrated in Figure 4-12(a) where the minimum and maximum delay between the receive event and the later send event of $O2$ is specified.

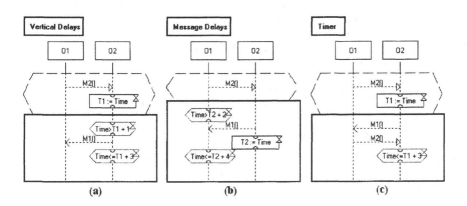

Figure 4-12. Expressing Timing Constraints

Figure 4-12(b) shows the specification of the minimal and maximal delays allowed from the moment a message is sent until the moment it is received. It works like the specification of the vertical delay between two consecutive events on a life-line as in Figure 4-12(a) except that here time is stored on one instance life-line ($O2$) and is checked on another ($O1$). We also note that here the first condition ($Time > T2 + 2$) and the assignment ($T2 = Time$) are not related in the LSC partial order and so the condition may be reached before the assignment. However, the LSC semantics regarding the binding of variables and their subsequent usage will ensure that the condition will not be evaluated before the assignment is performed. Finally, Figure 4-12(c) illustrates the specification of a timer along a life-line.

Many other means for expressing timing constraints and the techniques for handling them can be found in chapter 16 of [14].

REFERENCES

[1] R. Alur, K. Etessami, and M. Yannakakis, "Realizability and verification of MSC graphs", *International Colloquium on Automata, Languages and Programming (ICALP)*, 2001.

[2] R. Alur, G. J. Holzmann, and D. Peled, "An analyzer for message sequence charts", *Software Concepts and Tools*, 17(2), 1996.

[3] R. Alur and M. Yannakakis, "Model checking of message sequence charts", *Proceedings of the 10th International Conference on Concurrency Theory CONCUR'99, Lecture Notes in Computer Science 1664*. Springer-Verlag, 1999.

[4] H. Ben-Abdallah and S. Leue, "Timing constraints in message sequence chart specifications", *Proceedings of the Tenth International Conference on Formal Description Techniques, FORTE/PSTV'97*. Chapman & Hall, 1997.

[5] B. Caillaud, P. Darondeau, L. Helouet, and G. Lesventes, "HMSCs as partial specifications ... with PNs as completions", *Modeling and Verification of Parallel Processes 4th Summer School, MOVEP 2000, LNCS 2067*, 2001.

[6] W. Damm and D. Harel, "LSCs: Breathing life into message sequence charts", *Formal Methods in System Design*, 19(1), 2001.

[7] N. Halbwachs, *Synchronous Programming of Reactive Systems*. Kluwer Academic Publications, 1993.

[8] D. Harel, "Statecharts: A visual formalism for complex systems", *Science of Computer Programming*, 8, 1987.

[9] D. Harel, "From play-in scenarios to code: An achievable dream", *IEEE Computer*, 2001.

[10] D. Harel and E. Gery, "Executable object modeling with statecharts", *IEEE Computer*, 30(7), 1997.

[11] D. Harel and H. Kugler, "Synthesizing state-based object systems from LSC specifications", *International Journal on Foundations of Computer Science*, 13(1), 2002.

[12] D. Harel, H. Kugler, R. Marelly, and A. Pnueli, "Smart play-out of behavioral requirements", *International Conference on Formal Methods in Computer Aided Design (FMCAD)*, 2002.

[13] D. Harel and R. Marelly, "Playing with time: On the specification and execution of time-enriched LSCs", *Proceedings of the 10th IEEE/ACM Int. Symp. on Modeling, Analysis and Simulation of Computer and Telecommunication Systems MASCOTS 2002*. ACM Press, 2002.

[14] D. Harel and R. Marelly, *Come, Let's Play: Scenario-Based Programming Using LSCs and the Play-Engine*. Springer-Verlag, 2003.

[15] J.G. Hendriksen, M. Mukund, K.N. Kumar, and P.S. Thiagarajan, "Message sequence graphs and finitely generated regular MSC languages", *International Colloquium on Automata, Languages and Programming (ICALP), LNCS 1853*, 2000.

[16] J.G. Hendriksen, M. Mukund, K.N. Kumar, and P.S. Thiagarajan, "Regular collections of message sequence charts", *Mathematical Foundations of Computer Science (MFCS), LNCS 1893*, 2000.

[17] I-Logix Inc. Products Web Page. http://www.ilogix.com/fs_prod.htm.

[18] P. B. Ladkin and S. Leue, "Interpreting message flow graphs", *Formal Aspects of Computing*, 7(5), 1995.

[19] M. Lettrari and J. Klose, "Scenario-based monitoring and testing of real-time UML models", *International Conference on the Unified Modeling Language, Toronto*, 2001.

[20] P. Lucas, "Timed semantics of message sequence charts based on timed automata", In Oded Maler Eugene Asarin and Sergio Yovine, editors, *Electronic Notes in Theoretical Computer Science*, volume 65. Elsevier Science Publishers, 2002.

[21] J. Magee, N. Pryce, D. Giannakopoulou, and J. Kramer, "Graphical animation of behavior models", *International Conference on Soft. Eng. ICSE'00, Limeric, Ireland*, 2000.

[22] R. Marelly, D. Harel, and H. Kugler, "Multiple instances and symbolic variables in executable sequence charts", *Proceedings of the 17th ACM conference on Object-oriented programming, systems, languages, and applications*. ACM Press, 2002.

[23] A. Muscholl and D. Peled, "Message sequence graphs and decision problems on mazurkiewicz traces", *Proceedings of the 24th International Symposium on Mathematical Foundations of Computer Science MFCS'99, Lecture Notes in Computer Science 1672*. Springer-Verlag, 1999.

[24] A. Muscholl, D. Peled, Z. Su, "Deciding properties for message sequence charts", *Proceedings of the 1st International Conference on Foundations of Software Science and Computation Structures FOSSACS'98, Lecture Notes in Computer Science 1378*. Springer-Verlag, 1998.

[25] M. Nielsen, G. Plotkin, and G. Winskel, "Petri nets, event structures and domains", *Theoretical Computer Science (TCS)*, 13, 1981.

[26] M. Nielsen and P.S. Thiagarajan, "Regular event structures and finite petri nets: The conflict-free case", *Proceedings of the 23rd International Conference on the Applications and Theory of Petri Nets ICATPN 2002, Springer Lecture Notes in Computer Science 2360*. Springer-Verlag, 2002.

[27] A. Roychoudhury and P.S. Thiagarajan, "Communicating transaction processes", *Proceedings of Third International Conference on Applications of Concurrency to System Design ACSD'03 (to appear)*. IEEE Press, 2003.

[28] B. Selic, G. Gullekson, and P. Ward. *Real-Time Object-Oriented Modeling*. John Wiley and Sons, 1994.

[29] W. Thomas, "Languages, automata, and logic", In A. Salomaa G. Rozenberg, editor, *Handbook of Formal Language Theory, Volume III*. Springer-Verlag, 1997.

[30] S. Uchitel, J. Kramer, and J. Magee, "Detecting implied scenarios in message sequence chart specifications", *European Software Engineering Confernece and 9th ACM SIGSOFT International Symposium on the Foundations of Software Engineering ESEC/FSE'01. Vienna, Austria*, 2001.

[31] Z.120. ITU-TS recommendation Z.120: Message Sequence Chart (MSC), 1996.

Chapter 5

UML and Platform-based Design

Rong Chen[1], Marco Sgroi[1], Luciano Lavagno[2], Grant Martin[2], Alberto Sangiovanni-Vincentelli[1], Jan Rabaey[1]
[1]University of California at Berkeley [2]Cadence Design Systems

Abstract: This chapter presents a specification technique based on UML for the design of embedded systems and platforms. It covers stereotypes and extended notations to represent platform services and their attributes in embedded software development. It also presents a design methodology for embedded systems that is based on platform-based design principles.

Key words: platform-based design, embedded system design, UML

1.   INTRODUCTION

The embedded system design approach currently used in the industry is informal, especially in the initial phase, where the requirements and the functionality of the system are usually expressed in natural language. The inherent ambiguities of an informal specification prevent a meaningful analysis of the system and may result in misunderstandings with customers and in incorrect or inefficient decisions at the time when the design is partitioned and the tasks are assigned to different teams.

Hence, a key ingredient in a well defined methodology is a specification language with formally defined semantics that allows designers to describe the structure and the behavior of an embedded system at multiple levels of abstraction starting from the purely conceptual level. Embedded systems must satisfy tight performance and cost constraints. Therefore, embedded software design, in comparison with traditional software development, requires one not only to verify the functional correctness but also to check the satisfaction of these constraints. Performance and cost analysis depends on the selected architecture and therefore requires tools and models for a formal definition of the implementation platform resources and the quality of

L. Lavagno, G. Martin and B. Selic (eds.), UML for Real, 107-126.
© 2003 *Kluwer Academic Publishers.*

the services they offer. Furthermore, early stages of the design process would benefit from the use of graphical interface tools that visualize the system specification and allow multiple team members to share the relevant information.

This chapter presents a specification technique for the design of embedded systems and platforms that addresses these issues and is based on the Unified Modeling Language (UML).

1.1   Platform-based Design

Platform-based design has emerged recently as one promising approach to solve the problems caused by the ever-increasing complexity and time-to-market pressure in embedded system design. According to [1], a platform is an abstraction layer in the design flow that facilitates a number of possible refinements into a subsequent, lower-level abstraction layer (platform). In other words, a platform is an abstract representation of a set of possible implementations, which is used by the application designer as a design target, and is implemented by the platform provider.

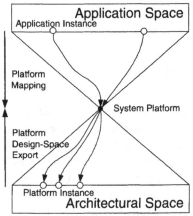

Figure 5-1. Platform-based Design

As shown in Figure 5-1, the basic tenets of the platform-based design methodology are:

1. the treatment of design as a "meet-in-the-middle process", where successive refinements of specifications meet with abstractions of potential implementations;

2. the identification of precisely defined layers, where the refinement and abstraction process take place. The layers then allow designs built upon them to be isolated from lower-level details, but let enough information be transmitted about lower levels of abstraction to allow design space

exploration with a fairly accurate prediction of the properties of the final implementation.

Among many platforms existing in a design flow, two important abstractions are identified at the articulation point between system definition and implementation: the (micro-) architecture platform and the application programming interface (API) platform. The (micro-) architecture platform concept originates from the fact that integrated circuits used for embedded systems are usually derived from some related micro-architectures rather than assembled from a collection of independently developed blocks of silicon functionality. Consequently, a (micro-) architecture platform is defined as a specific family of micro-architectures, possibly oriented toward a particular class of problems, which can be modified (extended or reduced) by the system developer. Examples are the AMBA/ARM platform, the CoreConnect platform, and family of FPGA chips. A platform instance can be derived from a platform by choosing a set of components from the platform library and setting parameters of configurable components. The choice of a platform is driven by cost and time-to-market considerations and is done after exploration of both the application and architecture design spaces. The API platform concept results from the fact that embedded software developers need a platform abstraction that hides architecture details and defines the services that the platform offers. More precisely, an API platform is the Programmer's Model for the abstraction of a multiplicity of computational resources and available peripherals contained within the architectural platform; it is a unique abstract representation of the architecture platform via the software layer. This abstraction usually consists of a software layer that wraps the essential parts of the architecture platform and includes, among others, RTOS and device drivers. Examples are the VxWorks platform, the OSEK platform, and the software DSP task control of the OMAP platform. On top of the API platform there is an application specific programmable platform, which consists of commonly used functionalities in a particular application domain. This platform usually consists of embedded software components and directly interacts with embedded system designers. Examples are the TCP/IP platform and the top level of the Nexperia platform. There are other platforms such as the silicon implementation platform (SIP), which is beyond the scope of this chapter, and the network platform, which is discussed in section 4.4.

1.2   UML and Embedded System Design

The Unified Modeling Language (UML) is an object-oriented modeling language introduced by Booch, Rumbaugh and Jacobson [2] to support software development. Recent work [3, 4, 5, 6] has shown the potential of

UML also for embedded system design. Due to its rich graphical notation and its modeling capabilities that allow the capture and visualization of the system structure and behavior at multiple levels of abstraction, UML has been used in the embedded system domain mainly as a documentation aid and a modeling language. UML includes a rich set of modeling elements that can be used for a wide range of applications and has already built in the capabilities to model the most relevant features of real-time embedded systems, such as performance (using tagged attributes or OCL [7]), physical resources (using Deployment Diagrams), and time (using classifiers and tagged attributes), as discussed in Chapters 11, 12 and 16. However, the following factors should also be considered.

- First, modeling specific applications would be easier using a more specialized (domain-specific) notation representing the basic elements and patterns of the target domain.
- Second, formally defined domain-dependent use semantics are required to avoid multiple interpretations of the same models and to support analysis tools.
- Third, multiple diagrams can be used to capture related aspects of a design. The possibility of viewing and describing the same object from different perspectives makes the system specification phase easier, but may result in inconsistencies between diagrams, when the use of UML is not coupled with a rigorous design discipline.

For these reasons, the use of UML for a specific application domain such as the design of embedded system platforms requires:
- a domain specific language, called a profile, built on the basic UML infrastructure and including domain-specific building blocks (defined using stereotypes) to model common design elements and patterns,
- a methodology that defines how and when the profile notation should be used.

A UML profile for embedded system platforms should include specialized notations to represent the structure and the behavior of the platform resources, and the services they provide, with particular emphasis on the performance and cost aspects. It should also have the capability to visualize multiple implementation alternatives of a specification to facilitate a quick comparison.

The rest of this chapter is organized as follows. First, we give an overview of related work, and describe the research project Metropolis, within which we are developing our concepts (section 2). Then, we describe a UML profile for embedded system platforms, called UML Platform, (section 3) and a methodology for using it (section 4). Finally we present its practical application to the design of wireless networks platforms.

2. BACKGROUND

2.1 Related work

The UML Profile for Schedulability, Performance and Time (also informally called the Real-Time UML Profile) [8], recently standardized by the Object Management Group (OMG) and summarized in Chapter 11, defines a unified framework to express the time, scheduling and performance aspects of a system. It is based on a set of notations that can be used to build models of real-time systems annotated with relevant Quality of Service (QoS) parameters. External tools can perform formal analysis based on these models and return information on performance and schedulability before the system is built. The profile consists of the Generalized Resource Modeling (GRM) Framework that defines a notation for modeling resources, time, concurrency and schedulability parameters. In addition to GRM, sub-profiles are defined with extensions to the basic notation that are specific to certain types of analysis, e.g. schedulability. The Real-Time UML Profile standardizes an extended UML notation to support the interoperability of modeling and analysis tools but does not define a full methodology for the use of this notation.

Several methodologies based on UML have been proposed. They all couple the UML notation with a formal model with precise semantics that allows the capture of system behavior and support simulation and synthesis. UML-RT [9] is a profile that extends UML with stereotyped active objects, called capsules, to represent system components. The internal behavior of a capsule is defined using statecharts; its interaction with other capsules is by means of protocols that define the sequence of signals exchanged through stereotyped objects called ports. Capsules have run-to-completion semantics and their execution is defined by the sequence of actions that are taken upon reception of messages from the input ports. The UML-RT profile defines a model with precise execution semantics, hence it is suitable to capture system behavior and support simulation or synthesis tools (e.g. Rational Rose-RT). UML-RT has limited architecture and performance modeling capabilities and therefore should be considered complementary to the Real-Time UML Profile standardized by OMG.

HASoC [10] is a design methodology based on UML-RT notation described in Chapter 6. The design flow begins with a description of the system functionality initially given in use case diagrams and then in a UML-

RT version properly extended to include annotations with mapping information. The authors argue that UML-RT is too restrictive a model because capsules' behavior is defined by statecharts and propose instead to associate capsules with additional models of computation (MoC) such as synchronous dataflow, codesign finite state machines etc. Another full system design methodology that uses UML is presented by de Jong et al. [4]. It consists of a flow from the initial specification phase to the deployment level that specifies the target architecture. The high-level system specification is first built using use-case diagrams; then the system components and their interactions are described using block diagrams and message sequence charts, respectively. As a next step the behavior of each module is specified using SDL that provides an executable and simulatable specification. This approach combines the informal notation of the UML Diagrams with the formal semantics of SDL and moves one step further the integration between these two models.

2.2   The Metropolis design environment

Metropolis [11] is an on-going research project at UC Berkeley that addresses embedded system design using the following novel approaches. First, Metropolis does not commit a priori to any particular communication semantics or firing rule. Hence, it leaves the designer free to use the specification mechanism of choice (graphical or textual language), as long as it has a sound semantic foundation (model of computation). Secondly, it uses a single formalism to represent both the embedded system and some abstract relevant characteristics of its environment and implementation platform. Finally, it separates orthogonal aspects, such as:

1. Computation and communication. This separation is important because:
a) refinement of computation is generally done by hand, or by compilation, or by scheduling or using other complex techniques;
b) refinement of communication is generally done by use of patterns (such as circular buffers for FIFOs, polling or interrupts for hardware to software data transfers, and so on).
2. Function and Architecture. They are often defined independently by different design teams (e.g. video encoding and decoding experts versus hardware and software designers in multimedia applications). Function (both computation and communication) is then "mapped" to architecture in order to derive an implementation.
3. Behavior and performance parameters, such as latency, throughput, power, energy.

All these separations result in better design re-use, because they decouple independent aspects that would otherwise tie, for example, a given functional specification to low-level implementation details, or to a specific communication paradigm, or to a scheduling algorithm. It is very important to define only as many aspects as needed at every level of abstraction, in the interest of flexibility and rapid design space exploration. They also allow extensive use of synthesis, system-level simulation and formal verification techniques in order to speed up the design cycle.

In Metropolis, a system is represented as a netlist, and a netlist can be further decomposed into subnetlists or components. Components of a netlist or a subnetlist include processes, media, ports, interfaces, constraints, and quantities. Processes are active objects (running on their own threads) used for modeling computation; media are passive objects used for modeling communication. Ports, specified as interface types, reside in processes and are the only places through which communication can take place. Interfaces declare all and only the methods that can be called through ports; constraints deal with coordination and performance specifications; quantities annotate behaviors so that constraints can be specified precisely.

3. UML PLATFORM PROFILE

3.1 Modeling Platforms Using UML

The UML Platform profile is a graphical language for specification of embedded system platforms. It includes domain-specific classifiers and relationships specialized with stereotypes, in addition to the notation defined in the standard UML [2] and in the UML Profile for Schedulability, Performance and Time Specification [12], to model the structure and the behavior of embedded systems and to represent the relationship between platforms at different levels of abstraction. The profile has been derived from the model and design of several wireless protocols and therefore is especially suited for this application domain.

UML Platform structural models capture the components of a system and their relationships using stereotyped modeling elements. The model of a platform, especially when it relates to another platform at a different abstraction level, often requires modeling elements of different types (e.g. classes to represent the logical functions, components for the software implementation and deployment nodes for the physical resources running them) and therefore is not identifiable with a specific UML Diagram.

The behavior of an embedded system can be captured at different levels of abstraction using Use Case, Interaction, State Machine and Activity

Diagrams. Use Case Diagrams provide an abstract representation of the services that the system as a whole provides to the environment, Interaction Diagrams define just the interaction among system components, and State Machine and Activity Diagrams allow the specification of the detailed action-level behavior of individual components. Specifying the behavior of a system requires one to choose a model of computation that formally defines the semantics of the execution and the interaction among the system components and to describe the behavior of the components. As discussed in Section 2.2, the specification mechanism should not commit *a priori* to a specific MoC but should be flexible enough to let the designer choose the most appropriate MoC for the application. The UML Platform profile defines stereotypes representing standard MoCs (such as Kahn Process Networks, Synchronous Dataflow etc.) and elementary building blocks, such as buffers, protocols etc., that can be used to specify a MoC. The behavior of individual components is specified using graphical (State Machine or Activity Diagrams) or textual notation.

The syntax of the UML Platform profile is defined by the set of standard and stereotyped UML modeling elements and by the rules for using and composing them. UML Platform follows the rules of UML for standard classifiers and relationships and explicitly defines composition rules for the newly introduced notation. The semantics of UML Platform is defined in terms of the Metropolis Metamodel [11] by establishing a direct correspondence between modeling elements of UML Platform and elements of the Metamodel.

3.2   Stereotypes

The UML Platform profile includes the following stereotypes:

- <<*Netlist*>> is a top-level class that identifies the overall system structure as a set of connected components
- <<*Resource*>> specializes classes, components or deployment nodes and is used to represent platform components. Resource attributes (for example, bus attributes such as width, number of masters/slaves, arbitration policy...) are specified by annotating tags or as attributes of the corresponding class. <<*Bus*>>, <<*Memory*>>, <<*Processor*>>... further specialize the <<*Resource*>> stereotype for deployment nodes and are used to model physical resources
- <<*Process*>> is an active class [2] modeling logical objects performing computation
- <<*Medium*>> is a class modeling logical or physical objects that implement a communication function

- <<*Scheduler*>> is a class modeling objects and algorithms that perform coordination and arbitration of access to shared resources
- <<*Port*>> represents a part of a resource that allows its interaction with its environment. A port has an aggregate relationship with the resource to which it belongs and is associated with the services it provides access to.

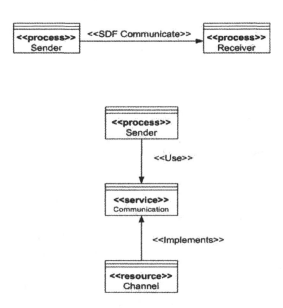

Figure 5-2. Stereotyped Relationships

The following stereotypes specialize the UML relationships:

<<*Communicate*>> specializes the association relationship and is used to relate classes of objects that interact and exchange messages. The <<*Communicate*>> relationship can be further specialized with stereotypes indicating a particular communication mechanism (e.g. Synchronous, Asynchronous, Buffered, Unbuffered) or a MoC (e.g. SDF, Kahn Process Networks, Synchronous FSMs, CFSMs...).

<<*Use*>> is a type of association that relates a service with a user of the service. <<*Need*>> is similar to <<*Use*>> and indicates that a user needs a service that is not currently available. Thus, it represents a request for future service extensions. An object may use multiple services and the same service may be used by multiple objects. A stereotyped relationship called <<*Share*>> can be used to relate the users of a service provided by the same resource. <<*Stack*>> and <<*Peer*>> specialize the relationship between a

service user and a service provider (a resource): *<<Stack>>* is used if the service user and service provider belong to different layers of abstraction, *<<Peer>>* if they belong to the same layer. *<<Transparent Stack>>* is used when the service user uses a service provided by a resource that is not in the adjacent lower layer.

<<Implement>> is a type of realization relationship between a service and a resource (or set of resources) implementing it. In figure 5-2, the channel resource is an implementation of a communication service. *<<Refine>>* is a type of realization relationship between an object (or set of objects) and an object or set of objects that describe it at a greater levels of details.

4.   UML PLATFORM DESIGN METHODOLOGY

The design methodology, based on the UML Platform profile and Metropolis [11], is shown in Figure 5-3. In the first step the design problem is formulated, i.e. the functionality of the system as a whole is specified using Use Case Diagrams and the constraints are annotated to the model. Then, the functionality is decomposed into components and captured using the UML Platform stereotypes within the Class (structure), State Machine, Activity and Sequence Diagrams (behavior). Constraints are propagated and budgeted to the components.

As a next step, the UML Platform specification is compiled into a Metropolis Metamodel specification to conjugate the convenience of using the graphical UML Platform interface for specification with the possibility of using the analysis and synthesis tools available in the Metropolis framework. The Metamodel functional specification can be validated using the Metropolis simulator [11].

Then, Communication Refinement and Mapping take place. Platforms that implement the functional components are specified in UML Platform as a netlist of resources providing services. The UML Platform model is compiled into a mapped Metamodel specification, and performance analysis and validation take place in the Metropolis simulation environment.

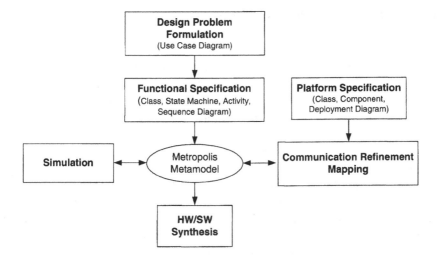

Figure 5-3. UML Platform Design Flow

4.1 Design Problem Formulation

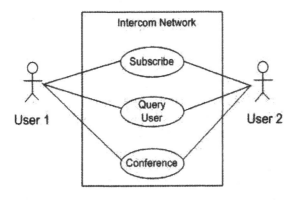

Figure 5-4. Intercom Use Case Diagram

The system requirements and the overall functionality are expressed using Use Case Diagrams. The system as a whole is described in terms of the services (modeled as use cases) it provides to the environment users (modeled as actors). Requirements are annotated to the model. Figure 5-4 shows the Use Case Diagram model of the Intercom Network [13]: use cases model the services provided by the network (subscription, conferences, query user status), and actors represent the mobile users of the Intercom network services.

4.2   Functional Specification

Specifying the functionality of a system usually requires one to identify a number of functional components (functional decomposition), select an MoC that defines the semantics of their interaction, and specify the behavior of each component.

In UML Platform the functionality of a system is specified in two steps.

–   First, a netlist of stereotyped classes and relationships is defined to capture the structural decomposition into interacting components. Computation objects are modeled as stereotyped *<<Process>>* classes, while their connectivity is expressed using *<<Communicate>>* relationships or explicitly using stereotyped *<<Medium>>* classes. When a stereotyped class is instantiated, its attributes, such as name of the process, number and type of its ports, internal variables, are set.
–   Second, the system behavior is specified refining the *<<Process>>* classes and the *<<Communicate>>* relationships to specific MoC types and describing the behavior of each process using State Machine Diagrams, Activity Diagrams or textual languages depending on what mechanism is more convenient for the target specification.

In UML Platform an MoC can be specified either using the stereotyped classes and relationships (e.g. *<<Kahn Process Networks Process>>*, *<<Kahn Process Networks Communicate>>*...) if it is a standard MoC or by composing finer granularity modeling elements such as types of channels (e.g. FIFO, shared memory...), interface functions (e.g. blocking/non-blocking read/write...) and coordination expressions (e.g. to specify synchronization or coordination of reads and writes...). A UML Platform model can be translated into a Metamodel description using the Metropolis Metamodel libraries, and instantiating the library elements that correspond to the stereotypes in the UML Platform model. The stereotyped classes of type process and medium have a corresponding Metamodel element. Ports and interfaces, which may be explicitly visualized in a UML Platform model, are part of the specification of processes and media in the Metamodel. The MoC's stereotyped relationship has a corresponding element in the library that includes a Metamodel description of the interface functions of the medium and the execution policy of the processes.

Let us consider the specification of the filter

$o(n) = k2 * i(n) + k1 * o(n-1)$.

The UML Platform model of the filter is shown in Figure 5-5. First, the computation components are described as stereotyped *<<Process>>* classes and are connected by *<<Communicate>>* relationships. The filter performs pure data processing functions, therefore the most suitable MoC is Synchronous Dataflow (SDF) [14]. SDF is an MoC that represents the system as a network of actors that communicate over single-reader, single-writer, blocking read, non-blocking write channels with infinite FIFOs holding tokens. The execution of an SDF model is based on a sequence of actor firings, each producing and consuming a fixed number of tokens.

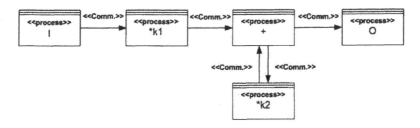

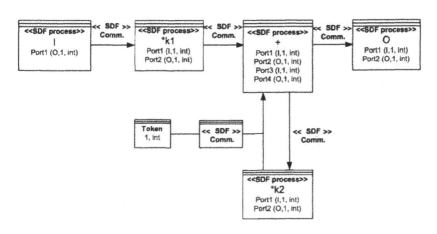

Figure 5-5. IIR Filter Model

The UML Platform model is refined using the corresponding SDF stereotypes, as shown in the lower part of Figure 5-5, so that the firing rules and the communication semantics of the specification are the ones of the SDF MoC. Parameters are set in the model for each class: the number of input and output ports, the data type and the number of the tokens produced or consumed at each port. The core function of each process in this case is conveniently specified with a fragment of code that describes the corresponding function (e.g. *o_adder = in1_adder + in2_adder*). The token class represents the one tap delay on one of the channels.

The information visualized in the UML Platform model is compiled together with the Metamodel description of SDF in the Metropolis library (built by H.Hsieh and L.Jin [15]). The SDF library defines:

1. the SDF medium, i.e. the interface functions read, write and n (that returns the token count) and the memory buffer (array list) storing the data,
2. the SDF process, i.e. the constructor, the declaration of the number and type of ports, and the functions readport, writeport defining the firing rules (e.g. SDF process executed when all the expected input tokens are present).

Figure 5-6 shows the Metamodel specification of the Adder process and a fragment of the netlist that corresponds to the UML Platform Class Diagram.

```
process Adder extends sdfprocess{
  Adder(String name){
    super(name,2,2);
    inports_token = new int[2];
    outports_token = new int[2];
    inports_token[0] = 1;
    inports_token[1] = 1;
    outports_token[0] = 1;
    outports_token[1] = 1;
  }
  void execute(){
    double vo0;
    double vi0;
    double vi1;

    vi0 = i_buffer[0].get(0);
    vi1 = i_buffer[1].get(0);
    vo0 = vi0 + vi1;
    o_buffer[0].set(0,(Object)vo0);
    o_buffer[1].set(0,(Object)vo0);
  }
}

public netlist IIRFilter{
  public IIRFilter(String name){
    ClassAdder Adder_instance = new ClassAdder("sdfadder");
    sdfchannel M0_instance = new sdfchannel("sdfchannel0");
```

```
        sdfchannel M1_instance = new sdfchannel("sdfchannel1");
        addcomponent(Adder_instance, this,"adder");
        addcomponent(M0_instance, this, "channel0");
        addcomponent(M1_instance, this, "channel1");
          ...
        connect(Adder_instance, inports[0], M0_instance);
        connect(Adder_instance, outports[0], M1_instance);
   }
 }
```

Figure 5-6. Metamodel Filter Specification

4.3   Platform Specification

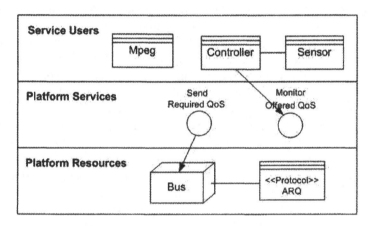

Figure 5-7. Key Elements of a Platform Model

The following components are usually part of a platform specification (Figure 5-7):

– the (physical or logical) resources modeled using the stereotyped classifiers defined in the UML Real-Time [5] and in the UML Platform profiles

– the services offered by individual or groups of resources modeled using standard UML interfaces; (an interface does not have attributes, but may have operations to specify the service primitives [2])

– the QoS performance expressed using tags that annotate the interface modeling the corresponding service

– the QoS constraints specified annotating OCL [7] or expressions to the modeling elements to which they are applied

– the relationships between resources, services and service users captured using the stereotypes defined in the UML Real-Time and UML Platform profiles

Packages are useful modeling elements. A package is "a general purpose mechanism for organizing elements into groups in order to manipulate them as a set" [2]. Hence, packages are used to provide abstractions and improve the readability of the models, as they group together modeling elements that are closely related.

4.4   Communication Refinement

Communication refinement is the procedure that defines, through a sequence of steps, how to implement the interaction among objects. A *Network Platform (NP)* is a library of resources that can be selected and composed together to form *Network Platform Instances (NPIs)* and to support the communication among a group of interacting objects, called NPI users. An NP library includes logical resources (e.g. protocols, virtual channels...) that are defined only in terms of their functionality and physical resources such as memory, processor, physical medium.

During communication refinement, UML Platform is used to model NPIs and their relationships. In the model of an NPI the platform users are the components in the upper platform layers and are represented as stereotyped classes, the services are of communication type (send and receive primitives) and are modeled as interfaces, the resources are protocols and channels and are represented as stereotyped classes of type <<*Process*>> and <<*Medium*>> respectively. These elements of the model are annotated with QoS requirements and may be related by the stereotypes <<*Use*>>, <<*Communicate*>>, <<*Implement*>> and <<*Refine*>>.

Figure 5-8 shows the UML Platform model of an Application Layer (AL) protocol and its refinement into a Network Layer (NL). The UML Platform model of the AL includes two Process classes representing a Controller and a Sensor, a (one-directional) <<*Communicate*>> relationship, a description of the communication services and a Medium modeling the AL network platform that provides the services. To communicate, the Sensor and Controller <<*Use*>> a communication service, whose primitives, send() and receive(), are accessible through the PortSensor and PortController ports. The service is implemented by a platform that consists of a medium with buffer size equal to 1. The platform is refined into a NL platform that includes a protocol entity at each node and a FIFO interconnecting them.

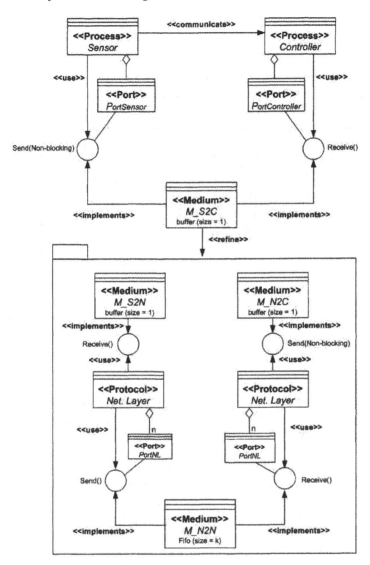

Figure 5-8. Network Platform example

4.5   Mapping

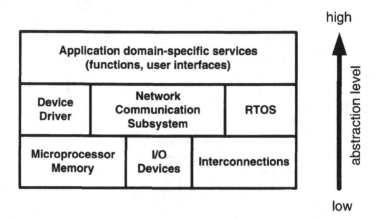

Figure 5-9. Platform Layers

Mapping a functional specification onto an architecture requires the definition of a model of the implementation platform and the establishment of the relationships of the platform resources and services with the application-level functional components. The components assigned to the HW partition are mapped directly onto a HW resource. The components in the SW partition are implemented as SW tasks that use the services provided by an intermediate SW layer. Hence, the elements of embedded system platform models can be conveniently grouped within the three layers shown in Figure 5-9: Architecture (ARC), Application Programming Interface (API) and Application Software (AS) Platforms, where the ARC layer includes a family of micro-architecture HW resources such as microprocessors, memories, ASICs, FPGAs, I/O devices and inter-connectors that in UML are typically modeled as deployment nodes; the API layer is a software abstraction layer and includes RTOS, device-driver, and network communication subsystem that in UML are represented as components; the AS layer includes the software tasks that implement application-level functional components.

Figure 5-10 shows the model of the embedded system platform implementing the Intercom Protocol Stack [13]. The Intercom protocol layers are visualized on the top part of the figure: they are modeled as classes and are annotated with QoS constraints on parameters like error rate (error-free transport layer connection) and throughput (the Mu-law Quantization block must process voice samples at 64 kbps, while the required throughput at the Physical Layer, due to the TDMA policy and the

CRC redundancy, is higher than 1.5 Mbps). Two layers, UI and Transport, are implemented as SW tasks and define the AS Layer; all other protocols are mapped onto HW resources (ASICs or FPGAs). The API Layer includes the RTOS and the Device Drivers. The RTOS implements the communication, arbitration and execution services used by the software tasks. Some of its parameters are the scheduling policy and the context switch overhead. It uses the services offered by the device drivers. The ARC layer includes the Tensilica Xtensa processor, the I/O devices, the Sonics Silicon backplane, ASICs and FPGA blocks that are implemented as deployment nodes. The processor provides to the upper layers ISA execution services, and the I/O devices provide HW interface services.

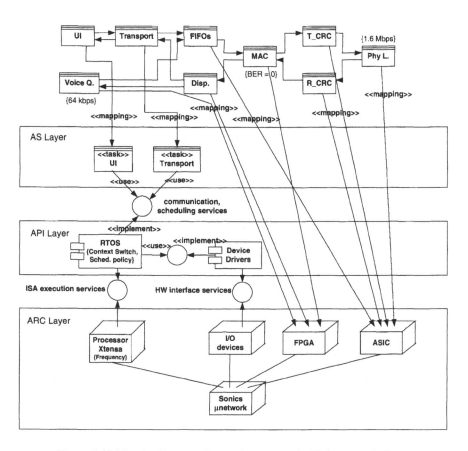

Figure 5-10. Mapping Intercom Protocol onto an embedded system platform.

5.   CONCLUSIONS

This chapter has discussed the issues of using UML in the context of platform-based design. A new UML profile, UML Platform, has been proposed by introducing new building blocks (e.g. new stereotypes) to represent platform resources and services. Further, an embedded system design methodology that uses UML Platform and follows the platform-based design principles was presented. We believe that industry convergence on a standard platform profile in UML will be vital for the development of a variety of tools and methods that will better support embedded system design and help automate the flow from specification to platform-based implementation.

REFERENCES

[1] A. Sangiovanni-Vincentelli, "Defining Platform-based Design", *EEDesign*, Feb. 2002.
[2] J. Rumbaugh, I. Jacobson, and G. Booch, *The Unified Modeling Language User Guide*, Addison-Wesley, 1998
[3] G. Martin, L. Lavagno, J. Louis-Guerin, "Embedded UML: a merger of real-time UML and co-design", *Proceedings of CODES 2001*, Copenhagen, April 2001, pp.23-28.
[4] G. de Jong, "A UML-Based Design Methodology for Real-Time and Embedded Systems", *Proceedings of DATE 2002*, Paris, March 2002.
[5] B. Selic, "Complete High-Performance Code Generation from UML Models", *Proceedings of Embedded System Conference*, San Francisco, CA, USA, March 2002.
[6] C. Raistrick, "Executable UML for Embedded System Development", *Proceedings of Embedded System Conference*, San Francisco, CA, USA, March 2002.
[7] J. Warmer, A. Kleppe, *The Object Constraint Language: Precise Modeling with UML*, Object Technology Series, Addison-Wesley, 1999.
[8] B. Selic, "A Generic Framework for Modeling Resources with UML", *IEEE Computer*, June 2000, pp.64-9.
[9] B. Selic, J. Rumbaugh, "Using UML for Modeling Complex Real-Time Systems", White paper, Rational (Object Time), March 1998.
[10] P. N. Green, M. D. Edwards, "The Modeling of Embedded Systems Using HASoC", *Proceedings of DATE 2002*, Paris, March 2002.
[11] F. Balarin, L. Lavagno, C. Passerone, Y. Watanabe, "Processes, interfaces and platforms. Embedded software modeling in Metropolis", *Proceedings of EMSOFT 2002*, Grenoble, France, October, 2002.
[12] ARTISAN Software Tools, Inc. et al., "Response to the OMG RFP for Schedulability, Performance, and Time", OMG document number: ad/2001-06-14, June, 2001.
[13] J. da Silva Jr., M. Sgroi, F. De Bernardinis, S.F Li, A. Sangiovanni-Vincentelli and J. Rabaey, "Wireless Protocols Design: Challenges and Opportunities", *Proceedings of CODES 2000*, SanDiego, CA, USA, May 2000.
[14] E. Lee, D. Messerschmitt, "Synchronous Data Flow", *Proceedings of the IEEE*, September, 1987.
[15] H. Hsieh, J. Lin. Modeling SDF in Metropolis, Private Communication.

Chapter 6

UML for Hardware and Software Object Modeling

Martyn Edwards and Peter Green
Department of Computation, UMIST, Manchester, M60 1QD, United Kingdom

Abstract: This chapter discusses the HASoC (Hardware and Software Objects on Chip) approach to the development of embedded systems. HASoC is an object-oriented method, which is based on an iterative, incremental lifecycle. The design process, which uses UML notation, begins with the development and validation of a partial, abstract, executable system model, in which the objects are *uncommitted* to implementation in either hardware or software. This model is then partitioned into hardware and software, on the basis of design constraints, to create a *committed* model, which is subsequently mapped on to a system platform, and evaluated against design constraints. Subsequent design iterations add further detail to the original model. The method emphasises the reuse of pre-existing hardware and software models to ease the development process. The chapter presents an overview of the method, and a partial case study based on the development of a digital camera. The use of SystemC in the development of executable platform models is also mentioned.

Key words: UML, SystemC, object-orientation, lifecycle modeling, platform modeling.

1. INTRODUCTION

An embedded system normally consists of a set of hardware and software components that interact to perform a set of prescribed operations in its host environment. Embedded applications include aerospace systems, washing machines, automobile control systems, multimedia systems (including personal digital assistants and TV set-top boxes), telecommunications (including mobile phones), and industrial controllers. In fact, any application that requires some form of internal intelligence is included. Systems normally contain a balance of hardware and software components that work together to achieve the specified behaviour, whilst meeting various design criteria, including cost, power, and performance targets [1]. Typical target

L. Lavagno, G. Martin and B. Selic (eds.), UML for Real, 127-147.
© 2003 *Kluwer Academic Publishers.*

architectures for complex embedded systems consist of one or more processors, memories, and custom co-processors, input and output transducers, as well as application and system software. In the past, such systems would have been implemented using multiple integrated circuits. Today, with the increasing complexity of integrated circuits it is now possible to implement a complete embedded system on a single integrated circuit – the so-called system-on-a-chip (SoC).

Today's SoC devices contain tens of millions of transistors and in a few years time high performance devices are predicted to contain well over one billion transistors [2]. These rapid advances in process technology have led to an increasing productivity gap between the number of transistors available and the number of transistors that can be integrated in a design – annual growth rates of 58% and 21%, respectively, have been widely reported [2]. This gap is, in part, due to the lack of power in current system development methods and tools to permit the design, verification, and implementation of increasingly complex systems within reasonable timescales. A major challenge is to produce innovative design methods that go some way to reducing this productivity gap. We address this challenge in this chapter.

In order to meet shortening time-to-market constraints and reduce the astronomical development costs for new complex SoCs, it is recognised that the design process must make increasing use of reusable hardware and software intellectual property (IP) components. Incremental design procedures, where ~ 25% of the final system contains newly developed IP, will become commonplace [3]. Such procedures will lead to the development of pre-characterised *platform* architectures [3] that are essentially the same for a specific class of applications, for example, wireless communications [4]. It is highly likely that an existing platform will need to be customised in order to meet the requirements of a particular instance of the application space by, for example, adding, removing, replacing, or tweaking the parameters of IP components [5, 6]. This implies that a SoC development method will need to support an incremental design strategy using existing platforms.

Tracking the evolution of a system specification, capturing requirements and constraints, modeling hardware and software architectures, and partitioning functionality into hardware and software sub-systems are major design challenges that should be incorporated into a single, consistent design method. In our research, we are developing the HASoC (Hardware and Software Objects on Chip) method that employs an object-oriented approach to the implementation of complete embedded systems (including hardware, software, and platform architectures) [7]. HASoC is a fusion of our existing MOOSE approach [8] with an extended UML notation [9], coupled with an iterative, incremental approach to embedded system development.

The next section reviews a number of different approaches to the development of embedded systems and places our work in the context of related current research. An overview of the HASoC modeling flow is discussed in Section 3. Section 4 introduces a digital camera case study that is used to illustrate the main features of the method. The final section summarises our work to date and presents our plans for future research.

2. EMBEDDED SYSTEM DEVELOPMENT METHODS

In recent years, a number of noteworthy design methods have emerged for the development of real-time systems that include facilities for requirements capture and analysis, design, implementation, and testing [10, 11, 12]. Whilst most of this work has been targeted at the development of real-time software, some researchers have proposed similar frameworks for the co-development of hardware as well as software [13].

Our approach to the development of SoCs is founded on past research and experiences within our MOOSE object oriented hardware/software development method [8]. Although MOOSE has been successfully applied to the implementation of a number of embedded systems [14], it suffered from a number of drawbacks that have been eliminated in HASoC. In particular the need to complete each design stage in a sequential manner, with no iteration loops, made the method unresponsive to changes in requirements. The development of a system platform was delayed until after the system objects had been committed to hardware or software. This runs counter to the incremental/reuse design procedures that have been identified as being necessary in the future. MOOSE also employed a proprietary graphical notation. Lately considerable attention has been focused on the Unified Modeling Language (UML) [15], which has become the standard object-oriented modeling language. For this reason UML has been chosen as the main modeling notation in HASoC.

In its basic form, UML is applicable to a wide variety of systems, but lacks specialist concepts for particular application domains. Hence a number of specialist extensions have been proposed for the modeling of real-time and embedded systems.

UML-RT [16] emphasises a hierarchical system organisation via *capsules*, a capsule being a stereotyped form of active class[32]. The internal behaviour of a capsule is represented by a single statechart, supplemented by

---

[32] The instances of an active class all contain their own thread of control and are therefore capable of autonomous activity.

passive objects whose operations may be invoked as transition actions or state-based activities. From a structural viewpoint, capsules may contain sub-capsules as well as, or instead of, the statechart. Capsules communicate via owned objects called *ports* that implement specific *protocols*. Protocols are named sets of *signals*[33] that are communicated in a point-to-point fashion between capsule instances, Finally, *connectors* between ports in different capsules indicate message communications paths. The execution model is based on the transmission and reception of signals through ports that cause state transitions within a capsule's statechart.

The "UML Profile for Schedulability, Performance, and Time Specification" [17], which is discussed in Chapter 11, defines, as its name suggests, standard paradigms for modeling time-, schedulability-, and performance-related aspects of real-time systems. They allow the generation of models that can be used to make quantitative predictions about the schedulability and performance of a system. A new profile to allow UML to be augmented with the concepts of platform-based design is proposed in [18], and discussed in Chapter 5, which builds on the concepts originally articulated in [19] to allow the modeling of embedded systems.

On the basis of our past work and experiences with MOOSE, we also believe that it is necessary to put forward extensions to UML to not only make the notation more suitable for modeling mixed technology embedded systems but also to allow the systematic development of such systems, including software, hardware, application, and platform.

Our original HASoC work was based on extensions to UML-RT, but recently many of the concepts introduced in UML-RT have been included in the proposal for UML 2.0 [20]. Certain aspects of this proposal facilitate the generalization of the capsule concept, and this is helpful in some parts of our work, particularly with respect to the use of alternative behavioural descriptions and communications mechanisms [9, 21]. However, in this chapter we will, for the most part, confine ourselves to the use of capsules, although we will indicate where a more general view is profitable.

3.   THE HASOC DESIGN LIFECYCLE

The HASoC design method utilizes an iterative, incremental lifecycle, based in part on the "Rational Unified Process" [15]. Figure 6-1 illustrates a simplified view of the HASoC lifecycle. A more detailed explanation of the lifecycle can be found in [7].

---

[33] Signals are UML's asynchronous communication mechanism.

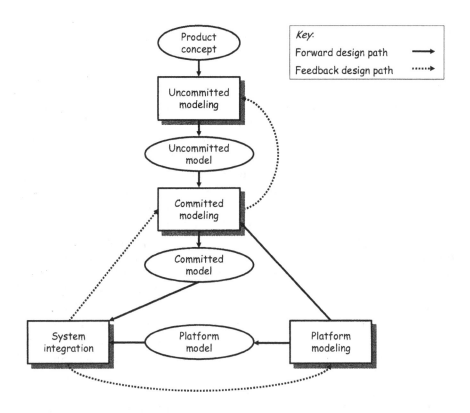

Figure 6-1. The HASoC Lifecycle

3.1   Product Concept

This initial stage informally defines the scope of the product as an *ad hoc* set of statements, in a natural language, which are not necessarily complete. The aim is to document what is known about the product, particularly in terms of its functional requirements, design constraints, and system platform.

This informal statement of requirements is used to create an initial use-case model for the system. Use-cases provide a simple way of stating functional requirements and can form the basis of an incremental design method [15]. Moreover, there are well-defined routes from use-cases to object models [22, 15]. The HASoC process is iterative, and in each iteration, a subset of use-cases is chosen for development, as described below. This leads to a prototype of the system that displays limited functionality, and which is elaborated with further use-cases in subsequent iterations.

The use-case model does not have to be complete at this stage, although the closer it is to completeness, the better.

3.2   Uncommitted Modeling

Uncommitted modeling consists of three separate phases: functionality selection, development of object and class models, and specification and validation of behaviour. In the *functionality selection* phase the use-case model is considered, and the use-cases to be developed in the current design iteration are selected. Decisions about the use-cases to assign to particular design iterations may be made on the basis of a number of criteria. For example, use-cases that represent core system functionality would typically be implemented in earlier iterations. Core functionality is deemed to be intrinsic to the purpose of the product, for example capturing an image in a digital camera, or video decoding in a set-top box. Other factors could involve perceived risk, for example, an element with a high complexity and for which no reusable Intellectual Property (IP) is available should be included at an early stage. The expertise of the design team would strongly influence how and when the many activities in a system were considered.

In the *objects and class models* phase, these models are developed for each selected use-case(s). A typical approach would be to generate sequence diagrams for key use-case scenarios, and then to create the UML class and collaboration diagrams corresponding to each sequence diagram.

A UML class model depicts the static structure of the application-specific part of the system, and the corresponding UML object model shows the run-time behaviour of instances of the classes, as they collaborate to deliver the functionality under development in the current iteration. Both class and object models provide information for the implementation of the executable model: the class model supports the generation of class interfaces, and interactions provide information about run-time inter-object communications. From these models a skeleton executable model can be constructed semi-automatically that supports the system-wide validation of object-level communications. A finer degree of behavioural validation can be achieved by adding detailed code fragments to the skeleton executable model in the *specification and validation of behaviour* phase of uncommitted modeling.

At some point during this phase the executable model from the current iteration is integrated with the one produced in the previous iterations, since at least some of the classes/objects will be common to different iterations. Further information concerning the detailed development and use of executable models can be found in [8].

The result of this design stage is an abstract executable model of the functionality of the proposed system. At this time, the system objects are not committed to either hardware or software implementations.

3.3   Committed Modeling

In developing a committed model, we are principally concerned with partitioning the abstract executable model into hardware and software implementations, and allocating the resulting 'committed objects' to the processing elements in the platform. Committed modeling consists of two separate phases: identification of the external interface mechanisms; and system partitioning. The first phase considers the *external interface* of a system. In some projects, interaction with the environment will be predefined at the start of the project, whereas in others it must be determined as part of the design process. In most embedded systems, design decisions must be taken about how to support human interaction, for example, whether to use voice input/speech output, or a keypad/LCD display. Additional objects must normally be added to the existing uncommitted model to support these design decisions.

Partitioning is performed at the capsule level, with some objects being identified for implementation in software, and others being targeted at a hardware implementation. The commitment of non-leaf capsules requires further comment since these may have their own behaviour, as well as containing simpler capsules. A difficulty arises when sub-capsules of a 'parent' are committed to different implementation technologies, and so there is then no obvious commitment for the behaviour of the parent. For reasons that are discussed in detail in [7] we take the view that elements that do not require ports for communication should be committed to the same technology and be 'co-resident'. Another way of looking at this is to say that elements of a capsule's behaviour (transition actions, passive objects, etc.) are so tightly bound that they should be committed en-bloc. A finer commitment granularity is likely to be accompanied by high communications overheads.

Our method is not prescriptive about how partitioning is to be achieved or what rules need to be applied in order to optimise performance, power consumption, etc. Since an executable model of the system is available, run-time measurements, code analysis, or examination of communication patterns can be employed to guide partitioning. Once a partition has been decided, the model must be reviewed, to ensure that inter-object communications are consistent with the chosen commitment, and that the identified concurrent activities have been implemented correctly.

The result of this design stage is a model of the functionality of the system with objects being assigned to software or hardware, and associated with specific platform components.

3.4   System Integration

System integration involves exploring the implementation space for a given application in order to find a suitable platform that satisfies a set of design constraints. The integration process maps a committed model onto the current incarnation of the platform model. Also included in this stage is an evaluation process that effectively carries out an assessment of the performance of the system in order to determine whether or not the current platform can execute the current committed model in a functional sense and satisfy the design constraints. The results of the integration process can be used to reconfigure the platform and/or modify the committed model (in terms of allocation of objects to hardware and software) so that the constraints are satisfied. System integration can be performed at multiple levels of abstraction, from a purely functional level to a detailed clock cycle accurate timing level as defined by the platform model – see Section 4. This is supported in HASoC through iterative mapping, evaluation, and platform development. Typically, the system integration process attempts to 'execute' the committed model on the hardware architecture model.

3.5   Platform Modeling

Elements of an application model are committed to hardware and software implementations on the basis of design constraints relating to, for example, performance and availability of IP elements. To construct a working system, however, consideration must be given to those components that provide the system execution environment, for example, processors, buses, memories, RTOS, and device drivers. A complete system requires a *hardware platform* to execute the application model, together with a significant level of *system software* support. In our context, both these elements make up the *platform model*.

The hardware platform is an architecture that satisfies the hardware and software constraints of an application. At one end of the spectrum, a pre-existing hardware platform may be used without change. It is, however, more likely that an existing platform would be customised for a particular application through the addition, removal, replacement, etc. of hardware and software objects. During the course of the design process it is envisaged that the capabilities of the hardware platform may also be updated to reflect any modifications to the functionality of the application.

The platform model describes the execution environment in sufficient detail to facilitate the implementation of the complete system. In HASoC, the platform model has two major elements: the *Software-Hardware Interface Model* (SHIM), and the *Hardware Architecture Model* (HAM). The relationships between these two models and their various internal components are shown in Figure 6-2.

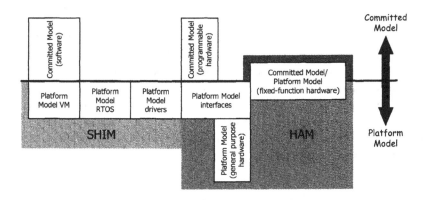

Figure 6-2. Relationship between the SHIM and HAM models

The SHIM typically consists of a virtual machine (VM) layer, a real-time operating system (RTOS), and device drivers. The objective of the VM is to support the execution of the committed model at a high level of abstraction, independently of the RTOS. Hence a key function of the VM is to provide a bridge between the committed model and the system software. A VM (such as the ROOM VM [12]), can be *heavy*, providing comprehensive model execution facilities, or *light*, in the sense of providing a thin layer of abstraction above the RTOS. A partial example of a light VM is provided in Section 4.4.1. The choice between a heavy, a light, or no VM at all is a trade-off of abstraction and portability against simplicity and higher performance.

In modeling the SHIM we are typically seeking to represent the configuration of existing software, along with modifications (for example new hardware drivers), rather than develop it from scratch. Hence we typically represent the SHIM as a component model. If OS-type software is to be developed as part of the project, then this must be stated early in the project as part of the use-case model, and the development of the OS should be scheduled into development iterations.

The HAM consists of general-purpose hardware (processors, memories, etc.), programmable hardware, and custom hardware, together with the interconnect and interfaces. The HAM is initially defined by a UML deployment diagram (DD). These are normally used in software projects to reason about issues such as distribution, and represent the hardware as a collection of static computational resources. Within HASoC, DDs play a similar role and for pre-existing platforms they are trivial to construct. Hence the DD is useful for indicating the basic structure of the platform, and can show where particular software components are executed, and where and how IP components are connected.

This representation forms a useful starting point in hardware development since it is possible to derive an object model from the DD that not only represents the hardware of the system but also supports its synthesis and simulation (see Section 4.4.2). Such a model provides a convenient framework for organising the platform definition, enabling elements to be added, removed, replaced or modified. Objects in the model are IP components that are assumed to have high-level, synthesisable functional hardware descriptions but which may not be able to interface to other blocks without, for example, bus wrappers.

4.   CASE STUDY: DIGITAL CAMERA

This case study discusses the development of a very simple digital camera system. The objective is to present sufficient detail to show clearly how the HASoC method works. It is not the intention to provide comprehensive details of the design of a real product!

The camera will enable still pictures and short video clips (up to 30 seconds duration) to be captured and stored. Pictures and video clips will be transferred to a desk-top computer, and the camera will not have any removable storage media. An on-camera display will be provided so that captured pictures and video clips can be reviewed, although there will be no live video feed to the display. The camera will have a fixed focus, provide automatic exposure control, use an optical view-finder, and implement an electronic shutter. A shutter release button will be provided, but decisions regarding other aspects of the user interface, for example, the method by which the user can navigate through an options menu to change camera settings, will be part of the design process. A important requirement is that the camera is responsive, and a key design objective is to minimise the time between the capture of successive still images. Furthermore, the camera must support image compression using the JPEG standard.

4.1 Uncommitted Model

A self-explanatory UML use-case model for this simple camera is given in Figure 6-3. The HASoC lifecycle subsequently requires the selection of an initial use-case(s) for the first iteration of the system development. For the digital camera we choose the "Take picture" use-case since it represents a major part of the core functionality of the system. A UML sequence diagram representing the successful taking of a picture is shown in Figure 6-4[34].

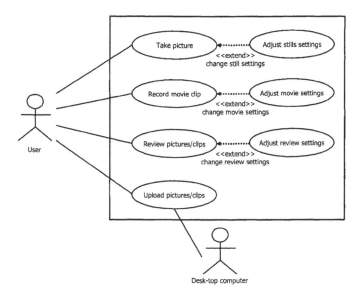

Figure 6-3. Use-case Model for the Digital Camera

The scenario is initiated by the user pressing the shutter release – modeled as the (asynchronous) signal "shoot". This triggers the (active) exposure controller object "exC", which reads light intensity from the metering cell object "mc"[35]. The exposure controller object is now able to determine the aperture and shutter speed. Since the product proposal specifies that an electronic shutter is to be used which is often integrated with the image capture device, the diagram only shows the adjustment of the aperture. The exposure controller object then sends a signal to the image controller object to initiate the capture of a still picture.

---

[34] The display of the picture after capture is omitted in the interests of clarity.

[35] In what follows, we use class names and object names interchangeably where the meaning is clear from the context.

The image controller object[36] is responsible for managing the entire picture capturing process. The sensor device object represents the physical device (which is typically a CCD sensor) at a high level of abstraction. Image capture is initiated by the image controller when it sends a "start" signal to the sensor device object. A "done" signal is returned when a picture has been captured. An image object is then created to hold the picture, and this controls the extraction of the image from the sensor device. The diagram shows the complete image being built before it is passed to the compressor object, which in turn creates a compressed image object. The compressed image object is subsequently stored in the album object "a".

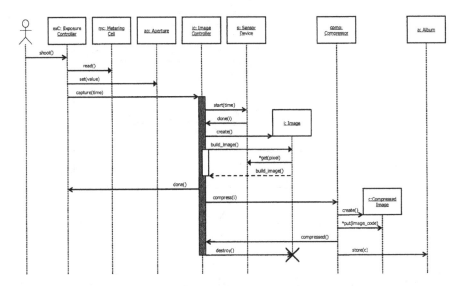

Figure 6-4. Sequence Diagram for the "Take picture" Use-case

4.1.1 The Capsule Model

The uncommitted capsule model corresponding to the Figure 6-4 is shown in Figure 6-5. The model indicates that passive objects are encapsulated in active objects. For example, the "exC" capsule contains the "mc" and "ap" capsules, and the "ic" capsule contains the capsule "s".

---

[36] This object is shown in more detail in Figure 6-4 as it is used to illustrate the development of capsule and platform models.

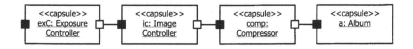

Figure 6-5. Uncommitted Capsule Model

The "exC" object receives an asynchronous input from the user ("shoot"), and, therefore, needs to be capable of autonomous action. However, after dispatching the capture signal to the "ic" object, it must enter a wait state which ignores inputs until it receives the "done" signal from the Image Controller object. Once the picture has been created in memory, picture acquisition can recommence, and be overlapped with the compression of the current picture.

The specification of a capsule can be refined, to show its internal structure. For example, the internal structure of the Image Controller capsule is shown in Figure 6-6, together with its state machine.

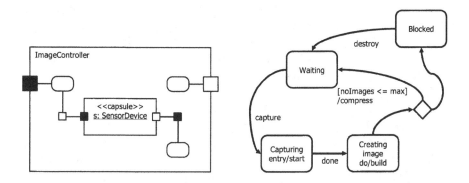

Figure 6-6. Internal Structure of the Image Controller Capsule and its State Machine

4.2 Committed Modelling

Developing a committed model involves the definition of external interface objects (see Section 3.3) and the partitioning of objects between hardware and software. With respect to the system use-case used in the first design iteration, there are no additional interface objects that need to be added to the model. Hence we focus on partitioning.

Some commitments are obvious, for example, the Sensor Device object cannot be anything other than hardware. Other partitioning choices are less clear cut, and require investigation through model execution or code analysis. For the purposes of illustration, we adopt the simple strategy of committing reactive elements to software and compute-intensive elements to hardware. This means that the compressor is assigned to hardware, and the other capsules to software. The only capsule that cannot be committed directly is the Image Controller, since it contains the hardware capsule Sensor Device. Here we commit the behaviour of Image Controller (its state machine and passive objects) to software, and its sub-capsule Sensor Device to hardware, in accordance with the discussion in Section 3.3. These commitments are summarized in Figure 6-7.

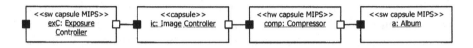

Figure 6-7. Committed Capsule Model

4.3   System Integration

The commitment must be done with some knowledge of the platform, except in the rare case where a new platform is to be developed, when an initial partition sets the requirements for the platform. In the case of our digital camera there are numerous SoC architectures that may be employed to perform the basic tasks required of such a device. Architectures include single-chip DSP devices that perform the necessary picture capture, processing, storage, and replay functions; for example, the TI TMS320DSC21 [23]. In this chapter, the hardware architecture is based on the DIGICAM chip, which is a reference design for digital camera applications developed as part of the Dalton project – see [5, 24] for further details. The associated DD is given in Figure 6-8. The processor *MIPS*, the memory *SRAM*, the devices *ISABridge*, *PPP*, and *PC16650* form the general-purpose part of the hardware platform. The *CCD* device implements the image sensor interface operations. The two buses *FastBus* and *SlowBus* define the two bus structures used to interconnect the hardware components, with the ISABridge device controlling the data transfers between them.

The software must be mapped to the single MIPS processor. If we assume the initial platform does not have a hardware-based JPEG picture compressor (CODEC), then we must consider the modifications to the platform that are needed to include such a device, since the compressor has been committed to hardware. Moreover, we would also need to investigate the overall performance of the system, and so hardware/software co-simulation is required in order to determine the allocation of the picture compression task to either hardware or software. How this can be accomplished is briefly considered in Section 4.4.

Figure 6-8 also illustrates that the processing elements in the platform share an address space. The uncommitted model in Figure 6-5 was developed at high level of abstraction and as such, makes no assumptions about whether the objects involved in image capture share an address space with those that are concerned with compression. Hence, pure message passing, which is the only form of inter-capsule communication that is supported by UML-RT, is used. As discussed in [12] this means that any object that is to be transferred between capsules must be copied. However, in an application such as our case study, this is clearly inefficient. There are a number of solutions to this problem. The first is to pass a pointer to the image data as the parameter of the compress call, rather than the image itself. This solves the problem by enabling the compressor to read the image directly, but runs counter to many object-oriented principles.

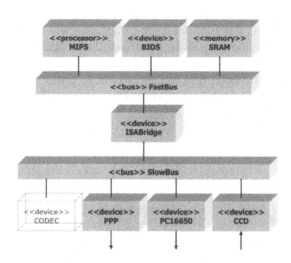

Figure 6-8. DIGICAM Platform Model, not including the hardware CODEC

A second possibility is to relax the UML-RT/ROOM rule requiring all passive objects to have a single owning capsule, and to introduce monitors [10] as an alternative to purely port-based communication. In this modified formalism, a monitor would be a boundary object in the same sense as a port, but with the key difference that it can enjoy aggregation relationships with several capsules. The purpose of such monitors would be to support rapid and safe sharing of data between concurrent entities when permitted by the platform configuration. The relationship between the monitor and the objects whose communication it facilitated would be analogous to the relationship between a port and a protocol role (or interface).

4.4 Platform Modelling

4.4.1 Software Hardware Interface Model

For the purposes of this case study, we assume that a small RTOS is available for use in the system. Hence an important issue is how the RTOS supports communication between software and hardware elements within the system. As indicated in Section 3.4, communications typically involve the RTOS, device drivers and some form of VM if one is being used. Here we will consider the use of a light VM. A light VM is simply a layer of proxy objects that mediate between the software in the committed model and the RTOS/device drivers. In the case of the compressor, we see from Figure 6-4 and Figure 6-7 that there is a direct communication between the software image controller and the hardware compressor. This can be realized via a software proxy object that represents the compressor within the SHIM, and a device driver that is developed on the basis of the actual interface of the hardware compressor, and which must be added to the RTOS. The message from the image controller is sent to the proxy object, which then utilizes the RTOS's I/O API to target the appropriate device driver. The configuration of these different system software elements is shown as a UML component diagram in Figure 6-9.

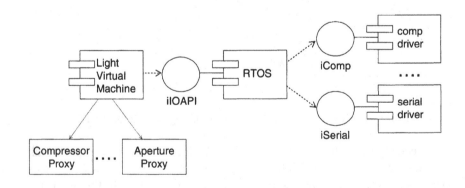

Figure 6-9. SHIM Component Model

According to [15], component diagrams are drawn to represent one aspect of software implementation, and Figure 6-9 is constructed from the perspective of communication with hardware. Details of most device drivers are omitted, but the control of the aperture is briefly considered. This case differs from the compressor in that it does not deal with committed model hardware. It can be inferred from Figures 6-4 and 6-7 that the aperture object is committed to software. This object adjusts the aperture of the camera, and we assume that the aperture mechanism is driven from the platform's serial port (PC16650 in Figure 6-8). Hence, although the model does not show the interaction between the software aperture object and hardware, it must still be managed and hence the aperture proxy appears in Figure 6-9.

4.4.2   Hardware Architecture Model

In the DD shown in Figure 6-8, the platform is simply represented as a set of static resources that support system execution. In order to pursue dynamic modeling and implementation of the platform, it should be possible to define additional notation and semantics for DDs to support these activities. A key observation, however, is that DDs normally represent the platform from the perspective of applications software. However, when viewed from a system perspective, DDs represent more than a simple collection of computational resources, they also represent a set of communicating elements that contain state and exhibit behaviour; that is, nodes of a DD represent objects. It now becomes possible to develop a high-level object model that represents the hardware platform, which uses the facilities of UML to model behaviour, and allows the generation of executable models, for example, in SystemC. Hence no extensions to UML are required. The platform can be modeled in terms of capsules, since the major elements of the platform execute concurrently and communicate through well defined interfaces. However, we choose to model platforms in terms of the constructs available in UML 2.0. This is shown to have certain advantages over UML-RT for our purposes, which are specifically concerned with communication and the representation of behaviour. For example, the communications behaviour of ports may be described by interfaces in UML 2.0, which can easily represent synchronous as well as asynchronous communications. The behaviour of active elements can be described, for example, using a programming language, hardware description language (HDL) or some appropriate model of computation, rather than a state machine.

The high-level HAM corresponding to the DD for the DIGICAM device is shown in Figure 6-10, in terms of active objects (represented by bold rectangles), ports, and connectors. The diagram indicates that there is a one-to-one correspondence between the nodes in the deployment diagram and the active objects. The main difference between the two representations is that the HAM can be made to be "executable" in order to verify the correct functioning of the system. This can be achieved by synthesizing the skeleton of an executable SystemC model of the system from the HAM. In HASoC, we propose that a "transaction level" (TL) model is defined in the first instance that is subsequently refined into a lower level "register transfer level" (RTL) model. A TL model allows the abstract communication between components of the HAM to be described as function calls. An RTL model is required in order to validate the actual communication between modules using the appropriate low level bus protocols. Such an RTL model, in SystemC, can be obtained by refining the communication structure developed in the SystemC TL model. Further details about this process are given in [21]. The resulting SystemC models can be utilized in a variety of ways. For example, they can be used with workload information derived from a model of the application to verify functionality, or co-simulated with the application software itself.

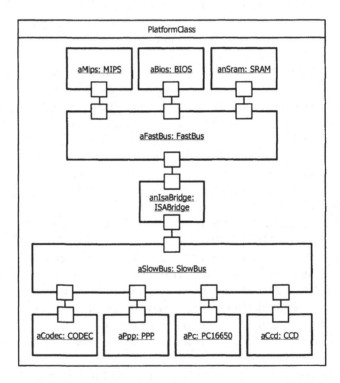

Figure 6-10. High Level DIGICAM Hardware Architecture Model

Different versions of the HAM may also be evaluated, using the above techniques, by modifying the model to include alternative implementations of active objects. For example, the JPEG CODEC could be implemented either as an IP core or a programmable logic block or software on the processor with different cost/performance tradeoffs. Figure 6-10 shows the CODEC included in the platform model as a custom hardware device.

5. CONCLUSIONS AND FURTHER WORK

The HASoC lifecycle for the development of embedded systems has been addressed in this chapter. By using ideas of iterative system construction, we have developed a lifecycle that is responsive to changing requirements, and where work on the underlying platform model can commence not only at an early stage but also concurrently with the iterative development of the application-oriented executable model. Indeed, there is significant concurrency within the complete lifecycle, enabling different specialist groups to work in parallel, but always in the context of a homogeneous model of the system.

Platform-based design continues to excite significant interest in the SoC community due to its potential to reduce development times. To date, however, platform descriptions have been ad hoc, ranging from informal block diagrams, through to HDL descriptions at varying levels of abstraction. A platform would typically have a number of such descriptions, each used for a different purpose, and without any formal link between them. This can lead to duplicated effort and inconsistencies between models. In this chapter we have shown that by reinterpreting the platform UML deployment diagram from the perspective of hardware development, we are able to produce an object model that can form the basis of further development of the platform itself. Definition of the interfaces between the objects of this model facilitates the construction of a skeleton SystemC model at the transaction level. The model can be completed via the addition of functional descriptions of the IP block represented by each object. This transaction-level model can subsequently be refined to a register transfer model that represents bus-based communications at the physical level.

We have proposed an outline framework for system and platform description, simulation, refinement and implementation, in which all these activities are linked via models that are transformations or refinements of one another. We are currently working on the development of a set of tools to support our design methodology which we hope will form the basis of a practical method for platform-based design.

REFERENCES

[1] R. Ernst, "Codesign of Embedded Systems: Status and Trends", *IEEE Design and Test of Computers*, 14 (3), 1998, pp. 45-54.

[2] Semiconductor Industry Association, *International Technology Roadmap for Semiconductors: 1999 Edition*, Austin, Texas: International Sematech, 1999.

[3] A. Ferrari and A. Sangiovanni-Vincentelli, "System Design: Traditional Concepts and New Paradigms", in *Proceedings of International Conference on Computer Design*, October 1999.

[4] J. M. Rabaey, M. Potkonjak, F. Koushanfar, S-F. Li, and T. Tuan, "Challenges and Opportunities in Broadband and Wireless Communication Designs", in *Proceedings of International Conference on Computer Aided Design*, November, 2000.

[5] F. Vahid and T. Givargis, "Platform Tuning for Embedded Systems Design", *Computer*, 34(3), pp. 112-114, March, 2001.

[6] H. Chang, L. Cooke, M. Hunt, G. Martin, A. McNelly, and L. Todd, *Surviving the SOC Revolution, A Guide to Platform-Based Design*, Kluwer Academic Publishers, 1999.

[7] Peter Green, Martyn Edwards, and Salah Essa, "HASoC – Towards a New Method for System-on-a-Chip Development", *Design Automation for Embedded Systems*, 6, 2002, pp. 333-353.

[8] D. Morris, D. G. Evans, P. N. Green, and C. J. Theaker, *Object-Oriented Computer Systems Engineering*, Springer-Verlag, 1996.

[9] Peter Green, Martyn Edwards and Salah Essa, "UML for System-Level Design: Extending the Object Model for Systems-on-Chips", in *Systems on Chip Design Languages*, Anne Mignotte, Eugenio Villar, and Lynn Horobin (Editors), Kluwer Academic Press, 2002.

[10] G. Booch, *Object-Oriented Design*, Benjamin/Cummings. 1991.

[11] D. J. Hatley and I. A. Pribhai, *Strategies for Real-Time System Specification*, Dorset House, 1988.

[12] B. Selic, G. Gullekson, and P. T. Ward, *Real-Time Object-Oriented Modeling*, Wiley, 1994.

[13] W. Wolf, "Object Oriented Co-Specification for Embedded Systems", *Microprocessors and Microsystems*, 1(20), 1996.

[14] P. N. Green, P. Rushton, and S .R. Beggs, "An Example of Applying the Codesign Method MOOSE", in *Proceedings of the Third International Workshop on Hardware/Software Codesign*, May, 1994.

[15] G. Booch, J. Rumbaugh, and I. Jacobson, *The Unified Modeling Language Guide*, Addison-Wesley, 1999.

[16] B. Selic and J. Rumbaugh, *Using UML for Modelling Complex Real-Time Systems*, ObjecTime Limited/Rational Software White Paper, 1998.

[17] Object Management Group, *UML Profile for Schedulability, Performance, and Time Specification*, Object Management Group, 2002.

[18] R. Chen, M. Sgroi, G. Martin, L. Lavagno, A. Sangiovanni-Vincentelli, and J. Rabaey, "Embedded System Design Using UML and Platforms", in *Proceedings of FDL'02, Volume 2*, September 2002.

[19] G. Martin, L. Lavagno, and J. Louis-Guerin, "Embedded UML: a merger of real-time UML and co-design", in *Proceedings of CODES'01*, May, 2001.

[20] Object Management Group, *Unified Modeling Language 2.0 Proposal (version 0.671)*, 25 January, 2002.

[21] P. N. Green and M. D. Edwards, "Platform Modelling with UML and SystemC", in *Proceedings of FDL'02*, September, 2002.

[22] K. Beck and W. Cunningham, "A Laboratory for Teaching Object Oriented Thinking", *ACM SIGPLAN Notices*, 24(10), 1989.

[23] Texas Instruments, *TMS320DSC21 – A High Performance, programmable, Single Chip Digital Signal Processing Solution to Digital Still Cameras*, Texas Instruments, 2001.

[24] Dalton Project: http://www.cs.ucr.edu/~dalton (July 2002).

Chapter 7

Fine Grained Patterns for Real-Time Systems

Bruce Powel Douglass, Ph.D.
I-Logix

Abstract: A design pattern is a generalized approach or solution to a commonly occurring problem. Design patterns are a way of capturing and codifying design expertise in the forms of solutions that have proven effective in solving specific kinds of problems in a various contexts. This chapter discusses how fine-grained patterns that solve specific kinds of problems common in real-time systems. These and other related patterns can be found in the references. Much of this material is adapted from the author's book *Real-Time Design Patterns: Robust Architecture for Real-Time Systems* (Addison-Wesley, 2002).

Key words: Real-time design patterns, resource management patterns

1. INTRODUCTION

Collaborations define the structural elements and their relations necessary to achieve a use case behavior. Patterns exist to provide common ways of wiring together collaborations that optimize some criteria of importance. Because the functional issues are addressed by the collaboration itself, design patterns optimize some quality of service (QoS) criteria such as performance, memory usage, reusability, robustness, safety, or reliability. Rather than exhaustively catalog all potentially useful patterns, let us concern ourselves with patterns that address some specific problems faced by real-time and embedded system developers. Catalogs of patterns useful for real-time systems are dealt with in more detail elsewhere [2, 3, 4] and the interested reader is referred there for a more complete set of real-time design patterns.

Experienced developers find when they approach a new problem, that the situation usually has something in common with a solution they have previously either created or seen. The problems are not identical and the

L. Lavagno, G. Martin and B. Selic (eds.), UML for Real, 149-170.

identical solution will rarely solve the new problems, but the problems are nevertheless similar, so a similar solution will probably work. The "similar solution," generalized and formalized, is called a *design pattern*. Creating design patterns is a problem of abstracting the similarities of the many specific instances of the problem and their solutions. The discovered generalized solution can then be applied to the new problem at hand.

Of the three fundamental concerns associated with patterns, the first has to do with the application of patterns. The problem of identifying the nature of the problem and examining the patterns "library" for the best ones to apply is called *pattern hatching*[10]. And, as John Vlissides, author of that excellent book points out, this name implies that we're not creating something new but "developing from preexisting rudiments." These preexisting rudiments are our captured design patterns that we can use to construct solutions that work in novel circumstances.

Another issue, of course, is the identification and capture of new patterns to add to the library. This process I call *pattern mining*. It involves the abstraction of the problem to its essential properties, creating a generic solution and then understanding the consequences of that solution in the problem context in which the pattern applies.

Lastly, patterns must be *instantiated* – that is, they must be applied to the application problem at hand. This is usually a combination of specialization of the general pattern roles, parametric instantiation of parameterized classes, and modification of application classes to take on properties of the pattern elements.

Patterns are not just software reuse, but rather a kind of *concept reuse*. Most patterns, such as those presented in this book are related to design. Design is always an optimization of an analysis model and design patterns are always a general concept for how to optimize an analysis model in a particular way with particular effects.

Optimization always entails improving some aspect of the system at the expense of others. For example, some patterns will optimize reusability at the expense of worst-case performance. Other patterns will optimize safety at the expense of system recurring cost (i.e., cost per shipped item). Whenever you optimize one set of aspects, you necessarily *deoptimize* others. This is a fact of life, else we would all be driving at the speed of sound using no gasoline and in perfect safety for zero cost.

1.1   What is a Design Pattern?

A design pattern is "a generalized solution to a commonly occurring problem." To be a pattern, the problem must recur often enough to be usefully generalizable. The solution must also be general enough to applied in a wide set of application domains. If it only applies to a single application domain, then it is probably an *analysis pattern*. An analysis pattern is similar to a design pattern but applies to a specific application domain such as finance or aerospace. Analysis patterns define ways for organizing problem-specific object analysis models within a single application domain. See [5] for some examples of domain-specific analysis patterns.

Analysis is driven by *what* the system must do while design is driven by *how well* the system must achieve its requirements. A design pattern is a way of organizing some aspect of a design to improve its optimality with respect to one or a small set of qualities of service. Some of the QoS that may be optimized by design patterns are:

- Performance
  - Worst case
  - Average case
- Predictability
- Schedulability
- Throughput
  - Average
  - Sustained
  - Burst
- Reliability
  - With respect to errors
  - With respect to failures
- Safety
- Reusability
- Distributability
- Portability
- Maintainability
- Scalability
- Complexity
- Resource usage, e.g. memory
- Energy consumption
- Recurring cost, i.e. hardware cost
- Development effort and cost

Of course, many of these QoS properties are to some degree conflicting. A design pattern always has a focused purpose – which is to take one or a small set of these QoS properties and optimize them at the expense of the others.

Patterns may be applied at the different levels of design abstraction. Architectural patterns have systemic scope and apply mostly to only one of the Five Views of architecture (Subsystem organization, Distribution, Safety and Reliability, Concurrency and Resource Management, or Deployment) [2, 3, 4]. At the next level down in design abstraction, mechanistic design patterns apply to individual collaborations, optimizing the same QoS properties, but in a more narrow context. This is the level of abstraction that we consider "fine-grained" patterns, such as those dealt with in this chapter. Patterns usually do not apply to detailed design (limited in scope to the optimization of a single object or class), but idioms and practices do.

The pattern literature deals primarily with *structural design patterns*. That is, they call for organizing systems or parts of systems in certain ways so that behavioral strategies can be applied to optimize the desired QoS. Patterns, however, need not be structural. The book *Doing Hard Time* [6], for example, provides a set of *behavioral* design patterns for ways in which state machines may be "behaviorally structured" to optimize how the state machine works.

Sets of interrelated patterns tailored specifically to work well together are called *frameworks*. In a framework-based development effort, the majority of the application is provided by the instantiated framework. This includes the "meat and potatoes" of the application, typically offering services to construct GUI elements, manage devices, manage concurrency, execute state machines and so on. The developer need only then build the elements of the system which are peculiar to that *particular* system, relying on the framework to support those application services.

Frameworks provide four primary usage strategies – instantiation, generalization, parameterization, and extension – and many frameworks use all four. The instantiation usage strategy uses some aspect of the framework – such as scheduling threads or executing state machines – directly with no change. The generalization strategy takes an abstract framework element and specializes it, adding problem-specific functionality. A real-time framework might provide a *Sensor* class that fits into a Model-View-Controller style pattern, with the expectation that you will subclass this *Sensor* class for your particular device and overwrite the inherited methods. This is a very common way of using patterns. Parameterization is applied when the framework provides parameterized classes – such as containers in C++'s STL – with the intention that you will provide the actual parameters when you instantiate that portion of the framework. Lastly, most frameworks have special places were you can plug in pieces and extend the framework. An example of this would be plugging in a CAN bus communications protocol or an HDLC (High-level Data Link Communications) protocol. The disadvantages of frameworks are that they limit the ways in which you do things and frameworks are *much* more difficult to design and construct than applications. However, once developed, they greatly simplify application development. Frameworks are prime examples of effective use of patterns.

1.2   Basic Structure of Design Patterns

According to Gamma, et. al. [6], a pattern has four important aspects:

- Name
  The name provides a "handle" or means to reference the pattern.

- Purpose
  The purpose provides the problem context and the QoS aspects the pattern seeks to optimize. The purpose identifies the kinds of problem contexts where the pattern might be particularly appropriate.

- Solution
  The Solution is the pattern itself, including the pattern elements, their roles, and their relations.

- Consequences
  The Consequences are the set of pros and cons of the use of the pattern

The pattern *name* brings us two things. First, it allows us to reference the pattern is a clear, unambiguous way, with the details present, but unstated. Secondly, it gives us a more abstract vocabulary to speak about our designs. The statement "The system uses a Layered structural architecture with Messages Queuing Concurrency distributed across a Symmetric deployment with a Broker pattern" has a lot of information about the overall structure of the system because we can discuss the design in terms of these patterns.

The *purpose* of the pattern brings into focus the essential problem contexts required for the pattern to be applicable and what qualities of service the pattern is attempting to optimize. This section specifies under which situations the pattern is appropriate and under which situations it should be avoided.

The *solution* of course, is the most important aspect. It identifies the elements of the pattern and their roles in relation to each other. As we'll see in the next section, these elements are used, replaced, or subclassed by your application objects to instantiate the pattern.

The *consequences* are important because we always make tradeoffs when we select one pattern over another. We must understand the pros and cons of the pattern to apply it effectively. The pros and cons are usually couched in terms of improvement or degradation of some qualities of service as well as a possible elaboration of problem contexts in which these consequences apply.

A pattern is a parameterized collaboration. That is, it is a collaboration in which some element or roles are not specified in the pattern but will be filled in later then the pattern is applied. The UML uses a dashed oval as a stand-in for a pattern with dependencies indicating the pattern roles. The application of a pattern supplies classes or objects for these roles resulting in an instantiable collaboration, as shown in Figure 7-1.

In Figure 7-1a, the pattern itself is defined. The dashed oval provides the name of the pattern and indicates the pattern roles with dependencies. The classes within the pattern are the structural elements of the pattern. Some of these roles, such as Owner and Element, come from the problem to which the pattern is being applied. Others, in this case Parameterized Container and Container, are provided by the pattern itself.

Figure 7-1b shows how the pattern is used. The upper part is a collaboration (in this case, a small one) from an application model. The lower part shows the collaboration elaborated with the Container pattern.

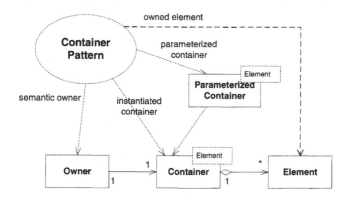

Figure 7-1a: Sample Pattern Definition

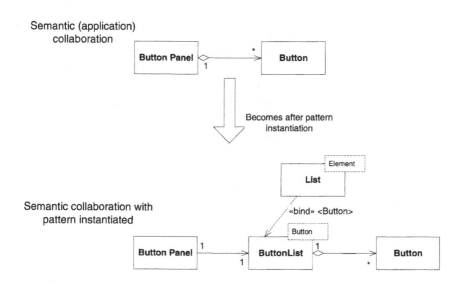

Figure 7-1b: Sample Pattern Usage

Figure 7-1. Sample Pattern

2.   USING DESIGN PATTERNS IN DEVELOPMENT

We have argued above that patterns aid us by providing strategies to optimize our designs against the various qualities of service. Let us now explore the ways in which we can use patterns. Patterns are used in one of three ways – they must be located (a process called *pattern hatching*), captured from design expertise (*pattern mining*), or applied (*pattern instantiation*).

2.1   Pattern Hatching – Locating the right patterns

You're facing a design problem. How do you find the patterns that can be applied to solve your particular design issues? We recommend an approach multi-step approach as shown in Figure 7-2.

1. First, before starting your design familiarizing yourself with the patterns literature. There are a number of books, papers, and web sites devoted to patterns in many application domains. A few of those patterns are briefly described here and others are given in the references. Once you have increased your vocabulary to include patterns likely to be relevant to your application domain, you have more intellectual ammunition to face your design challenges.

2. Apply Linear Thinking. Characterize the nature of the design problem you face. What is the scope of the problem – architectural, mechanistic, or detailed? What are the relevant quality of service issues – Worst case performance? Reusability? Safety? Portability? Memory usage? Rank them according to criticality. Sometimes once you've done this, a design solution will suggest itself.

3. Apply pattern matching. This is the fun part. Your cerebral cortex is a wonderful pattern-matching machine. It operates autonomously from your linear thought processing. This is why you have the "Eureka!" experience when you're in the shower, getting ready for bed, or eating dinner. Once you've applied the linear thinking step, your unconscious pattern matching machinery has enough information to go to work.

4. "A miracle occurs." The pattern matching machinery identifies a potential solution, usually the application of a pattern, whether that pattern was explicitly formulated as a general solution or not. This doesn't mean that the proposed solution is a good one, just that it matches the desired properties closely enough for further evaluation.

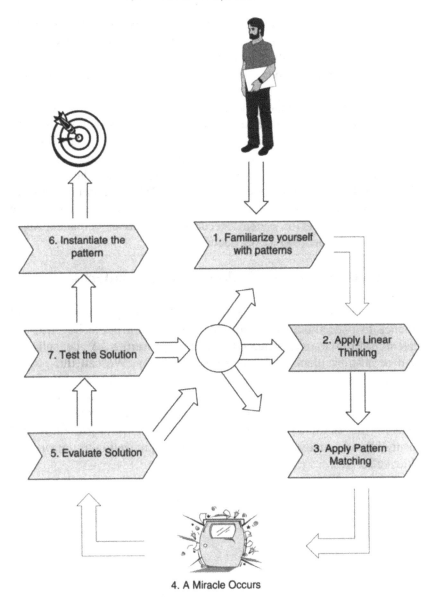

Figure 7-2. Pattern Hatching

5.   Evaluate the proposed solution. This is another application of linear reasoning, in which you logically analyze and evaluate the pattern suggested. If the solution is good, then you apply it (step 6), if not, you clearly go back to step 3, or perhaps even step 2.

6. Instantiate the pattern. Organize your structural elements to be consistent with the pattern. This may involve breaking objects apart, merging them together, reassigning collaboration responsibilities or the introduction of new elements all together (a process commonly known as "refactoring").

7. Test the solution. Elaborate your analysis scenarios with the elements of the collaboration and demonstrate that they meet the functional and behavioral requirements. Once you're satisfied that the collaboration is doing the right thing, measure the desired qualities of service, if necessary, to ensure that the pattern is achieving your quality of service goals. This is especially true for performance and resource usage goals. This measurement may be done via model or system execution, simulation, or mathematical analysis depending on your needs.

2.2   Pattern Mining – Rolling your own patterns

Creating your own pattern is useful especially when you have a depth of experience to understand the optimization issues in a particular area, and sufficient breadth to understand the general properties of the solutions enough to abstract them into a generalized solution. We call this *pattern mining* (see Figure 7-3). Pattern mining isn't so much a matter of invention as it is discovery and abstraction – seeing that this solution in some context is similar to that solution in another context and abstracting away the specifics of the solutions. Keep in mind that to be a useful pattern, it must occur in different contexts and perform a useful optimization of one or more qualities of service.

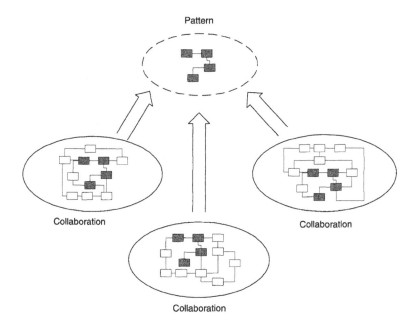

Figure 7-3. Pattern Mining

2.3   Pattern Instantiation – Applying Patterns in your designs

Pattern instantiation is the opposite of pattern mining. It is applying the pattern to a particular collaboration to gain the benefits of the pattern (see Figure 7-4). Patterns are normally applied to an object collaboration. A collaboration is a set of objects (at some scope these may be small low-level objects while at others they may be large-grain objects such as subsystems and components). The purpose is to organize, and possibly elaborate, this already existing collaboration with the pattern.

The application or instantiation of a pattern in your design is a matter of defining the elements that will fulfill the collaboration roles in the application. For some of the patterns you may create the role as a superclass, from which you subclass to instantiate that pattern. In other patterns, you may simply replace the pattern element with one from your application domain, adding in the required operations and behavior. Or, you may choose to create objects just as they exist in the pattern itself to provide services to your application objects.

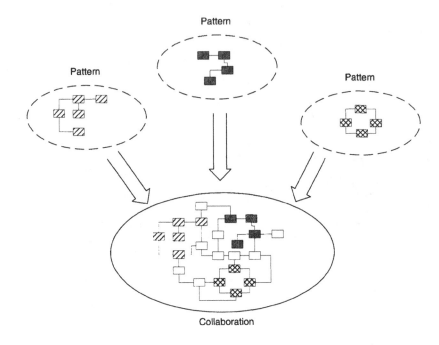

Figure 7-4. Pattern Instantiation

3.   CATEGORIES OF MECHANISTIC PATTERNS

Given that fine-grained, mechanistic patterns are about optimization of some properties of a collaboration at the expense of others, we can catalog patterns on the basis of what they seek to optimize. Since we are focusing on design patterns helpful for the development of real-time and embedded systems, the patterns discussed here will fall into one of the following categories:

- Resource Management
- Concurrency
- Distribution
- Safety and Reliability
- Reuse and software quality patterns
- Reactive (behavioral) patterns

These categories are not mutually exclusive, nor an exhaustive list, but they provide a convenient way to categorize patterns based on the primary QoS aspect they attempt to optimize. It should be noted that there are also architectural patterns that fall into these categories as well. Readers interested in those kinds of patterns are referred to the references for more detail [1, 4].

3.1   Resource Management

One of the most important kinds of optimization required in real-time and embedded systems is the correct management and optimization of resource usage, whether that resource is memory, CPU, hardware, or bus. A resource, or more precisely a resource instance, is defined in the so-called Real-Time UML Profile [12] as

> a run-time entity that offers one or more *services* for which we need to express a measure of effectiveness or quality of service (QoS).

A large portion of the real-time literature is in fact devoted to ensuring that the delivered qualities of service for a resource can be demonstrated to match its client's requirements.

The fundamental aspect of resources is that they are limited or constrained in some way. One of the most common (hardware) resources is, of course, memory. There are many patterns that deal with memory usage. [7] provides a number of patterns specifically around memory usage such as reference counting smart pointers (Reference Counting Pattern), and various allocation schemes such as Fixed Allocation Pattern, Pooled Allocation Pattern, and Garbage Compaction. [3] offers a number of resource management patterns around memory usage (although tending more towards architectural scope), but also provides patterns for the sharing of resources in a concurrent environment, including Priority Inheritance and related patterns for bounding priority inversion and other patterns, such as Critical Section, Simultaneous Locking, and Ordered Locking Patterns, to avoid deadlock.

Figure 7-5 shows one simple access pattern – called the smart pointer pattern. Pointers have many positive qualities, but they are a low-level primitive, error-prone aspect of programming. It is very easy to lose track of memory (memory leak), access memory after it has been reclaimed (dangling pointer) or use a pointer when it has not yet been initialized (uninitialized pointer). These problems arise because pointers have invariant preconditions for their usage but because they are language primitives they have no means to ensure these invariants remain adhered to. The Smart Pointer pattern [3, 7] solves these problems by making the pointers into objects and the operations, including the constructor and destructor, execute to ensure that these preconditions remain valid. The reference count attribute of the target object identifies when it is safe to reclaim the memory of the target object (i.e. when the reference count is decremented to zero accessing pointers).

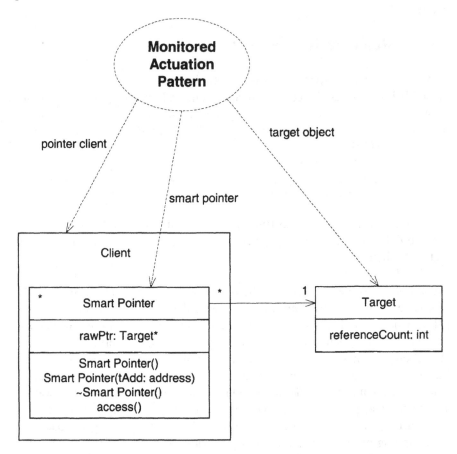

Figure 7-5. Basic Smart Pointer Pattern

3.2 Concurrency

Concurrency is, of course, a critical aspect of real-time systems and it's management is far from trivial. There are excellent references on concurrency issues, such as [13, 14, 15] although they are rarely expressed as patterns *per se* ([3] is an exception to that rule). The primary issues around concurrency are either (or both) overall performance or schedulability. By performance, we mean the ability of a system to perform as many calculations and actuations as possible in a given time – the higher the number of calculations and actuations, the greater the performance. By schedulability, we mean the ability of a system to meet its timeliness requirements regardless of task loading. Such timeliness requirements are normally couched in terms of meeting deadlines, but that is not the only possible criteria [2, 15]. Average execution time is usually the optimzation criteria for so-called soft real-time systems, which an occasional late or even missed computation being tolerable. In hard real-time systems, the optimization criteria is that every computation is performed within a specified static constraint, called a deadline.

The concurrency patterns provided in the literature tend to be focused in two areas. The first is scheduling policies, such as the Interrupt Pattern, Guarded Call Pattern, or. Message Queuing Pattern [3], or mechanisms to optimize schedulability of sporadic tasks [14, 15]. The second area has to do with patterns around limiting blocking and priority inversion. These patterns overlap with the resource patterns (discussed above) because the primary reason for blocking to occur is because of the locking of resources in a concurrent situation.

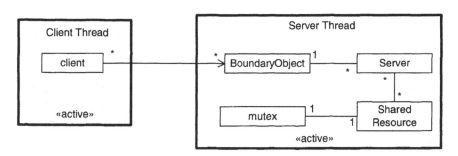

Figure 7-6. Guarded Call Pattern

The Guarded Call Pattern is shown in Figure 7-6. The classes with heavy borders are «active», meaning that they are the roots of OS threads. The objects they contain via composition (shown as "nested classes" in the figure) run in the thread of their composite «active» object. This pattern allows the classes running in different threads to with a direct call across the thread boundaries. To ensure data integrity, the Shared Resource (which contains the data or service that must be protected) associates with a mutual exclusion semaphore which guarantees that at most only a single client will access the data or service at a time. The boundary object provides a public façade for clients to invoke the server operations that manipulate the resource. If a client tried to invoke the server operation while the Share

Resource is locked, the OS will suspend it until the resource becomes available.

3.3   Distribution

Distribution is crucial to many of today's complex real-time and embedded systems. By "distribution" we mean the separation of collaborating objects across multiple address spaces. The goal of many distribution patterns is to make this separation as transparent as possible while making the communication among objects as efficient as possible. Many patterns in this area are architectural [1, 4, 16] but many smaller patterns fit in as well.

Distribution is often categorized into two types – *asymmetric*, meaning that the location of the objects is decided at design time, and *symmetric*, in which run-time mechanisms load and execute the objects in potentially different locations depending on run-time conditions. Asymmetric is certainly less complex overall, but suffers from a lack of flexibility. For example, it isn't possible to perform dynamic load balancing among several processors if the each object is dedicated to a single processor during design. On the other hand, the simplicity of asymmetric distribution is appealing. The primary concerns with asymmetric distribution are the kind of protocols used to deliver the messages to maximize different qualities of service (such as throughput and reliability, to name only two) and the patterns by which the distribution will be made transparent to the designer and/or programmer.

The observer pattern [4, 6] is a common basis for distribution because it simplifies the communication between a server (an object providing information or service) and its clients. Figure 7-7 shows the very simple observer pattern from which many distribution patterns, such as Proxy and Broker are derived.

The Observer Pattern optimizes the response time of a client to a change in value in the server. If the client repeatedly polls the server, especially for slowly changing values, most of these probes will consume CPU (or in the distributed version, bus) bandwidth, even though the value doesn't change. The observer pattern allows the Concrete Client (the application client class) to subscribe to the Concrete Server (the application server class). It passes off a Notification Handle (logical address of some kind) so that the Server can notify its' clients when the value changes.

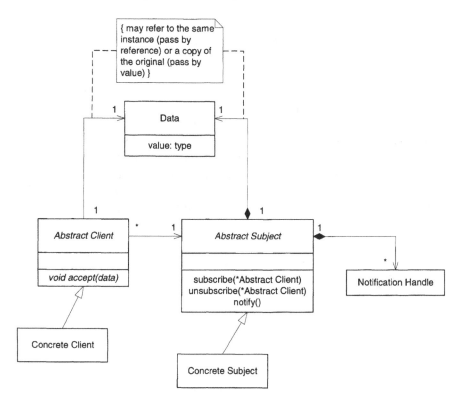

Figure 7-7. Observer Pattern

3.4   Safety and Reliability

Safety and reliability are two categories of quality of service that are crucial in many real-time and embedded systems. Safety refers the "freedom from accidents or losses" while reliability is "the probability that a computation will be completed successfully" [2]. While these aspects are importantly different and distinct, some of the same underlying design patterns are used to address both. Safety and reliability tend to be managed at two levels – architecturally and in detailed design. [3] provides a number of architectural patterns for this purpose while [2, 17, 18, 19] discuss the issues and many common solutions, although these are not cast in the form of patterns *per se*.

The patterns in this genre focus primarily on the violation of so-called invariants – things that are supposed to be always true – and on taking appropriate action when such violations are detected. In reliability patterns, these tend to be completely internal; that is, they look for corruption or obviously incorrect results. This is the purpose of the Redundant Storage Pattern, shown in Figure 7-8. The Numeric Basis class provides the fundamental structure of a server of numeric data – which might be monitored heart rate in an ECG machine or controlled yaw of a satellite. The fundamental type of the *value* attribute is deferred for later specification. This parameterized class is then subclassed into two different kinds of redundancy. The simple form stores the value twice – once in its normal form and once in a one's complement form – and either sets both when the *set()* operation is called or checks one against the other when the *get()* operation is called. This identifies if the value has been corrupted. Note that for a given value *either* the one's complement or the CRC class is subclassed, not both. That is the meaning of the { XOR } constraint between the two relations.

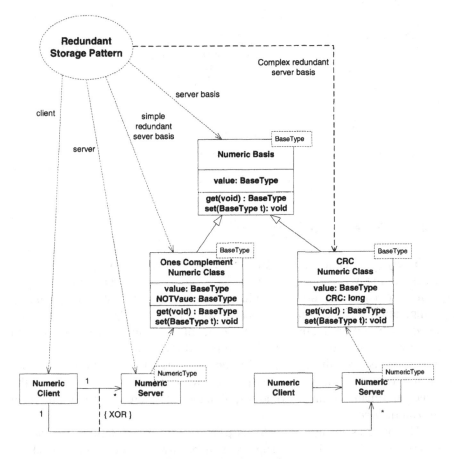

Figure 7-8. Redundant Storage Pattern

Safety patterns, on the other hand, tend to compare an independent observation of what the system is doing in the real world with and expectation of what it ought to be doing. This requires a separate sensor from any used in the actuation control to ensure an independence of fault effects. This is often done at the architectural level, but it can be done at the mechanistic level of abstraction as well, as shown in Figure 7-9.

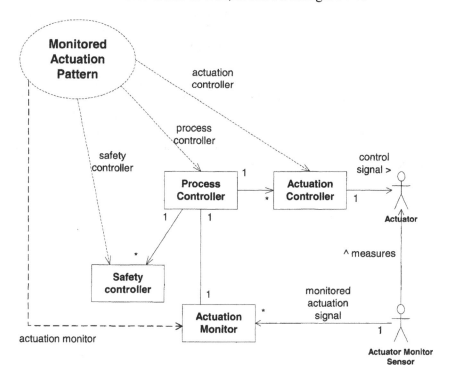

Figure 7-9. Monitored Actuation Pattern

The concept of the pattern is that the Actuation Controller affects the real world by commanding the Actuator actor. This actuation might be controlling the amount of drug injected into a patient or the pressure in an industrial press. An error in the chain of computations or in the actuator hardware itself could lead to an unsafe situation. The Actuation Monitor is told what the actuation should be via the association to the Process Controller. It uses an independent sensor to monitor the physical process to ensure the match is "close enough" to what is expected (in practice the monitor or the Process Controller must take into account actuation delays and measurement inaccuracies). The pattern provides single-point failure safety. If the Actuation Controller fails then the Actuation Monitor detects it and the Process Controller can invoke the appropriate safety action. On the other hand, if the Actuation Monitor fails, then the actuation continues properly.

3.5   Reuse and Software Quality Patterns

Real-time and embedded systems have all the same issues that traditional IT software has in terms of non-time related qualities of service, such as reusability, correctness, portability, simplicity and so on. Virtually all of the patterns defined for these qualities work for real-time systems just as well. [6] is perhaps *the* classic reference of such patterns. The Adapter pattern of [6], for example, performs "impedance matching" when the interface of one class doesn't match what is needed. This allows high-quality tested classes to be reused in new situations. It does this by providing an Adaptor that subclasses both the desired interface and the actual server class (or it's interface); then the subclassed request() operation is specialized to invoke the original operation (specificRequest()).

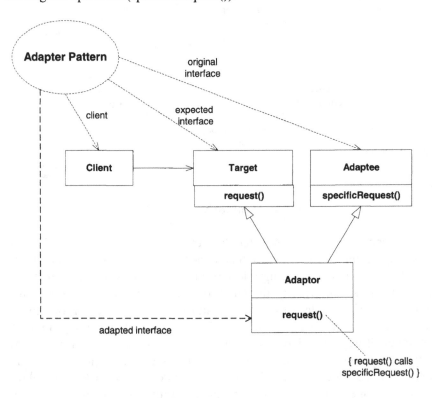

Figure 7-10. Adapter Pattern

3.6   Reactive (behavioral) patterns

The last category of fine-grained patterns are the behavioral patterns. The behavioral patterns of [6] define how to add structural elements (classes) to control or facilitate the behavior of the collaboration. The Command Pattern is once such as this in which inter-object messages are abstracted into classes themselves. The State Pattern (ibid) reifies high-level states of a class into classes themselves as a way of controlling the execution of the object's state machine.

[2] provides different kind of behavioral pattern – organizations of statecharts in various ways to achieve different behavioral benefits referred to collectively as *state patterns*. These patterns define common ways to organize statecharts to get different kinds of behavioral effects, such as synchronization of behaviors with other object (Rendezvous State Pattern), remembering the occurrence of events or states (Latch State Pattern), and so on. Figure 7-11 shows one such pattern, the Polling State Pattern, which is used when an object is responsible for both the execution of a periodic activity, such as the acquisition of data, and data processing, such as the filtering or manipulation of that data. The upper and-state performs the data manipulation functionality while the lower and-state is responsible for periodically polling. Once it acquires the data it creates a new event (GEN(DataReady)), that is consumed by the top and-state to crunch the incoming data.

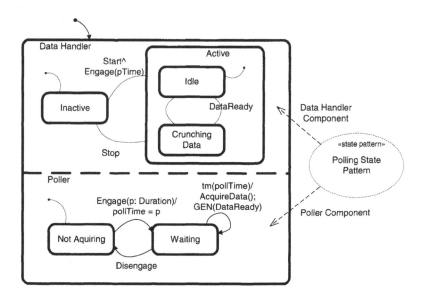

Figure 7-11. Polling State Pattern

REFERENCES

[1] Buschmann, Meunier, Rohnert, Sommerlad, and Stal. *A System of Patterns: Pattern Oriented Software Architecture* New York, NY: Wiley and Sons, 1996.

[2] Douglass, Bruce Powel, *Doing Hard Time: Developing Real-Time Systems with UML, Objects, Frameworks, and Patterns* Reading, MA: Addison-Wesley, 1999.

[3] Douglass, Bruce Powel, *Real-Time UML 2nd Edition: Developing Efficient Objects for Embedded Systems* Reading, MA: Addison-Wesley, 1999.

[4] Douglass, Bruce Powel, *Real-Time Design Patterns: Robust Scalable Architecture for Real-Time Systems* Reading, MA: Addison-Wesley, 2002.

[5] Fowler, Martin, *Analysis Patterns: Reusable Object Models* Reading, MA: Addison-Wesley, 1996.

[6] Gamma, E., Helm, R., Johnson, Vlissides, J., *Design Patterns: Elements of Reusable Object-Oriented Software* Reading, MA: Addison-Wesley 1995.

[7] Noble, James and Weir, Charles, *Small Memory Software: Patterns for systems with limited memory* Reading, MAL Addison-Wesley, 2001.

[8] *OMG Unified Modeling Language Specification Version 1.4* Needham, MA: Object Management Group, 2001.

[9] Rumbaugh, Jacobson, and Booch, *The Unified Modeling Language Reference Manual* Reading, MA: Addison-Wesley, 1999.

[10] Vlissides, John, *Pattern Hatching: Design Patterns Applied* Reading, MA: Addison-Wesley, 1998.

[11] Zalewski, Janusz, *Real-Time Software Architecture and Design Patterns: Fundamental Concepts and Their Consequences* Annual Reviews in Control, Vol. 25, No. 1, pp. 133-146, July 2001.

[12] *UML Profile for Schedulability, Performance and Time Specification ptc/02-03-02* Needham, MA: Object Management Group, 2001.

[13] Stankovic, Spuri, Ramamritham, and Buttazzo, *Deadline Scheduling for Real-Time Systems: EFT and Related Algorithms* Norwell, MA: Kluwer Academic Publishers, 1998.

[14] Briand and Roy, *Meeting Deadlines in Hard Real-Time Systems: The Rate Monotonic Approach* Los Alatimos, CA: IEEE Computer Society, 1999.

[15] Lui, Jane, *Real-Time Systems* Upper Saddle River, NJ: Prentice Hall, 2000.

[16] Mowbray and Malveau, *CORBA Design Patterns* New York, NY: John Wiley and Sons, Inc, 1997.

[17] Storey, Neil, *Safety-Critical Computer Systems* Reading, MA: Addison-Wesley, 1996.

[18] Hatton, Les, *Safer C: Developing Software for High-integrity and Safety-critical Systems* Berkshire, England: McGrall-Hill International, 1995.

[19] Leveson, Nancy, *Safeware* Reading, MA: Addison-Wesley, 1995.

Chapter 8

Architectural Patterns for Real-Time Systems
Using UML as an Architectural Description Language

Bran Selic
Rational Software Canada Co.

Abstract: Design patterns capture proven solutions, which, if applied intelligently, can result in significant benefits in terms of productivity and reliability. Architectural patterns are patterns that are useful for defining architectures. In this chapter, we describe several key structural patterns that have proven themselves quite useful in defining the architectures of complex real-time systems. We also show how these patterns can be modeled using the new structural modeling capabilities defined in the proposed new version of UML (UML 2.0).

Key words: software design patterns, software architectures, layered architectures, software structure

1. INTRODUCTION

Software architecture is a topic that is rightly receiving much attention these days. It has become obvious that this is a crucial aspect of any software system that has a major impact not only on how that system is constructed but, even more importantly, how easily it can be maintained and evolved. Despite the well-known flexibility of software, it is often the case that evolutionary changes that were not anticipated in the original architecture of a system are prohibitively expensive or otherwise practically infeasible to implement. Since most complex systems have long lifetimes during which they undergo significant evolutionary growth, architecture is clearly a major concern.

However, one of the essential difficulties with software architecture is that, for a given system, it is often very difficult to identify precisely what it

L. Lavagno, G. Martin and B. Selic (eds.), UML for Real, 171-188.

looks like. Once the coding of an application is complete, the only concrete manifestation of the architecture is in the source code itself, hidden among the thousands or even millions of lines of detailed code. Even if the architecture is well documented, using some high-level block diagram formalism, there is no guarantee that the documentation is faithful to the reality of the code. If there is no formal link between an architectural specification and its realization in code, it is easy for the two to diverge and difficult to spot when that happens. Programming is a task that involves thousands of low-level decisions and it is impossible to track each one to ensure that it is consistent with the intent of an architectural specification. This leads to a phenomenon knows as "architectural decay", whereby the original architecture of the system is gradually changed over time without any alarm bells going off when key elements of the architecture are corrupted.

UML and model-driven development methods can play a significant role in this situation. First, the language can help by providing modeling facilities that allow direct and easily understood means of specifying architectures. By using those specifications as the source from which code is generated, the problem of architectural decay can be avoided.

In this chapter, we will explain how the new structural modeling capabilities of UML 2.0, described in Chapter 3 of this volume, can be used to specify software architectures. Specifically, we shall demonstrate this ability on a number of key architectural patterns. These are common structural configurations that are at the core of many different software architectures.

2.   THE BASIC STRUCTURAL MICRO-PATTERNS

With all the fuss and anxiety devoted to the topic of software architecture, it may come as a surprise that, when it comes to rendering structure, there are only three fundamental architectural forms, or structural *micro-patterns,* out of which all architectures can be constructed. Like children's blocks, these micro-patterns can be combined in different ways to produce a vast spectrum of different architectural patterns to suit different domains, requirements, and tastes.

The term "structure" here has a strictly topological connotation in the sense that it deals with sets of elements, their types, and their adjacency relationships. In software development, there are many different kinds of structures, such as conceptual structures (e.g., layers of abstraction), compilation dependency structures, software file structures, and inheritance hierarchy structures. All of these play significant roles in software development and each needs to be designed ("architected") with care. However, in this chapter we will deal exclusively with run-time structures that comprise concrete run-time entities—things such as subsystems, components, objects, as well as the interconnections (e.g., communication channels) and relationships between them.

2.1   The Peer-to-Peer Micro-Pattern

The most basic micro-pattern is the *peer-to-peer* pattern, shown in Figure 8-1.

Figure 8-1. The peer-to-peer micro-pattern

This pattern captures the situation where two run-time entities, PeerA and PeerB, collaborate via the communication channel between them to accomplish some joint purpose. Note that even though the two participants depend on each other to accomplish their objective, the two exist independently of each other.

This pattern is readily captured in UML using a collaboration diagram with two parts and a connector. If the parts represent structured classes, then they may be interconnected via appropriate ports as shown in Figure 8-2.

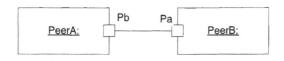

Figure 8-2. The peer-to-peer pattern realized with UML ports

2.2   The Container Micro-Pattern

In this micro-pattern, one entity is contained within the other as depicted in Figure 8-3.

Figure 8-3. The container micro-pattern

The interpretation of this pattern depends on the semantics of the containment relationship and has two basic variants. In general, however, the purpose of the *part* is to contribute in some way to the overall functionality of its container, possibly through interaction with other parts in the same container. (This is true even if the functionality of the part is defined independently of the functionality of the container.) We often say that the part belongs to the *implementation* of the container. A primary role of the container is to encapsulate its parts (i.e., its implementation) and, thus, to eliminate potential dependencies between its environment and its implementation.

It is worthwhile distinguishing this encapsulation role of run-time container entities from their abstraction role, although the two roles are often combined. In its abstraction role, the container provides a single conceptual unit for the collection of parts and interconnections that constitute its implementation. Note, however, that abstraction does not actually require a concrete run-time container entity.

Can a part exist independently of its container? One possibility is that the existence of the part is predicated on the existence of the container (although the reverse does not necessarily apply, since the part may be created dynamically some time after the container has been created). This means that, if the container is destroyed, the part will be destroyed with it—a common requirement in software systems. For example, in most object-oriented programming languages, when an object is destroyed dynamically, it is often the case that all of its directly contained attributes are also removed. This simplifies application code since it automates some basic housekeeping functionality.

In UML, this type of containment is represented by the "black diamond" relationship (Figure 8-4). We will refer to this form of containment as *composition.*

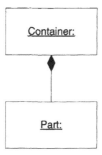

Figure 8-4. Representing composition in UML

The alternative is for the existence of the part to be independent of the existence of the container. We will call this variant *aggregation*. In this case, if the container is destroyed, the part entity remains. A common way of modeling this with UML is through the "white diamond" relationship[37].

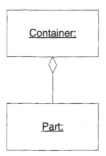

Figure 8-5. Representing aggregation in UML

Given that the container and the part have an independent existence, it is reasonable to ask why we don't just use the peer-to-peer pattern to model aggregation. The main reason is that the peer-to-peer relationship does not involve encapsulation and, hence, does not capture the full semantics of the relationship between containers and their implementation.

---

[37] Given that the semantics of the "white diamond" notation are not fixed in standard UML, this is merely a convention that we shall use in this chapter.

2.3   The Layering Micro-Pattern

The final basic structural micro-pattern is called *layering* and is shown in Figure 8-6.

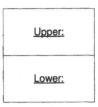

Figure 8-6. The layering micro-pattern

The adjacency of the upper- and lower-layer entities in Figure 8-6 indicates, among other things, that the two interact with each other. Based on that, one could easily conclude that this is merely a different rendering of the basic peer-to-peer pattern. However, this is misleading, as there are some key differences. The first of these is that the existence of the two entities is not independent: the upper-layer entity depends on the presence of the lower-layer entity for its proper functioning and, in many cases, even for its existence. On the other hand, the lower-layer entity can exist independently of the upper. This might lead us to deduce that layering is similar to composition, with the lower-layer entity corresponding to the container and the upper-layer entity to the part. But, this too is incorrect, since there is no encapsulation here—the lower-layer entity does *not* encapsulate the upper-layer one. In fact, in most cases, lower layers are designed and implemented completely independently of any entities that use them. Clearly then, we cannot consider upper-layer entities to be part of the implementation of the lower layer.

We expand on the layering pattern and its UML representation in the following section.

3.   THE VIRTUAL-MACHINE LAYERING PATTERN

Practically every software system, and, in particular, any complex software system involves layering. If nothing else, there is the fundamental layering of an application over an underlying operating system, as shown in Figure 8-7. In most cases, the layering goes beyond that, with the applications themselves (as well as operating systems) structured into multiple internal layers. In fact, the topmost level of the vast majority of software architectures comprises a set of layers—each layer dealing with a different set of concerns and realizing different abstractions.

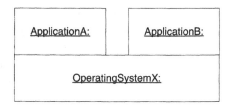

Figure 8-7. Typical software application architectures

The conceptual simplicity provided by layering make it a very convenient and commonly used tool for architects. Unfortunately, despite its prevalence, the concept is often poorly understood. Layered diagrams are often used to depict very different concepts and, due to their notational similarity are often confused with each other. To illustrate the kind of confusion that can occur, let us examine two well-known examples from the public domain.

The first is the popular seven-layer Open Systems Interconnection (OSI) Architecture standardized by the ISO [1]. This is an architecture that describes the layering structure of communication mechanisms in distributed software systems (Figure 8-8). It defines the conceptual framework for defining a set of related communications protocol standards.

| Application |
| Presentation |
| Session |
| Transport |
| Network |
| Link |
| Physical |

Figure 8-8. The OSI 7-layer architecture

The second example is also from an international standard: the Reference Model for Open Distributed Processing (RM-ODP) published by the ITU-T [2]. This model is broken down into five viewpoints of a given system, each viewpoint dealing with a different set of abstractions. To illustrate the relative degree of abstraction of the viewpoints, they are sometimes drawn as a vertical stack, with the level of abstraction increasing from bottom to top. Thus, the technology view at the bottom describes a system in terms of the specific hardware and software technologies used in its realization, whereas the topmost enterprise viewpoint describes it purely from a business purpose perspective and is devoid of any technology-specific aspects.

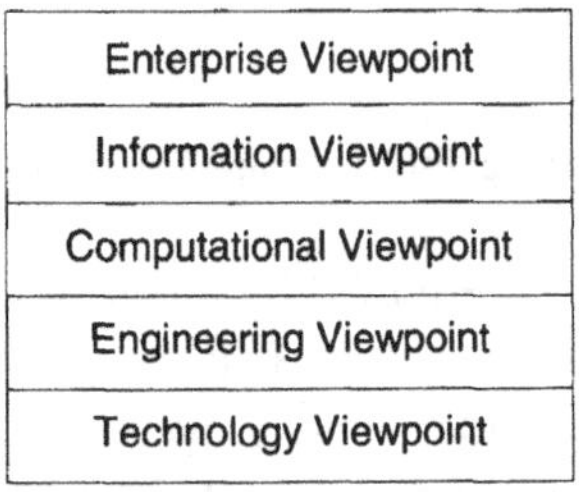

Enterprise Viewpoint
Information Viewpoint
Computational Viewpoint
Engineering Viewpoint
Technology Viewpoint

Figure 8-9. The RM-ODP viewpoints framework

Except for the different number of levels and different names, the two diagrams in Figure 8-8 and Figure 8-9 look quite similar and one might easily conclude that they mean the same thing. However, the two diagrams are quite different and have completely different interpretations.

The RM-ODP architecture uses layering to distinguish different *levels of abstraction*. The technology level is closest to the actual implementation and farthest from its business considerations. As we move up the hierarchy, more and more implementation and technology details are abstracted out. At the computational level, for instance, details of physical distribution across computing nodes are removed and the application is viewed merely as a network of collaborating objects. The information level abstracts this further and represents only the nature of the information that needs to be represented and the necessary relationships, independently of any technical considerations. Thus, each level is a model of the *complete system* but from a different viewpoint addressing a different set of concerns.

In contrast, each of the layers in the OSI model represents distinct entities not present in any of the other layers. The complete system is the sum of all of the layers. Thus, the physical layer specifies the hardware, while the link layer describes the software entities responsible for point-to-point link-level communications. At the next level up, we have specifications of software that is not present in the link layer, and which is responsible for communications across distributed networks. In this case, the layer above does not represent a more abstract view of the layer below. In other words, these are *not* abstraction layers. The same holds for the layers shown in figure 8-7: applications most certainly are not abstract views of the operating system and the code in the two layers is completely distinct and results in distinct run-time entities.

In this chapter, we are only interested in talking about run-time layering; that is, the modeling of layering relationships between run-time entities. A common term that can be used to describe this type of layering is *virtual machine* layering. This is because each successive layer provides a virtual machine for the software in the layer directly above it. Since each layer takes us further away from the technological realities of the lower layers, it can be said that this too represents a kind of abstraction layering—which is why the two are so often confused. However, it should be clear that the two kinds of abstraction taking place in the two cases are different.

In what circumstances is the layering pattern useful? To answer that, we consider the example of a typical real-time component responsible for controlling an individual communications line that is part of a complex telecom switching system (Figure 8-10).

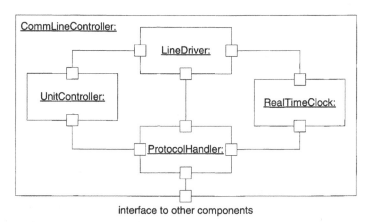

Figure 8-10. The structure of a telecom line controller

For conceptual simplicity and ease of management, the entire software component is packaged in a container called CommLineController (an application of the Container micro-pattern). The implementation of this component consists of four sub-components collaborating through peer-to-peer relationships. The LineDriver is responsible for interfacing and controlling the hardware. Since some of its functionality is time-dependent, this sub-component needs to interact with the RealTimeClock sub-component. This is a sub-component that controls a physical clock device, and which provides general-purpose timing services (e.g., generation of time-out signals, reading and writing of the current value of the real-time clock device). The ProtocolHandler sub-component is used by the other sub-components for interaction with other components in the system via some internal protocol (e.g., sockets). Since it too has time-dependent functionality, it needs to interact with the RealTimeClock sub-component. The UnitController is responsible for synchronizing the operation of the LineDriver and ProtocolHandler. For example, if an external command is given to run a maintenance diagnostic on the communications line, the UnitController would ensure that the other sub-components are properly coordinated for this task.

Standard engineering practice and common sense tell us that the four parts constituting the implementation of this component should be fully encapsulated within the component. However, in trying to do this, we run into a problem: the real-time clock component cannot be monopolized by this particular component since it is likely to be useful to other line controller instances as well as other types of components. In fact, we want the real-time clock functionality to be a shared service, even though it is part of the implementation of the line controller.

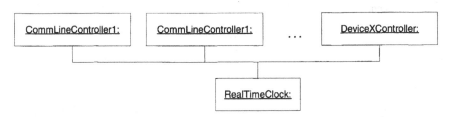

Figure 8-11. The shared RealTimeClock component

In practice, there are many different kinds of shared services such as the real-time clock. This includes different inter-process communications services, error and alarm reporting services, file system services, event-notification services, billing services, and so on. What is common to all of them is that they are used to *implement* application components but are not themselves a direct part of the application. Because they may be shared by many different kinds of components, they are usually defined generically and, in many cases, independently of the applications that use them. The most prototypical examples are operating system services.

This suggests that *a supporting run-time layer is really a packaging of shared implementation-support services*—a convenient virtual machine environment that entities in the layer above can use in their realizations.

However, it may seem that extracting shared implementation services and grouping them into virtual machine layers has one significant drawback: that changes to the internal implementation of a component may be reflected in changes to its interface. For example, if we change the implementation of the communications line controller to use an internal real-time clock service rather than the shared one, the component's interface to the shared service needs to be removed. This appears to defeat the primary objective of encapsulation, since a change of interface generally implies corresponding changes to the environment.

In practice, though, the ripple effect from such implementation changes hardly ever occurs. Recall that the interfaces for supporting layers are usually defined and exist independently of applications that use them. In designing application components, designers most often tend to structure their implementation to take advantage of the services already defined in supporting layers rather than requiring new ones. So, an implementation change at the layer boundary implies either the removal of an existing interface or its replacement by a different (usually already existing) interface. In either case, the peers of the component are unaffected by the change.

This does indicate, however, that it is useful to distinguish between the *layer* (implementation) interfaces of a component and its *peer* interfaces. Layer interfaces are used to access to shared services of supporting layers, whereas peer interfaces are interfaces through which a component interacts with its peer components. This distinction will help us to better determine the impact that an interface change on a component might have on its environment.

This distinction is supported in UML through its concept of ports, and it enables direct modeling of the layering pattern. Specifically, it is possible to designate a behavior port defined on a UML class or component as a "service" port. This means that the interface represented by this port is a layer interface, which can be connected via a connector to any corresponding port on an element of a supporting layer. Ports not designated as service ports default to being peer ports. An example of this can be seen in Figure 8-12, which uses the "diamond" notation to indicate service ports[38]. In this case, the two ports labeled "rtclk" on sub-components ProtocolHandler and LineDriver are service ports that can be connected to any matching ports on other components (usually those in supporting layers).

---

[38] Note that the UML standard does not define a standard notation for service ports.

Service ports have public visibility, which allows them to be connected to external entities (although they may also be connected to parts inside the component, if desired). Furthermore, they are always visible regardless of how deeply their corresponding sub-components are nested. This reflects the nature of layering relationships where the layers are assumed to be directly adjacent to each other, unhampered by application-level nesting. This is a reflection of the fact that layer ports are in a different "plane" from peer ports.

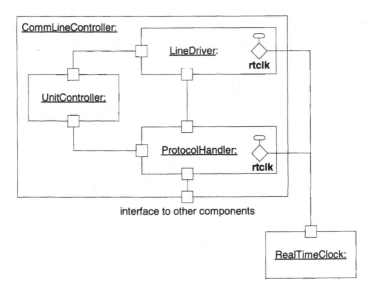

Figure 8-12. Using service ports to denote layering structures

4.   THE RECURSIVE CONTROL PATTERN

Like the term "layering", the concept of "control" is also much used to cover a range of different meanings. In this chapter we shall use it strictly to mean the following:

The set of mechanisms and activities required to bring a system into the desired operational state and to maintain it in that state despite various disruptive events and situations that might force it out of that state.

It is helpful to distinguish the *control* behavior of a system from its *functional* behavior. The term "functional behavior" denotes activities that directly realize the primary functionality of a system; that is, the functionality for which the system has been constructed. Functional behavior represents the *raison d'être* of the system. Control behavior, on the other hand, is behavior that is required to enable and support functional behavior.

Consider, for example, a relatively complex real-time system such as a private branch exchange (PBX). This is a telecommunications switch whose purpose is to make connections between individual telephone lines on request. For such a system, establishing and removing of connections, handling various call features (call forwarding, call transfer, conferencing, etc.), and transmission of voice and data between users are all examples of functional behaviors. Control behavior is represented by activities such as configuring new telephone lines and features, performing equipment maintenance diagnostics, detecting and recovering from failures, powering up and powering down the system or its components, and so on. The only reason why such activities are necessary is to enable functional behavior.

Since control plays a supporting role, there is a tendency to view it as a second-order concern; something that is only addressed after the functional design has been resolved. This is unfortunate, since it often leads to embedded software systems that are difficult to monitor and control. In fact, in systems where high levels of reliability are required, as much as 80% of the overall system functionality and implementation effort may be dedicated to control. In such systems, for example, the choice and implementation of fault-tolerance mechanisms (fault detection, fault recovery, fault diagnosis) must be factored into the architectural design to ensure consistency and effectiveness of recovery. In general, fault tolerance is not something that can be successfully retrofitted onto an existing design. Consider, for instance, the case of access to a high-integrity database, that is, a database whose contents must be kept consistent in the face of possible failures. The classical solution to this is to use all-or-nothing transaction mechanisms. These mechanisms typically have to be factored into the design of the application[39].

While this means that control and functional behavior are interdependent, it is still seems useful to separate the two sets of concerns as much as possible, so that one can be changed independently of the other. How can we achieve this separation?

Before we propose a solution to this, it is helpful to make two additional observations about control. The first is to note that there is a distinction between control policies (e.g., recovery strategy) from the mechanisms used

---

[39] There is an important argument, known as the "end-to-end argument", that suggests that the application is often the best arbiter of what kind of fault recovery is most appropriate in a given situation, given that (a) it is often not possible to fully mask out the effects of certain types of failures from applications and (b) general-purpose fault-tolerance mechanisms are typically unaware of the specific needs of individual applications [3].

to realize that control policy. While control policy clearly depends on the availability of suitable control mechanisms, it is certainly possible to realize different policies with a given set of control mechanisms. An everyday example of this can be seen in automobiles: the various control mechanisms of a car (gas pedal, brake, steering wheel, etc.) can be used in a variety of ways to effect very different driving styles (control policies). By keeping control policies and mechanisms separate, we provide the flexibility to change policies without necessarily requiring a change of mechanisms.

The second relevant observation about control is that, in principle, centralized control is easier to implement and generally more effective than distributed control. Centralized control here means that control policies are administered by a single decision-making entity. In contrast, distributed control allocates responsibility for a control policy to a number of separate entities that work in concert. The main problem with distributed control is that it requires the various entities to agree on the current state of the system, and the appropriate control measure for that state. This not only introduces overhead, that can slow down control responses to disruptive situations, but, especially in distributed systems, it may not always be possible to even reach agreement[40].

These considerations, along with the notion of keeping functional and control aspects separate, lead us directly to the *recursive control pattern*. We shall illustrate the pattern using the structured class concepts of UML 2.0 as shown in Figure 8-13.

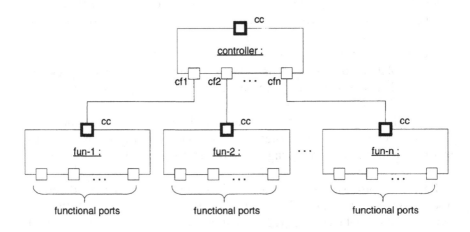

Figure 8-13. The basic recursive control pattern

---

[40] The impossibility of guaranteeing agreement in certain common categories of distributed systems has been proven theoretically [4, 5].

In this case, parts fun-1 through fun-n is a collection of components each of which realizes specific functional behavior. Furthermore, for some reason, there is a need to synchronize the operation of these components according to some joint control policy. For instance, they may need to be activated in a particular order during startup. Whatever the reason, all the functional components report to a single common controller component (controller), which is responsible for realizing the desired control policy.

The policy is effected using the control mechanisms provided by the functional components through their individual *control ports* (cc). The controller receives status information from the functional components through its unit control ports (cf1 through cfn) and responds with appropriate control messages through the same ports in the opposite direction.

The functional behavior of the functional components may be accessed through their *functional ports*. (Note that some of these functional ports on different components may be connected to each other but such connections are not depicted in the diagram since they are application specific.)

In larger systems, there can be numerous control clusters such as this, each with its own set of functionalities and a control policy. If the operation of the clusters also has to be controlled, then, applying the same reasoning as before, we can provide a "super" controller that coordinates the operation of the individual cluster controllers. In this case, the mechanisms for controlling the cluster controllers are provided by their own control ports (cc) while the control policy is executed by the super controller.

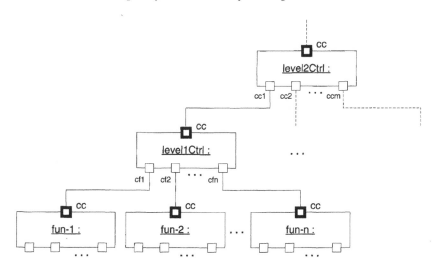

Figure 8-14. Recursive application of the recursive control pattern

This pattern can be applied at any number of control levels as shown in Figure 8-14, which is why it is called the *recursive* control pattern. One of the advantages of such a uniform structure is that it provides a lot of opportunity for exploiting various commonalities. For example, the control protocol occurring between controllers and their controlled components may be quite similar or even identical regardless of the entity that is being controlled. This is because such control protocols typically consist of generic directives such as *start, stop, reset,* etc. Furthermore, it is often the case, that the control behavior is the same or similar at different levels, implying that a common abstract class may be defined as the root class of all controlled components. This not only provides reuse and saves effort, but also ensures consistency of control policies across the system. The net result is systems that are inherently more controllable.

Note that there is another way of realizing the pattern using the structured class concept of UML. Namely, the role of the controller can be taken on by the behavior of a structured class that incorporates the functional components as parts (Figure 8-15). This has the advantage of ensuring that the components cannot exist and function independently of their controller, so that the system is guaranteed to always be under control. It also provides the convenience of packaging the entire cluster as a single complex and fully reusable component.

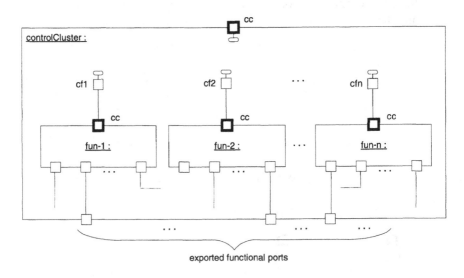

Figure 8-15. A variation of the recursive control pattern with increased controllability

The recursive control pattern is independent of the functionality of the controlled components. It also has the advantage that, due to its recursive nature, it can be applied to arbitrarily complex real-time systems, including heterogeneous "systems of systems". These features make it eminently suitable as the top-level architecture for practically any embedded or real-time system that needs to be dynamically controlled.

5. SUMMARY

The primary purpose of this chapter was to introduce the ability of UML to serve as an *architectural description language*, capable of describing architectures at all levels of granularity—from the topmost level down to the smallest of subsystems. To that end, we first identified the fundamental structural relationships (micro-patterns) that represent the alphabet of software architecture. We also showed how these basic patterns can be expressed, in a straightforward manner, using the structured class concepts of UML 2.0. Two highly significant architectural patterns were described in detail. The "layering" pattern deals with "vertical" structures of hierarchically organized virtual machines, while the "recursive control" pattern describes structures that might occur within any given layer or even across multiple layers. Both of these patterns are applicable to complete systems as well as to parts of such systems (e.g., a layer may itself be layered internally).

Of course, there are many other important architectural patterns beyond the ones described here (including some covered in other chapters of this volume), which can be expressed using these features of UML. Such high-level descriptions can be combined with other UML specifications (e.g., behavioral specifications) to produce complete system specifications encompassing the full range of detail required in a real system. This has the major advantage that all the various viewpoint specifications that comprise a system can be formally aligned with each other (since they are all part of the same UML model). This avoids the reconciliation problems that commonly occur when a complex system is described from different viewpoints based on different formalisms.

REFERENCES

[1] International Telecommunications Union, *Information Technology—Open Systems Interconnection—Basic Reference Model*, ITU-T Recommendation X.200 (ISO/IEC 7498-1), Geneva, Switzerland 1994.

[2] International Telecommunications Union, *Information Technology—Open Distributed Processing—Basic Reference Model: Architecture*, ITU-T Recommendation X.903 (ISO/IEC 10746-3), Geneva, Switzerland 1995.

[3] J. Saltzer, D. Reed, and D. Clark, "End-to-end Arguments in System Design", ACM Transactions in Computer Systems, (2, 4), pp. 277–288, 1984.

[4] M. Fischer, N. Lynch, and M. Paterson, "Impossibility of Distributed Consensus with One Faulty Process", Journal of the ACM, (32, 2), pp. 374–382, 1985.

[5] J. Halpern, and Y. Moses, Y, "Knowledge and Common Knowledge in a Distributed Environment", *Proceedings. of the 3rd ACM Symposium on Principles of Distributed Systems*, pp. 50–61, 1984.

Chapter 9

Modeling Quality of Service with UML
How quantity changes quality

Bran Selic
Rational Software Canada Co.

Abstract: The quality of service of software is usually expressed as a quantitative measure and, in case of real-time systems, it may be as important as logical correctness. Therefore, for software models of such systems it is of critical importance to be able to specify this information. In this chapter we introduce the standard UML profile that enables the specification of quality of service information directly in UML models.

Key words: Quality of service, QoS, resource modeling, time modeling

> *"Knowledge of what is possible is the beginning of happiness"*
> — George Santyana

1. INTRODUCTION

The original UML standard evolved from a primordial soup of numerous object-oriented analysis and design notations of the late 80's and early 90's. These, in turn, were inspired by the previous generation of software modeling techniques, such as structured analysis and structured design. The dominant concern of these early modeling techniques was to expose the high-level "logic" of the application; that is, to impart, in as clear and concise form as possible, a qualitative understanding of how the modeled system operated. In particular, analysts and designers were exhorted to defer implementation-specific aspects, such as specifics about the programming language, the operating system, or the hardware to be used, until the high-level program logic was defined and verified. The principle behind such "platform independent" design is that it is not only simpler because of fewer concerns, but that it also assures relatively smooth migration of applications

L. Lavagno, G. Martin and B. Selic (eds.), UML for Real, 189-204.

to new or different platforms. Consequently, there was very little if any support in these early languages for modeling platforms or their quantitative characteristics.

However, this was unsatisfactory for many real-time and embedded systems whose quantitative characteristics, such as response time or throughput, are often just as important as system functionality. After all, real-time systems that do not produce timely outputs have little practical value. In these systems the functional and non functional are significantly intertwined and mutually dependent. The design of the application logic is often determined by the platform. Therefore, languages that did not have the ability to accurately model both platforms and their key characteristics were typically inappropriate for this domain.

Standard UML does provide some capabilities for modeling platforms, primarily in the form of deployment diagrams, with concepts such as nodes and connections. However, these diagrams are based on relatively simple models of deployment, showing direct mapping of software components to hardware. This is often inadequate for the complex deployment relationships that exist in larger real-time systems, in which software layers may be mapped onto each other before they are mapped to hardware. The deployment modeling concepts of UML simply do not have the expressive power to accurately model these scenarios.

In addition, although there are mechanisms in the language, such as tagged values, which can be used to associate quantitative measures with model elements, these were not standardized and, consequently, of limited value. A shared method of annotating models was necessary.

These deficiencies of the general UML standard prompted an initiative to define a *standard* UML profile for real-time based applications. This profile, formally named the UML Profile for Scheduling, Performance, and Time, is usually referred to as the "real-time" UML profile [1]. It defines standard means for modeling platforms and their time-related mechanisms and quantitative characteristics. In the remainder of this chapter we provide an overview of the contents of the profile and describe its conceptual foundations. The more advanced aspects of the profile dealing with its application to specific types of model analysis are described in subsequent chapters.

2.   REQUIREMENTS FOR THE REAL-TIME PROFILE

A first-order requirement for the real-time UML profile was to allow the construction of *predictive* UML models, that is, models that can be used to compute important real-time characteristics of the final system, such as response times and throughput. In particular, it was deemed necessary to be able to perform such analyses very early in the development cycle on very high-level models. This would allow quantitative requirements to be properly addressed during the selection of a software architecture. The inability to do this in a direct and systematic way has been the root cause of numerous software disasters (see [2, 3] for some high-profile examples).

In traditional engineering, this predictive quality of models is considered fundamental and is supported by numerous mathematical analysis methods. However, in software engineering the use of quantitative analysis methods—except for the crudest estimates mostly based on intuition—is still relatively rare. Apart from the fact that many practitioners do not even know that such methods exist, one of the primary reasons for this is that they are often quite sophisticated (because software is a difficult thing to model accurately) and require very specialized skills. Hence, experts who can apply these methods successfully are quite scarce.

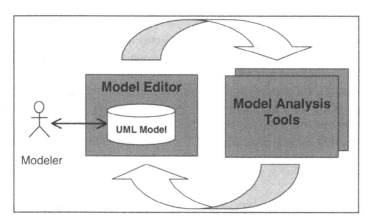

Figure 9-1. Automating model analysis

To get around this hurdle, the formal requirements for the real-time UML profile specifically sought solutions that were open to automation, eliminating the need for a human expert to a certain extent (see Figure 9-1). The intent is for system developers to construct their UML models in the usual way using a UML editor, annotate them using the conventions defined by the real-time profile, and then pass the annotated models over to a specialized analysis tool for quantitative analysis. In most cases, the analysis tool will first transform the model into a form suitable for analysis (e.g., a queuing network model), perform the analysis, and return the results. Of course, since the designers are not expected to be experts on the analysis methods used, the results must be expressed in the context of the original model. The simplest way to do that is to return to the editing tool a model that is the same as the original model except that it has the results of the analysis embedded in the appropriate places.

The role of the standard is crucial here since it allows independently designed tools from different manufacturers to be used together.

In terms of specific modeling capabilities, the requirements also asked for the following general capabilities [4]:

- A means for representing time and time values
- A means for modeling concurrency support mechanisms of the kind encountered in most standard real-time operating systems (operating system threads and processes, schedulers, conflict resolution mechanisms, etc.)
- A means for modeling platforms (both hardware and software) suitable for complex real-time and embedded applications.
- A means for specifying precisely how a software application is mapped to its platform.

In addition, the following specific requirements were included:

- Support for common schedulability analysis mechanisms, such as rate-monotonic analysis [5, 6]
- Support for common performance analysis mechanisms based on queueing theory techniques [7] (see also Chapter 11 in this volume).
- Support for analysis of models based on the real-time CORBA middleware standard [8] and the CORBA enhanced timing service [9].

3.   COMPONENTS OF THE REAL-TIME PROFILE

The real-time UML profile consists of three main parts:

1. A general framework for modeling resources and quality of service—this provides the foundations for the rest of the profile and for possible future extensions.
2. A set of "analysis sub-profiles", individual profiles for specific types of analyses.
3. A UML model of the real-time CORBA middleware standard; this is included as an example of the kind of model that vendors of real-time technologies are expected to provide for their software, comparable to the VHDL models that chip manufacturers publish for use by CAD analysis tools.

The first two of these are organized further into multiple subparts. The subparts and the dependencies between them are shown in the UML package diagram in Figure 9-2.

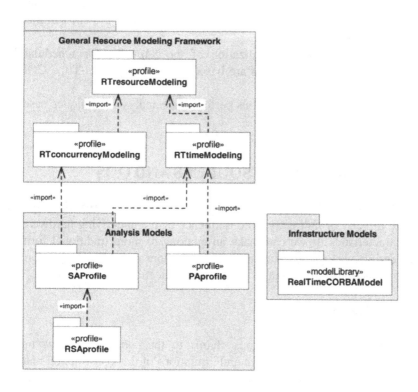

Figure 9-2. Main components of the real-time profile

The requirements for the real-time profile ask for models of the hardware and software infrastructure (platform). Rather than address these in an ad hoc fashion, the submission team decided to provide a general framework for modeling elements of platforms, regardless of whether they are directly related to modeling time-related features. This provides for extensibility of the profile to cover other aspects as well, such as reliability, availability, or safety. This is the function of the General Resource Modeling Framework. It consists of several specialized frameworks that cover aspects common to all time- and resource-sensitive systems. In turn, the core of this framework is the *RTResourceModeling* package. This package defines the two related notions that are used throughout the rest of the profile: the concept of *resource* and the concept of *quality of service* (QoS). The *RTtimeModeling* package extends these general concepts with facilities for modeling time and timing mechanisms. Finally, the *RTconcurrencyModeling* package defines the concepts used in modeling concurrency and concurrency mechanisms.

The *Analysis Models* package contains the following sub-profiles.

- *SAprofile* supports a variety of established schedulability analysis techniques that determine whether or not a given system will meet all of its deadlines.
- *RSAprofile* is a specialization of the *SAprofile* for schedulability analysis of systems that are based on the OMG Real-Time CORBA standard.
- *PAprofile* supports various performance analysis techniques based on queuing network theory.

4.   MODELING RESOURCES AND QOS

As noted earlier, the quantitative characteristics of real-time systems are all, directly or indirectly, a consequence of the underlying hardware and its characteristics. If we can make an analogy to more traditional forms of engineering, we can view the hardware, and, more generally, the platform, as the construction material out of which our application software is built.

4.1   Resources

Although there are numerous claims to the contrary [10], as in any engineering endeavor, the nature and limitations of this construction material can have a fundamental impact on our design. A good designer is aware of this and takes that into account. While idealizations of platform capabilities are often useful they are not always appropriate. At the very least, the hardware part of any platform is finite. It has finite speeds, finite capacities, and finite reliability. These "finities" can, in some cases, impose restrictions on what we can achieve with software. Even at computer speeds, real programs are not infinitely fast, bandwidth limitations constrain how much information can be transferred in a given time interval, and the amount of memory and CPU speed at our disposal is limited.

The general resource framework captures this through the notion of a *resource*. This is the common basis for the modeling all quantitative aspects of software systems. Note, however, that resources do not necessarily have to be physical devices. For instance, virtual memory and software connections are common examples of logical resources, Still, there is ultimately a physical underpinning in all these cases.

The real-time profile represents a resource as playing the server role in a client-server relationship. This means that it provides one or more services that can be accessed by its clients. The limitations of a resource service and the resource itself are represented by *quality of service (QoS)* attributes. In general, these attributes characterize either *how well* a resource service can be performed or how well it needs to be performed.

The client-server model suggests that we need to distinguish between *offered QoS* on the server (resource) side and *required QoS* on the client side. In essence, most quantitative analyses methods serve to answer the simple question whether the supply (offered QoS) meets the demand (required QoS). Of course, even though this question is simple to formulate, providing an answer to it is not simple by any means. This is primarily because in most software systems there are many complex and dynamic interference patterns between otherwise independent clients due to the fact that they may be competing for the same resources (the same CPU, the same physical memory or communications device). This greatly complicates the analysis.

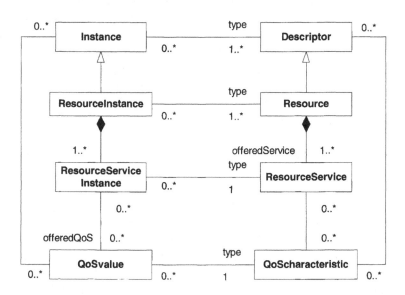

Figure 9-3. The basic concepts of the general resource model

The UML class diagram in Figure 9-3 captures this core conceptual model consisting of resources, services, and QoS. (Note that UML is being used here as a convenient means to represent abstract concepts, such as resources and services, and their relationships. Readers should distinguish these conceptual "domain" diagrams from the actual UML extensions (stereotypes, etc.) defined in the profile. In general, each concept shown in such diagrams maps to a stereotype of some appropriate UML concept, while the associations between them map to corresponding associations between those concepts. For example, the Descriptor concept might be represented by a stereotype of the UML concept of Classifier, Instance might be specified by a stereotype of the UML concept of Object, and the association between Descriptor and Instance is represented by the standard association that exists between Object and Classifier in the UML formal definition of UML[41].)

This model makes a fundamental distinction between the notion of a *descriptor,* which represents *specifications* of things that may exist at run time, and *instances,* which are the actual run-time things. The relationship between these general concepts is exemplified by the relationship between a blueprint for a building (a descriptor) and an actual building constructed from that blueprint (an instance). Although this distinction is common and usually well understood, in practical situations people often confuse the two.

This distinction runs through the set of UML concepts, although it is not explicitly noted in all cases. For example, the UML concepts of Class, Association, and Action are all descriptor-type concepts, whereas Object, Link, and ActionExecution are their corresponding instance concepts. In Figure 9-3, each of the elements on the right-hand side of the diagram is a kind of descriptor. To the left of each is its corresponding descriptor type.

4.2   Analysis contexts

Most useful analysis methods are instance based; that is, they work on models or model fragments that describe situations involving instances rather than descriptors. For example, in performance analysis it is necessary to know precisely how many server instances exist, their individual service rates, and the precise interconnection topology between them. The fact that two or more of those instances may be of the same class is not particularly relevant. In fact, they may have different quantitative characteristics due to differences in their underlying processors, relative scheduling priorities, etc. Descriptor-based diagrams, such as UML class diagrams, usually abstract out this type of information, which means that they are not particularly useful for such analyses.

A specific configuration of interconnected resource and client instances interacting in a particular way at a given intensity level is referred to as an *analysis context* in the real-time profile. An analysis context is a generic formulation of the standard supply-demand matching problem common to

---

[41] For pedagogical reasons, these mappings have been somewhat simplified from the more complex ones that are actually defined in the standard.

most analysis methods. The conceptual model of an analysis context is shown in Figure 9-4. This abstract model is further refined by each sub-profile for its specific needs.

Each *resource instance* participating in an analysis context offers one or more resource service instances. As indicated in Figure 9-3, these may be characterized by their offered QoS values (e.g., response time). The clients of these resources and the details of how they use the resources is captured in the concept of a *resource usage*. This can be expressed in a number of different ways depending on the type of analysis desired. The simplest usage models are static, typically consisting of a list of clients matched against the resources that they use. More sophisticated usage models may describe the dynamics of resource usage, such as the order in which the resources are used by clients, the type of access, holding time, etc. The final element of this generic model is the concept of *usage demand*, which specifies the intensity with which a usage is applied to the set of resources (e.g., arrival frequency). The task of analysis is to determine if a given concrete model—involving specific resource instances, usages, and demands and explicit required and offered QoS values—is internally consistent or not. If not, this is an indication that demand exceeds supply and that a different model is required.

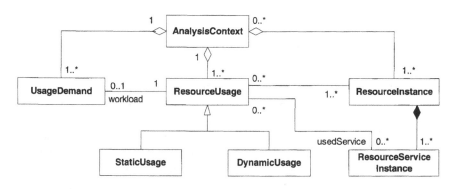

Figure 9-4. The general model of analysis

Static usage models are usually very simple. A static model consists of a list of clients and their characteristics), a list of resources and their characteristics, and a specification of the allocation of resources to clients. There are no details of the order in which individual clients approach individual resources, how long they hold on to them, etc. Instead, a homogeneous usage model is assumed so that the results obtained tend to be very general and not particularly precise. Static models are typically used for quick but rough "ballpark" estimates.

Dynamic usage models (Figure 9-5) are more detailed and capture at least some of the dynamics of resource usage. A typical usage comprises one or more concrete scenarios—ordered sets of actions that access the resources and their services in a specific pattern. These accesses might include specifications of the required QoS values (e.g., timing deadlines, holding times, maximum delays, throughput rates), which can be matched against the offered QoS values of the resources. This type of analysis takes into account the interference between individual scenarios in some way and, therefore, generally produces more precise results than static models.

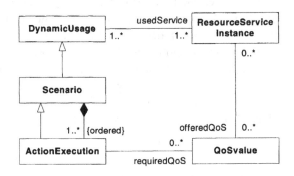

Figure 9-5. The dynamic resource usage model

One aspect of note in the conceptual model in Figure 9-5 is that an action execution is represented as a kind of scenario. This allows a complex action at one level of abstraction to be expanded into a full-fledged scenario, consisting of an ordered set of lower-level fine-grained action executions. The choice of abstraction level and level of decomposition is determined by the modeler, based on the level of accuracy desired from the analysis.

4.3   Categories of resources

The real-time profile allows the modeling of many different kinds of resources in a variety of ways. The general taxonomy of resources supported is shown in Figure 9-6.

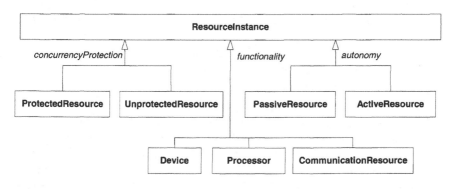

Figure 9-6. Resource taxonomies

Resources are classified in different ways. Based on their primary functionality, they may be *processors* (devices capable of executing code), *communication resources* (for transfer of information), or general *devices* (e.g., specialized sensors, actuators). Depending on whether or not they require controlled access, they may be either *protected* or *unprotected* resources. Finally, depending on whether or not they are capable of initiating activity or not, they may be *active* or *passive*. The different categorizations can be combined for the same model element. For example, an element representing a physical CPU might be designated simultaneously as a processor resource that is both active and protected.

5. MODELING TIME AND TIMING MECHANISMS

The general UML standard does not impose any restrictions on the modeling of time. It neither assumes that time is discrete or continuous nor makes any assumptions about global or distributed time sources. This flexibility is retained in the real-time profile, with the difference that the profile allows some of those aspects to be specified explicitly according to need.

5.1 The model of time

The time model supported in the profile is shown in Figure 9-7. Physical time is considered an abstraction—a relationship that imposes a partial order on events. It is modeled as a continuous and unbounded progression of *physical time instants* perceived by some observer comprising a set such that

- The set is fully ordered, which means that, for any two distinct elements of the set, p and q, either p precedes q or q precedes p;
- It is a dense set, which is to say that there is always at least one instant between any pair of instants (in other words, the basic time model assumes a continuous model of time)

Out of this can be derived a discrete model of time, or time that is broken up into quanta. Dense time can be represented by the set of real numbers, whereas discrete time corresponds to the set of integers.

Physical time is assumed to progress monotonically (with respect to a specific observer) and only in the forward direction. Note that these restrictions apply to our model of physical time but not necessarily to other models of time that may be useful in modeling. For example, there exist "simulated" time models in which time does not necessarily progress monotonically or "virtual time" that may even regress under certain circumstances.

Since physical time is incorporeal, its progress is typically measured by counting the number of expired cycles of some strictly periodic reference clock starting from some origin. This way of measuring time necessarily results in a discretization effect in which distinct but temporally close physical instants are associated with the same count value. However, since our physical time model is dense, this is not a restriction and any desired time resolution can be obtained simply by choosing a sufficiently fine resolution for the reference clock.

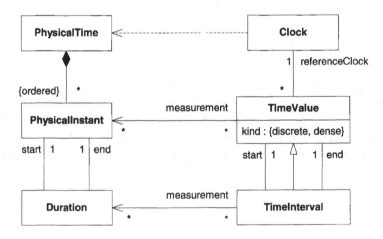

Figure 9-7. The conceptual model of time

The count associated with a particular instant is called its *measurement*. In the conceptual model, a time measurement is represented by a special value called *time value*. The profile provides for a rich variety of forms for specifying time valued including simple integers, real numbers, as well as by more sophisticated structured data types such as dates.

Duration is the expired time between two instants. Since this too is represented by time values, it is useful to be able to distinguish it from a time value that represents a specific instant. Hence, the profile introduces the concrete notion of a *time interval*.

5.2 Modeling timing mechanisms

In addition to the model of time, the real-time profile permits the modeling of two different kinds of timing mechanisms: clocks and timers. A *clock* is an active resource that periodically generates clock interrupts in synchrony with the progress of physical time. A *timer* is also an active resource but one that detects the expiration of a specific duration after which it generates a timeout signal. The model of timing mechanisms is shown in Figure 9-8.

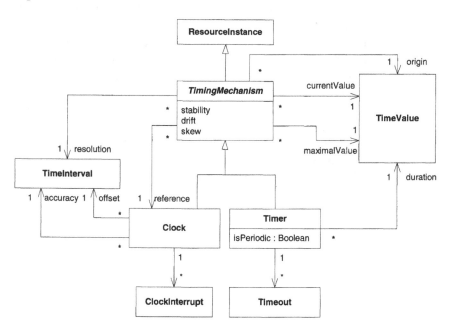

Figure 9-8. Model of timing mechanisms

Note that both clocks and timers are derived from a more general concept of an abstract timing mechanism. This captures the common characteristics of all timing mechanisms, such as resolution, origin, maximal value, etc.

6.   MODELING PLATFORMS

As noted earlier the language of UML deployment diagrams is not rich enough to accurately model capture the kinds of platforms and deployment situations found in complex real-time and embedded systems. One approach, therefore, would be to enrich this language by adding the missing concepts. However, this would likely lead to a very complex language. For instance, the platform might be an operating system, which implies that a full-fledged operating system modeling language is required. This strategy seems pretty futile, since platform technologies will invariably keep getting more sophisticated and more specialized.

Fortunately, a much simpler solution is possible. Namely, instead of devising a new set of specialized platform modeling languages (such as deployment diagrams), we can simply use UML to model platforms of all kinds. With its rich repertoire of general-purpose modeling concepts it has all the expressive power that is needed for this.

This is exactly the approach taken in the real-time profile. UML can be used to define models of software applications as well as models of platforms (which might themselves be software applications). The only additional capability required is the specification of the mapping between an application model and a platform model, representing the deployment model. For this purpose, the real-time profile defines a special kind of dependency between elements of two (or more) models, called *deployment*. An example of the use of the deployment dependency is shown in Figure 9-9, in which three distinct software objects are deployed onto a single processor object.

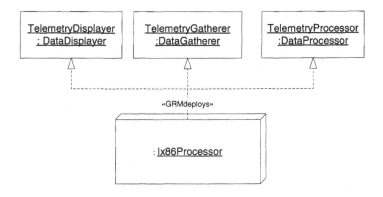

Figure 9-9. Example of the deployment dependency

There is also a tabular form of the deployment dependency that is used for complex deployment specifications which can be used when a graphical rendering might be impractical.

7. SUMMARY

The standard real-time UML profile enhances standard UML with two important capabilities that are of particular significance to real-time and embedded system designers:

1. It provides a means for associating time-related and other quantitative information to a UML model; this in turn, provides the ability to formally analyze models to verify a system's compliance (or non-compliance) with its key non-functional requirements. This capability is particularly important in the early stages and may have a fundamental influence on the choice of architecture.

2. It provides a simple yet very effective solution to the modeling of platforms and the specification of deployment relationships.

Examples of the application of this profile to specific situations are described elsewhere in this volume.

ACKNOWLEDGEMENTS

The author would like to recognize the contributions of his colleagues with whom he collaborated in the design and documenting of the real-time UML profile. In particular, many thanks are due to Alan Moore, Ben Watson, and Mark Gerhardt.

REFERENCES

[1] Object Management Group, *UML Profile for Schedulability, Performance, and Time,* OMG document ptc/02-03-02, Needham MA, 2002.

[2] R. Britcher, *The Limits of Software: People, Projects, and Perspectives,* Addison Wesley Longman, Inc, Reading MA, 1999.

[3] L. Lee, *The Day the Phones Stopped,* Donald I. Fine, Inc., New York NY, 1991.

[4] Object Management Group, *RFP for scheduling, performance, and time*, OMG document ad/99-03-13, Needham MA, 1999.

[5] M. Klein, T. Ralya, B. Pollak, R. Obenza, and M. Gonzalez Harbour, *A practitioner's handbook for real-time analysis: guide to rate monotonic analysis for real-time systems,* Kluwer Academic Publishers, Boston, MA, 1993.

[6] J. W. S. Liu, *Real-Time Systems,* Prentice-Hall Inc., Upper Saddle River, NJ , 2000.

[7] L. Kleinrock, *Queueing Systems, Volume 2: Computer Applications,* John Wiley & Sons, New York NY, 1976.

[8] Object Management Group, *Dynamic Scheduling Final Adopted Specification*, OMG document ptc/01-08-34, Needham MA, 2001.

[9] Object Management Group, *Enhanced View of Time Specification – V 1.1,* OMG document formal/02-05-07, Needham MA, 2002.

[10] W-L. Wang, "Beware the engineering metaphor," *Communications of the ACM,* (45, 5), pp. 27–29, May 2002.

Chapter 10

Modeling Metric Time

L.Motus

Tallinn Technical University, leo.motus@dcc.ttu.ee

Abstract: Following a short discussion on the essence of time and on the applicability of dense time for modeling software, the paper focuses on the time model that has been suggested for the UML profile for Schedulability, Performance, and Time. It is suggested that the profile be extended with timing analysis of interactions. Potential extensions of the time services, required for description and analysis of timing requirements on interactions and validity intervals of events and data are explained in a separate section. Some open research problems are listed in the conclusion.

Key words: metric time, dense time, point and interval semantics of time, multiplicity of times, timing of interactions, UML.

> A man with a watch knows what time is; a man with two watches isn't
> so sure -- Anonymous

1.   INTRODUCTION

Any particular science can always abstract away dynamic problems and focus on static characteristics of the studied phenomena. For instance, think of the implicit assumption of a static environment that forms the foundation for science and requires a static axiomatic basis for a formal theory to be applicable. This assumption is usually satisfied if the theory is applied to a homogeneous domain (e.g. natural processes, computer engineering, mathematical algorithms). As soon as the theory is to be applied to several inhomogeneous domains simultaneously (e.g. to a computer and a chemical process, or to a computer and a moving vehicle), the assumption of a static

L. Lavagno, G. Martin and B. Selic (eds.), UML for Real, 205-220.

environment may be violated unless certain constraints are imposed [1]. These constraints usually limit changes in values of some intrinsic attributes of those domains, and are quite often approximated by time constraints, based on the estimated dynamics of the corresponding domains.

Conventional computer science has essentially assumed a static environment, like most other sciences (e.g. mathematics, physics, and chemistry). Ordering observed events and applying causal relations in a proper order was for a long time, the only substitute for time in computer science – often also called logical time, or topological time. Metric time has been gradually introduced to computer science and software engineering in order to:

1. satisfy requirements on overall time of computations -- performance estimation (explicit interest since 1965, see also [2])
2. invoke programs so as to meet their deadlines, improve performance of the computer system, and in some cases to verify certain time-dependent liveness and safety properties – scheduling, performance estimation, and temporal logic since 1973, e.g. [3]
3. directly monitor and influence the environment – timing of interactions, scheduling, performance, and temporal logic, since 1977, see for instance [4] and [5].

An additional argument for introducing metric time into software development is the need to approximate incompletely known causal relations by time constraints. Such a need is typical in real-time applications where computers are to monitor and influence their environment, as well as in many applications of computational modeling.

The use of metric time and its derivatives for modeling real-time software reached sufficient complexity in 1977, as described in [4]. Since then many seemingly disparate approaches to formal analysis of timing issues can be reduced to a small number of time modeling principles or to choosing appropriate model of computation. For instance, the fundamental similarity of basic theoretical problems in analyzing the behavior of real-time software, and those related to models of interactive computation [6] and [7], are examples. Close connections between UML and models of interactive computation are pointed out in [8].

Theoretical advances combined with technological development and persistently increasing Quality of Service (QoS) requirements from applications have created a situation where the role of time and time models in computer science, and in software engineering is gradually being re-evaluated. The evolution of the role of time in software is similar to the evolution of relations between observers and observed phenomena in physics, as pointed out by Wegner in [9]. Time as used in performance analysis is comparable to an observer as an external recorder of the world in

Newtonian physics. Scheduling (especially in a distributed environment) needs more sophisticated handling of time – comparable with observers in relativity theory, where some phenomena have meaning to a single observer while other phenomena may have meaning for all observers.

Increasing numbers of component-based computer systems exhibit emergent behavior, i.e. dynamically generated behavior, not completely describable at the specification and design stages of development. The emergent behavior depends on interactions between the components and on the system's interaction with its environment. With increasing autonomy and "intelligence" of system components, the impact of emergent behavior becomes more noticeable. This leads us to the case where each "intelligent" component (agent) needs its own time counting system, and the correspondence between those time counting systems is established via negotiations (and/or interactions) of components. The resulting steep rise in complexity of the required models for metric time is one factor that has hindered wider application of time analysis of interactions, and the associated analysis methods [10].

At the moment the most advanced, and widely accepted by computing community, model of time has been developed by the OMG, in its concerted effort to promote wide applicability and interoperability of object-oriented methods. OMG has compiled and accepted two detailed documents specifying the basics of time handling in a computer system.

The first document [11] is on required time readings as obtained via a set of clocks. The document defines the basic characteristics of clocks – for instance resolution, precision, stability – and also characteristics that are needed to synchronize several clocks with required accuracy. The second document [12] is on a selection of time services to be used by clients, such as:
- obtaining current time with an error estimate
- ascertaining the order in which events occur
- computing the interval between two events.

The third document [13] – "UML™ Profile for Schedulability, Performance, and Time" (further denoted in this text as RT UML) – discusses clocks and time services in the context of UML, provides necessary UML constructs, and adds some explanations where necessary.

This chapter comments on the aforementioned OMG documents, attempting to narrow the gap between time description and its usage in tackling real world phenomena, and time as modeled in UML. The secondary message of this chapter is a warning about dangers of mixing models and reality, or in some cases of a necessity to use models as real-world objects that certainly puts additional responsibility on modelers.

Section 2 suggests that we should distinguish philosophical and physical metric time, whereas physical metric time cannot be dense. This pragmatic point of view helps to reduce the danger of potential integration errors caused by *ad hoc* transformations from continuous time based theories to discrete time theories.

Section 3 discusses time as used in OMG products. Some minor enhancements in defining the context of time usage for software modeling are suggested. It is hoped that this will reduce potential ambiguity in interpretation of the role of continuous time in software modeling.

Section 4 considers timing analysis from the user perspective. The basic message of this section is that, in addition to performance and schedulability analysis, the necessity for timing analysis of interactions is emerging in an increasing number of applications. Analysis of interactions enables us to shift the timing analysis closer to the specification stage and forms the theoretical basis for studying the coherence of the time requirements and constraints imposed by (or elicited from) the environment and computer system.

Section 5 concludes the presentation and lists some open research topics.

2.   PHILOSOPHICAL AND PHYSICAL TIME

The contemporary world has become sophisticated mostly because real things, their models and virtual things are getting more and more mixed – mostly due to the increasing interaction of the natural and artificial worlds. Quite often it does not matter whether we talk about models or real things; in some cases we do not care, in some cases it is difficult to tell the difference between a model and a real thing. For instance, an algorithm A that describes certain features of a natural phenomenon P is its mathematical model. When we implement the algorithm A in a computer we get a program C that is a model of algorithm A – since it corresponds only approximately to the mathematical algorithm. When we build a real-time system that influences the behavior of natural phenomena interacting with the phenomenon P by using the program C as a substitute for P and A, we actually mix the models and the real world things.

Similar confusion can be noticed when handling time. It is highly questionable whether time exists as a real world phenomenon, although time is essential in understanding the essence of those phenomena. Increasingly, time is believed to be an abstract notion introduced by observers to describe more precisely models of natural and artificial phenomena and their interactions. Nowadays time is used to enable and foster control over the behavior of things and to synchronize interactions between those things in the case of incomplete information about causal reasons (that truly rule the world), and in presence of random disturbances.

Similar things have also happened in mathematics and philosophy – for instance, real numbers are an extremely useful abstraction that hardly exists in Nature. There are a number of physicists claiming that our Universe comprises only a finite number of atoms, thus questioning the existence of continuity in our Universe.

In the light of the above, physical time as used in [13] should rather be called philosophical time.

2.1 Continuous and discrete time

All intelligent beings are intrinsically lazy – this is the major reason for introducing the notion of continuous time. Continuous time is dense. This means that between any neighboring points in continuous time we can insert a new point, and at the same time maintain a complete order of time points. If we project events onto a dense timeline, we can always insert a new event in between two events, which have already occurred and thus maintain a complete order of events – a real dreamland for modelers.

Quite often complete ordering of events is not sufficient; for pragmatic purposes it might be necessary to know the distance between any two events in the observed history. In that case we model the dense timeline with real numbers, thus introducing a natural metric for measuring distance between two points in time. Ironically for the real-time systems community, some philosophers call a metric dense time, modeled with real numbers, *the real time.*

Continuous time is very comfortable while we remain in the domain of philosophy, mathematics, and abstract modeling. Many mathematical theories provide more efficient methods in the continuous time domain (e.g. differential equations, optimization, etc.), as compared to their discrete time counterparts. Many interesting academic problems can be stated and solved in the continuous time domain, although several pragmatic aspects of those solutions may often remain slightly mystical -- for instance, a study of operational semantics of programs in continuous time to be run on discrete time computers [14].

Problems start to emerge as soon as we transit from abstract theory closer to the real world – e.g. when transforming an algorithm, based on continuous time theory to a respective algorithm based on discrete time theory, a change in algorithm properties can often be observed. Guaranteeing equivalent behavior of a discrete time theory based algorithm and its computer implementation is not always a trivial task. In some cases even the loss of stability in a proven stable algorithm may occur [15] – this can partly be explained by the influence of unavoidable jitter of a discrete time unit as implemented in a computer. The jitter of a time unit is caused by a cumulative effect of fluctuations in coordinated clocks, random delays in program control mechanisms (schedulers, interrupt handlers) and in the context changing mechanism of a computer. Jitter of a time unit becomes noticeable in multi-programmed processors (and in distributed applications), and can be neglected, in less critical applications, in a processor used by a single program.

A *very simple example* of a time unit jitter: A program P has to measure a signal value at regular time intervals (for further signal processing). A clock in a computer generates interrupt signals at (almost) regular intervals, the interrupt handler processes interrupts and invokes the scheduler at (not so) regular intervals, the scheduler takes some time and invokes context switching in order to activate program P, and eventually program P gets started (at not necessarily sufficiently regular intervals).

There is a principal difference whether we model clocks generating time for "basic" time services, or for "derived" time services. In the aforementioned example, the time unit for generating time interrupt signals has minimal jitter, and the time unit for measuring the value of the signal from the environment has a remarkably larger jitter (that may not always conform to the Shannon-Nyquist criteria).

In order to reduce the number and complexity of problems related to the transition from continuous time to discrete time, it is recommended to use discrete-time based methods and algorithms from the very first steps of software modeling. This brings forward many common real world difficulties, and inconveniences – like the loss of dense time and the capability of establishing a complete order of events occurring in the real world and in the computer system. However, the major advantage of those new problems is that they are explicitly visible and therefore less dangerous than the usually implicit continuous-to-discrete time *ad hoc* transition-caused problems.

3.   METRIC TIME AS USED IN *OMG* PRODUCTS

The approach to time modeling in OMG documents [11] and [12] is very rational. They avoid discussions on the nature of time and focus on time measuring devices and time measurements only, strictly following a set of requirements carefully collected from a number of applications. The documents define the origin of the absolute time (15.10.1582, 00:00:00). The progress of the absolute time is measured by counting periods of a certain line in a spectrum of a cesium atom. Since different applications need a variety of time-related services, and different resolutions of time, the documents define a variety of clocks and timers together with required parameters and synchronization methods that can be accessed by clients.

The document on RT UML [13] tackles a more sophisticated issue of unified time, jointly processed in the informal world of a client and the (semi-)formal world of UML. This has led to some questionable statements about a physical world with physical time (as named in [13]) in it. It is not easy to imagine something unbounded (and continuous) that physically exists and is used as an object for modeling – like physical time as defined in [13]. The concept of unified time forces upon the systems and software engineers a rather widespread, but not very realistic belief that real numbers and continuous processes truly exist in the real world.

I rather suspect that in many cases such an assumption actually leads to superfluous approximations in modeling the physical entities from the natural and artificial worlds. A system developer models the real world phenomenon by a mathematical model (usually based on continuous time) by abstracting away unnecessary details. Then the mathematical model (based on continuous time) is approximately transformed into another model based on discrete time; in the worst case, this transition is left to a programmer to complete. Then the discrete time based mathematical model is approximately transformed into a computer program where the mathematical discrete time is slightly distorted by (unwillingly) adding jitter to the time unit's length (see section 2.1 for details). Such cumulative inaccuracies caused by approximate transformations of time are often one of the causes of integration errors.

Do we really need the assumption of a continuous metric time when modeling software and/or other artificial systems? Pragmatically speaking we want to build a system where computers interact with real world entities with the purpose of maximizing the satisfaction of the system designer's specifications. Computers work in discrete time (with "random length" of time unit), without real numbers, and with bounded rational numbers only.

One should be careful with the true meaning of time-related terms as used in practice – the meaning varies from case to case. The minimal time unit of a clock that measures physical time is often important, but vaguely related to the time model as used in the system, achievable synchronization precision of generated events, and verifiable timing properties. The application-related time model is often not checked, because a small time unit of the system's clock is so impressive (see section 4 for more information).

None of our measuring devices can provide measurements in real numbers; it is possible to fix only a partial order of events due to large numbers of concurrently running (in the environment) processes generating events that are of interest to the system. In addition, it is impossible to build a clock with arbitrarily small resolution. Philosophically we admit the convenience of real numbers, complete order of events, and dense time for describing and understanding the essence of real world phenomena. Many scientific theories and computational algorithms rely heavily on continuous time. Pragmatically, however, we have to admit that in computers we can manage only non-dense metric time, and/or non-metric, non-dense topological time for ordering events.

It would be reasonable to accept the difference between the philosophical description of the world, the ideal capabilities of the virtual world of (mathematical) models, and the pragmatically realizable properties, confess that those three are complementary to each other, and avoid mixed use of those three descriptions. Instead we should fix a clear border between those three descriptions with a strict interface between them.

In the case of RT UML this means that we should admit the existence of a philosophical time that is dense and can be modeled with real numbers (or at least with unbounded rational numbers). We also accept the existence of a physical time that cannot be dense, is modeled by integers because of our limited instruments, and can be measured by clocks (e.g. the cesium clock). We also should admit that physical time as measured in different parts of a computer and/or software system has different jitter for different observers. In some cases the time unit jitter may substantially influence the results of computations and should be included in models of time.

Such pragmatic assumptions help to avoid potential confusion introduced by physical time, as defined in [13], as incorporeal and measured by real numbers. The explicit distinction between philosophical and physical time will not change the constructs of the time model as defined in [13] for software modeling. At the same time, it helps to demystify many time related notions used in analyzing time correctness of interactions -- e.g. multiplicity of time concepts [10] and [16], multiplicity of time measurements and their relations to observers, and partially simplify the matching of topological and non-dense metric times. The latter problem cannot be fully neglected when modeling applications.

3.1 Point *versus* interval semantics of time

In RT UML the software developer (modeler, analysis method provider, or infrastructure provider) handles timed events and time-tagged variable values. The assigned time-tags could, in principle, come from three different sources – from the computer, from the UML model specification, or from a real-world process – i.e. from different, not necessarily coordinated clocks. For many, not too time-critical, applications it is acceptable that we interpret a time-tag as a point on a timeline. For more demanding applications a more pedantic interpretation is necessary. For instance, this is true in the cases where the measurements' precision and their timing are both important, or the computer system has to monitor/control an environment that comprises physical processes with different dynamics, and/or a computer system itself is essentially distributed and remote clocks are used for time-tagging. Just think of a moving vehicle with computer-controlled brakes, and the notion of simultaneous generation of distributed events in a computer network, as an example.

Any measurement of a physical characteristic provides us with a value that is an average for a time interval. The length of this interval depends on the application and on the measuring device. Assignment of a time-tag is a process that starts with a request for the service and completes with the actual arrival of the time-tag. The actual time instant is somewhere between the starting and completion instants of the time-tag assignment process.

In many cases such uncertainties must be assessed quantitatively since they may be decisive for timing correctness of emergent behaviors (see for instance, [10]). Similar problems may emerge when interpreting statements of user requirements – e.g. the simultaneity requirement of two events does not always means that those events should occur (or be generated) at the same time instant. Usually this means that the "simultaneous" events should occur (be generated) in a time interval of a certain acceptable length. In modeling software it is most likely that whenever we say a time instant, we actually mean a time interval. The dynamic properties of the application and QoS requirements define the acceptable length of that time interval.

The time model in RT UML [13] does not state explicitly the semantics of time it assumes, but the selection of properties characterizing all timing devices and time services indicates a strong bias towards the interval semantics of time.

Philosophers and theoretical computer scientists support both point semantics and interval semantics of time. Engineers tend to prefer interval semantics of time, since this is the only way the actual time counting and measuring can be realized. Readers with interest in the details of semantics of time are recommended to read books by van Benthem [17], and Shoham [18].

4. TIMING ANALYSIS IN RT UML – THE USER PERSPECTIVE

RT UML provides a safe and productive development and analysis environment for the user, once the system's specification is stated in terms of

UML. In addition to design, RT UML also supports schedulability and performance analysis at various design stages. However, a real-time system is not only concerned with what happens inside a computer system; equally important is the interaction of the computer system with real world processes. So far, in this chapter, the time model and time services have been considered from the software developer's perspective – i.e. focusing on what happens in the computer system and not paying too much attention to what happens in its surroundings.

The questions of how to acquire feasible estimates for time characteristics of, and requirements from the real world processes, and how to enforce dynamic coordination of time counting in a computer with time counting systems used by real world processes, have gained less attention. These estimates and requirements are usually made under incomplete knowledge about the precise nature of real world phenomena and processes. Quite often they are based on expert assessment, and/or rough indirect measurements. These estimates are often presented in substantially different time scales [19], or based on disparate time counting systems. Imagine, for instance a generic synchronization example of an approaching train and a gate lowering at the crossing – precise information for computing the appropriate time for gate lowering can be given as a n-tuple (speed and weight of a train, weather conditions, distance to the crossing), and usually a worst-case estimate is given (fixed distance to crossing in meters). Railway people are interesting in safety, car drivers are interested in safety and in how many minutes they have to wait when the gate is closed. The software developer has to find a compromise in this situation, make a feasible design decision, and compute (dynamically?) the instant for gate lowering.

The potential incoherence of time requirements acquired from the real world is one of the threats that need to be addressed as early in the design process as possible. For truly time-critical applications, equally important is the necessity of maintaining time correctness of events and data, and time correctness of interactions between components of the system. These additional services can, in principle, be included into RT UML – in the same way as performance and scheduling analysis are. Unfortunately the corresponding methods need more research before they reach the required level of maturity.

4.1   Interaction-centered models of computation

Systems, including software-intensive systems, are increasingly built from components (e.g. COTS) since this reduces time spent on testing and verification, and improves economic feasibility of systems. Object-oriented programming is one of the examples, where the majority of components comprise several objects. The acceptable (sometimes required) autonomy of components increases quickly – e.g. intelligent agents used as components, and multi-agent systems.

Component-based systems tend to display "emergent behavior" very clearly – in addition to individual component generated behavior, a large share of the system's behavior is invoked dynamically by interactions between components. The emergent behavior cannot be expressed by finite descriptions. Therefore traditional algorithm-centered models of computation are pretty helpless in handling emergent behavior, and interaction-centered models of computation are gaining more popularity, see for more information references [20] and [21].

Component-based systems, increasing "intelligence" and autonomy of components naturally leads to the necessity of time-wise autonomy of components – each component may have its own time counting system (and, of course, its own time model). In the case of real-time systems, for analysis purposes certain processes from the surrounding real world should also be considered as components of the system. Coordination of components' time counting systems and matching dynamic characteristics of the interacting components is a key to verifying time-correctness of interactions, and is still a challenge for researchers (see next section of this chapter). This shift of the time modeling paradigm has some analogy to what happened with the role of observers in physics in the first half of the last century (see [9], section 5, for a quick survey).

4.2   Time modeling in interaction-centered model of computation – an example

In this section we describe one of the cases, where each component may have its own time model. The example stems from a time-sensitive interaction-centered model of computation, see [7] and [10], that is based on an elaboration of results published in [4]. The generic time model for an autonomous component comprises:

- *Single universal time for a neutral observer*, common for all the components of system (e.g. a clock that represents *UTC* (*Universal Time Coordinated*) time signals, used as a reference clock for the "physical time" in [13]).
- *Discrete, strictly increasing time for each component of a system*; resolution (granularity) of this time corresponds to execution time of the component; stability properties of this clock's time unit characterize the actual (or acceptable) jitter of a single execution time of the component; in other words, in this time the designer counts the number of activations, fixes deadlines for any execution of the component, and measures actual

execution time; this time may be compared to mission time [11], as applied for countable number of executions of this particular component.
- *Fully reversible relative time* is used for monitoring component's detailed behavior during a single execution, within limits of a granule of the strictly increasing time (as defined in the previous paragraph). For instance, start instant of interaction, completion instant of interaction, cumulative duration of time spent on exception handling, and expected duration required to recover from errors via returning to checkpoints are typical characteristics measured in this time. This time enables one to guarantee the termination of each execution of a component within given time budget; it may be compared to mission time [11], as applied for a single execution of the component, with slight modifications that cater for reversibility of time.
- *Relative time for each in-component and/or inter-component interaction* enables one to measure relative age of events and data involved in the interaction with respect to the instant of invoking the interaction. It is a necessary precondition for applying time-selective interaction – i.e. the consumer can subscribe to messages of a certain age only. This time links timing characteristics of events and data in interacting partners (operating potentially under different time counting systems) and may be compared to mission time [11], as applied for a joint action of two interacting components within a single execution of the consumer component.

While the first two time concepts can be readily modeled by using the existing OMG time services, the fully reversible time needs some comments. In real-time systems it is important to guarantee that time is reversed only within the permissible limits – so that the deadline can be met. During run time we have to deal with a branching time under the constraint that any acceptable path in the time-tree must be shorter than the deadline for termination of a particular execution of this component. Usually we should avoid reverse over the time interval that includes an interaction – in many cases it is not possible to undo the influence of an interaction. In the specification and design stage we need to guarantee that sufficient time is left for exception handling, error correction, and other unexpected activities – depending on the estimated properties of the application. During run-time the fully reversible time measurements support actual decisions on whether to start corrective measures, or not. It is important to notice that the fully reversible time is embedded in a granule of strictly increasing time.

A relative time for measuring interaction-related time attributes is not a readily available service in RT UML. Its role is to coordinate time counting in the interacting partners and to measure the age of transferred messages (time-tagged by the producer-partner) relative to the instant when the consuming partner receives (or is scheduled to receive) the message. Similar time – based on the concept of relative time with moving origin – forms the time-basis of many studies in psychology and is used for reasoning about time-sensitive events by our consciousness.

Due to its inter-component nature such a relative time is ideal for checking the coherence of imposed time constraints and other time parameters, specified in interacting components of the system and in its environment. As demonstrated in [7], there are many subtle timing properties that cannot be detected by testing, but can be studied analytically by using such a relative time – e.g. non-transport delay (whose behavior can be approximated by a saw-tooth function) of messages, achievable minimal length of simultaneous interval for computer-generated events, and detection of potential violations of validity intervals for events and data at the specification and design stages of a system development. Analytical timing analysis consumes very little resources. Therefore it is recommended that analytical timing analysis be repeated each time the existing estimates are improved in the system development process.

5. CONCLUSIONS

Computers, programs, computer science, and specialists in those areas have traditionally not been interested in time – the introduction of metric time complicates many issues. Besides, a sophisticated notion of time can be avoided until we deal with statically (pre-)specified, and finite behaviors, and with completely known causal relations -- in other words, until we stick to the world of algorithms and algorithmic thinking. It has never been possible to avoid metric time in real-time systems; its avoidance is very questionable in artificial intelligence due to the increasing role of the agent-based paradigm, and is getting more difficult in traditional software due to the wide application of object-oriented methods and data-stream processing.

During the last decade OMG has introduced a sophisticated time model into software engineering and software applications via its CORBA and RT UML initiatives. The time model has been widely accepted and can be applied for performance and schedulability analysis in real-time applications – since for those methods a relevant link to UML is already specified. However, not all the time model's capabilities are used when analyzing performance, and/or schedulability.

At the same time, interaction-centered models of computation are gradually gaining popularity in computer science – for reasoning about software-intensive systems resulting from the application of object-oriented, component-, and agent-based technologies. Many new emerging computing paradigms – e.g. pervasive computing, proactive computing, and autonomous computing – operate in an environment with incompletely known causal relations and depend essentially on time awareness. The new models of computation have pointed out many subtle issues, including timing properties – e.g. related to timing of interactions and validity intervals of events and data -- that traditionally have been neglected.

The time model introduced by OMG has inherent capabilities for supporting timing analysis of interactions. However, timing of interactions cannot readily be applied in practice since there are several open questions related to understanding the essence of time-sensitive interactions. For instance, in the case when interaction is automatically established (e.g. autonomous components, agents) the partners have to coordinate their understandings of the world (their ontologies). Hopefully some analogy to adaptation and learning can be revealed when studying this process. Automatic adaptation and learning of ontology will inevitably introduce the time dependence of ontology. It is not quite clear what is the role of time in this process since the ontology of interaction, as well as interacting ontologies, have not been studied seriously. In addition to that, the already existing timing analysis methods for interactions, as described in [7] and [10] need more research and practical testing.

Time has a dual role in the software development process, at least in analysis of interactions. The time model is used for matching dynamic properties of the environment and the computer system by specifying time constraints and requirements imposed by both parties followed by the coherence analysis of those constraints and requirements. The coherent set of time constraints and requirements forms the basis for design and implementation, and is an implicit assumption for performance and schedulability analysis.

In many time-critical applications it is also required to have on-line monitoring of the operating conditions of the implemented system – to detect timing abnormalities and errors in due time. Monitoring itself is not much different from the analysis of specification and design; care should be taken that resources spent on monitoring and operation of the clock system in the application, fit into the constraints pre-scheduled at specification and design.

ACKNOWLEDGEMENTS

Partial financial support from ETF grant 4860, and Estonian Ministry of Education grant no. 0140237s98 is acknowledged. Fruitful discussions on topics of time, interaction and ontologies with M. Meriste in many different places of this world are appreciated. Comments and questions to the author from the editors of this book have pointed out many things that still need further studying.

REFERENCES

[1] H.A. Simon, *The Science of the Artificial*, The MIT Press, Cambridge, MA, 3rd edition, 1996.

[2] E. Ashcroft and Z. Manna "Formalization of Properties of Parallel Programs", *Machine Intelligence*, vol.6, 1971, 17-41.

[3] C. L. Liu and J.W. Layland "Scheduling Algorithms for Multi-Programming in a Hard Real-time Environment" *Journal of the Association for Computing Machinery* vol.20, no.1, 1973, 40-61.

[4] W.J. Quirk and R. Gilbert "The Formal Specification of the Requirements of Complex Real/time System", AERE, Harwell, UK, report no. 8602, 1977.

[5] A. Pnueli "The temporal logic of programs", in *Proceedings of the 18th IEEE Annual Symposium on Foundations of Computer Science*, 1977, 46-57.

[6] P. Wegner and D. Goldin "Co-inductive Models of Finite Computing Agents", *Electronic Notes in Theoretical Computer Science*, vol. 19, 1999, www.elsevier.nl/locate/entcs/.

[7] L. Motus, and M.G. Rodd *Timing Analysis of Real-time Software*, Pergamon/Elsevier, Oxford, UK, 1994

[8] D. Goldin, D. Keil, P. Wegner "An Interactive Viewpoint on the Role of UML", in K. Siau and T. Halpin, (editors) *Unified Modeling Language: Systems Analysis, Design and Development Issues*, Idea Group Publishing, Hershey, PA, 2001.

[9] P. Wegner "Towards Empirical Computer Science", *Monist,* 82 (1), 58-108, 1998, www.cs.brown.edu/people/pw, 25.09.2002.

[10] L. Motus "Timing Problems and their Handling at System Integration", in Tsafestas S.G. and Verbruggen H.B. (editors) *Artificial Intelligence in Industrial Decision Making, Control, and Automation,* Kluwer Academic Publishers, 67-87, 1995.

[11] OMG document formal/02/05/07 "Enhanced View of Time", version 1.1.

[12] OMG document formal/02/05/06 "CORBA services: Time Service Specification", version 1.1.

[13] OMG document ptc/02/03/02 "UML^{TM} Profile for Schedulability, Performance, and Time", specification, version 1.0.

[14] I. Ulidowski and Y. Shoji (2001) "Timed Properties for Process Languages with Time", *Proceedings of the 5th World Multi-conference on Systems, Cybernetics and Informatics*, Orlando, USA, on CD, 6 pages

[15] L. Motus, M.G. Rodd, C. Neill "The Impact of Software Timing Correctness on Systems Safety", *Proceedings of the IFAC 2nd Workshop on Safety and Reliability in Emerging Control Technologie*s, Florida, 1995, 193 – 201.

[16] K.G. Denbigh *Three Concepts of Time*, Springer Verlag, Berlin 180 pp., 1981

[17] J.F.A.K. van Benthem *The Logic of Time*, Kluwer Academic Publishers, Dordrecht, 1991

[18] Y. Shoham *Reasoning about Change*, MIT Press, Cambridge, MA, 1988

[19] E. Corsetti, E. Crivelli, A. Mandrioli, A. Montanari, A.C. Morzenti, P. San Pietro, and E. Ratto "Dealing with Different Time Scales in Formal Specification", *Proceedings of the 6th International Workshop on Software Specification and Design*, Como, 92-101, 1991.

[20] P. Wegner and D. Goldin "Interaction as a Framework for Modeling", in Chen et alii (eds), *Conceptual Modeling: Current Issues and Future Directions*, Springer, Berlin, LNCS no.1565, 1999.

[21] M. Meriste and L. Motus "On Models for Time-sensitive Interacting Computing", *International Conference on Computational Science*, Lecture Notes in Computer Science, vol. 2329, Springer, Berlin, 156-165, (2002).

Chapter 11

Performance Analysis with UML

Layered Queueing Models from the Performance Profile

D. C. Petriu, C. M. Woodside

Dept. of Systems and Computer Engineering, Carleton University, Ottawa, ON, Canada

Abstract: The performance of a software design specified in UML is analyzed to estimate the delays, throughputs and resource utilizations, and such measures as the probability of missing a target response time. A case study that defines scenarios for the important responses is described by using the recently adopted UML Profile for Schedulability, Performance and Time. Using the Profile, stereotypes and annotations are added to the UML model to define desired values for performance measures such as response time, and estimated or budgeted values for performance parameters such as the CPU demand for an operation. From this information a performance model is created (a Layered Queueing Model, in this case) from which the performance estimates are computed, either by simulation or by analytic techniques.

Key words: UML, Performance analysis, Non-functional requirements, Scenario, Layered Queueing Model

1.   INTRODUCTION

One of the essential requirements in many software systems is to meet some performance targets that may be defined in terms of delay or throughput capacity. Performance model-based techniques can be used at an early stage of design, and experience has shown that they give useful early-warning information even when they are based on high-level designs and rough estimates of CPU demand parameters. Estimates do not have to be accurate to be useful; sometimes an order-of-magnitude is enough to identify basic problems with an architectural concept, that can be dealt with during high-level design. As the design is refined and demands are better understood through testing and prototyping, the performance predictions can be made more accurate.

L. Lavagno, G. Martin and B. Selic (eds.), UML for Real, 221-240.

The barrier to analysis is the labor of creating a performance model which accurately represents the design, and the obvious line of attack is to create the model directly from the design specification. To make this possible for specifications in UML, OMG has adopted a UML Profile for Schedulability, Performance and Time (which we will term the SPT Profile) [1]. The part of the profile for general performance analysis deals with statistical models for non-deterministic behavior. It defines stereotypes which are used to identify those response paths (scenarios) which are important for performance, their parameters and the target values for the scenario performance. Additional stereotypes describe the resources used by the system (that may limit performance), which include hardware resources such as processors and networks, and logical resources like threads and buffers.

The SPT Profile is envisaged to be used with some performance modeling tools, which could include tools for schedulability analysis, simulation, queueing [2], layered queueing [3, 4], Petri Nets [5], stochastic process algebra [6], etc. Figure 11-1 shows a UML tool, a performance tool, and examples of the quantities that are input and output for statistical modeling.

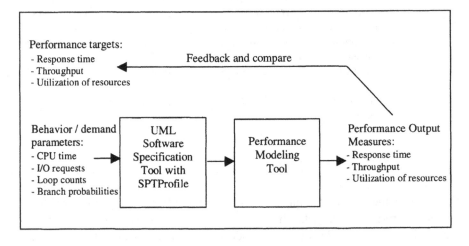

Figure 11-1. Performance measures: targets, input and output

This chapter will explain the SPT Profile and how to use it, by analyzing a high-level UML specification for a system that manages security in a building such as a hotel. It manages access control to the rooms using magnetic cards, and it collects and stores frames from digital video monitors. We will consider two Use Cases from the diagram shown in Figure 11-2.

The Access Control Use Case responds to card reader events by checking the access rights of the card-holder in a database, and triggering an actuator in the door frame to permit access. It should be able to process a random stream of card accesses at an average rate of 2 per minute, with 95% of responses being completed within one second.

The Acquire/Store Video Use Case addresses a given number $N of video surveillance cameras one at a time, polls each one to send its latest frame, and then stores it in a database of frames. (Note that in the STP profile the variable names begin with ' $ ') Each camera should be polled at least once per second, and this is interpreted into a requirement that 95% of polling cycles for all $N cameras should be completed in one second. Also, the system should be capable of handling 50 cameras.

For simplicity, other interesting use cases, such as video display and management of the access rights, will not be considered here.

The planned deployment shown in Figure 11-3 has one application processor and a database with a separate processor, plus peripherals accessed over a local network. The scenario to acquire and store the video frames is defined in a Sequence Diagram in Figure 11-4, and annotated using stereotypes from the SPT Profile. The scenario for access control is shown later in Figure 11-5. The following sections describe the performance quantities that are used, and the stereotypes related to scenarios and to resources.

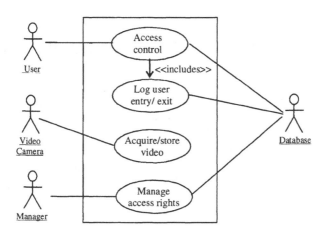

Figure 11-2. Use Cases for the Building Security System

The purposes to be addressed by the performance analysis are:

- feasibility of the performance goals for the system with 50 cameras and two door accesses per minute,
- scalability to a higher volume of activity
- the impact of different buffering schemes for the video frames waiting for storage,
- the impact of alternative deployments.

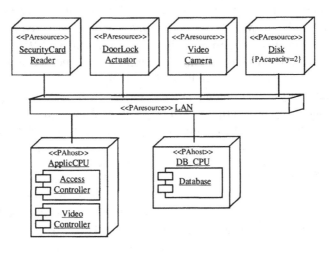

Figure 11-3. Deployment of the Building Security System

2.   DEFINING PERFORMANCE REQUIREMENTS AND MEASURES

Performance measures are intimately connected with the uses of the system as described by use cases. Response time is usually the end-to-end delay of a particular Use Case, and throughput or capacity is the frequency of execution of a Use Case, or a set of related Use Cases. The actual measures may express an aspect of the requirements on performance, such as a required deadline value for some responses. Examples of measures related to end-to-end delay are:
- the maximum value
- the mean delay, or the mean and variance
- the probability of exceeding a given threshold or soft deadline
- a value of jitter for multimedia quality of service.

In the SPT Profile, response time or rate requirements can be attached to the entire scenario by attaching them to the first scenario step. In Figure 11-4 the first step has a tag `PAinterval` which refers to the interval between successive repetitions of the same scenario. The tag is of the type PAperfValue, and represents a tuple which defines:

- a qualifier string: one of `req`, `asmd`, `pred`, or `meas`, respectively, standing for required, assumed, predicted, or measured;
- a string identifying the measure of response time, which offers many possibilities including `mean` for mean, `sigma` for standard deviation, `percentile`'x for the x-th percentile, or `dist` for a distribution;
- a time value of type RTtimeValue that may be given by a numerical literal and a string defining its units, or by a histogram, etc.

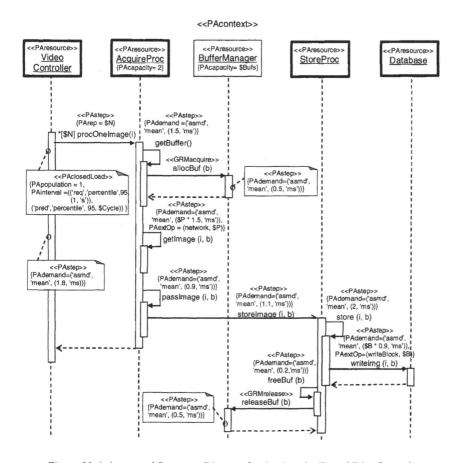

Figure 11-4. Annotated Sequence Diagram for the Acquire/Store Video Scenario

The tag PAinterval is used in Figure 11-4 to express the scenario requirement that the video camera polling cycle should repeat once per second, with a 95% probability of a cycle time less than 1 second:

```
PAinterval=('req', 'percentile', 95, (1, 's'))
```
The same tag also defines a variable $Cycle to contain the response time value predicted by the performance model solver:
```
('pred', 'percentile', 95, $Cycle)
```
Alternatively the tag PArespTime may be used to refer to the response time (i.e., the total duration) of the scenario. An example of PArespTime tag is given in Figure 11-5. It defines the requirement for the Access Control scenario that 95% of the responses to card access requests should be completed within one second:
```
PArespTime =('req','percentile',95,(1, 's'))
```
The same tag also defines also a variable $UserR for reporting the response time result predicted by the performance model:
```
('pred','percentile', 95, $UserR).
```
Besides the end-to-end performance measures associated with scenarios, measures can be defined for resources, as described in section 3.1.

To summarize, the performance requirements for the Building Security System are:
a) it should respond to the card reader input within one second, with a peak-hour rate of generating events at each reader of 2 per minute;
b) it should be able to scan 50 video cameras once per second, such that the probability of exceeding one second for a complete scan is less than 5%.

3.   INPUTS TO ANALYSIS: WORKLOAD PARAMETERS

The attributes of the system that define the load on its resources are called its workload parameters. They define the intensity of the arriving requests, the relative frequency of alternative paths in the scenario, and the resource demands of individual steps in the scenario. Most of these parameters are tagged values for Steps of the Scenario. The use of SPT Profile annotations for workload parameters is illustrated in Figures 11-4 and 11-5 for two scenarios expressed as Sequence Diagrams, and in Figure 11-6 for a scenario expressed as an Activity diagram.

3.1   Resource Annotations

Before describing the workload parameters, it is useful to discuss the annotations for different kind of resources.

The hardware resources used in the system (such as processors, I/O devices, networks, etc.) are represented in UML deployment diagrams as nodes, and can be stereotyped either as <<PAhost>> or as <<PAresource>>.

A processor is stereotyped as <<PAhost>> (see, for example, the processor nodes ApplicCPU and DB_CPU from Figure 11-3). PAhost has associated tag values that define its scheduling policy, processing rate, context switching time and performance measures, such as utilization and throughput.

The hardware devices that are not processors can be stereotyped as <<PAresource>> (see, for example, the network LAN and the I/O devices Disk, VideoCamera, SecurityCardReader, and DoorLock Actuator from Figure 11-3). Such a resource has associated tag values that define its capacity, scheduling policy, time to acquire/release it, and performance measures such as utilization, throughput, response time and waiting time. For example, in Figure 11-3 the tag PAcapacity is used to indicate that there are two disk nodes in the model. This is necessary because the deployment diagram nodes are considered instances, and therefore cannot have a multiplicity attribute. The response time of a resource, defined by the tag PArespTime, is the total time to complete a service (including the waiting for the resource and for other nested resources, if any), and is a measure of the "offered Quality of Service" (QoS). PArespTime may represent a requirement on the resource, an assumed value, or a result computed by the performance model. It is important to remember that, in general, the achieved QoS depends on the load placed on the resource.

The tag <<PAresource>> can be also used to stereotype software resources, which are modeled as UML active or passive objects (classes) participating in the scenarios. While objects (classes) are used to represent resources, the class operations represent services offered by those resources. An active object (represented in the interaction diagram by thicker boxes) owns its own execution thread, and models resources such as operating system processes and threads. In the case of active objects the tag PAcapacity can be used to indicate the number of execution threads (i.e., active object instances) available in the system. For example, there are two AcquireProc threads indicated in the Acquire/Store Video scenario (see Figure 11-4).

Passive resources do not execute any action, but play a supporting role; they must be acquired, then used in a number of scenario steps and finally released. Software passive resources are usually represented as passive objects. The role of managing a certain kind of passive resources is played by a "resource manager", which is in charge of implementing the acquire/release operations according to a certain policy. Examples of passive software resources used in the case study are the buffers needed for the video data, which are allocated/deallocated by the BufferManager component.

The tag `PAcapacity` associated with `BufferManager` in Figure 11-4 represents the number of buffers in the pool.

Besides the services offered by resources represented explicitly in the UML model, there may also be external services offered by resources in the environment that are not explicitly modeled. Such services may be invoked as "external operations" by different scenario steps (see Section 3.2), and their offered QoS may be an assumed value.

Notice that performance modeling is intrinsically instance-based, and components (resources in this case) are usually instances rather than classes. If a class is shown, the stereotypes and tags apply to all instances, and this must be interpreted correctly in modeling.

3.2   Annotations for a Step on a Sequence Diagram

In a Sequence Diagram like Figure 11-4, a Step is an operation which can be shown in two ways: by the message that invokes it, and by the resulting focus of control indicated by a vertical rectangle over the lifeline of the instance which executes it. Either can be stereotyped as `<<Step>>`, and both are used in the figure.

The workload parameters of a `<<Step>>` are defined by tagged values. The `PAdemand` tag gives the "host demand" (the CPU demand, in most cases) as a `PAperfValue` type, with the same fields as described above for a response time. For example, the `getBuffer` step has an assumed mean host (CPU) demand of 1.5 ms expressed as:

> `PAdemand=('asmd', 'mean', (1.5, 'ms'))`

There may be multiple values defined for the same tag, for example to show both the measured mean and the standard deviation, or to define a requirement and a placeholder for the predicted result.

The value of a demand (given in a `RTtimeValue` type, as described above) may be a real value like 1.5 ms, or an expression using a simple syntax called Tag Value Language [1]. In this language, variables may be used to represent quantities that are not known at the time of specification, or that may be varied during the performance analysis. These variables are identified by a string name beginning with '`$`'. In Figure 11-4 there are three variables:

- `$N` is the number of video cameras,
- `$P` is the mean number of packets in a video frame,
- `$B` is the mean number of disk blocks needed to store a video frame.

Using the Tag Value Language the mean host demand of the `getImage` step in Figure 11-4 is (`$P* 1.5, 'ms'`), meaning 1.5 ms per packet.

Other resource demands can be shown as requests for external operations (such as file operations) by the `PAextOp` tag, which has a string to give the name of the operation (this is of significance to the performance evaluation only), and an integer for the number of operations it invokes. If the <<Step>> includes a pure time delay, this can be indicated by a PAextOp tag with no string, and a time value for the delay. In Figure 11-4, the write step executed by the database component makes $B requests to a disk device (which is not defined in the UML model), to write $B blocks. The performance modeling tool must represent the disk device and model the handling of these requests.

Other kind of resources used by a step include process thread resources (indicated indirectly by stereotyping an active object instance as <<PAresource>>) and logical resources (acquired/released by <<GRMacquire>> and <<GRMrelease>> operations, respectively, and used by all steps in between). For example, the buffer resource is used by all steps between allocBuf and releaseBuf in the Acquire/Store Video use case.

3.3   Annotations for Load Intensity and Path Probability

The intensity of the workload for a scenario is attached to the first scenario step. The workload can be open or closed. The stereotypes used are either <<PAopenLoad>> as in Figure 11-5 (with a tag for the arrival rate of requests to the scenario) or <<PAclosedLoad>> as in Figure 11-4 (with a tag for the population size). For example, the scenario Acquire/store Video has a closed workload with a population size of 1, because there is just one controller looping through all cameras in a cycle. There may also be a tag for a delay between the end of one operation and the request for the next.

Where a scenario has an OR-fork there is a set of alternative messages from a branching point, which are associated with the first step of each branch. For each of these Steps, the PAprob tag gives the probability of the branch (e.g., the step readData in Figure 11-5, which has a probability of 0.4).

Where there is a loop, the first step has a mean loop count defined by the PArep tag (e.g., the step procOneImage in Figure 11-4 has a loop count of $N).

4.   DEFINING A SCENARIO IN UML

A Scenario is a sequence of Steps, which may include:
- alternative paths (OR forks and joins)
- parallel paths (AND forks and joins)

- loops with a mean repetition count
- refinement of a Step by a Scenario (a sub-scenario)

Scenarios can be modeled in UML either by interaction diagrams or by activity diagrams. An interaction diagram refers to either a sequence or a collaboration diagram; in spite of their differences in the graphical notation, they have similar representations at the UML metamodel level. Due to this reason, we discuss here only scenarios represented as sequence diagrams.

Sequence diagrams have the ability to represent scenarios as an ordered collection of steps; however, sequential ordering is more easily represented then branch/merge and fork/join (see a more detailed discussion below). An advantage is the fact that it is very straightforward to relate the actions executed in different steps to class operations (methods). A major disadvantage is that there is no refinement mechanism defined for UML sequence diagrams (see section 4.1 for a more detailed discussion).

Activity diagrams have the advantage that they represent naturally the execution flow of scenario steps, which includes sequence, fork/join and branch/merge. Also an advantage is that an activity block can be refined by another activity diagram, so it's easy to move between different levels of abstraction. A disadvantage of the activity diagrams is that they don't show very well who is responsible for various actions, although swimlanes do mitigate this drawback to a certain extent. Another disadvantage is that the actions described in the diagram cannot be related to the operations defined for different classes (objects). This is important because, as mentioned before, classes (objects) represent resources, and their operations represent services offered by these resources. More details on the modeling of scenarios as activity diagram are discussed in section 4.2.

4.1   Defining a Scenario by a Sequence Diagram

Annotated Sequence Diagrams have already been introduced in Figure 11-4, showing the Acquire/Store Video Scenario. The structure of the scenario is defined by the sequence of messages and by the foci of control (the vertical rectangles in the component lifelines). Figure 11-5 shows a second Sequence Diagram for the Access Control scenario.

Simple sequencing of steps is easily represented. Alternative paths (with OR forks and joins) are shown in two ways. In the first, conditional messages (i.e., annotated with guards) branch from a point message (see Figure 11-5); the probabilities of taking each branch are tags of the following. An OR-join of alternative branches is shown by messages arriving at the same point. In the second, the lifeline of the component forks into alternative parallel lifelines and then rejoins. The probabilities of taking each branch within the component can be indicated on the next step in each case.

An AND fork can be indicated by two messages without guards leaving from the same point; an AND join similarly can be inferred when two unconditional messages arrive in the same point.

Refinement of a Step by a sub-scenario is more difficult to show. However a subsystem or collection of components can be represented in a high-level diagram by a single lifeline, which is then expanded in another diagram. This gives a limited capability to express refinement.

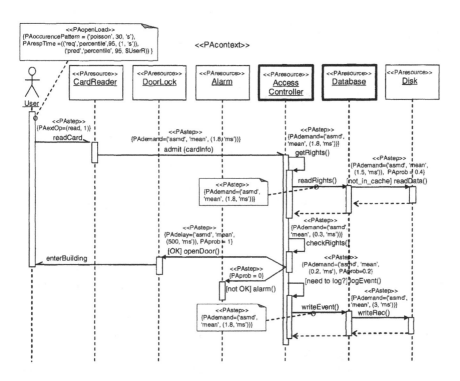

Figure 11-5. Annotated Sequence Diagram for the Access Control Scenario

4.2   Defining a Scenario by an Activity Diagram

An Activity Diagram may have a swimlane or vertical track for each participating component. Activities are shown as rounded rectangles called ActionStates, which can be stereotyped as <<PAstep>>, and flow and precedence are indicated by transition arrows. Figure 11-6 shows an activity diagram for the Acquire/Store Video use case modeled in Figure 11-4 as a sequence diagram. The tags for a Step can be indicated as part of an activity label. An activity which acquires (releases) a resource, performed by a resource manager or the resource itself can also be stereotyped as <<GRMacquire>> (<<GRMrelease>>), as shown in Figure 11-6.

Refinement of an activity by another activity diagram directly represents refinement of a Step into a sub-Scenario, and is indicated by a dumbbell symbol in the activity label, as shown for procOneImage in Figure 11-6. The top-level Activity Graph is stereotyped as an analysis context <<PAcontext>>, and its start point is stereotyped as a workload (either <<PAclosedLoad>> or <<PAopenLoad>>), with tags identifying the intensity of workload and its overall performance measures.

Among the UML diagrams describing behavior, the Activity Diagram is the closest to the Scenario stereotype, as it explicitly shows alternatives, parallel branches and refinement of an activity by a sub-diagram.

5.   PERFORMANCE MODELING

The scenario and resource information described above can be used to build many different kinds of performance model, such as:
- queueing or extended queueing network model, solvable by tools such as RESQ [2]
- layered queueing network (LQN) model, solvable by tools such as LQNS [3]
- simulation model, solvable by tools such as Hyperformix Workbench [7]

The steps to build a performance model from software specifications have been described by many authors. For instance, Smith and Williams [8] build queueing network models from a scenario notation of their own; Petriu and Woodside [9] describe an algorithm and tool for reducing annotated scenarios to layered queueing networks (LQNs); Petriu and Shen [10] derive LQN models from a certain style of UML models. LQN is a kind of extended queueing model adapted for software resources, with queues for concurrent task resources buffers, locks, semaphores, etc. [3, 4, 11]. We will consider building and solving an LQN model for the Building Security System, to illustrate the use of the UML models discussed so far and of the SPT Profile.

In practice, automated extraction of the performance model will be essential, and work is underway in our lab and elsewhere to do this.

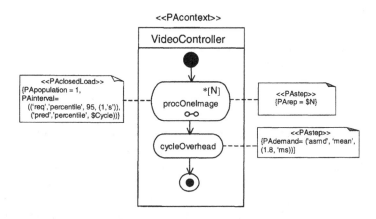

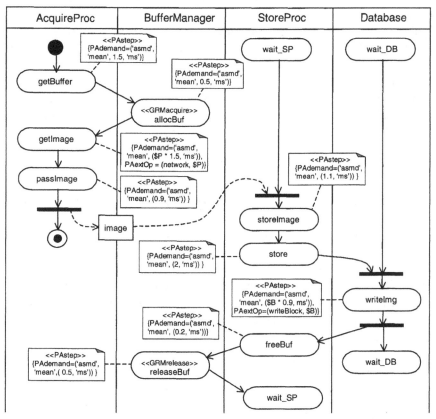

Figure 11-6. Annotated Activity Diagram for the Acquire/Store Video Scenario

5.1   Layered Queueing Model

To build an LQN model, we trace the scenario from the beginning, and for each Step we identify the concurrent component that executes it, which we will call a Task. Also the messages between Tasks are analyzed to identify blocking (call-reply) interactions such as remote invocations or remote procedure calls, and asynchronous (call-no-reply) interactions. Blocking is inferred when a task waits between an asynchronous request and an asynchronous reply, as seen in the first interaction in the access control sequence diagram. A third interaction type, called forwarding, may occur in LQN, in which a caller blocks for the reply, but the server Task forwards the request (asynchonously) to a third party, or through a chain of Tasks, before there is a reply. The Task deployment to host processors and Task priorities are included in LQN models, as well.

The acquisition and release of other kinds of logical resources is also identified, and such resources also become Tasks in the model. Pure layered queueing applies if the use of resources is nested, so that the last resource acquired is released first.

An additional Task is defined for the logical interface of an attached device such as a Disk; its entries define the operations of the device and its host processor represents the device itself.

5.2   LQN for the Building Security System

The LQN for the present example is shown in Figure 11-7. The notation in the figure shows each Task (that is, each software resource) as a bold rectangle, with one or more Entries representing Steps or subsequences of Steps carried out by the task, as attached rectangles. VideoController is a Task representing the VideoController active object in the behavior diagrams. It implicitly executes an endless loop (since it receives no requests). In each cycle it makes $N requests to AcquireProc for a video frame, one from each camera. AcquireProc is a server with one or more threads; two threads means that two frame-acquisitions can be underway concurrently. It requests a buffer from BufferManager, which forwards the request (the dashed arrow) to a "pseudo-task" Buffer representing the buffer pool and the number $Nbuf of buffers. Notice that the logical resource BufferManager stereotyped in the sequence diagram has been divided into a manager task with a host workload, and a separate pseudotask for the buffers themselves. The forwarding arrow indicates that the buffer is held (blocked) during the succeeding operations but the manager is not.

Once a buffer was obtained, the remaining operations are initiated as being associated with the Buffer resource, although some of them are actually executed by `AcquireProc`, indicated by a pseudo-task named `AcquireProc2`. The first operation `getImage` requests a camera to send a frame which occupies an average of `$P` packets; the second operation `passImage` hands the buffer of data over for storage. Then `Buffer` signals `AcquireProc` by replying, and in "second phase" (still holding the buffer), requests `StoreProc` to store the frame in the database. The `Database` operation `writeImg` uses an "external operation" `writeBlock` in the UML scenario from Figures 11-4 and 11-6, which is represented in the LQN by the `writeBlock` entry of the task `Disk`.

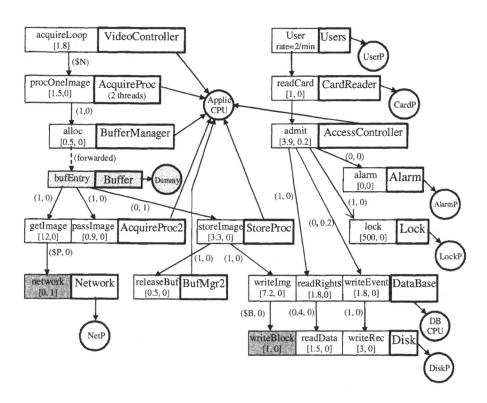

Figure 11-7. Layered Queueing Network Model for the Building Security System

The external operations are not explicitly defined in the UML model, so their mapping to the performance model must be supplied externally by a modeling library or by the modeling team. Finally `StoreProc` releases the buffer.

On the right side of Figure 11-7, the `Access Card` submodel has open arrivals initiated by User entities at the rate of 2 arrivals/min to `CardReader` (one per door), and a single `AccessController` task which makes security related database queries, triggers the door lock, and in second phase optionally (with probability 0.2) writes a log to the database. In `Access Control` scenario there is an option to trigger an alarm task, but its probability is set to zero, so it is not represented in the LQN model.

The parameters of form [s1, s2] shown on the task entries give the processor execution demands (in msec) of the entry before and after it replies to its caller, called phase one and phase two demands. These are taken from the host demands of the Steps. The parameters (y1, y2) on the arcs are the mean numbers of calls generated in phase one and phase two, and are taken from the message patterns, the repetition counts and probabilities on Steps. Some parameters are variables, taken from the UML tag values: $N cameras in a cycle (nominally exactly 50), $P data packets per video frame (nominally random with a mean of 8), and $B disk blocks written per video frame (nominally random with a mean of 8).

An interaction probability is shown through a mean frequency of less than one on a request, for instance the probability of having a cache miss on the `readRights` operation was defined as 0.4, which is shown as the mean number of requests for the `readData` entry to the `Disk`.

The LQN has a different appearance from the UML behavior descriptions, but a scenario can be read from it. For the video scenario, follow down from `VideoController`, following the arrows; the `Buffer` pseudo-task makes three requests, first to get the image from the camera (follow down and back $P times for the request/return operations to bring packets to the interface), then down and back for the operation to pass the image to the storage, then `Buffer` sends a "reply" to `AcquireProc` (because its first phase is now over, and the call to `Buffer` was forwarded; this pattern is evident in the sequence diagram). Finally, `Buffer` sends a request in its second phase to `StoreProc`, which executes storage operations on the database, after which the `Buffer` resource is released when the blocking "requests" made from it are all completed.

5.3   Analysis Results

Often the first question posed about performance is just a point estimate of delay or throughput, for a single set of parameter values. However more can be learned by scanning over ranges of values, and by looking deep into the results for the base case to identify how the resources are loaded. Table 11-1 shows some sets of cases.

The first group of cases in Table 11-1 shows results for different numbers of buffers, with six threads in the acquisition task, $N = 40$ cameras, $B = 8$ disk blocks/video frame, and $P = 8$ packets/frame. Additional task threads were added to the numbers shown in the UML diagrams (six threads for `AcquireProc` instead of two, three for `StoreProc` and `AcquireProc2`, and 10 for `DataBase`), when initial results showed inadequate concurrency in processing.

The cycle time of `VideoController` (called Cycle) is the time between successive frames of the first camera (or, if cameras are all similar and the loop is continuous, then for any camera). The first case with just one buffer has a mean cycle length of 1.31 seconds and a probability of 100% of missing the deadline of one second, which is clearly unacceptable (the requirement is 5%). The access-control delays UserR have almost zero probability of exceeding one second, which is fine.

Additional buffers give satisfactory performance with 40 cameras. Two buffers, as in a double-buffered scheme, reduce the miss probability to 6%, which is not quite acceptable. 3 buffers allow 40 cameras to achieve the required performance, without endangering the access-card response requirement on UserR.

However, a series of results for 3 buffers and one CPU shows that more than 40 cameras makes the 5% miss requirement infeasible (the 50-camera-case has a probability of 32% of missing the deadline). In this case, the high utilization of processor ApplicCPU shows that the bottleneck moves from software to hardware. Using two processors, however, the final set of results shows that the desired capacity of 50 cameras can be supported with acceptable performance, with 3% probability of missing the deadline.

The utilizations for multiple resources like the dual CPU are reported as the mean number of busy resources. For the dual CPU cases, none of these resources shows saturation. Thus the performance is not limited by a resource bottleneck, but by a design limitation. The limitation might be that the VideoController task can only launch one frame acquisition at a time.

The table also illustrates a performance effect that may appear when two separate use cases compete for the same resources (in this case, for the processor and the database). Increasing the number of buffers makes things better for the `VideoAcquisition` use case, which will lead to higher resource consumption on its behalf, and consequently will decrease the performance of the `AccessControl` case. The effect is not strong here, but it can be observed from the first sub-table that, for 40 cameras, `UserR` tends to get longer whereas `Cycle` gets shorter when the number of buffers

Table 11-1. Results from LQN simulations

Columns are: Bufs : number of buffers; Cycle: mean camera scan cycle (sec)
                 UserR: mean door access response time (ms); UAcpu: ApplicCPU utilization,
                 Uaqc: AcquireProc task utilization; Ubuf: Buffer utilization
                 Ustor: StoreProc task utilization; Sstor: service time of storage task;
                 PCam: Probability camera cycle > 1 sec; PDoor: Prob door response > 1 sec

For 40 cameras

Bufs	Cycle	UserR	UAcpu	Uacqp	Ubuf	Ustor	Sstor	PCam	PDoor
1	1.31	8.78	0.543	0.965	1.000	0.583	19.8	1.00	0
2	0.87	10.27	0.816	0.942	1.683	1.683	22.7	0.06	0
3	0.77	10.70	0.923	0.931	2.035	1.242	24.8	0	0

For 3 buffers, single ApplicCPU

Cams	Cycle	UserR	UAcpu	Uacqp	Ubuf	Ustor	Sstor	PCam	PDoor
30	0.58	10.74	0.923	0.93	2.034	1.242	24.8	0	0
40	0.77	10.70	0.923	0.931	2.035	1.242	24.8	0	0
50	0.96	10.71	0.923	0.932	2.036	1.243	24.8	0.32	0
60	1.16	10.69	0.923	0.932	2.037	1.244	24.8	0.96	0

For 3 buffers, 2 ApplicCPUs

Cams	Cycle	UserR	UAcpu	Uacqp	Ubuf	Ustor	Sstor	PCam	PDoor
40	0.67	8.23	1.057	0.994	2.086	1.314	22.2	0	0
50	0.84	8.15	1.056	0.994	2.088	1.317	22.2	0.03	0
60	1.01	8.20	1.057	0.995	2.087	1.314	22.1	0.52	0

goes up. However, by adding more processors, the performance of both use cases improves.

The accuracy of these results depends on good estimates of the CPU demands for the Steps. However, even if the estimates are not highly accurate, they point to saturated or nearly saturated software and hardware resources: the Acquire process is fully saturated, and the Application CPU is saturated for high concurrency levels (i.e., many buffers and execution threads). This suggests that a coordinated change in both software architecture (replicated subsystems to gather simultaneously from more cameras) and hardware (more or faster processors) is indicated in order to achieve the original goal.

6.   CONCLUSIONS

The example system described here illustrates many points that must be considered in capturing performance data and concerns in a UML model, using the SPT Profile. Examples include:
- physical resources,
- logical resources such as active objects and the buffer pool,
- synchronous, asynchronous and forwarding interactions between active objects,
- services that are offered by resources outside the UML model.

The example goes on to show how each is represented in the performance model, and how issues are studied by varying parameters supplied with the data.

To gain insight into the performance properties of a design, one should plan sets of experiments over a range of design alternatives, parameters, and configurations. One can systematically identify trouble spots (such as system bottlenecks), study the sensitivity of the overall performance measure to different parameters, propose solutions to mitigate the bottlenecks, investigate alternatives, and study trade-offs.

Tool support for model transformation from UML to LQN (or other performance models) is essential, and there are several research projects working on the problem. Such a project in which the authors are involved is called Performance from Unified Model Analysis (PUMA) (www.sce.carleton.ca/rads/puma). We have not shown here how results may be returned into the UML presentation, but this will presumably, also be supported by UML tools in the future.

ACKNOWLEDGEMENTS

The authors wish to acknowledge the support of the Natural Sciences and Engineering Research Council (NSERC) of Canada through its Discovery Grant Program. Jing Xu helped greatly with the model computations.

REFERENCES

[1]   Object Management Group, "UML Profile for Schedulability, Performance, and Time Specification," OMG Adopted Specification ptc/02-03-02, July 1, 2002.

[2]   Edward A. MacNair, "An introduction to the Research Queueing Package", *Proc. 17th Winter Simulation Conference*, San Francisco, 1985, pp 257 – 262.

[3] G. Franks, A. Hubbard, S. Majumdar, J.E. Neilson, D.C. Petriu, J. Rolia, C.M. Woodside, "A Toolset for Performance Engineering and Software Design of Client-Server Systems", *Performance Evaluation* (special issue on Performance Tools), Vol. 24, No.1-2, pp.117-135, Nov. 1995

[4] G. Franks, S. Majumdar, J. Neilson, D.C. Petriu, J. Rolia, and C.M. Woodside, "Performance Analysis of Distributed Server Systems," in *The Sixth International Conference on Software Quality (6ICSQ),* Ottawa, Ontario, pp. 15-26, 1996

[5] S. Bernardi, S. Donatelli and J. Merseguer, "From UML Sequence Diagrams and Statecharts to analysable Petri Net models", in *Proc. of 3rd International Workshop on Software and Performance (WOSP'02),* Rome, Italy, July 2002.

[6] C. Canevet, S. Gilmore, J. Hillston, and P. Stevens, "Performance modelling with UML and stochastic process algebras", in *Proceedings of the UK Performance Engineering Workshop (UKPEW'2002)* Glasgow, July 2002.

[7] R. Gimarc and Amy Spellman, "Modeling Microsoft SQL Server 7.0", *Proceedings of Computer Measurement Group International Conference CMG'98*, December 1998.

[8] C. U. Smith, L. G. Williams, *Performance Solutions: A Practical Guide to Creating Responsive, Scalable Software,* Addison-Wesley, 2001.

[9] D.B. Petriu and M. Woodside, "Software Performance Models from System Scenarios in Use Case Maps," in *Computer Performance Evaluation - Modelling Techniques and Tools*, (T. Fields, P. Harrison, J. Bradley, U. Harder, Eds.) Lecture Notes in Computer Science 2324, pp.141-158, Springer, 2002.

[10] D.C. Petriu, H. Shen, "Applying the UML Performance Profile: Graph Grammar based derivation of LQN models from UML specifications", in *Computer Performance Evaluation - Modelling Techniques and Tools*, (T. Fields, P. Harrison, J. Bradley, U. Harder, Eds.) Lecture Notes in Computer Science 2324, pp.159-177, Springer, 2002.

[11] G. Franks, C.M. Woodside, "Performance of Multi-level Client-Server Systems with Parallel Service Operations", *Proc. of 1st Workshop on Software Performance (WOSP'98)*, pp. 120-130, October 1998.

Chapter 12

Schedulability Analysis with UML

Marco Di Natale[1], Manas Saksena[2]

[1]Computer engineering dept., Scuola Superiore S. Anna, Pisa, Italy,
[2]TimeSys Corp., Pittsburgh, USA

Abstract: The growing complexity of real-time software is generating an increasing demand for (specialized) UML as a modeling language for real-time systems. Verification of non-functional properties is key in hard real-time systems, which are required to perform correctly both in the value and time domains. Schedulability analysis provides algorithms and methods for assigning physical and logical resources to the software objects and for analyzing and guaranteeing their time properties at design time. Furthermore, it provides guidelines on the deployment of logical architecture into physical architecture. Unfortunately, UML behavioral models are based on an implicit event-triggered model, quite unlike those assumed in real-time scheduling research. Furthermore, until the recent development of a specialized UML profile for schedulability analysis, the use of UML has been hindered by the lack of explicit support for common hard real-time abstractions. This chapter shows how fixed and dynamic priority scheduling theory can be applied to designs developed using a specialization of UML for real-time software. It provides a reference architecture for the development of real-time systems amenable to schedulability analysis and features a short survey on the most common real-time scheduling and analysis concepts and policies.

Key words: scheduling, resource management, deadlines, predictability, guarantees

1. INTRODUCTION

The correctness of many software applications, especially embedded applications, depends (explicitly or implicitly) on non-functional requirements, dealing with, for example, reliability, robustness, and timing constraints. This chapter focuses on applications that require results to be produced within a specified delivery time (or require other forms of timing constraints) in order to be correct. These systems are commonly identified as

L. Lavagno, G. Martin and B. Selic (eds.), UML for Real, 241-269.

hard real-time (HRT) systems in that they require guaranteeing beforehand (most often at design time) the ability to achieve the timing behavior.

Schedulability analysis is a fundamental tool for checking the correctness of hard real-time applications. It allows checking timing constraints given the (hardware and software) resources available for the execution of the application tasks and the resource allocation and scheduling policies. The OMG UML profile for Schedulability, Performance and Time (SPT) [1] addresses the definition of *"standard paradigms of use for modeling of time-, schedulability- and performance related aspects of real-time systems"*. Its resource model package defines schedulability analysis as a Quality of Service (QoS) matching problem between a client and the resources it uses. The profile provides two interpretations: in the *peer interpretation* the client and the resource coexist at the same level; in the *layered interpretation* (more useful to our concerns), the resources are used to implement the client.

Figure 12-1 shows an example of a peer interpretation: the analysis problem consists of finding suitable expressions for (schedulability- and time-related) QoS demands and offerings and of finding a rule for matching the two. As we shall (unfortunately) see, the schedulability analysis problem does not always translate into such a simple QoS-oriented model. Nonetheless, the OMG profile captures well the distinctive aspect of schedulability analysis as a match between the timing (or, in general QoS) requirements of *logical entities* in the *logical layer* and the corresponding QoS offers of an implementation or *engineering layer* (Figure 12-2) and consequently raises the fundamental problem of mapping logical-level entities into architecture-level entities.

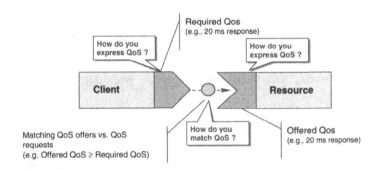

Figure 12-1. The peer model: matching QoS requests and offers

For the sake of simplicity we concentrate on the most common situation where three layers are defined: a *logical architecture level*; a *concurrency description layer* and the *hardware layer* (Figure 12-2).

The *logical architecture* contains the design of the objects implementing the system functionality and their interactions. The *concurrency description layer* contains an implementation description consisting of all the threads that are running in the system and of the policies for managing resources (possibly implemented in the operating system). Finally, the *hardware layer* describes the hardware and its QoS features. The two bottom layers collectively define the so-called *physical architecture layer,* describing the mapping of the object design to a particular real-time execution environment.

In the OMG Profile the mapping between the logical entities and the physical architecture supporting their execution is a form of *realization layering* (synonymous with *deployment*). The semantics of the mapping provides a further distinction between the «deploys» mapping, indicating that instances of the supplier are located on the client and the «requires» mapping, which is a specialization indicating that the client provides a minimum deployment environment as required by the supplier (Figure 12-2).

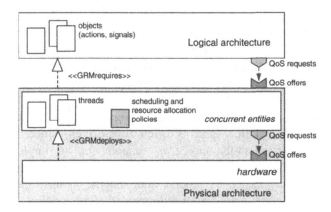

Figure 12-2. Schedulability analysis requires creating a correspondence between logical and physical architecture

Designers of hard real-time object-oriented systems should be able to exploit the degrees of freedom that are available at the different layers of the architecture and to understand the options for mapping logical objects onto concurrent threads (or the consequences of the mapping when the implementation is dictated by an underlying CASE tool).

This capability requires being familiar with the schedulability analysis techniques that are available at the concurrent entities level, and to understand the restrictions that they impose on the logical architecture design and the definition of the mapping (the three design levels are tied to each other). This phase of the design can be supported by schedulability analysis tools providing not only validation of timing constraints but also automatic synthesis of at least some of the design parameters.

In the remainder of the chapter, the logical and concurrent level are briefly introduced; then, for those not familiar with schedulability analysis, an (as short as possible) introduction to Rate Monotonic Analysis (or RMA, probably the best known real-time analysis methodology) is provided. Given the restricted applicability of pure RMA analysis, more realistic models and algorithms for schedulability analysis and logical-to-physical level mapping are presented in the following sections. A discussion of the (unfortunately many) problems that are still open and a very short review of other research results in the field end the chapter.

1.1   The logical model

In standard OO modeling, the class model is the main constructive model and the focus of development. In contrast, quantitative analysis in UML (timing and schedulability analysis makes no exception) requires *all the instances of the classes to be statically known in number, operations, and relations and the system topology needs to be made explicit.*

Hence, the starting point for HRT system analysis is the topology of the objects and their links and the synchronous/asynchronous semantics of messages. The object model and the behavioral models come to the foreground and the class model rests in the background.

At the logical level, most real-time systems feature a control and a dataflow part. The dataflow part is often time-driven, since inputs are sampled at regular intervals and it is suitable for an implementation consisting mainly of periodic activities. The predictability of event arrivals makes these models easier to predict and analyze against their timing constraints. In contrast, the control-dominated functionality is highly asynchronous and state-dependent. This software part typically executes in loops where it waits for an event, reacts to it by issuing an action and then blocks, waiting for the next event (event-driven). The non-deterministic arrival of events makes this model harder to analyze, but schedulability analysis is possible provided all events have a minimum interarrival time.

The design of the logical model mostly requires standard UML abstractions. This general UML model features objects communicating with each other using messages. Messages may be *asynchronous* (signals) or *synchronous* (call messages). In the latter case, according to the UML semantics, the sender object releases its thread of control to the recipient object by calling one of its operations and continues only after a reply message. The reception of a message is said to generate an event. The behavior that specifies the processing of a message in an object is called an action and the actual processing of the action is called an action-execution.

The objects defined in the logical layer are often classified as active objects or passive objects to represent the logical concurrency in the design. Conceptually, each active object has a life of its own, i.e., it executes concurrently with other active objects in the system. The behavior of active objects is usually modeled using a finite state machine supplemented with code. They act asynchronously and may be the recipient of asynchronous signals. Passive objects, on the other hand only respond to synchronous operation requests and are often modeled (and implemented) as a data class.

Schedulability analysis is performed on snapshots of the system as it is working expressed by means of behavioral diagrams. This is a less standard part, since it requires domain-specific entities and the specification of timing attributes and constraints.

Finite state machine models of objects are useful for code-generation but focus on a design level, which is inappropriate for reasoning about end-to-end timing behaviors. UML offers sequence diagrams (or collaboration diagrams) to model end-to-end system behaviors. In many real-time research papers [2, 3, 4] and in specialized modeling environments for real-time systems [5] this notion is partly captured by the term *transaction,* which refers to the entire causal set of actions executed as a result of an external event (including timer events.)

The notion of transaction is captured in the OMG profile SPT using the concept of scheduling jobs. A scheduling job consists of an event *trigger* (stereotyped as «SATrigger») that models how often the scheduling job is to be executed. The computational part of the scheduling job is represented by a *response* (a sequence of action-executions, where each action is stereotyped as «SAAction»). Figure 12-3 shows the conceptual model for schedulability analysis in the SPT profile and depicts the relationships between these entities. Interaction diagrams (stereotyped as «SASituation») are used to show the behavior of a scheduling job. Figure 12-4 shows the modeling of an end-to-end behavior as an extended sequence diagram showing the triggers and actions, and their properties (expressed as tagged-values in the SPT profile).

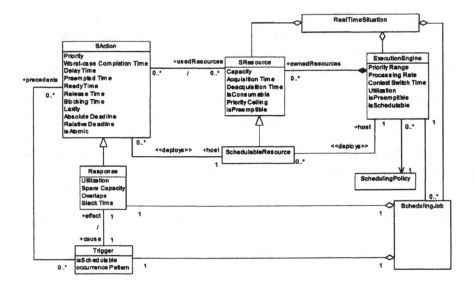

Figure 12-3. The Conceptual Model for Schedulability Analysis (from [1])

1.2   The physical architecture

If the logical architecture primarily focuses on functional constraints, the *physical architecture level* is where physical concurrency and schedulability requirements are expressed. At this level, the units of computation are the processes or threads (or in general, tasks), executing concurrently in response to environment stimuli or prompted by an internal clock. Threads cooperate by exchanging data and synchronization or activation signals and contend for use of the execution resource(s) (the processor) as well as for the other resources in the system. The physical architecture level is also the place where the concurrent entities are mapped onto target hardware. This activity entails the selection of an appropriate scheduling policy (for example, offered by a real-time operating system), which must be clearly supported by techniques for analyzing schedulability.

The conceptual model of OMG Profile SPT uses the concepts of execution engine, scheduling policy, resources, and schedulable resources to model the elements of a physical architecture. An execution engine models the processing resource and has a scheduling policy that determines how the tasks will be scheduled.

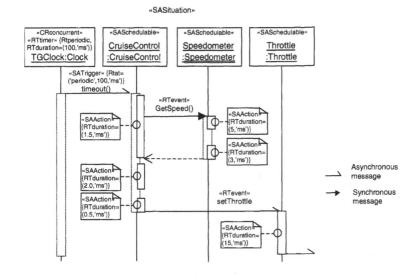

Figure 12-4. A sample sequence diagram defining a real-time transaction

The SPT profile uses the term resource (stereotype «SAResource») to model mutex-protected resources. It also introduces the concept of a schedulable resource (stereotype «SASchedulable») to model tasks. The concurrency model defined by the SPT allows for inter-object concurrency but explicitly prohibits intra-object concurrency (by defining the mutex-protected stereotype «SAResource» as the parent class for the «SASchedulable» scheduling entities). In other words, operations within a task-object are atomic. This allows programming the object without needing to worry about protecting the object attributes from concurrent access. This assumption is quite common as it may be found in many other real-time object-oriented methodologies, such as ROOM [6] and HRT-HOOD [7].

The mapping from a logical model to the elements in the physical architecture is done in UML through the concept of realization or deployment. In practice, this may be accomplished by directly using elements of the physical architecture (e.g., schedulable resources and shared resources) in the logical model.

The schedulability analysis model concepts of schedulable resources («SASchedulable») and resources («SAResource») have straightforward mapping to most standard operating environments including POSIX, OSEK, Real-Time Specification for Java (RTSJ) and Ada.

Before the advent of the OMG profile PST, many proposals for UML-based metamodels, like MAST [5] had defined their own set of stereotypes representing abstract components for modeling the hardware (computers, networks, devices, timers, etc.) and software (threads, process, servers, drivers) resources that constitute the platform of the system

The standard UML model, supplemented by the schedulability analysis model from the SPT profile, should hopefully provide a new unified standard for qualitative and quantitative modeling of realtime systems behavior. However, the current version still lacks enough expressive power for describing all the OS-level components and the hardware components involved in this level.

2.   INTRODUCTION TO SCHEDULABILITY ANALYSIS

The need for scheduling arises in all those cases where the number of logical or physical resources is not sufficient to support the concurrent execution of all the threads. In single processor systems, which are the target of our discussion, a scheduler is necessary to assign the execution engine (the CPU) to threads (tasks). The main objective of real-time scheduling policies is to formally guarantee the timing constraints (deadlines) on the system response to external events. This step implies not only the selection of a policy for assigning the parameters affecting scheduling and resource usage (such as the priority by which threads are executed), but also an analysis methodology for validating the timing constraints by means of mathematical reasoning.

2.1   Rate Monotonic Analysis

Rate Monotonic Analysis (RMA) [8, 9] is by far the most common real-time scheduling and analysis methodology. It provides a very simple procedure for assigning static priorities to a set of *independent periodic tasks* together with a formula for checking schedulability against deadlines. The RMA rule for assigning priorities to tasks is the following:

Assign the higher priority to the task having the higher rate

Rate Monotonic (the name means that the priority ordering is a monotonic function of the rate of execution) is optimal among all the policies based on static priorities. Optimality in this case means that if a task set cannot be scheduled using the RMA algorithm, it cannot be scheduled using any other fixed-priority algorithm.

If the priority assignment rule is simple, so is the formula for checking the schedulability of any task set. Suppose the system consists of a set $\Gamma=\{\tau_1, \tau_2, \dots ,\tau_n\}$ of real time tasks to be executed on a processor. A task τ_i is an infinite sequence of periodic jobs (or instances). Each task is characterized by a worst case execution time C_i, a period θ_i, a relative deadline d_i and a priority π_i. Each job instance is released at time $r_{i,j} = r_{i,j-1} + \theta_i$. RM assumes that the relative deadline of a task is equal to its period ($d_i=\theta_i$).

The schedulability analysis is based on the concept of *processor utilization*. Given a set of periodic tasks the utilization demand of task τ_i is defined as

$$U_i = \frac{C_i}{\theta_i}$$

and the processor utilization is the sum of the utilization demands of all tasks.

$$U = \sum_{i=1,n} \frac{C_i}{\theta_i} \tag{1}$$

Given a scheduling algorithm and a task set, the upper bound U_{lub} on the processor utilization is the maximum U that can be possibly achieved without violating the deadline constraints. In order for a task set to be schedulable under Rate Monotonic Analysis, it suffices that the processor utilization is lower than the bound $U_{lub} = n(2^{(1/n)} - 1)$ where n is the number of tasks in the system. U_{lub} decreases as n increases, eventually approaching the limit value of $ln(2) = 0.693$. This well-known limit value tells that, if the RMA policy is used and the processor utilization is below 69%, than any task set is schedulable.

The utilization-based schedulability check only gives a sufficient condition. If the set is not schedulable a sufficient and necessary condition on RMA needs to be evaluated. This (more complex) kind of analysis is based on the concepts of *critical condition* and of *busy period*. Given a schedulability algorithm the critical condition is the worst case scenario. If the set of tasks is schedulable in the critical condition, then it is schedulable under all circumstances. For RMA the critical condition happens when all tasks are released at the same time instant ($t=0$). A busy period (of level π) is a continuous time interval when the processor is busy executing tasks (of priority higher than or equal to π). By analyzing the busy period originating at the time $t=0$ it is possible to derive the *worst case completion time* W_i («SAWorstCase» according to the SPT terminology) for task τ_i. If the task can be proven to always complete before or at the deadline ($W_i \leq D_i$) then it can be guaranteed to be schedulable under all circumstances.

W_i can be computed by adding up the computation time of the task to the *Interference time,* that is the time used by all tasks having a priority higher than or equal to π_i. The interference time can be computed by considering that each task τ_j with a priority $\pi_j \geq \pi_i$ executes W_i/θ_j times in the π_i-level busy period W_i and contributes with a term

$$I_i = \left\lceil \frac{W_i}{\theta_j} \right\rceil C_j$$

Hence, the formula for computing W_i is an iterative formula of the form

$$W_i = C_i + \sum_{\forall j \in hp(i)} \left\lceil \frac{W_i}{\theta_j} \right\rceil C_j \qquad (2)$$

where $hp(i)$ are the indices of those tasks having a priority higher than or equal to π_i. The formula can be solved by letting $W_{i(0)} = C_i$ and iterating the computation for the generic term $W_{i(k)}$

$$W_{k+1} = C_i + \sum_{\forall j \in hp(i)} \left\lceil \frac{W_k}{\theta_j} \right\rceil C_j$$

until a stable point $W_{i(k+1)} = W_{i(k)}$ is found or until the value of $W_{i(k+1)}$ exceeds the deadline d_i proving the task is not schedulable.

RMA only applies to sets of independent periodic tasks where deadlines are equal to the periods. If at least one of the previous conditions is not met, then the policy is not optimal and the schedulability analysis does not apply. In order to cope with this problem, the original model has evolved and it has been extended with results that allow the handling of aperiodic activation events (spawning sporadic tasks) or resources shared in an exclusive way. A sporadic task is a task activated by an event characterized by a minimum interarrival time θ_i (the same notation for task periods is used.)

There is not enough space here for discussing sporadic tasks and the server mechanisms that are used to perform their guarantee in the context of the sufficient schedulability formula (1) (please refer to [10] or [11]). For the purpose of this tutorial, it suffices to say that the sufficient and necessary schedulability check (2) can still be used, provided the interarrival time is used in place of the period.

When the relative deadline is different from the period, a variation of RMA called *Deadline Monotonic Analysis* can be used. The priority assignment rule of Deadline Monotonic Analysis simply states that higher priorities must be assigned to tasks having shorter relative deadlines. If deadlines are shorter than periods, the guarantee formulas (1) and (2) can still be used provided that in (1) d_i is used in place of θ_i. If, on the other hand, deadlines are arbitrary (and possibly larger than periods or the minimum interarrival times) a more complex kind of analysis is needed [12, 13]. We'll go back to this case after discussing the shared resource case.

2.2 Shared resources and priority inversion

Rate Monotonic scheduling was developed starting from a very simple model where all tasks are periodic and independent. In reality, many tasks require access to shared resources (apart from the processor), that can only be used in an exclusive way. Furthermore, in most applications, tasks need to be synchronized. The general-purpose semaphore mechanism is not adequate for real-time systems since it introduces possibly unbounded blocking times (and even deadlocks, if not prevented by some additional mechanism). The need for avoiding unbounded blocking times and the ensuing priority inversion led to the development of algorithms for controlling the use of shared resources in an exclusive way. Among these algorithms, the Priority Inheritance algorithm and the Priority Ceiling Protocol are the most common.

Suppose tasks are allowed to access mutually exclusive resources through critical sections. Let $R=\{\rho^1, \dots, \rho^p\}$ be the set of shared resources («SAResource»). The k-th critical section (operation) of task τ_i on resource ρ^j is denoted by χ^j_{ik} and its maximum duration (of the corresponding call action) is denoted by ω^j_{ik}.

The first, unavoidable consequence of mutex protected (shared) resources is priority inversion by direct blocking. Figure 12-5 shows an example of priority inversion (top half). Suppose a low priority task τ_2 is released at time $t=0$ and at time $t=10$ locks a shared resource R1. At time $t=20$ the high priority task τ_1 is activated. τ_1 preempts τ_2 and executes for 10 time units before trying to lock resource R1. Since the lock is already held by τ_2, τ_1 suspends and waits until τ_2 releases the resource (at time $t=40$). The usage of R1 results in Task τ_2 being executed in place of τ_1 for 10 time units inverting the priority order. Task τ_1 is said to experience *direct priority inversion*, which is an unavoidable consequence of sharing resources in exclusive mode.

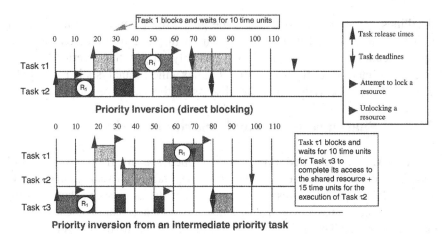

Figure 12-5. Direct blocking and push-through blocking

The purpose of a good scheduling and resource management algorithm is not to avoid priority inversion but rather to bound the worst case blocking time that Task τ_1 (or, in general, any high priority task) must experience. Direct priority inversion is not the only kind of priority inversion that can possibly happen in a real-time system. The *Priority Inheritance* algorithm (PI for short) was devised to avoid the additional blocking from intermediate priority tasks, as represented in the bottom half of figure 12-5. In this second example, high priority task τ_1 blocks when trying to lock the shared resource held by the low priority τ_3. τ_1 not only waits for τ_3 to finish using the resource (direct priority inversion) but also adds to it the time it takes to execute any middle priority task (τ_2) arriving while τ_3 is inside its critical section (and preempting it). The PI solution consists of letting the low priority task inherit the highest priority among all tasks that are waiting on the resources it holds. In the example in this figure, this means raising the priority of τ_3 to π_1 while holding the lock on the resource, thereby preventing τ_2 from executing. This allows the reduction of the blocking time for τ_1 but forces τ_2 to wait for a lower priority task executing inside a critical section it does not require access to (*push-through blocking*). Even if the OMG profile includes Priority Inheritance among the algorithms of choice, its use in the context of hard real-time systems is strongly questionable since the worst case blocking time it guarantees is way higher than the worst case blocking time that can be possibly guaranteed (at no additional implementation costs) [14] by using the Priority Ceiling algorithm.

The priority ceiling policy (PCP) [15] improves priority inheritance by further restricting the access to shared resources and by allowing a better estimate of the worst case blocking time for high priority tasks. Each resource is associated a static ceiling $\Omega(\rho^j)$ defined as the maximum priority among all the tasks that may lock it: $\Omega(\rho^j) = \max_k\{\pi_k : \tau_k \text{ uses } \rho^i\}$. Furthermore, a dynamic system ceiling is defined as the highest ceiling among the currently locked semaphores. The resource locking rule is the following: a task is allowed to lock a shared resource only if its priority is greater than the dynamic system ceiling. The priority of a task executing a critical section can be raised to the highest priority among the tasks blocked on it (standard PCP) or it can be raised to the ceiling of the mutex resource (immediate PCP).

PCP provably permits a task τ_i to be blocked by lower priority tasks only once and for only one critical section executed with a ceiling priority higher than or equal to π_i. Hence, the blocking factor B_i is the worst case length of any critical section used by tasks having a priority lower than τ_i and accessing a semaphore with a ceiling higher than or equal to π_i.

If the priority ceiling protocol is used, then the guarantee formulas can still be used provided a factor depending on B_i, which is the worst case blocking time for the task, is added to the utilization or the busy period time. The sufficient condition formula can now be evaluated for all tasks as follows

$$\forall i = 1..n, \sum_{j=1,i-1} \frac{C_j}{\theta_j} + \frac{C_i}{\theta_i} + \frac{B_i}{\theta_i} \le U_{\text{lub}}(i)$$

and the sufficient and necessary schedulability check (evaluation of the worst case completion time) is now the following

$$W_{k+1} = C_i + \sum_{\forall j \in hp(i)} \left\lceil \frac{W_k}{\theta_j} \right\rceil C_j + B_i$$

In both cases $B_i = \max\{\omega_{l,m}^r : l \in lp(i) \wedge \Omega(\rho_r) \ge \pi_i\}$ where $lp(i)$ are the indices of those tasks having a priority lower than π_i.

Putting it all together

The last case in our introduction to schedulability analysis features periodic and sporadic tasks with arbitrary deadlines sharing resources in exclusive mode. Assume a preemptive scheduling where priorities are assigned statically and resources are protected by PCP semaphores.

In the case of *arbitrary deadlines* multiple instances of the same task may be scheduled simultaneously and there is no guarantee that the worst case response time happens on the first task instance after the critical instant ($t=0$) but we need to consider all instances inside the π_i-level busy period starting in t=0 (alternatively, until we find an instance that has a worst case response time lower than the interarrival time of the corresponding task.) If m is the number of instances inside the πi-level busy period, the worst-case response time is the maximum value found for each $q=1..m$:

$$W_i = \max_{q\in[1,...,m]} \{W_{i,q}\} \tag{3}$$

The term $W_{i,q}$ of the q-th instance of τ_i is given by its worst case completion (or finishing) time minus the ready time (the time instant when instance q is released):

$$W_{i,q}=F_{i,q}-r_{i,q}. \tag{4}$$

$F_{i,q}$ can be computed by dividing the π_i-level busy period in two parts: the time interval from the critical instant ($t=0$) to the time instant when the q-th instance of τ_i starts executing, $S_{i,q}$, and the time interval from $S_{i,q}$ to $F_{i,q}$. The worst case start time $S_{i,q}$ is given by the sum of a blocking term B_i, the interference from the (q-1) previous instances of τ_i and the interference from the instances of all tasks with a priority higher than τ_i.

$$S_{i,q} = B_i + (q-1)C_i + \sum_{j\in hp(i)} \left(1+\left\lfloor \frac{S_{i,q}}{\theta_j} \right\rfloor\right)C_j$$

Once $S_{i,q}$ is computed, it is possible to compute the worst case (absolute) finish time $F_{i,q}$ by adding the computation time of the q-th instance of τ_i and the interference from the higher priority instances of the other tasks in the time interval [$F_{i,q} - S_{i,q}$]

$$F_{i,q} = S_{i,q} + C_i + \sum_{j\in hp(i)} \left(\left\lceil \frac{F_{i,q}}{\theta_j} \right\rceil - \left(1+\left\lfloor \frac{S_{i,q}}{\theta_j} \right\rfloor\right)\right)C_j$$

Once $F_{i,q}$ is computed, the worst case response time is derived by applying (4) and (3) and schedulability against the deadline d_i can be easily checked.

3. SCHEDULABILITY ANALYSIS OF OO DESIGNS USING RMA: TASK CENTRIC DESIGN

RMA is the method of choice for analyzing hard real-time UML models in the OMG SPT as well as in other design methodologies [7] and texts [16]. Unfortunately, even if it is simple and effective in some contexts, this approach has many limitations.

Consider the example of Figure 12-6 (adapted from the example in [1].) The behavior of each task is relatively simple and consists of a combination of reading input signals, performing computation and producing output signals (Figure 12-6). Each task is logically concurrent, it is activated periodically, and performs a single activity. This design paradigm is called *task centric design*.

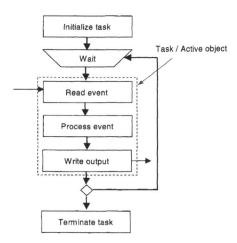

Figure 12-6. In task-centric design, each task performs a single activity

Rate Monotonic Analysis can be applied without effort and the analysis fits very well the logical layer/engineering layer QoS negotiation pattern.

In our sample case only three concurrent «SASchedulable» objects are defined: TelemetryDisplayer (τ_1), TelemetryGatherer (τ_2), and TelemetryProcessor (τ_3). They all access the shared «SAResource» object RawDataStorage by means of the call action gatherData() with a worst case execution time of 2 ms.

The sufficient schedulability test fails for task τ_3 since the result is:

for τ_1: $U_1 - B_1 \approx 0.2083 - 0.033 \approx 0.2413 < 1 = U_{lub}\,(n = 1)$

for τ_2: $U_1 - U_2 - B_2 = 0.2083 - 0.335 - 0.02 \approx 0.5453 < 0.828 = U_{lub}\,(n = 2)$

for τ_3: $\displaystyle\sum_{i=1..3} U_i = 0.2083 + 0.335 + 0.2425 \approx 0.7858 > 0.7798 = U_{lub}\,(n = 3)$

but the exact schedulability analysis formula for RMA returns the following worst case completion times.

$W_1 = 14.5$ ms; $W_2 = 58$ ms; $W3 = 153.0$ ms.

Since all the W_i are lower than the corresponding deadlines, the tasks are schedulable.

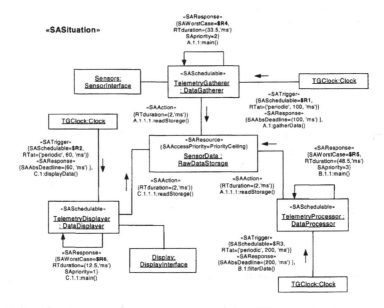

Figure 12-7. A sample collaboration instance representing a situation suitable for Rate Monotonic analysis (adapted from the OMG profile document).

If we see schedulability analysis in the context of the QoS matching rule, our simple RM analysis case corresponds to the general pattern in Figure 12-7 (shared resources are omitted for clarity but they could easily be added). The QoS demand of each thread results in a demand for utilization U_i from the operating system/scheduling policy and a demand for a target worst case computation time C_i from the hardware. The QoS offer from the RM scheduling policy is the guaranteed least upper bound on the utilization U_{lub} and the QoS matching rule easily follows. On the hardware side things are more complicated. Let's say that, as a first order approximation, the QoS offer of the hardware can be modeled as the instruction set table of the CPU with the clock cycle count for each instruction (more sophisticated as well as less sophisticated models are possible) and the matching rule for our C_i demand consists of the static analysis of the thread worst case execution time or, simply, of experimentally measuring the worst case execution times.

Unfortunately, as our example shows, necessary and sufficient (exact) RMA analysis is sometimes necessary to verify the schedulability of the system. Exact RMA analysis makes it very difficult to identify what could be the QoS offer of the schedulability method (since the guaranteed maximum U_{lub} does not apply).

3.1   Single event synchronization

RMA is simple and effective, but assumes a quite restrictive tasking model. It can only be applied (as is) to design models where each thread (periodic or sporadic) handles a single event and where active objects cooperate only by means of pure asynchronous messages, possibly implemented by means of memory mailboxes, a kind of protected (shared resource) object.

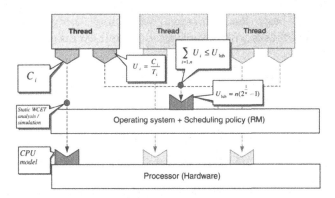

Figure 12-8. QoS matching for our example.

This is quite unlike the structure of many UML design models, where each action is part of multiple end-to-end computations and timing constraints. Abstracting from details, most OO models of real-time systems consist of a possibly complex network of cooperating active objects, implementing state machines and exchanging asynchronous messages. Furthermore, from a performance perspective (especially in control-dominated applications) putting each active object in a single task may lead to excessive scheduling overhead (context switching). The limitations in using Rate Monotonic Analysis for object oriented methods (please refer also to the HRT-HOOD design rules [7] or the ADA Ravenscar profile [17, 18]) prompted an effort for a more comprehensive approach to scheduling of UML models.

The first option is a straightforward extension of the single-task model to the so-called *linear model*, where each task is activated by the arrival of a single event or message, possibly sent by another (single) task. In this case, the only possible transactions are pipelines of tasks, possibly distributed among different processors. The activation rate of internal tasks cannot be periodic, due to precedence and schedulability constraints, but advanced schedulability analysis techniques such as Holistic analysis [19] or Offset based scheduling [20] allow handling the case of jittery task activations in the context of fixed-priority scheduling. These technique provide an evaluation of the worst case completion times of activities (tasks) with some (limited) pessimism.

3.2   Multiple-event synchronization

The *linear model* does not allow complex interactions among the responses to different event sequences. The authors of [21] provided an extension to the base Rate Monotonic scheduling theory that allows the synchronization of tasks with the arrival of multiple events or messages.

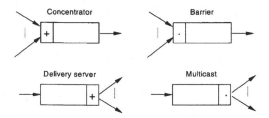

Figure 12-9. Additional action classes for the multiple-event model in [20].

The analysis allows a *multiple event model* in which an action can not only be a linear action with a single input and a single output (according to the model in Figure 12-6), but possibly belongs to one of the types of Figure 12-9.

The *multiple event model* is representative of a larger number of systems provided that there is a one-to-one correspondence between actions and tasks. The schedulability analysis techniques that apply are those found for the linear model. In fact, the authors proved how a large subset of all possible *multiple event* models could be transformed into an equivalent linear model (for a list of the restrictions that apply see [21]). Hence, schedulability analysis is possible, although at the price of some pessimism in the evaluation of the worst case completion times of all actions.

To summarize, and to clarify the cross dependencies that exist among scheduling policies, physical and logical architecture meta models, the following table represents the applicability context for the scheduling and resource management policies defined in the previous sections (in the context of fixed priority scheduling schemes).

Scheduling policy	HW architecture requirements	Logical architecture requirements	Mapping restrictions
Classic Rate Monotonic	monoprocessor	Single task transactions d = θ	
Deadline Monotonic	monoprocessor	Single task transactions d ≤ θ	
Generalized response time	monoprocessor	Single task transactions d ≥ θ	
Holistic analysis	multiprocessor	Linear transactions	
Offset based analysis	multiprocessor	Linear transactions	
Multiple-Event analysis	multiprocessor	Multiple event transactions, no event cycles	
Additional resource management policy			
Priority Inheritance		Any of the above + protected objects	Protected objects only used by threads running on the same cpu
Priority Ceiling		Any of the above + protected objects	Protected objects only used by threads running on the same cpu

Table 12-1. Dependencies among scheduling policies, hardware and logical meta models.

4.   EVENT CENTRIC DESIGN

In the last of a series of papers [22, 23, 4], Saksena, Karvelas and Wang present an integrated methodology that allows dealing with more general OO models where multiple events can be provided as input to a single thread. According to their model, each thread has an incoming queue of events possibly representing real-time transactions and the associated timing constraints (Figure 12-10). Consequently, scheduling priority (usually a measure of time urgency or criticalness) is attached to events rather than threads. This design and analysis paradigm is called *event centric design*. Each event has an associated priority (for example, deadline monotonic priority assignment can be used.) Event queues are ordered by priority (i.e. threads process events based on their priority) and threads inherit the priority of the events they are currently processing. This model entails a two-level scheduling: the events enqueued as input to a thread need to be scheduled to find their processing order. At system level, the threads are scheduled by the underlying real-time operating system (a preemptive priority-based scheduler is assumed).

Schedulability analysis of the general case is derived from the analysis methodology for generic deadlines, only it is much harder. This chapter provides an introduction to the reasoning and the formulas that can be used to test a more general UML model for schedulability. The overview skips many details (the interested reader should refer to [4]), nonetheless, it requires a few additional definitions and it features formulas that may (in some cases) look quite elaborate.

Definitions

Formally, let $\mathcal{E} = \{E_1, E_2, ..., E_n, E_{n+1}, ..., E_m\}$ be the set of all events in the system, where $E_1, E_2, ... E_n$ denote external (asynchronous) events, and the remaining internal ones. Each external event E_i may originate a transaction T_i. Associated with each event E_i is an action A_i. All events and actions are part of a transaction. Action A^T and event E^T belong to transaction T. Each action A_i is characterized as either asynchronously triggered or synchronously triggered and executes within the context of an active object $O(A_i)$. A_i is also characterized by a priority π_i, which is the same as the priority of its triggering event E_i.

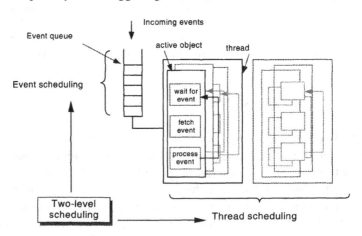

Figure 12-10. Two-level scheduling in the general case.

Each action A_i is characterized by a computation time $C(A_i)$ (abbreviated as C_i). $\Theta(A_k)$ denotes the synchronous set of A_k, that is the set of actions that can be built starting from action A_k and adding all actions that are called synchronously from it. $C(\Theta(A_k))$ is the sum of the execution times of all the actions in $\Theta(A_k)$. Each external event stream E_i is characterized by a function $\Psi_i(t)$ that gives the maximum number of event arrivals in any interval $[x, x+t)$, where the interval is closed at the left, and open at the right. $\Psi^+_i(t)$ indicates the maximum number of event arrivals in any right-closed interval $[x, x+t]$.

In [4] many implementation options are discussed, namely, single thread implementation, multithread implementation with fixed priority or dynamic priority multithreaded implementation and schedulability analysis is provided or at least discussed for each of these models. This chapter contains a short summary of the main results. The details of the schedulability analysis as well as its application to a sample case are omitted for lack of space but can easily be found in the original reference.

4.1 Schedulability analysis approach

Schedulability analysis of the general model is carried out by computing response times of actions. The response time of an action A^T_i is derived relative to the arrival of the external event that triggers the transaction T. The analysis is based on the standard concepts of critical instant and busy-period for task instances with generic deadlines (adapted to the transaction model.)

The analysis of the worst case response time of A^T_i requires computing the response times of all the instances of A^T_i inside the busy period. If $r^T_{i,q}$ is the release time of the instance q of the external event E^T_i, starting from the critical instant $t=0$ (assuming the events arrive at the maximum rate) we need to compute $S^T_{i,q}$, the worst case start time for an instance q of A^T_i (i.e., when the instance q of the action gets the cpu for the first time) and its worst-case finishing time $F^T_{i,q}$.

The worst-case response time of action A^T_i is given by:

$$W_i^T = \max_{q \in [1,\ldots,m]} \{ F_{i,q}^T - r_{i,q}^T \}$$

If W^T_i is lower than the deadline of A^T_i, then the action is schedulable (Figure 12-11).

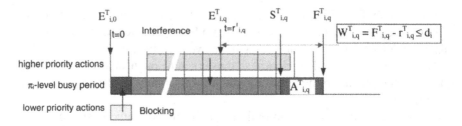

Figure 12-11. Computing the worst-case response time for $A^T_{i,q}$.

In computing the busy period we need to evaluate all the factors that contribute to it: the interference factor (from processing all the events with higher priority) the computation time of the action A^T_i itself and the blocking factor (from processing events with a priority lower than A^T_i). The first term can be further specialized in an interference factor from actions belonging to the same transaction T and interference from actions belonging to transactions other than T.

4.2   Single thread implementation

In a single thread implementation, the only application thread processes pending events in priority order. Since there is only one thread, there is only one level of scheduling. Actions inherit their priorities from the priorities of the triggering event. Also, a synchronously triggered action inherits its priority from its caller.

Blocking

Since intra-task preemption is not allowed, in single threaded implementations, any synchronous set that starts executing must be completed with no interruption. Hence, the worst case blocking time of an action is bound by the longest synchronous set of any lower priority action that started prior to *t*=0.

$$B(A_i) = \max_k \{C(\mathsf{E}(A_k)) :: \pi_i > \pi_k\}$$

Interference

Suppose, for now that action A^T_i is activated asynchronously (please refer to [4] for the case of synchronous activation) and let $A^T_i \xrightarrow{path} A^T_l$ denote the condition for which there exists a path of (call or signal) events and actions that makes A^T_1 causally dependent on A^T_i. In this case, the interference from $t=0$ to $t=S_{i,q}$ can be computed as the sum of the interference term from other transactions and the interference from actions in the same transaction. For each transaction $T' \neq T$ the highest arrival rate of external events is assumed and the sum of the computation times of all actions $A^{T'}_1 \in T'$ with a priority higher than π_i is considered.

$$I^{T' \neq T}(A^T_i) = \sum_{T' \neq T} [\Psi^+_{T'}(S) \cdot \sum_l (C^{T'}_l :: \pi_l \geq \pi_i)]$$

As for transaction T, we need to consider the term from all the higher priority actions in the previous $q-1$ instances and the interference from the actions belonging to the instances from $q+1$ to the last one that can be possibly activated before $S_{i,q}$. For all instances after q, only the higher priority actions that are not successors of $A_{i,q}$ contribute to the interference.

$$I^T(A^T_i) = (q-1) \cdot \sum_l (C^T_l :: \pi_l \geq \pi_i)$$
$$+ (\Psi^+_T(S) - (q-1)) \cdot \sum_l (C^T_l :: \neg(A^T_i \xrightarrow{path} A^T_l) \wedge \pi_l \geq \pi_i)$$

Once the blocking and the interference factors are known, the worst case start time can be computed with the iterative formula

$$S_{i,q} = \min S :: S = B(A_i) + I^{T' \neq T}(A^T_i) + I^T(A^T_i)$$

The analysis is now almost complete. Once A^T_i starts executing, no other action can interrupt it other than any synchronous calls that A^T_i makes. Consequently, the worst-case finish time for instance q of A^T_i is

$$F^T_i = S^T_{i,q} + C(\Theta(A^T_i))$$

and schedulability can be guaranteed provided

$$W^T_i = \max_{q \in [1,...,m]} \{F^T_{i,q} - r^T_{i,q}\} \leq d_i \qquad (5)$$

4.3 Multi-thread implementation: dynamic thread priorities

In multi-threaded implementations the run-to-completion semantics makes threads behave as special mutual exclusion (mutex) resources. This insight allows using threads and threading priorities in a way that facilitates response time analysis.

If threads behave as mutexes, then it makes sense to associate with each thread a ceiling priority as the priority at which the highest priority event is served. As prescribed by PI or PCP, threads inherit the priority of the highest priority event in their waiting queue. As in the Priority Ceiling algorithm, this allows us to bound priority inversion. In this case, the worst case blocking time is restricted to the processing of a lower priority event. Furthermore, before processing an event, a thread locks the active object within which the event is to be processed (this is necessary when multiple threads may handle events destined to the same object), hence a ceiling priority and a priority inheritance rule must be defined for active objects as well as for threads.

The ceiling priorities of an object and a thread are defined as follows:

$$\Omega(O_i) = \max_k \{ \pi(A_k) :: O(A_k) = O_i \}$$
$$\Omega(\Gamma_i) = \max_k \{ \pi(A_k) :: \Gamma(A_k) = \Gamma_i \}$$

where O and Γ represent the set of objects and threads respectively. The preemption threshold of an action is defined as the maximum of the two ceiling values.

$$\gamma(A_i) = \max(\Omega(O(A_i)), \Omega(\Gamma(A_i)))$$

The preemption threshold is the priority that is dynamically assigned to actions when executing in the context of a thread and/or active object. In order for another action A_j to preempt A_i it must true that $\pi_j > \gamma_i$ (hence the name preemption threshold.)

In this case, the *blocking time* is restricted to the worst-case synchronous set of actions originating from A_k that started prior to $t=0$ and have a priority lower than π_i but a preemption threshold $\gamma_k \geq \pi_i$ (A_i cannot preempt them.)

$$B(A_i) = \max_k \{ C(\Theta(A_k)) :: \gamma_k \geq \pi_i > \pi_k \}$$

The computation of the worst case start time $S_{i,q}$ for the q-th instance of action A^T_i, is performed exactly the same as in the single-threaded case except for the difference in $B(A_i)$.

The main difference with the single-threaded case is in the evaluation of the worst case time elapsed between the start $S^T_{i,q}$ of A^T_i and its completion time $F^T_{i,q}$. In addition to the term $C(\Theta(A_i))$ we need to consider the interference from actions mapped to higher priority threads. This interference is given by all the actions arriving in the time interval $(S_{i,q}, F_{i,q})$ and having a priority higher than the preemption threshold of A_i. The interfering actions must also be executed in a different thread and in a different object (otherwise, they would not preempt A_i). This term can be recursively computed by using the following formulas (please refer to [4] for further details)

$$\sum_{k \neq i} (\Psi_k(F) - \Psi_k^+(S_{i,q}^T))L_k(A_i^T)$$
$$+ (\Psi_i(F) - \Psi_i^+(S_{i,q}^T))L_i(A_i^T)$$

where

$$L_k(A_i^T) = L(A_i^T, A_k^k)$$
$$L(A_i^T, A_j^k) = \begin{cases} 0 & if\,(\Gamma(A_j^k) = \Gamma(A_i^T)) \vee (O(A_j^k) = O(A_i^T)) \vee (\pi_j < \gamma_i)) \\ C(\Theta(A_j^k)) + \sum_{g::A_j^k \rightarrow A_g^k} L(A_i^T, A_g^k) & else \end{cases}$$

As in the previous case, once the worst case finishing time $F_{i,q}$ is computed by adding the blocking time, the interference factors and the computation time of the action itself, the action can be checked for schedulability by applying (5).

4.4 Multi-thread implementation: problems with static thread priorities

Assigning static priorities to threads is tempting (static priority assignment is supported by most RTOSes) and quite a common choice (Rational Rose RT and other tools use this method). Unfortunately, when threads are required to handle multiple events it is not clear what priority should be assigned to them. A good rule of thumb is to assign a thread a priority that is the maximum among all the events that are input to it. Unfortunately, in this case the computation of the worst case response time is very hard due to the two level scheduling and the difficulty of constructing an appropriate critical instant. The problem in this case is multiple priority inversion that arises from all the lower priority events handled by a higher priority thread. Still, however, it may be perfectly acceptable to use static thread priorities in specific situations where it is easy to estimate the amount of priority inversion.

5.   AUTOMATED SYNTHESIS

Real-time systems designers can clearly benefit from the techniques for schedulability analysis that have been presented in this chapter, but the degrees of freedom that these algorithms leave to the designer are simply too many. What is truly required is a set of design rules, or even better an automatic synthesis procedure that helps in the construction of a logical design and in the mapping of the logical entities to the physical architecture.

The problem of synthesizing a schedulable implementation is actually a complex combinatorial optimization problem. In [23] the authors propose an automatic procedure for synthesizing the three main degrees of freedom in a real-time UML design subject to schedulability analysis:
–   the priorities of events;
–   the number of tasks;
–   a mapping of events to tasks.

The synthesis procedure uses a heuristic strategy based on a decomposition approach, where priorities to events/actions are assigned in a first stage and mapping is performed in a separate stage.

6.   OTHER APPROACHES

The methods presented in this chapter represent a quick overview ranging from the very fundamental algorithms for schedulability analysis to a quite complex and general model that highlights most of the problems and some of the solutions available in the context of UML models. Other works have been performed in the context of schedulability analysis of object-oriented models. Traditional real-time scheduling theory results have been applied in [7, 16, 24]. In other cases, the analysis of UML models is made possible by restricting the semantics of the analyzable models (e.g., the treatment of event sequences [25, 26]).

As for the closely related topic of schedulability analysis of entity-based models, it is worth recalling the work that has been done in the context of the POLIS and Metropolis projects [27, 28]. In [29, 3] a priority assignment algorithm is presented that prevents dropping real-time events in networks of active objects. More recently, a general methodology for the worst case analysis of systems with discrete observable systems has been proposed [30]. Even if, in this case, the analysis method is quite different from the deadline-based model of conventional real-time research, the proposed methodology allows one to evaluate a bound on the response time of actions given the worst case arrival rates of external events.

7. CONCLUSIONS

This chapter discusses the issues of using UML for schedulability and time analysis of real-time systems.

Schedulability analysis techniques provide algorithms, methods and tools for verification of timing properties and can guide the deployment of logical architecture to a physical architecture by adding (limited) support for the synthesis of the architecture design levels. The recent development of a specialized UML profile for schedulability performance and time (SPT) introduces new stereotypes to represent common (hard) real-time abstractions and allows the use of timing analysis in the context of UML models.

To this purpose, background knowledge on fundamental real-time schedulability results is not sufficient, unless it is supplemented by an understanding of how the logical architecture meta-model, physical architecture meta-model, and the analysis techniques are all tied to each other. For example, the use of standard RMA analysis techniques requires fixed priority tasks and protected objects to be the core abstractions in the physical architecture meta-model. This, in turn, limits what is allowed at the logical level (e.g., no direct communication between active objects).

Schedulability analysis can today provide response time (deadline) analysis and optimal priority assignment. Ultimately, we foresee its use for the automated synthesis of architecture-level entities and parameters, embodied in a variety of tools and methods that will seamlessly allow analysis, develop (or assist) a deployment mapping and generate code based on the mapping

REFERENCES

[1] *UML Profile for Schedulability, Performance and Time Specification*. OMG Adopted Specification, July, 1, 2002, http://www.omg.org

[2] A. Burns. *Preemptive Priority Based Scheduling: An Appropriate Engineering Approach*. Advances in RealTime Systems, pages 225-248, S.H.Son, Prentice Hall, 1994.

[3] M. Di Natale, A. L. Sangiovanni-Vincentelli, F. Balarin. "Task scheduling with RT constraints" *Proceedings of the DAC Conference 2000*. Los Angeles. 483-488.

[4] M. Saksena and P. Karvelas. "Designing for Schedulability: Integrating Schedulability Analysis with Object-Oriented Design" *Proceedings of the Euromicro Conference on Real-Time Systems*, Stockholm, June 2000.

[5] J.L. Medina, M. González Harbour, and J.M. Drake. "MAST Real-Time View: A Graphic UML Tool for Modeling Object-Oriented Real-Time Systems", *Proceedings of the 22nd IEEE Real-Time Systems Symposium (RTSS 2001)*, London, UK, IEEE Computer Society Press, pp. 245-256, December 2001.

[6] B. Selic, G. Gullekson, and P. T. Ward. *Real-Time Object-Oriented Modeling.* John Wiley and Sons, 1994.

[7] A. Burns and A. J. Wellings. "HRT-HOOD: A Design Method for Hard Real-Time" *Journal of Real-Time Systems,* 6(1):73–114, 1994.

[8] M.H.Klein and others. *A Practitioner's Handbook for Real-Time Analysis: Guide to Rate Monotonic Analysis for Real-Time Systems.* Kluwer Academic Publishers, Hingham, MA, 1993.

[9] C. Liu and J. Layland. "Scheduling algorithm for multiprogramming in a hard real-time environment" *Journal of the ACM,* 20(1):46–61, January 1973.

[10] G. Buttazzo: *Hard Real-Time Computing Systems: Predictable Scheduling Algorithms and Applications,* Kluwer Academic Publishers, Boston, 1997.

[11] B. Sprunt. *Aperiodic task scheduling for real-time systems.* Ph.D. Dissertation, Dept. of Electrical and Computer Engineering, Carnegie Mellon University, Pittsburgh, PA, August 1990.

[12] J. Lehoczky. "Fixed priority scheduling of periodic task sets with arbitrary deadlines" *Proceedings Real-Time Systems Symposium 1990,* pages 201-209, 1990.

[13] K. Tindell, A. Burns, and A.J. Wellings. "An extensible approach for analysing fixed priority hard real-time tasks". *Real-Time Systems Journal,* 6 (2), pp. 133-151, 1994.

[14] V. Yodaiken. "Against Priority Inheritance". *FSMLABS technical report,* July 9th, 2000 (available at http://www.linuxdevices.com/files/misc/yodaiken-july02.pdf).

[15] L. Sha, R. Rajkumar and J. P. Lehoczky. "Priority Inheritance Protocols: An Approach to Real-Time Synchronization". *IEEE Transactions on Computers,* Vol. 39, No. 9. Sep. 1990.

[16] B. P. Douglass: *Doing Hard Time: Developing Real-Time Systems with Objects, Frameworks, and Patterns.* Addison-Wesley, 1999.

[17] A. Burns. "The Ravenscar Profile" *ACM Ada Letters,* XIX(4):49–52, Dec 1999.

[18] A. Burns and A. Welling: "Restricted tasking models" *Proceedings of the 8th International Real-Time Ada Workshop,* pages 27–32. ACM Ada Letters, 1997.

[19] K. Tindell, and J. Clark, "Holistic Schedulability Analysis for Distributed Hard Real-Time Systems". *Microprocessing & Microprogramming,* Vol. 50, Nos.2-3, pp. 117-134, 1994.

[20] J. C. Palencia Gutiérrez and M. González Harbour, "Schedulability Analysis for Tasks with Static and Dynamic Offsets", *Proceedings of the 19th Real-Time Systems Symposium,* IEEE Computer Society Press, pp 26-37, December 1998.

[21] J. J. Gutiérrez García, J.C. Palencia Gutiérrez and M. González Harbour, "Schedulability Analysis of Distributed Hard Real-Time Systems with Multiple- Event Synchronization" *Proceedings of 12th Euromicro Conference on Real-Time Systems,* Stockholm (Sweden), IEEE Computer Society Press, pp. 15-24, June 2000.

[22] M. Saksena, P. Freedman, and P. Rodziewicz. "Guidelines for Automated Implementation of Executable Object Oriented Models for Real-Time Embedded Control Systems" *Proceedings, IEEE Real-Time Systems Symposium 1997,* pages 240–251, December 1997.

[23] M. Saksena, P. Karvelas, and Y. Wang. "Automatic synthesis of multi-tasking implementations from real-time object-oriented models". *Proceedings, IEEE International Symposium on Object-Oriented Real-Time Distributed Computing,* March 2000.

[24] L. Kabous and W. Nebel. "Modeling hard real-time systems with uml the ooharts approach". *Proceedings, International Conference on Unified Modeling Language (UML'99),* 1999.

[25] M. Awad, J. Kuusela, and J. Ziegler. *Object-Oriented Technology for Real-Time Systems: A Practical Approach using OMT and Fusion*. Prentice Hall, 1996.

[26] H. Gomaa: *Software Design Methods for Concurrent and Real-Time Systems*. Addison-Wesley Publishing Company, 1993.

[27] F. Balarin, M. Chiodo, P. Giusto, H. Hsieh, A, Jurecska, L. Lavagno, C. Passerone, A. Sangiovanni-Vincentelli, E. Sentovich, K. Suzuki, B. Tabbara: *Hardware-Software Co-Design of Embedded Systems: The Polis Approach*. Kluwer Academic Press , June 1997.

[28] F. Balarin, L. Lavagno, C. Passerone, Y. Watanabe: "Processes, Interfaces and Platforms. Embedded Software Modeling in Metropolis" *Proc. of the EMSOFT Conference 2002, Grenoble, France*: 407-416.

[29] F. Balarin, Alberto L. Sangiovanni-Vincentelli: "Schedule Validation for Embedded Reactive Real-Time Systems". *Proc. of the Design Automation Conference DAC 1997*: 52-57.

[30] Felice Balarin: "Stars in VCC: Complementing Simulation with Worst-Case Analysis". *Proc. Of the ICCAD Conference 2001*: 471-478.

Chapter 13

Automotive UML
A (Meta) Model-Based Approach for Systems Development

M. von der Beeck[1], P. Braun[2], M. Rappl[2], and C. Schröder[3,4]
[1]BMW Group, München, Germany, [2]Technische Universität München, Germany [3]Ames Laboratory, Ames, Iowa, USA, [4]University of Applied Sciences Bielefeld, Germany

Abstract: In this chapter a recent approach is described which utilizes the Unified Modeling Language (UML) within the automotive specific systems development. In particular it presents the Automotive Modeling Language (AML), a modeling language tailored to the development needs of automotive embedded systems. A focus is set on the definition of a metamodel for the AML, as well as on a system of abstraction levels, and on a tight integration between requirements engineering and model-based descriptions. Furthermore the concrete AML representation is given by a concrete UML subset, which is called "Automotive UML". The application of the introduced language concepts is illustrated by means of a realistic case study from the automotive domain.

Key words: Abstraction Levels, Architecture Description Language (ADL), Automotive Modeling Language (AML), Electronic Control Unit (ECU), Metamodel, Requirements Engineering, Unified Modeling Language (UML)

1. THE AUTOMOTIVE DOMAIN

For about thirty years electronic control units are of increasing use in automobiles. The first electronic control unit was introduced to control fuel injection of an engine. This control unit set great expectations which were met with regards to the enhancement of the engine's performance, while simultaneously reducing fuel consumption at the same time. About ten years

L. Lavagno, G. Martin and B. Selic (eds.), UML for Real, 271-299.
© 2003 *Kluwer Academic Publishers.*

later, a programmable microprocessor based control unit was deployed for the first time: the Anti-Lock Braking System (ABS). At that time nobody could anticipate the present car-wide use of microprocessor based control units, including all applications within the powertrain, chassis electronics, body car electronics, infotainment, and driver assistance. Nowadays, in high end cars a vast number of control functions is executed on a network of up to 80 control units, each fulfilling a dedicated task. This situation is slightly different from other application domains such as avionics where redundant full fledged microprocessors like the Motorola 68030 take care of different tasks at the same time.

In nearly every application domain innovative functions are the key potential for competitive advantage, though their merits will be limited if they are not subject to a permanent cycle of innovation and change. Recent studies [15] show that the amount of the electronic content in the net value of a car will double by the year 2005. Furthermore, to meet customers' wishes as well as safety and performance requirements isolated functions have to be combined together to build up car-wide applications which are executed on a distributed network of control units. Despite the integration of functions and the increasing complexity of the systems, car-wide applications have to be easily maintainable, changeable, and customizable according to the manufacturers' and drivers' demands.

1.1   Reconciling the Needs of Automotive Software Development with Model-Based Approaches

Along with the evolution of the complexity of automotive embedded systems, the development processes of car manufacturers have been redefined to large degree. In the very beginning, electronic functions were developed in isolated development teams at the manufacturer's site. As long as these functions had to fulfill a truly isolated task, the corresponding development processes were *localized*, i.e. easy to control and to maintain. However, with the increasing number of functions and the increasing number of interactions resulting in complex communication protocols the integration task for these functions failed due to insufficient support provided by the actual local development process in use. As a result severe technical problems such as incorrect feature interactions and timing latencies emerged. This lead to the well known symptoms of the "software crisis": blown budgets, late delivery, and unfulfilled requirements.

To overcome these difficulties one has to take into account the specific needs of a distributed development of automotive systems leading to a truly *delocalized* development process. Accordingly, the obtained development artifacts have to be communicated properly across the different development teams on a regular basis in order to gain an understanding of mutual dependencies between subsystems. Unfortunately, most developed systems lack well defined documentation, so that typically just the source code of realized functions would be exchanged. However, this is not sufficient to achieve a deeper understanding of the system's functionality. Abstract models that could help to constitute an improvement were hardly ever used.

The complexities of a distributed development scenario were reinforced when third party suppliers took over the development of parts and components. In addition to the evolving deficiencies during the integration of those components into existing systems, car manufacturers complained about a progressive lack of knowledge of their own systems.

About 15 years ago, model-based techniques [17] were employed with great expectations to overcome the recognized difficulties of current development processes. Whereas in "traditional" engineering disciplines such as electrical and mechanical engineering, model-based techniques, like CAD (Computer Aided Design), FEM (Finite Element Method), and hardware design tools were employed with enormous success, a discipline called "software engineering" was hardly established. Since then various tools supporting visual modeling languages, configuration management tools, requirements management tools, and test tools were brought in, but the great diversity of model-based techniques, their abstract nature, and the strict focus of these tools on usually just one aspect of the development process limited their success and effectiveness within the actual development environment. As a consequence, car manufacturers started expensive integration projects to realize a model-based approach with the goal to achieve a seamless development process technically supported by a tailored tool chain.

Step by step car manufacturers developed a new perception of their systems' architectures [4]. Nowadays, the partitioning of the system's architecture into different abstraction levels, introducing a domain specific terminology, concepts for the formation of variants, and the understanding of model-based configurations seem to be potential steps towards a successful deployment of model-based techniques. In order to achieve a comprehensive and tightly-bound model-based paradigm for the automotive domain, only a well defined so called "metamodel-based" approach can be successful (cf. Section 1.3).

The AML includes abovementioned issues of a rigorous metamodel-based approach to simultaneously cover all different aspects of the heterogeneous system development needs within the automotive domain by providing a common conceptual framework.

Concepts such as signals, functions, electronic control units, real-time operating systems, communication infrastructure, and processors now build up the automotive specific terminology that characterizes automotive embedded systems. Each of these notions constitutes a fragment of the architectural model at a certain level of abstraction. Signals, for instance, are elementary entities which can be exchanged between actors, sensors, and control units. Each signal can be measured or computed from a physical context. For the construction of architectural models, a model-based management of all signals occurring in a car is essential since their number nowadays goes far beyond ten thousand. Another important aspect of architectural models is the specification of data dependencies between control functions. Since functions are potentially distributable entities that can be deployed on different control units, the consistent and complete capture of model information in terms of data dependencies between functions supports the collaboration of distributed development teams in a delocalized development process. By defining the required and offered signal interfaces, one forms the basis for a description of possible interaction patterns. Finally, model-based deployment of functions on different control units, and model-based association of functions and control units to the underlying technical infrastructure (processors, real-time operating systems, communication infrastructure) are essential for an automotive-specific support of a distributed - or in other words *global* - development process.

In the next paragraphs a metamodel-based approach is presented and its practical usage illustrated by means of an example including parts of the body car electronics. However, the presented approach is not at all restricted to the automotive domain although it was developed for applications within this domain.

1.2   Automotive Specific Constraints

In general, the design space spanned by all possible architectural models is reduced by automotive specific non-functional constraints. These constraints originate from technical, quality, economic, and even political requirements for automotive systems and already imply characteristic architectural models.

Technical constraints, for instance, generally restrict the deployment of functions. Function deployment depends to a large extent on the transmission of signals. Since most of the sensors and actuators do not have any logic for their linkage to a bus system, they are "hard-wire" connected to their control units. The deployment is therefore limited with respect to the availability of signals. Their transmission is generally impeded by geometric constraints due to the installation of the wiring harness.

Quality constraints, as another example, can be discussed in conjunction with up-coming X-by-wire systems, which are already used in avionics for quite some time. These safety-critical systems replace a mechanical control by an electrical control. As an advantage, these technologies allow one to realize comfortable driver assistance systems. However, these systems have to satisfy very strict safety and quality requirements e.g. on availability and robustness since there might exist no mechanical fallback solutions. The requirements on availability therefore affect the formation of architectural models with regard to a redundant realization of these safety critical systems. Generally, new safety-critical systems must adhere to regulations stated in safety standards like the IEC 61508 [12].

Economic constraints are imposed according to the large number of cars which are manufactured. Therefore, the cost of any hardware used has to be minimized which usually means that old-fashioned control units with low memory and processor resources are still in use. However, these control units are very often not capable of executing all of the newly developed functions; a fact which influences the specification of architectural models to a large extent.

Eventually, *political constraints* such as road traffic acts influence the use of technologies or require the implementation of certain dedicated systems. At this point, the controller for the regulation of the lighting distance can serve as an example.

1.3 (Meta) Model-Based Development Processes

Within the automotive industry model-based specification techniques are becoming more and more popular allowing the complete, consistent, and unambiguous specification of software and hardware parts of automotive specific networks of control units. In this context model-based approaches provide methodical support to manage the integration of logical functions and the deployment of functions on distributed networks of ECUs. In addition, well-defined models form the very source for analysis, validation, and verification activities within the development process.

In contrast to conventional structured programming methods model-based methods provide a comprehensive support for all kinds of issues imposed by modern system development processes. This support comprises activities ranging from the modeling task itself to requirements tracing as well as versioning, configuration, and change management.

A prerequisite for the design of a model-based specification methodology is a precise knowledge of the architecture of the target system class. Therefore, a well-defined architecture centric development language has to support all issues of automotive embedded systems by providing modeling concepts in terms of an automotive specific terminology. Upon this rests the construction of a metamodel by precisely defining relationships between model elements as well as their classification within abstraction levels and their embedding in a development process. During modeling all information is stored in an integrated and consistent model. To cope with the complexity of this model a system of domain specific abstraction levels provides an appropriate structuring mechanism for the specification of networks of control units on different technical levels.

Metamodel: The AML metamodel is defined on a mathematical basis and is structured by a system of automotive-specific abstraction levels. The metamodel represents abstract modeling concepts which are used to build an integrated model. A model contains all necessary information about the functional logic, the distributed network of electronic control units, the actors, the sensors, and the environment. The metamodel structures this information and describes the possible interrelationships. For representing the metamodel of the AML a limited subset of UML class diagrams is used together with metamodel patterns as a rationale. In addition, OCL-like constraints are used to define a basic consistency level.

1.4   Structure of the Chapter

This chapter is structured as follows: in Section 2 the AML is introduced at a glance: this covers the motivation for developing the AML, its history, as well as its prominent features. Following that, Section 3 provides a deeper insight into the AML structure: it illustrates the set of abstraction levels, the definition of AML metamodel fragments, and the use of the AML metamodel for model-based requirements management as well as metamodel-based tailoring of the standard UML. As a practical AML-application the model based development of a window lifting system is presented in Section 4. Finally, in Section 5 conclusions are drawn.

2.   AML SURVEY

According to the abovementioned brief tradition of software engineering techniques and the increase of complexity of automotive embedded systems, the need for adequate methodologies and languages supporting the development process within the automotive industry is enormous. As a matter of fact, the AML originates as a result of intensive research within the project AUTOMOTIVE initiated by automotive industry partners, tool vendors, and universities.

2.1 The AML History

The results presented in this chapter emerged from research carried out within the project FORSOFT *AUTOMOTIVE - Requirements Engineering for embedded systems* [1]. In this context the Technische Universität München, the tool providers Telelogic and ETAS, the car manufacturers BMW and Adam Opel, as well as the suppliers Robert Bosch and ZF Friedrichshafen are closely working together on specific aspects of the methodology, on the adaptation of the UML and ASCET-SD notations in the context of automotive systems development, and on the realization of a tightly coupled tool chain including the tools ETAS ASCET-SD, Telelogic UML Suite, and Telelogic Doors.

2.2 AML Features in a Nutshell

First, we summarize characteristic language features offered by the AML for the modeling of distributed embedded systems.

2.2.1 Abstraction Levels

Abstraction levels define confined views of models to structure and filter information. Each abstraction level is based upon higher, i.e. more abstract levels. In this context, a more technical level access to the information contained on a more abstract level is permitted. Every view shows the system at a uniform technical level. At each abstraction level semantic properties are considered which are characteristic for automotive embedded systems. In the development process, the transition from one abstraction level to another abstraction level is used to restrict the design space by finding a solution for a specified problem.

2.2.2 Architecture Specific Modeling Concepts

Well known architecture description languages (ADLs) offer recurring modeling concepts for representing certain architectural aspects of a system. After a comprehensive evaluation of previous ADL surveys, Medvidovic and Taylor ended up with an ADL classification framework [13]. According to this framework an ADL must explicitly model components (including ports), connectors, and their configurations. These mandatory ADL modeling concepts are described as follows:

- A *component* in an architecture represents a unit of computation or a data store. It must provide an interface which specifies the services (messages, operations, and variables) the component provides. This interface can also specify needed services. Interfaces are described by *ports*.

- A *connector* is an architectural building block used to model interactions among components and rules that control those interactions.
- (Architectural) *configurations* are connected graphs of components and connectors that describe an architectural structure.

In the AML these concepts are applied to various kinds of architectural elements as they are contained in the metamodel.

2.2.3   Formation of Variants

The modeling concept of variants allows specializing architectural elements according to the context in which the element is actually used. From a methodological point of view a strict relation between elements and their variants allows the management of complexity by abstracting specialized details to generally needed model information. In contrast to the concept of inheritance in object orientation, building variants from model elements just means to select specific sub-elements from the available set of all sub-elements. This concept will be discussed in more detail in Section 4.2.2.

2.2.4   Requirements Classification

A central part of an architectural language is to provide a fixed terminology for reasoning about architectural issues. The AML introduces a terminology which is well suited for systems in the automotive domain. The requirements classification rests upon this terminology, and is used itself as a tool to manage the transition from informal, loosely structured requirements to model-aligned and structured requirements. With this classification at hand, different architectural entities of a system can be identified.

2.2.5   Semantic Domain

Each AML modeling concept can be represented by various notations. Notations may be of a textual or tabular form, or they may be graphically aligned. In particular, visual notations, also known as box and line drawings, are a focus for the definition of a mapping to AML. Each visual representation of such a notation symbolizes one AML modeling concept and therefore inherits its semantics. Within the project AUTOMOTIVE, mappings between the AML and the UML, the ASCET-SD, and textual notations are defined. In fact, these mappings also define the transformation of models between the tools UML Suite, ASCET-SD, and DOORS.

2.3 Using AML for Automotive Systems Development

In general, the concrete syntax of notational elements used within the AML has to be aligned with the AML metamodel. Within the AML only a restricted subset of the current UML notation standard (UML 1.4), called Automotive UML, is used to represent some parts of a model (see Figure 13-1). Other parts are represented by a subset of notations offered by ASCET-SD [8], a tool supporting technical-oriented modeling, prototyping, as well as target code generation for embedded systems. Furthermore, textual notations such as structured (hyper-)text and tables are used to enrich the system model, especially in earlier phases of the system development process.

The main reason for using UML in the automotive context is the growing acceptance of this language as a modeling standard within the area of software engineering. The Automotive UML subset is used to represent parts of the AML model by using concrete graphical syntax elements provided in different UML notations. To be aligned to the actual language standard a UML profile is defined. The resulting modeling concepts have been selected with respect to their applicability and expressiveness in the realm of automotive software development.

However, examining the expressiveness of the UML (version 1.4) with respect to its application to the development of embedded systems, one already realizes that there are fundamental weaknesses which consequently have an impact on the expressiveness of the AML representation as a UML profile [7]. There are several efforts addressing that issue, which are currently being elaborated and evaluated by the U2 partners group during the ongoing UML 2.0 standardization [21].

Figure 13-1 shows fundamental parts of the AML centric, metamodel-based approach for automotive systems development and their interrelations. The figure is divided into two columns: the left column contains AML relevant packages of the modeling theory, whereas the right one shows the corresponding UML packages. The diagram shows the relevant aspects which are of major concern in this chapter and which are used to define the corresponding modeling language. The separation of the metamodel level (upper one) and the concrete model level (lower one) exposes the use of a metamodel-based approach. The metamodel level displays the tailoring relation between the AML metamodel and the UML metamodel and defines the structure of models to be instantiated in both languages. The Automotive

UML model is used to represent concrete AML models (see concrete-level). Both kinds of models are instances of the corresponding metamodels.

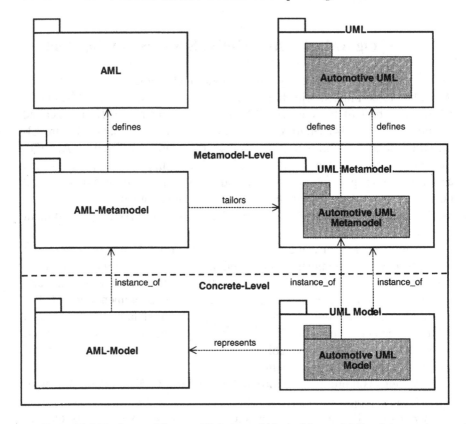

Figure 13-1. Fundamental Parts and Relations within the Metamodel-Based Approach

3. THE AML

Current research in the field of embedded automotive systems shows the importance of automotive specific concepts in terms of a reference archi- tecture. As long as commonly accepted abstractions, understood in terms of reusable ontological entities, are not available, we consider domain specificity as desirable. In fact, collaborating in a domain specific manner might well be the only way to identify generally applicable abstractions.

3.1 Abstraction Levels

The AML consists of concepts which are well known in the automotive domain such as signals, functions, electronic control units, real-time operating systems, communication infrastructure, and processors for assembling the automotive embedded systems architecture. Each of these notions constitutes a fragment of the architectural model at a distinct level of abstraction.

In the following, all notions of this ontology with respect to their classification within a system of AML relevant abstraction levels are listed. Their semantics and their use as modeling concepts are described informally. In addition the AML offers generally applicable modeling patterns such as hierarchical structuring, instantiation, formation of variants, formation of configurations, and model composition for each presented ontology.

3.1.1 Signals

The abstraction level signals contains model information about the system with the least amount of technical details. The core modeling concepts at this stage are signals and actions. Signals are elementary entities which can be exchanged between actors, sensors, and control units. Each signal can be measured or computed from a physical context. Separate management of all signals occurring in a car is essential to construct architectural models, since their number goes far beyond ten thousand. Actions also allow signal configurations to be modified with respect to a managed set of operations. Both concepts together provide in addition to an ordering mechanism enough modeling power to describe scenarios. Scenarios are ordered sequences of actions which are necessary to achieve a determined goal in a certain context.

3.1.2 Functions

Functions constitute basic building blocks at a high level of abstraction. They are independent of implementation techniques or target languages. These functions behave as abstractions for control units, actors, sensors, or the environment, used later. Each function has an interface stating the required and the offered signals. Those interfaces are used to model in- and outports of functions. For reusability reasons functions prohibit access to local signals. Therefore communication has to be handled explicitly via signals passing between ports.

Explicit representation of signal dependencies between different control functions is an essential content of architectural models. Function instances are potentially distributable units that can be deployed on different control units. So, their consistent and complete description in terms of signal dependencies allows the analysis of functional networks.

3.1.3   Logical Architecture

The logical architecture is determined by the specification of logical partitions where parts of the functional network are deployed. These logical partitions characterize potential control units (called functional clusters in AML terminology), actors, sensors, and the environment. At this stage, dealing with the entire system as a whole transforms into dealing with a set of independent subsystems working together interactively.

Extensive experience based on the development of electronic control units shows that a clear separation between the logical system architecture level and the technical system architecture level is a very helpful distinction during the deployment of functions on ECUs. At the logical architecture level only a subset of partitioning criteria is applied in order to achieve a clear view of the functional structure - without identifying the set of functions which constitutes an ECU. However, finally the complete set of partitioning criteria (e.g. also those which consider geometric, and topological requirements) has to be applied.

3.1.4   Technical Architecture

The technical architecture level is determined by two steps: (1) finalizing the responsibility of each control unit by applying the full set of partitioning criteria in terms of technical, economic, quality, and political constraints, and (2) connecting model-based functions and functional clusters to models of the technical infrastructure (processors, real-time operating systems, and communication infrastructure).

3.1.5   Implementation

At the implementation level the model is realized in hardware and software. This level has an exceptional place in the system of abstraction levels since no further information is added to the model. Code generation and the installation of hardware go far beyond the realization of first prototypes which could be generated from the models created above. Although there are many examples of how to successfully apply simulation and code generation facilities in the areas of testing and rapid prototyping, nevertheless code generation often fails to fulfill domain specific constraints for production use. For this reason, at implementation level the size and execution time of the generated code has to be optimized manually.

3.2 Definition of Metamodel Fragments

Corresponding to other model-based approaches the abstract syntax of the AML is defined by a metamodel. Within this chapter only some noteworthy fragments are shown (see [4] for a more complete description). The AML metamodel fragment shown specifies modeling concepts such as functions, their tailoring to variants, and the formation of function instances as well as different kinds of signal dependencies.

Similar to design patterns so called metamodel patterns are used for the definition of the metamodel on every abstraction level. For example an intuitive hierarchy pattern is used for the definition of hierarchically structured functions. Further, relations between elements, variants, and instances are expressed by a variant and an instance pattern.

For a better understanding we have chosen different colors to distinguish between elements, variants, and instances. Elements are displayed in light grey, variants are displayed in medium grey, and instances are displayed in dark grey and white letters. These colors are used both on the metamodel level and on the concrete model level. In the sequel names are written in Arial to denote model names in the referenced diagram.

3.2.1 Functions, Ports, and Connectors

Functions are basic building blocks of systems, whereas instances of functions are used to build up the overall system. Functions are a prerequisite for the definition of variants. From a model oriented point of view functions are labeled with a name, they are hierarchically structured and they can therefore be decomposed into subfunctions (see Figure 13-2).

Analogously to UML classes AML functions aggregate attributes called variables. A variable is characterized by a name and a type. The explicit interface specification is given by so called in- and outports. Ports describe sets of signals which can be exchanged. Inports comprise those signals which are received from other functions. This concept is comparable with the definition of interface classes in the UML. Outports comprise signals which are sent to other functions. Signal dependencies between two functions on the same hierarchical level are described by a caller-callee relationship between outports and inports. Delegation and propagation is used to specify the signal flow between functions belonging to different hierarchical levels. Note that these relationships are used to represent connectors. These concepts can be directly mapped to the concepts used in other ADLs or those defined in the UML 2.0 standard [21].

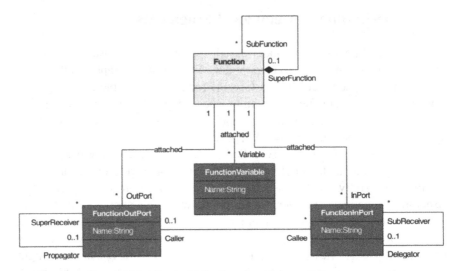

Figure 13-2. Metamodel for Functions, Ports, and Connectors

3.2.2   Function Variants

As functions are general and reusable building blocks of systems, they often need to be tailored to specific situations. Variants allow the specialization of general functional behavior. In contrast to the concept of inheritance in object orientation, building variants means to select specific subfunctions or variants from the admissible set of functions. Each function can be tailored to many different variants (see Figure 13-3). A variant selects a set of functions or variants. The selected functions have to be direct subfunctions of the function which is tailored. Similarly the selected variants have to be variants of those subfunctions. From the modeler's point of view, variants and functions appear to be the same during the construction of a model as both may be instantiated to function instances. Variants also contain variables as well as in-, and outports. These too may be variants of those defined by the tailored function itself. As already mentioned above both are used for the construction of a system in a similar role. To ensure consistency an abstract superclass VariableFunction is introduced in the metamodel.

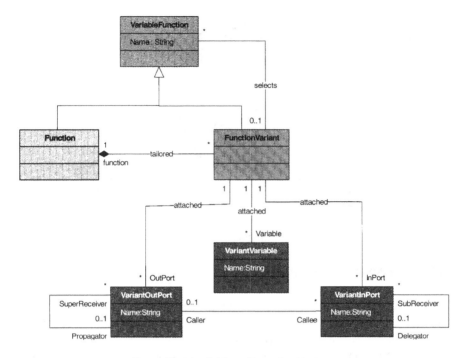

Figure 13-3. Definition of Function Variants

Corresponding to signal dependencies between functions, in addition signal dependencies between VariableFunctions have to be specified at the variant level. Again in- and outports are used for the interface definition.

Note that Figures 13-2, 13-3, and 13-4 only show simplified fragments of the AML metamodel. For example the common relations between specific in- and outports are inherited in the complete metamodel which is not shown in the presented metamodel fragments.

3.2.3   Functional Network

By the definition of functions and variants different element types of the basic building blocks used within a model are specified. As usual, those types have to be instantiated before they can be deployed. Both functions and variants can be instantiated (see Figure 13-4). On the instance level new signal dependencies specifying the horizontal (caller-callee) and vertical (delegation/propagation) communication have to be defined. The resulting information is represented as the functional network.

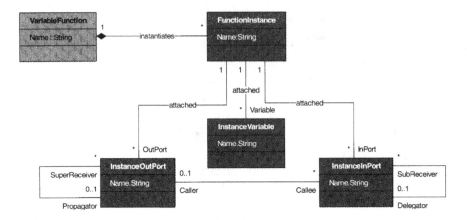

Figure 13-4. Definition of Function Instances

3.3 Use of the Metamodel

Nowadays model-based design techniques are becoming more and more common for software and systems development within the embedded area. These techniques are commonly aligned to standard modeling languages such as UML. The abstract syntax of such a modeling language can be defined using a metamodel. The metamodel specifies the concepts used and their relationships. Next to the definition of abstract modeling concepts the metamodel can be used for the definition of further model-based development techniques. Within this chapter the focus is set on two different aspects for which the AML metamodel is used (see Figure 13-5).

The concepts of the AML metamodel are strictly and uniformly used throughout the whole development process (see Figure 13-5). In particular, this means that the metamodel is used to define a model-based requirements management. Therefore, requirements are classified by the concepts of the metamodel and are tightly related to model elements. The AML metamodel also defines the UML metamodel subset (Automotive UML metamodel), which is used for building concrete AML models. Thereupon, the AML uses a tailored version of the UML for the representation of models. However, within the automotive domain further notations are needed which are not at all supported by the standard UML. These are especially notations for coping with continuous system parts. As a result only a fraction of a complete AML model can be expressed as an instance of the UML metamodel subset. The strength of the AML metamodel lies in the fact that it defines the overall semantics of all model fractions regardless of their origin. Furthermore, the AML metamodel serves as a common metamodel for combining different CASE tools, so that models can be exchanged between them. Moreover, it is also the basis for defining invariant, variant, and semantic consistency constraints, which describe different levels of well-formed models which are closely related to a development process model.

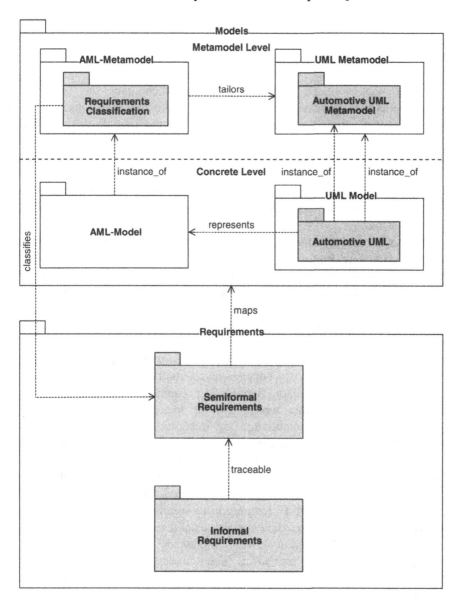

Figure 13-5. Role of the AML Metamodel

In the next sections the use of the AML metamodel for the definition of a model-based requirements management process is sketched. To give an impression of the used Automotive UML dialect the concrete syntax of some AML elements is shown in Section 3.3.2. The use of this notation is explained by a case study in Section 4.

3.3.1   Model-Based Requirements Management

Along with software and system design techniques the scope of requirements management methodologies has continuously increased in the last few years, aiming at an improvement of the overall development process. As a merger of both model-based design techniques and requirements management methodologies, a new kind of requirements engineering methodology has been proposed. However, due to the complexity of this methodology and due to the high degree of informal aspects, a unique and integrated methodology for requirements engineering is still missing.

The AML requirements engineering process distinguishes between three major phases (see Figure 13-5) to manage the transition from informal requirements to a model-based specification. First, the existence of informal requirements is assumed, which are usually unstructured and are not at all aligned to a specific syntax. With the help of the requirements classification fraction of the AML metamodel, semiformal requirements can be created. This process can only be done manually and results in a loose coupling between informal requirements and semiformal requirements. The traceability between these two adjacent levels can be established by a semi-automatic linking mechanism. Semiformal requirements are enriched by nonfunctional requirements which can be found in several high-level structuring conventions, elaborated by different organizations, such as VDMA, IEEE, or DOD. As a result some parts are now classified according to the AML metamodel and are therefore structured by a formal syntax. The last step deals with the mapping to the model-based specification where the complete syntax of all notations is considered. By using AML based structuring rules a tight "1:1" integration of semiformal requirements with the model-based system specification can be achieved.

In Table 13-1 a fragment of the template describing the structure of semiformal requirements is shown. The template focuses on a section describing functions, variants, and instances. It consists of two columns: the left one contains functional requirements and the right one nonfunctional requirements. The template includes predefined headings and variable headings (marked by angle brackets). The last ones have to be replaced by names of model elements. Every heading is followed by a textual description, which contains mostly informal information. By the strict definition of this template a tight integration of model elements describing functions with their textual requirement description can be established. As a result, starting with this semiformal requirements definition the function hierarchy can be computed and stored within a model. In contrast starting from a function hierarchy one can also compute the structure of the semiformal requirements document. Even more, existing textual descriptions and models can be related, to synchronize changes in the model with changes in the requirements document and vice versa.

Table 13-1. Parts of the Template for Semiformal Requirements Describing Functions

<Function Name>

Functional Requirements	*Nonfunctional Requirements*
1. Short Description	**1. Quality Attributes**
1.1 Super-Function	*1.1 Usability*
1.2 Responsibility	*1.2 Timings*
1.3 Interfaces	*1.3 Capacity*
2. Applications	*1.4 Reliability*
2.1 Basic Scenarios	*1.5 Security*
2.2 Extended Scenarios	**2. Technical Constraints**
3. List of Subfunctions	*2.1 Deployment*
4. Cooperation of Subfunctions	*2.2 Technology*
5. Variants	**3. Management Characteristics**
5.1 <Variant Name>	*3.1 Scheduling*
5.1.1 Short Description	*3.2 Expenses*
5.1.2 Scenarios	*3.3 Human Resources*
5.1.3 Instances	**4. Legal Obligations**
5.2 ...	*4.1 Demands*
6. Instances	*4.2. ...*
6.1 <Instance Name>	
6.2 ...	

Table 13-2. Using UML Notation for AML Representation

UML-Syntax	Description
Folded classes **WindowRegulator**	Classes are used to represent functions. Usually they are depicted in a folded way for clarity reasons. The chosen kind of visualization hides information about (private) attributes and methods. Light grey is used to mark functions.
Environment class «environment» @WindowRegulator	Each function or variant can be hierarchically structured. The hierarchical structure is achieved by decomposing classes. Within class diagrams the environment of the decomposed function or the decomposed variant is shown as a marked class attached with the stereotype <<environment>> and "@" symbol as a name prefix. The environment depicts the complement of the function or variant itself. It symbolizes all specified functions or variants except the function respectively variant itself. This external model element is needed for the specification of the vertical communication, i.e. delegation and propagation, within the hierarchy of functions or variants.
Lollipop SwitchMovement [Movement] ——o	Inports are represented as lollipops which are linked to classes. In UML the lollipop notation stands for an abstract class containing an interface specification inherited to the linked class. In AML the "types" of ports are described by interface classes. Since functions can use several instances of a port definition, not only the type name (in square brackets) is stated but also the instance name is declared.
Dependency arrow ···············>	Signal dependencies meaning call, propagation, or delegation relationship between different functions, variants, and instances are shown by dependency arrows. The arrow starts at a class and ends at a lollipop.
Variants **DriverDoor**	Classes are used for the representation of variants as well. Analogously to functions they are depicted in a folded way for clarity reasons. The chosen kind of visualization hides information about (private) attributes and methods. Medium grey is used to mark variants.
Variant dependency arrow ········«variant»········>	The definition of variants of a function is done by a marked dependency arrow attached with the stereotype <<variant>>. The arrow starts at the defined variant and ends at the tailored function.
Function instance WR_FrontLeft [DriverDoor]	Instances of functions and variants are drawn with component symbols and they are marked by a dark grey together with white text. The function or variant name which is instantiated is given in square brackets concatenated to the instance name itself.

3.3.2   Tailoring of the Automotive UML Dialect

The AML metamodel is not only used to describe the abstract syntax of the AML, it also defines the mapping to concrete modeling languages, in our case the UML. Within the AML specification a rule-based and metamodel-based mechanism is used to formally define the mapping between those languages. In Table 13-2 an informal definition of this mechanism is given. In the left column the concrete UML 1.4 syntax is shown. In the right column the meaning of the used syntactic construct is explained in AML terminology. Note that the AML uses the UML constructs only by restricting and not by enhancing their UML meaning which results in a subset dialect of UML, called Automotive UML.

Unfortunately, this alignment leads to some cumbersome yet inconvenient modeling artifacts. The most important one deals with the representation of hierarchical structures and signal flow. The explicit representation of the function environment as an external entity, i.e. a class, rather than a true hierarchical "box within box" representation (as it is commonly realized by other ADLs) is required since UML 1.4 does not fully support this paradigm. As a matter of fact this restricts the applicability of the UML within embedded system development to a large extent. However, this drawback has early been recognized by the OMG and hence became part of the ongoing standardization work for the UML 2.0 standard [21].

4.   CASE STUDY

After the introduction of the AML framework this section shows an application to a realistic case study in the automotive domain. The example shows a fragment of the functionality within the body electronics of a car, namely the window regulator system. The case study reflects domain specific requirements such as data and functional dependencies with other functions and timing constraints.

4.1   The Window Regulator System

The control software operates the window pane by opening and closing it. The opening and closing action is performed by a motor and triggered by pushing the control switch in a certain position. The window regulator action has to be stopped automatically when the lower or upper bound is reached.

The window regulator function offers a normal operation mode, i.e. the control switch has to be pressed during operation. An additional automatic mode is provided to open or close the window until the limit is reached. This may happen by pressing the switch for a very short time or by some comfort functionality in connection with the central locking system.

4.2   Modeling

The model of the window regulator system is developed in three major steps involving major AML concepts. First, the functional structure is developed incorporating the use of common architectural modeling elements. Second, the elaborated functional framework is tailored by variants. Finally, the modeled variants are instantiated to a functional network. The functions are explained in the style of the AML requirements classification template. Herewith the description of functional requirements is more extensive than stated in the classification template due to readability reasons. Nonfunctional requirements are stated by means of the template. To demonstrate the applicability to hierarchical structures, two subsequent functions within the functional hierarchy are described in detail.

4.2.1   Functions, Ports, and Connectors

The WindowRegulator function is responsible for the operation of the window pane and interacts with other functions of the body car electronics such as the sunroof control, the central locking logic, and comfort functions. The function WindowRegulator performs basic services such as (automatically) opening and closing and offers extended services for functional and operational safety.

Figure 13-6 shows a decomposition of WindowRegulator into five subfunctions, namely BasicOperation, ChildProtection, RepetitionLock, BlockDetection, and Motor. BasicOperation analyses the switch positions and determines the MotorMovement direction. Its operation may be interrupted by a control signal. These signals may be generated by RepetitionLock and BlockDetection. RepetitionLock monitors the operation time of the window regulator motor. If the operation exceeds the time limit of 60 seconds, the operation is immediately stopped by sending the Control.Stop signal. Similarly BlockDetection monitors the current drain of the window regulator motor and stops the operation when it exceeds the activation current by more than 2 Amperes. Both functions together are responsible for providing functional and operational safety services. The function Motor can be further decomposed into two subfunctions. The first one contains algorithms describing the physical model of the controlled motor and the second one comprises functionality describing measured sensor values. All functions together build up a closed system.

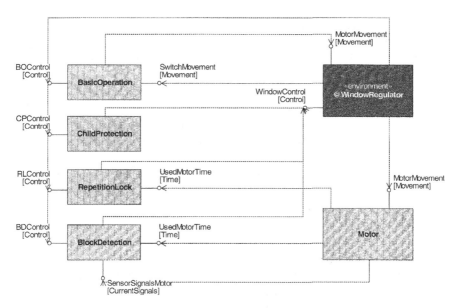

Figure 13-6. Decomposition of the WindowRegulator Function

Furthermore, Figure 13-6 shows the class @WindowRegulator attached with the stereotype <<environment>> to denote the environment of the function WindowRegulator. The environment symbolizes the set of all specified functions except the function itself. This model element is used to visualize the vertical signal flow between the environment and the function itself and its aggregated subfunctions. So for example the interface MotorMovement of @WindowRegulator shows the delegation and the propagation of signals with the type Movement to subfunctions of WindowRegulator and to the environment of WindowRegulator. By using an explicit model element for the representation of the environment, the symmetric port concept of the AML between the horizontal and the vertical signal flow can be realized in the UML subset.

As stated above interfaces are described by means of ports in AML. Figure 13-6 shows the function BlockDetection attached with three in- and one outport (at least the outport is not visible in the diagram due to limited presentation capabilities of UML 1.4). The inport SensorSignals is of signal type CurrentSignals and aggregates three methods described in a separate interface class description. The methods are measure_Amperage, measure_ Voltage and measure_Power. Each of these methods aggregates a parameter such as measured_I, measured_U, and measured_P. In the case of a UML 1.4 representation of ports as lollipops dependency relations provide an appropriate mechanism for stating bilateral signal dependencies.

Table 13-3. Nonfunctional Requirements for WindowRegulator

Quality Attributes	
Usability	— The window pane must be operated by a single switch
	— The switch must have 5 positions
	— The automatic mode is activated by a short movement of the switch
Timings	— For a convenient operation of the system, the movement of the window pane has to be started 10 ms after switch activity
	— After reaching the upper or lower bound the motor has to be stopped within 500 ms
Capacity	— The fulfilled services are regarded as a standard functionality and the implementation must be as small as possible with respect to memory utilization
Reliability	— A long term operation has to be ensured by all components
Security	— Access of unauthorized components must be prohibited
Technical Constraints	
Deployment	— All subfunctions of WindowRegulator have to be deployed on the same control unit
Technology	— The function has to be realized by the OSEK compliant operating system "tiny and superfast"
	— The Processor Infineon C167 is obligatory
Management Characteristics	
Scheduling	— Development deadline is scheduled at 15.12.03
Expenses	— The development cost is limited to 400,000 EUR
Human Resources	— 2 engineers are committed with the development
Legal obligations	
Demands	— The system must protect passengers from unauthorized attacks from outside

BlockDetection monitors the current drain of the motor to avoid a motor failure caused by over-operation. BlockDetection is a subfunction of WindowRegulator for which a set of nonfunctional requirements is shown in Table 13-3. BlockDetection gets sensor values and the operation time as an input and observes the current drain during operation. If the current exceeds the limit by more than 2 Amperes the motor operation is cancelled by sending a Control-Stop signal to all subfunctions of WindowRegulator. Table 13-4 shows nonfunctional requirements attached to model element BlockDetection.

Table 13-4. Nonfunctional Requirements for Function BlockDetection

Quality Attributes	
Usability	— ./.
Timings	— The initialisation phase is finished after 22 ms
	— After detecting a motor blocking the motor has to be stopped within 150 ms
Capacity	— The function must be realized with 8 Byte RAM and 256 Byte ROM
Reliability	— Without a proper operation of BlockDetection the window pane must not be moved
Security	— Sensor values of BlockDetection may not be accessed by other components
Technical Constraints	
Deployment	— BlockDetection is deployed together with other subfunctions of WindowRegulator
Technology	— → WindowRegulator
Management Characteristics	
Scheduling	— Development deadline is scheduled at 15.06.03
Expenses	— The development cost is limited to 50,000 EUR
Human Resources	— 1 engineer is committed with the development
Legal obligations	
Demands	— The function is responsible for the protection of passengers from unauthorized attacks from outside

4.2.2 Function Variants

This section demonstrates the use of the modeling concept variant when applied to functions. For the development of product lines, families of functions are considered. Families of functions share some identical functionality and each family member has some individual functionality which characterizes its variations. In the AML one distinct function is selected which incorporates all functionality. This function is treated as a generic framework on the element level and can be tailored to variants. In the case study the function WindowRegulator constitutes this framework. The functions DriverDoor and PassengerDoor (Figure 13-7) are variants of WindowRegulator. All three functions together make up the WindowRegulator family.

From a methodical point of view the framework serves as a source to reuse activities within different parts of a model. The framework itself contains a consistent and correct specification of all possible subfunctions and their signal dependencies. For the purposes of reuse the whole framework can be taken or only a fragment. Each fragment constitutes a variant.

During specification the tailoring of functions to variants is one essential step. Figure 13-7 shows the definition part of two variants related to WindowRegulator. Each of the defined variants selects a certain subset of subfunctions. The diagram also shows the interface specification provided by a variant. The set of offered ports attached to a variant is a subset of the ports attached to the corresponding function. The same holds for the subfunctions of WindowRegulator. For example the DriverDoor does not include the ChildProtection. The explicit declaration of subfunctions of a variant is identical to the specification of the framework function depicted in Figure 13-6.

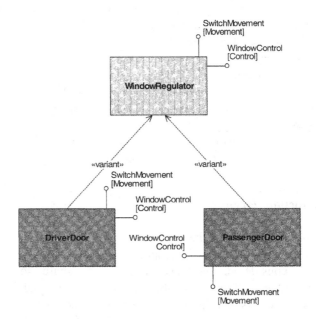

Figure 13-7. Declaration of Variants

4.2.3   Functional Network

At the functional network level the specified functions and their associated variants are instantiated as often as they are needed to fulfill control tasks in the overall system. At this level functions from different development teams can be integrated to validate their interoperation. The AML metamodel section for handling the functional level supports the development of correct and interoperable functional specifications. At the end this facilitates the realization of interacting control units at the technical level.

By composing different functional instances, signal dependencies between these instances have to be specified. This information is not contained in the model so far, and complements the signal dependency information at the functional level.

Figure 13-8 shows the definition of four window regulator function instances on the basis of two variants, namely DriverDoor and Passenger-Door. Again the signal dependencies occurring between these instances are described by means of ports and connectors. For representation of function instances UML components have been chosen. This ensures two properties: (1) the possibility of attaching ports to function instances and (2) the comprehension of engineers who are used to model in a conventional UML style. The meaning of the dependency arrows is exactly the same as it is at the functional level.

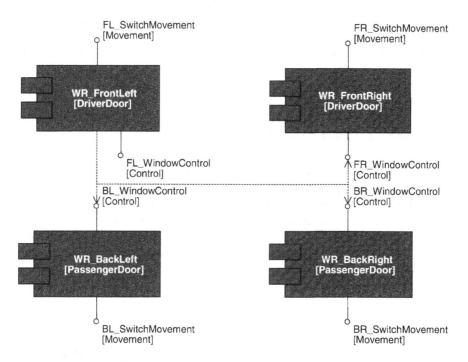

Figure 13-8. Fragment of the Functional Network

5.   CONCLUSIONS

Motivated by the need to comply with the challenges of developing complex networks of heavily interacting ECUs, a metamodel-based approach has been presented. This approach provides an elegant and common conceptual framework. Essential ingredients of this framework are the following:

- a system of abstraction levels for structuring AML models,

- the metamodel-based abstract syntax of the AML,

- the representation of the AML by means of the UML aligned to the UML 1.4 standard, and

- a model-based requirements management technique which leads to a tight integration of requirements descriptions and model elements.

The application of these concepts to a realistic example, a window regulator control system, reveals the benefits of applying the presented approach.

ACKNOWLEDGEMENTS

We thank Ulrich Freund, Luciano Lavagno, Grant Martin, and Bernhard Schätz for carefully reading draft versions of this chapter. We are much obliged to our colleagues of the project Automotive for many fruitful discussions and we thank Manfred Broy for directing this research. This work has been partially funded by the Bayerische Forschungsstiftung (BayFor) within the Forschungsverbund für Software Engineering II (FORSOFT II).

REFERENCES

[1] Peter Braun and Martin Rappl, "Model based Systems Engineering - A Unified Approach using UML, Systems Engineering - A Key to Competitive Advantage for All Industries", *Proceedings of the 2nd European Systems Engineering Conference (EuSEC 2000),* Herbert Utz Verlag GmbH, München, 2000.
[2] Peter Braun, Martin Rappl, and Jörg Schäuffele, „Softwareentwicklungen für Steuergerätenetzwerke – Eine Methodik für die frühe Phase" (in German), *VDI-Berichte,* Nr. 1547, S. 265 ff., 2000.

[3] Michael von der Beeck, Peter Braun, Martin Rappl, and Christian Schröder, „Modellbasierte Softwareentwicklung für automobilspezifische Steuergerätenetzwerke" (in German), *VDI-Berichte*, Nr. 1646, S. 293 ff., 2001.

[4] Michael von der Beeck, Peter Braun, Martin Rappl, and Christian Schröder, "Automotive Software Development: A Model-Based Approach", SAE Technical Paper Series 2002-01-0875, Detroit, 2002.

[5] Brodsky, Clark, Cook, Evans, and Kent, "Feasability Study in Rearchitecting the UML as a Family of Languages Using a Precise OO Meta-Modeling Approach", The pUML Group, 2000.

[6] Manfred Broy et al., "The Design of distributed Systems: An introduction to FOCUS – Revised Version", Technical Report, TUM-I9202, Technische Universität München, 1993.

[7] Manfred Broy, Michael von der Beeck, Peter Braun, and Martin Rappl, "A fundamental critique of the UML for the specification of embedded systems", unpublished, 2000.

[8] ETAS, ASCET-SD User's Guide Version 4.2; ETAS GmbH; Stuttgart; 2001.

[9] David Garlan, Shang-Wen Cheng, and Andrew J. Kompanek, "Reconciling the needs of architectural description with object-modeling notations", In *Science of Computer Programming* 44, P. 23-49, Springer Elsevier, 2002.

[10] Bernd Gebhard and Martin Rappl, "Requirements Management for Automotive Systems Development", SAE Technical Paper Series 2000-01-0716, Detroit, 2000.

[11] Derek Hatley and Imtiaz Pirbhai, *Strategies for real-time system specification*, Dorset House Publishers, New York, 1988.

[12] IEC, Functional safety of electrical/electronic/programmable electronic safety-related systems - IEC 61508, International Electrotechnical Commission, 1999.

[13] Nenad Medvidovic and Richard N. Taylor, "A Classification and Comparison Framework for Software Architecture Description Languages", *IEEE Transactions on Software Engineering*, vol. 26, no. 1, January 2000.

[14] Object Management Group, OMG Unified Modeling Language Specification, Version 1.4, 2003.

[15] Christine Rosette, „Elektronisch gesteuerte Systeme legen weiterhin zu" (in German). *Elektronik AUTOMOTIVE*, pages 22-23, 2002.

[16] Bernhard Rumpe and Andy Schürr, "UML + ROOM as a Standard ADL?, Engineering of Complex Computer Systems", *ICECCS'99 Proceedings*, IEEE Computer Society, 2000.

[17] Bernhard Schätz, Alexander Pretschner, Franz Huber, and Jan Philipps, Model-based development, Technical Report TUM-I0204, Institut für Informatik, Technische Universität München, 2002.

[18] Bran Selic, Garth Gullekson, and Paul T. Ward, *Real-Time Object Oriented Modeling*, John Wiley, 1994.

[19] Desmond F. D'Souza and Alan C. Wills, *Objects, Components and Frameworks with UML – the CATALYSIS approach*, Addison-Wesley, 1998.

[20] Christian Schröder and Ulf Pansa, „UML@Automotive - Ein durchgängiges und adaptives Vorgehensmodell für den Softwareentwicklungsprozess in der Automobilindustrie" (in German), Praxis Profiline, *IN-CAR COMPUTING*, 1. Auflage 2000, Vogel Verlag, ISBN 3-8259-1909-9, 2000.

[21] U2-Partners, Unified Modeling Language: Superstructure, version 2.0, OMG doc# ad/03-01-02, http://www.u2-partners.org/, 2003.

Chapter 14

Specifying Telecommunications Systems with UML

Thomas Weigert[1] and Rick Reed[2]
[1] Motorola, Inc .[2] TSE Ltd.

Abstract: The ITU service description methodology is widely used to specify the services of telecommunication systems and the equipment providing these services. Separate languages, such as SDL, MSC, or ASN.1 have traditionally been used to express specifications at the various stages of this methodology. Motivated by the ongoing convergence between telecommunications and computing and the increasing popularity of UML, these languages have been described as UML profiles. In this chapter, we show how the UML can be leveraged as the notation to capture specifications for network services and elements.

Key words: Modeling, Telecommunications, UML, ITU, Service Description

Telecommunications software has the following characteristics: Most often, the software runs as an *embedded system*, on a hardware platform dedicated to a specific task (e.g. a switch). Naturally, the hardware imposes limits on what the software can do. A large portion of telecom software can be considered *reactive* – the system is sent a message and it is supposed to give a response, which may involve a change in the state of the controlled hardware. Such software is usually *real-time* but the performance requirements are more often statistical than absolute. Equipment is often required to handle many independent transactions at the same time involving physically distributed network elements. As a rule, this software is *parallel* and *distributed*.

Modeling such software systems has a long history in telecommunications, beginning with work done in the 1970s. At that time electromechanical switching systems started to be replaced with program controlled systems and the industry was therefore starting to do software engineering. The high throughput requirements compared with the processing power and storage costs of the day were key factors that determined that most software was actually written in assembly language

L. Lavagno, G. Martin and B. Selic (eds.), UML for Real, 301-322.

and sometimes was wired logic. Equipment makers were therefore keen to make sure that the logic of the software did what was expected and introduced a number of modeling and design techniques such as top down and state based modeling to be applied before coding was undertaken. It was agreed that there would be benefit to the industry in general to share techniques. In the following, we give an overview of the ITU service description methodology that became the foundation of the standardization of ISDN services and is now widely used throughout the industry. We then demonstrate that UML is well suited as a notation to capture specifications following this methodology.

1.   ITU SERVICE DESCRIPTION METHODOLOGY

The description and implementation of telecommunication services and supporting networks has to support equipment from multiple vendors and multiple architectures. Service characteristics are specified by interaction (user-network, or network-network) and interfaces, rather than by the architecture, configuration, or technology of the network elements. This approach allows network technologies and internal configurations to evolve separately from the service requirements and has fostered the evolution of a service description methodology which is technology independent, and which does not impose implementation and configuration guidelines upon the network architect. While this methodology was originally intended by the ITU to derive standards relevant to these services, it has been adapted by the industry for the specification of telecommunication products implementing these services. [42, 43]

The overall ITU description methodology for telecommunication services (see Figure 14-1) is divided into three stages: service aspects, functional network aspects, and network implementation aspects [1].

Stage 1 gives the service description from the user point of view, Stage 2 describes the user-network interface and the interfaces between different service access points within the network, and Stage 3 gives the description of the physical switching and service nodes, as well as of the protocols and

---

[42]   The International Telecommunications Union (ITU) was formed in 1865, only twenty years after the invention of the telegraph, to determine common rules to standardize equipment to facilitate international interconnection, uniform operating instructions which would apply to all countries, and common international tariff and accounting rules. The ITU became a United Nations specialized agency in 1947 and is responsible for Telecommunication Standardization (ITU-T), Radiocommunication (ITU-R), and Tele-communication Development (ITU-D).

[43]   References to standards will be to the version currently in force.

message formats. Within each stage, several more detailed steps have been identified.

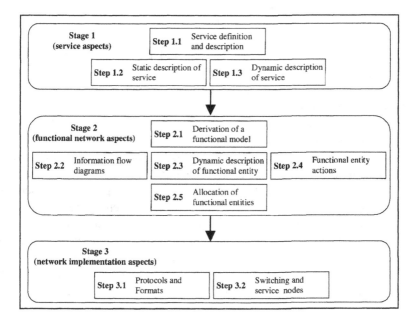

Figure 14-1. ITU Method for Service Description

At Stage 1, the overall service is modeled from the user point of view. As in UML, the "user" may be some other equipment or a person that interacts with the system but in any case the model does not concern itself with the details of the human interface. Stage 1 service descriptions are independent of the functionality in the user's terminal.[44] For example, the conference calling service description is designed to be independent of whether the conference bridge is in the terminal, in the local service node (e.g., a base station, an ATM switch), or elsewhere in the network (e.g., a central office switch) [1]. The descriptions at Stage 1 should be given in generic terms that do not constrain the design of either terminal or network. This description not only includes the operational, control, interworking, and administrative aspects of the service, but also specifies the resolution of interactions with other services. The steps at Stage 1 describe:

---

[44] In telecommunications lingo, "terminal" refers to any equipment that is capable of acting as a terminal point on a voice grade channel. This includes telephones, fax machines, modems, base stations for cordless phones, or any other customer premise equipment to be connected to the public network.

- The perceptions of both the user receiving the service as well as any other user involved in the service.
- The static (time independent) structure of the service in terms of independent, salient features (termed attributes in [2]) and their functional variations.
- The dynamic information that is sent and received by the user from activation or invocation of the service to completion of the service.

The Stage 1 descriptions treat the network (which could include some capability in the user terminal) as a single entity that provides the services to the user. No information flows within the network are considered. In other words, the service is defined as an interface between network and user(s).

Stage 2 identifies the functional capabilities and the information flows needed to support the service as described in Stage 1. At this stage, the network is decomposed into functional entities which group the functions required to provide the service.[45] Each functional entity represents the control of one instance of a service at a single location. For each basic service (e.g., bearer or teleservice) and for each supplementary service, a set of functional entities and the relationships between these functional entities is identified. These functional capabilities are then mapped onto physical network elements. The steps at Stage 2 describe:

- The functional entities that group the functions required to provide a service in a single location.
- The information flows between functional entities for both successful operation and for error situations.
- The dynamic description of the behavior of each functional entity.
- The actions each functional entity performs between communications with other entities.
- A mapping of each functional entity onto physical network elements.

The Stage 2 descriptions define functions required and their distribution within the network. These descriptions remain independent from any implementation or signaling system. Typically, a (small) number of physical realizations, or scenarios, to physical network elements are identified.

In Stage 3, for each network element, the functional requirements of these elements are defined. In addition, the relationship supported between two functional entities located in different physical locations must be realized by protocol(s) supported between those network elements. The steps at State 3 must be performed for each service and describe:

- The messages to be exchanged between network elements and the detailed message elements comprising these messages.

---

[45] The detailed procedures and formats used and the concepts needed for the Stage 2 descriptions are found in [3].

– The functional requirements for each network element.

2.   ITU SPECIFICATION LANGUAGES

In engineering practice, various variants of state diagrams as well as message sequence diagrams (often referred to as "ladder diagrams", "bounce diagrams", or "information flow diagrams") were typically used to represent a system. For example, following the ITU service description methodology, the system entity at Stage 1 was usually represented as a single state machine process or a sequence diagram with a single instance, depending on the complexity of the system. At Stage 2, behavior and actions are usually described by a number of communicating state machines, each corresponding to a functional entity. More detailed sequence diagrams and state machine diagrams are usually produced at Stage 3.

The first standardized notation for state diagrams was the ITU (then CCITT) Specification and Description Language (SDL), originally approved in 1976 [4,5,6]. It recognized that a telecom system would be built of blocks (we might say "objects" today) with a well-defined boundary (today we might say an "interface") across which explicitly indicated signals (or messages) pass.

The SDL language has evolved since 1976, part of which was the definition of the message sequence chart (MSC) notation, first as an auxiliary diagram to SDL, then as a separately defined standard Z.120 [7] in 1992. MSC later became the basis of UML sequence diagrams. The behavior models of SDL are extended finite state machines represented as state transition diagrams, and subsume and expand upon the UML 1.x hierarchical state charts. The most common use of these diagrams is to define the behavior of objects that can be scheduled separately for concurrent processing, independently of any underlying computing infrastructure. ASN.1 (in the separate X.680 series of standards) defines the logical layout of data communicated between such objects and the mapping of logical data onto a physical realization as determined by the encoding rules of the protocol. The ASN.1 data definitions can be used within SDL models following the ITU Z.105 standard of 1995 and its subsequent updates [8].

Even in the original 1976 version of SDL, the units of composition (referred to as "blocks") communicated in an object-like way: that is, by message passing. In the late eighties, more support was given to object based modeling by including class descriptions that could be inherited, elaborated and redefined. At the same time, there was a realization that the way SDL was used in the design approaches of different organizations was very similar and there would be benefit from sharing these ideas. One effort in this direction was the European SPECS project 1987-1993 [9,10]. This project contributed to ETSI and ITU studies which were eventually distilled into a framework methodology for SDL with other languages, published as SDL Supplement 1 in 1997 [11]. This framework suggested using OMT [12] to capture the entities needed in a system and analyze the relationships and attributes between these entities while doing the more detailed engineering using ASN.1, MSC, and SDL.

OMT became the basis of class/object modeling in UML and therefore when SDL-96 was updated to SDL-2000, the notation was extended to recognize UML class diagrams as legal SDL.

3.   ENTER UML

Until recently, mirroring the respective business domains, the software development methodologies deployed in the telecom industry have evolved quite disconnectedly from the software development methodologies in the computing industry. The developers in these two areas focused on tools and techniques that differed significantly.

In the computing industry, support for the code developer seemed the predominant concern. The artifacts were primarily produced by coders, individual developers who defined themselves by their skills in crafting code. Tools merely aided the developer in this activity: modeling tools helped the developers to document and visualize their artifacts. Consequentially, the notations used to model applications were rich in descriptive constructs that allowed to capture the many variations, subtleties, and nuances of implementations. Automation, if applied at all, helped to alleviate the tedious chores, such as generating header files. Construction of software artifacts is not even mentioned as an afterthought. Popular tools share this style of development: heavy emphasis is placed on the manual development of code. If coding is automated at all, it is done according to the paradigm of "round-trip engineering": code artifacts that might have been produced by tools are manually edited and can later be again examined from within the context of the tool and its model.[46]

In contrast, in the development of telecom applications, coding was considered an awkward necessity, at best, and tools quickly focused on eliminating this activity. SDL had emerged as the dominant modeling notation in this domain providing the user with representational means close

---

[46] The UML community has only recently recognized the importance of the automated generation of software artifacts from designs and adopted *Model Driven Architecture* as a goal of modeling [13,14].

to the concepts familiar in telecom application development. This was further supported by plenty of evidence that the really expensive mistakes were those where there was an error in the stimulus response specification. Rather than having many degrees of freedom in describing an application, telecom developers limited themselves to a few, but powerful, domain-specific constructs from which they assembled their applications. These concepts were given precise operational interpretation, originally to allow the abstract interpretation of system models for purposes of verification by simulation. Tools are now available that generate complete applications for network elements from SDL models, with no need for manual code development. In addition, due to stringent reliability demands on telecommunications equipment, much emphasis was placed on formal verification and validation of such systems, to ensure quality levels that simulation and testing could not guarantee.

For example, the introductory section of the UML 1.4 specification as the state of the art of modeling in the computing domain explicitly states that the primary focus for modeling is communication, visualization, and documentation [15, p. I-4]. Compare this with the methodology guidelines for Z.100 [11], which feature extensive discussions on the derivation of implementations from SDL specifications and on validation and verification of specifications through simulation and state space exploration.

Telecommunications and computing are converging, and the development communities now overlap. Some organizations have reported a period of culture clash amongst developers [16]; however, in 1999 the ITU adopted recommendation Z.109, making SDL the first standardized UML real-time profile. Z.109 leverages the mind share and analysis capabilities of the UML while maintaining the domain-specific characteristics of SDL.

4.   SPECIFYING SERVICE DESCRIPTIONS

While the methodology described in Section 1 originally was envisioned to be applied only to the definition of services provided by a telecommuni-cations network, it can easily be seen that this methodology is equally applicable to any application that emerges from the interaction of a set of fundamental functional building blocks. It is also important to recognize that the methodology is inherently recursive. While [1] holds that at Stage 1 the entity interacting with the environment is the network, actual engineering practice applies this methodology also to the design of the individual network elements, and even their subcomponents. In other words, the cycle of describing service aspects, functional system aspects, and system implementation aspects can be (and is) applied to any complex system, independent of whether the system is in fact the network, a single network element, or a subsystem of a network element.

UML is well suited to capture system descriptions following this methodology. In the following, we demonstrate the use of UML notations to specify the service description of the Call Waiting (CW) supplementary service.[47] The Call Waiting service permits a subscriber to be notified of an incoming call that is waiting for an interface information channel ("there is a call waiting"). The user then has the choice of accepting, rejecting, or ignoring the waiting call. The Call Waiting service is specified at Stage 1 in [16] and at Stage 2 in [18].

Modeling of the CW service begins by describing each behavior that the network offers, from the user point of view. The UML notation to describe the system behavior at this level is that of a *Use Case*. The subject of the use cases that jointly comprise the CW service is the network. Each use case specifies a unit of useful functionality that the network provides to the users, i.e., a specific way for the users to interact with the network. These use cases involve three users that interact with the network, represented in UML as actors: User *A* is engaged in a call with User *B* (this call can be in any state), User *C* originates a call to User *B* which causes the CW supplementary service to be invoked, and User *B* reacts to the waiting call. Figure 14-2 shows the uses case diagram for the CW service. Each of the use cases represents a complete sequence of interactions between the affected users and the network. After the execution of a use case, the network will be in a state in which no further inputs are expected and any use case can be initiated again. Use cases define the offered behavior without any references to the internals of the subject (i.e., the network). For example, [16] describes the *Invocation* use case as follows:

> When an incoming call from user C arrives at the access of subscriber B and encounters the channels busy condition, and a network determined user busy condition does not result, then the Call Waiting service will be invoked and the call shall be offered to subscriber B with an indication that the channels busy condition exists.

---

[47] Supplementary services represent a class of telecommunications services which modify, supplement or enhance a bearer service or teleservice, but which cannot be offered as a stand alone service without the companion capabilities of the higher level telecommunications service. The same supplementary service may be provided in common with a number of telecommunications services. Supplementary services deal with functions that relate to the interactions of a terminal device with the network (e.g., modifying the way a call is set up or charged for).

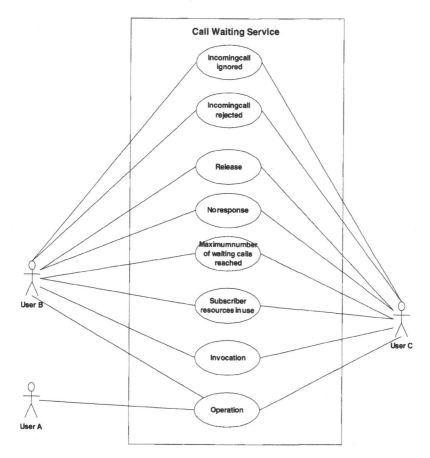

Figure 14-2. Stage 1.1 description for CW service: Use cases.

For additional clarification, a behavior description, such as an interaction diagram, a state machine, or an activity diagram may be associated with each use case. In addition, at Stage 1.2, we break each use case down into a number of salient features, where each feature is independent of the others so that a change to the value of one feature will not affect the others. In accordance with [1], these features are represented as attributes of the use case. A set of attributes and enumerated types of attribute values for bearer services and for teleservices can be found in [19], Annexes B and C.

At the final step in Stage 1, a state machine is defined that covers all possible interactions between the users and the network.[48] Figure 14-3

---

[48] The method of using state diagrams for Stage 1.3 service descriptions is given in [20], Annex D.

shows part of the Stage 1.3 specification for the CW service, excerpted from
[16].

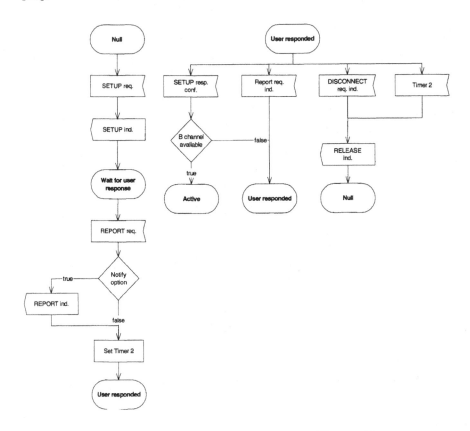

Figure 14-3. Stage 1.3 description for CW service: State machine.

This diagram shows the state changes the network undergoes in response
to user input. Each of the signal receptions and sends indicated in this
diagram are between the network and the users. Stage 1 behavior is often
rather straightforward, as it involves only a single process (the network)
interacting with its environment. In simple cases, sequence diagrams may
also be chosen to describe the dynamic behavior of the network.

The first step at Stage 2 is the development of the functional model for
the service under design. We use a collaboration diagram to describe the
functional model. A collaboration diagram specifies a set of participants that
conspire to bring about a particular functionality. As Figure 14-4 indicates,
the CW service results from three participants, referred to as *FE1*, *FE2*, and
FE3 in [18], communicating through two information channels r_a and r_b. In

any network providing the CW service, instances having the properties ascribed to *FE1*, *FE2*, and *FE3* will be found. The type of these instances must realize the types of the corresponding functional entity.

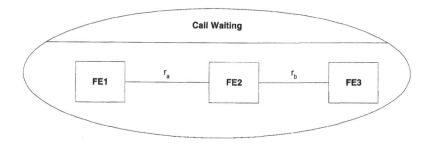

Figure 14-4. Stage 2.1 description for CW service: Collaboration diagram.

Step 2.2 identifies the interactions between the functional entities that permit the distribution of the service as defined by the functional model. Sequence diagrams are used to show the interaction between the functional entities identified in Step 2.1.

For example, in Figure 14-5, each of the functional entities collaborating to produce the CW service are represented as a life line. The diagram shows the messages interchanged between these functional entities when notifying User B of the call waiting request. This diagram makes use of the structuring capabilities now introduced in UML.[49] Upon receipt of the setup request indication primitive, if a B-channel is available (as indicated by the guard described in functional entity action *920*), a setup request indication is created, otherwise the scenario terminates.[50] The use of the alternative and optional combined interaction fragments allows a compact representation of the variability inherent in the CW notification scenario. Figure 14-5 also shows the use of a timer.

---

[49] The structuring capabilities introduced in UML 2 are critical in enabling the use of UML in Stage 2 service descriptions. Earlier versions would result in a significant blowup in the number of sequence diagrams required to describe even simple scenarios.

[50] The specification in [18], somewhat unintuitively, uses numbers to identify functional entity actions.

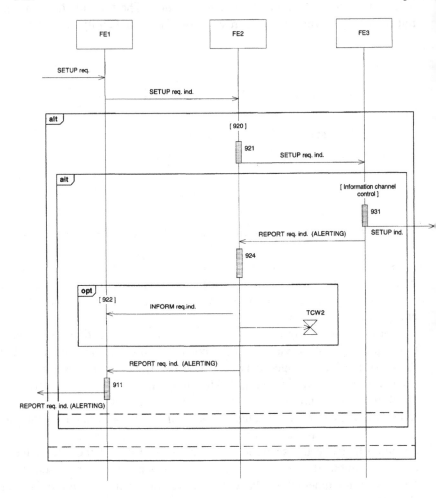

Figure 14-5. Stage 2.2 description of CW service: Notification Sequence Diagram.

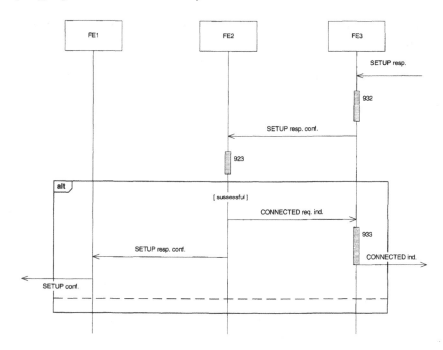

Figure 14-6. Stage 2.2 description of CW service: Acceptance Sequence Diagram.

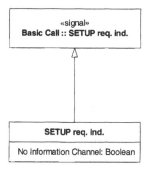

Figure 14-7. SETUP req. ind. primitive

These sequence diagrams depict part of the behavior of the CW service. Any implementation of the CW service has to obey the sequence of message interchanges described in Step 2.2 sequence diagrams.

In addition, the information conveyed by messages between the functional entities is elaborated at this step. As shown in Figure 14-7, the CW service augments the *SETUP req. ind.* primitive of the underlying bearer service to carry information as to whether an information interface channel is available.

In Step 2.3, the functions performed within a functional entity are identified and represented in the form of a state machine diagram. The inputs and outputs of the state diagram are to and from the users, as described in Stage 1 and are message exchanges to and from other functional entities, as described at Step 2.2. For each functional entity identified at Step 2.1, a state machine diagram is produced.

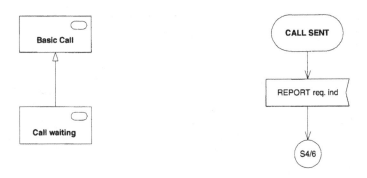

Figure 14-8. Relationship to the Basic Call Stage 2.3 description.

For supplementary services, the states and state transitions extend the state machines defined for the underlying bearer or teleservice. The CW service is an enhancement of the Basic Call service defined in [19]. The Stage 2.3 description of the Basic Call service specifies a state machine. The CW service Stage 2.3 description, in turn, specifies a state machine that inherits from the Basic Call state machine, as shown on the left side of Figure 14-8. The CW state machine inherits all the states and transitions of the Basic Call state machine.

In addition, the CW state machine redefines some of the transitions of the Basic Call state machine by extending these with additional behavior. For example, Figure 14-9 shows that the transition invoked by receiving the *REPORT req. ind.* primitive in state *CALL SENT* will check whether, in the case of a CW service, the inform option has been selected, in which case the *INFORM req. ind.* primitive is sent before setting the call waiting timer and continuing as in Basic Call. (The right side of Figure 14-8 shows the above transition as specified for Basic Call.) Using state machine inheritance, we can show how a supplementary service extends the underlying bearer or teleservice in a concise manner, without repeating detail from the specification of the underlying service.

The actions performed within a functional entity are represented in Step 2.4 as a sequence of functional entity actions. These actions will be described in terms of an action language (such as the action subset of SDL) or activity diagrams, as is shown in Figure 14-10 for the functional entity action *920* in [18]. This action is shown to be the entry condition to the CW Notification scenario, see Figure 14-5.

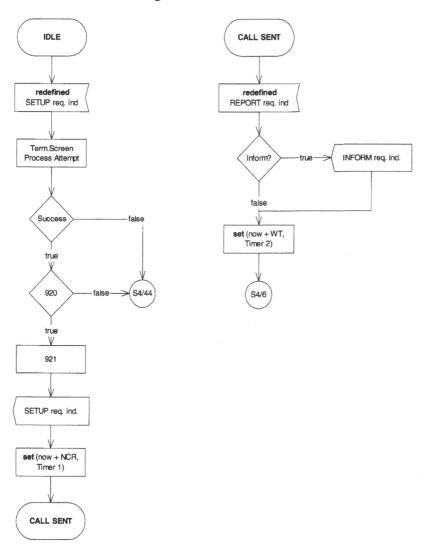

Figure 14-9. Stage 2.3 description of CW service: State Machine for *FE2*.

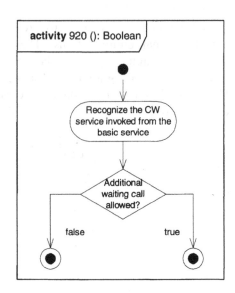

Figure 14-10. Stage 2.4 description of CW service: Functional entity action *920*.

Finally, in Step 2.5, the functional entities and messages identified in the previous steps are allocated to specific physical locations within the network. A UML collaboration is used to depict the various physical locations within the network interacting to produce the overall behavior of the network. In Step 2.1, we have identified the functional model of the CW service, also in the form of a collaboration between functional entities. A collaboration occurrence represents one particular use of a collaboration to explain the relationships between the participants of an underlying collaboration (or some other classifier). In Figure 14-11, the *Use Call Waiting* occurrence indicates the participants that cooperate within the ISDN network according to the *Call Waiting* collaboration representing the functional model (see Figure 14-4). For example, the *FE2* role of the CW service will be played by the local exchange (LE) participant in the ISDN network. Different functional entities may be allocated to the same location in the network, albeit every functional entity will be allocated completely to a single location.

The entities that will eventually implement the physical network locations will have to exhibit the properties and behaviors ascribed to the functional entities allocated to each physical location. Figure 14-11 shows that both TE_1 and TE_2 roles will be played by instances of terminal equipment (TE). Any such instance will have to support behavior satisfying both the properties of *FE1* and *FE3*, for the case of the CW service.

At Stage 3, each of the physical network locations will be designed separately. Each network location has to be able to exhibit the behavior of all functional entities allocated to it, for each service to be performed by the network. Similarly, the messages that will be interchanged between these network locations will have to carry the information specified for all services performed by the network.

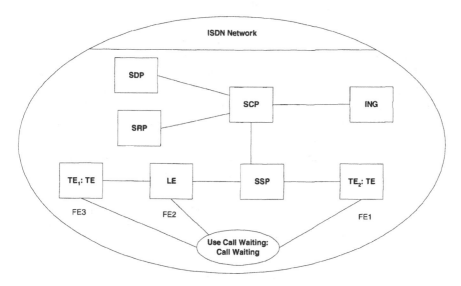

Figure 14-11. Stage 2.5 description of CW service: Collaboration occurrence.

As described earlier, this methodology can now in turn be applied to the design of each network location. For each network element, we can describe its behavior from the point of view of its environment, again considering the network element as a single, indivisible entity and then decompose its behavior into smaller components that collaborate to bring about the behavior of the network element.

5. THE UML TELECOM PROFILES

UML aims to be applicable to a wide range of application domains, ranging from health and finance to aerospace to e-commerce. In order to subsume the possible variances of application domains, UML does not define all language concepts (such as its concurrency semantics) to the level of detail necessary to allow unambiguous interpretation. As such, UML defines not a language per se, but a family of languages from which a specific language must first be instantiated by possibly selecting a subset of the modeling concepts, providing a dynamic semantics for these concepts suitable to the application domain, and possibly adding certain concepts unique to the application domain. The mechanism to instantiate a particular language from the UML language family is referred to as a "profile." In addition to giving detailed semantics where the UML definition is intentionally vague, a profile can also provide notations suitable for the instantiated language.

The SDL UML profiles focus on the modeling of reactive, state/event driven systems typically found in telecom applications.[51] They give precise, formal semantics for all concepts and constitute a language for specifying executable models independently of an implementation language. While inheriting the traditional strength of UML in object-oriented data modeling, the SDL UML profiles provide the following concepts that are of particular importance in the telecommunications domain.

- Modeling of active objects executing concurrently or by interleaving, the hierarchical structure of active objects, and their connection by means of well-defined interfaces.
- A complete action language that is independent of implementation languages. In practice, actions may be translated into target languages, but (correct) translation does not change the behavior. Actions are specified in imperative style and may be mixed with graphical notation.
- Object oriented data based on single inheritance and with both polymorphic references (objects) and values, even in the same inheritance hierarchy. Type safety is preserved in the presence of covariance through multiple dispatch.
- Mapping of the logical layout of data to a transfer syntax per the encoding rules of a protocol.
- An exception handling mechanism for behavior specified either through state machines or constructs of the action language that makes it suitable as a design/high-level implementation language.
- Composite states that are defined by separate state diagrams (for scalability); entry/exit points are used instead of state boundary crossing (for encapsulation), any composite state can be of a state type (for reuse), and state types can be parameterized (for even more reuse). Composite states may have sequential or interleaving interpretation.

---

[51] Formally, SDL is the acronym for the language defined by ITU Recommendations Z.100 to Z.107. However, following engineering custom, SDL is taken to mean ITU "System Design Languages" – the combination of SDL, MSC, and ASN.1, which are typically used jointly to develop telecommunication applications. The set of profiles for these notations is referred to as the "SDL profiles."

- Roadmaps (High-level MSC) for improved structuring of sequence diagrams; inline expressions for compactness of description, and references for better reuse of sequence diagrams.
- Object-orientation applied to active objects including inheritance of behavior specified through state machines and inheritance of the (hierarchical) structure and connection of active objects.
- Constraints on redefinitions in subclasses and on actual parameters in parameterization that afford strong error checking at modeling time.

At the time of writing, telecommunications companies consider the appropriate engineering approach is to use UML as specialized by the SDL profiles, so that these profiles are providing a formal semantics that can be directly implemented. Convergence continues, as UML 2.0 provides a better basis for integration with the ITU languages and ETSI and ITU studies already underway have objectives to update the Z.109 profile, define similar profiles for MSC and ASN.1, and update the methodology guidelines.

By relying on the SDL profiles, additional support for the development of telecommunication services and systems is gained. Figure 14-12 shows the SDL profiles to be used at the various steps of the ITU service description methodology.

In contrast to the UML, the SDL profiles provide an operational semantics for all the constructs of the UML. Developers can rely on the precise description of these constructs to unambiguously understand the meaning of their specifications. In addition, a number of tools have been developed that leverage the formal operational semantics to enable the verification and validation of specifications and to generate applications from the specifications.

As each of the steps in the ITU service description methodology is manual, defects might be introduced. A number of techniques have been presented [21] that allow one to verify that the more detailed specifications at later steps in fact describe behavior consistent with the earlier specification steps. In particular, we should verify the consistency between the Step 1.3 state diagrams, the Step 2.2 message sequences, and the Step 2.3 state diagrams. While each subsequent step may introduce additional detail, the systems specified in later steps should exhibit the behaviors prescribed in earlier steps. Similarly, the system resulting from Stage 3 must exhibit these behaviors.

The sequence diagrams developed at Step 2.2 also provide an excellent starting point for the development of test cases for the final system. Techniques have been developed for deriving test suites from the message sequences captured at this stage, together with the definition of the information content of each message. By selecting different network locations to serve as the *instance under test*, test suites for each network element can be derived from the Step 2.2 specifications.

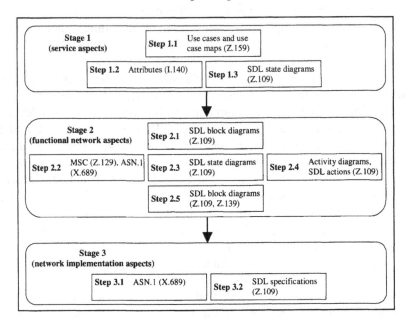

Figure 14-12. Using SDL profiles at the stages of the
ITU service description methodology.

At Stage 3, all services allocated to a network location are assembled into the behavior of each network element. While during the development of each individual service limited attention is paid to the possibility of services interfering with each other, any potential interaction between services must now be eliminated. (Such feature interactions, e.g., by multiple services being triggered by the same message primitive, or the same message primitive having different meaning in concurrently active services, have been recognized as the source of the most costly defects of telecommunication systems.) Tools can be deployed to pinpoint mutual interaction between services executing on a network element.

Finally, the operational semantics of the SDL profiles allow the derivation of product code for applications implementing the various network elements. SDL provides sufficient expressive power to fully specify such systems, and many commercial systems have been delivered to customers with code generated by tools directly from Stage 3 specifications. ASN.1 provides the necessary expressive power to allow messages between network elements to be specified abstractly at Step 2.2 and to allow the automated generation of data marshaling code imposing the encoding rules of the network protocol.

A tool chain leveraging the SDL profiles and supporting the verification and validation steps between stages of the ITU service description methodology as well as the generation of complete applications code from Stage 3 specifications is available. A number of vendors have shipped telecommunication equipment implemented with high levels of automation following this methodology.

REFERENCES

[1] International Telecommunications Union, *Method for the Characterization of Telecommunication Services supported by an ISDN and Network Capabilities of an ISDN*, Recommendation I.130, 1988

[2] International Telecommunications Union, *Attribute Technique for the Characterization of Telecommunication Services supported by an ISDN and Network Capabilities of an ISDN*, Recommendation I.140, 1988.

[3] International Telecommunications Union, *The unified functional methodology for the characterization of services and network capabilities*, Recommendation Q.65, 2000.

[4] International Telecommunications Union, *Specification and Description Language (SDL)*, Recommendation Z.100, 2002.

[5] J. Ellsberger, D. Hogrefe, and A. Sarma, *SDL*, Prentice Hall, Hemel Hempstead, 1997.

[6] A. Olsen, O. Færgemand, B. Møller-Pedersen, R. Reed, and J.R.W. Smith, *Systems Engineering Using SDL-92*, North-Holland, Amsterdam, 1994.

[7] International Telecommunications Union, *Message sequence charts (MSC)*, Recommendation Z.120, 1999.

[8] International Telecommunications Union, *SDL combined with ASN.1 modules (SDL/ASN.1)*, Recommendation Z.105, 2001.

[9] R. Reed (ed.), *Specification and Programming Environment for Communication Software*, North Holland, Amsterdam, 1993.

[10] M. Dauphin, G. Fonade, and R. Reed, "SPECS: Making Formal Techniques Usable", *IEEE Software*, Vol. 11, 1993.

[11] International Telecommunications Union, *SDL+ methodology: Use of MSC and SDL (with ASN.1)*, Recommendation Z.100, Supplement 1, 1997.

[12] J. Rumbaugh, M. Blaha, W. Premerlani, F. Eddy, and W. Lorenson, *Object-Oriented Modeling and Design*, Prentice Hall, 1992.

[13] Object Management Group, *Model Driven Architecture*, ORMSC/01-06-01, 2001.

[14] D. Frankel, *Model Driven Architecture*, Wiley, 2003.

[15] Object Management Group, *OMG Unified Modeling Language Specification*, 1.4, 1997.

[16] B. Møller-Pedersen and T. Weigert, "Towards a Convergence of SDL and UML", *Proc. 2nd Intl. Conf. on the Unified Modeling Language*, Ft. Collins, 1999.

[17] International Telecommunications Union, *Call Waiting (CW) Supplementary Service*, Recommendation I253.1, 1990.

[18] International Telecommunications Union, *Stage 2 Description for Call Completion Supplementary Services Section 1 – Call Waiting (CW)*, Recommendation Q.83.1, 1991.

[19] International Telecommunications Union, *ISDN Circuit Mode Switched Bearer Service*, Recommendation I.71, 1993.

[20] International Telecommunications Union, *Principles of telecommunication services supported by an ISDN and the means to describe them*, Recommendation I.210, 1993.

[21] A.Letichevsky and D.Gilbert, "A Model for Interaction of Agents and Environments", In D.Bert, C.Choppy, and P.Moses (Eds), *Recent Trends in Algebraic Development Techniques*, Lecture Notes in Computer Science 1827, Springer, 1999, pp. 311-328.

Chapter 15

Leveraging UML to Deliver Correct Telecom Applications

Sergey Baranov[1], Clive Jervis[1], Vsevolod Kotlyarov[1], Alexander Letichevsky[2], and Thomas Weigert[1]
[1]*Motorola, Inc.* [2]*ISS Ltd.*

Abstract: Stringent reliability demanded of telecommunications systems requires that the absence of defects be ascertained as extensively as possible. In this chapter, we present techniques we have developed to verify specifications expressed in sequence diagrams: formal verification of specifications can demonstrate the consistency and completeness of a set of sequence diagrams. Automated test case generation can produce a test suite that is able to establish that a system exhibits the traces implied by a set of sequence diagrams.

Key words: Modeling, Validation and Verification, Telecommunications

In order to allow the specification of telecommunication services and systems independent from the underlying network technologies, the ITU service description methodology was defined and standardized [1]. This methodology describes a telecommunication system in three stages: it begins with a service description from the user point of view, proceeds to describing a functional model of the network and the interfaces between user and network, as well as between the functional elements of the network, and finally, gives a description of the physical network elements and the protocols and message formats relied upon for communication between these network elements.

A key assumption when developing telecommunication services and systems following this methodology is that specifications at the various stages of abstraction are consistent. The specifications at lower (later) stages of abstraction must exhibit all the behaviors specified at higher (earlier) stages of abstraction, and they must not include behaviors that violate behaviors specified at higher stages of abstraction. In addition, Stage 3 service descriptions assemble the specification of network elements from the

L. Lavagno, G. Martin and B. Selic (eds.), UML for Real, 323-342.

Stage 2 specifications of the functional elements that are allocated to each network element. The services supported by a network element must not interfere with each other, either by the same message primitive having different meanings for several services provided by the same network element, or incompatible services being triggered by the same message primitive. Such difficulties arise due to the limited number of inputs available to the network in original terminal equipment as well as due to the distributed nature of telecommunication systems, where network elements need to infer the state of other devices from the history of their interaction.

The stringent reliability requirements on telecommunications equipment demand that the correctness of telecommunication services and systems be assured as much as possible.

1.   VERIFICATION AND VALIDATION

UML is well suited to express the specification of telecommunication services and systems following the ITU service description methodology [2]. However, UML proper does not give a precise dynamic semantics to its constructs, in order to be able to support a wide variety of application domains that demand incompatible interpretations for various UML modeling constructs. UML provides a mechanism (referred to as a "profile") to assign a precise, domain-specific meaning to its constructs. The telecom community has developed such a UML profile to support the particular needs of the development of telecommunication services and systems. This profile was standardized as ITU Recommendation Z.109 [3] and became the first standardized real-time profile for UML. Additional UML profiles for message sequence diagrams, deployment diagrams, use case diagrams, and interface definitions are under development at the ITU and ETSI (Recommendations Z.129, Z.139, Z.159, and X.689, respectively).

Specifications captured in terms of these UML profiles can be given their interpretation in terms of Labeled Transition Systems [4]. The total behavior of such systems can be examined by model checking, where the behavior of the system is computed and represented in terms of a reachability graph [5].

While model checking is powerful in that it can verify whether assertions about the system (including propositional temporal claims) hold, traditional model checking techniques have not been successfully applied to industrial sized feature scenarios and specifications because they are complex, resulting in too large a state space for the tools to search. This is compounded by specifications typically being intentionally partial, which can cause traditional techniques to detect many insignificant conflicts and to miss some significant ones. Table 15-1 shows the impact of state space explosion on the performance of popular tools (using both global state compression or on-the-fly techniques) with a test case characteristic for large distributed systems.[52]

*Table 15-1.*State space explosion and its impact on tools

Processes	States	Total CPU time (seconds)				
		SDT	Geode (BFS)	Geode (DFS)	Spin	FDR2
5	243	1	2	3	< 1	1
6	729	2	3	3	< 1	2
7	2187	6	4	7	1	3
8	6561	20	11	19	3	7
9	19683	71	33	62	19	22
10	59049	250	110	211	119	71
11	177147	DNF	377	716	1034	229
12	531441	DNF	1322	2501	6977	734

In the following, we discuss techniques we have implemented in tools that reflect engineering understanding of such specifications, yet give tractable analysis techniques reporting significant conflicts. We focus on using message sequence charts (MSC) as the starting point for analysis. MSC are central in the ITU service description methodology as they are used to capture Stage 2.2 service specifications. At this stage, the interactions between the functional entities comprising the system are captured in the form of message exchanges between the functional entities. The Stage 2.2 MSC describe behavioral scenarios that any subsequent system specification has to satisfy.

1.1 A UML MSC Profile

UML 2.0 has significantly enhanced the capabilities of UML sequence diagrams by subsuming most of the structuring capabilities of MSC [6]. However, UML sequence diagrams still lack the precise trace semantics of MSC; therefore, we rely on an MSC profile for UML. In addition, this profile extends the standard semantics of MSC in the following way.
– Conditions are used as synchronization primitives, such that all events following after some condition on the instances involved in this condition also follow after all events preceding this condition.

---

[52] A number of techniques have been proposed to reduce the effects of state space explosion: partial order reduction, state abstraction, partial analysis, system partitioning. Unfortunately, even applying a combination of these techniques has not brought the state space required to represent realistic systems to a manageable size.

- Events can be given a time specification, which defines the relative or absolute time of an event and its duration. The time is defined by means of numerical intervals indicating when an event can happen. The time specification of an event can be correlated with another event, marked by a label or with the previous event that occurred at the same instance. Time specifications can depend on parameters. The formal semantics of time extension of MSC has been defined in [7].
- Conditions can be augmented with logical expressions specified in a first order language. These expressions are interpreted on the set of states of a process induced by an MSC diagram. States are represented by means of state variables and constraints on their values changing over time.
- We distinguish two kinds of logical expressions. Control expressions are used in control constructs such as conditionals or loops. The possible values of control expressions define possible continuations of a process dependent on the current state or its properties. Annotation expressions are used for checking the correctness of MSC diagrams. They must be valid at the points where they are placed for any execution of this MSC diagram.

We distinguish three kinds of MSC diagrams: basic protocols, scenarios based on these protocols, and independent diagrams.

Basic protocols are composed of messages and local actions. Each protocol has preconditions placed just after initialization of the instances involved and postconditions placed just before termination of the corresponding instances. Basic protocols can be parameterized by the instances participating in the basic protocol; instances can also be parameters to conditional expressions and messages.

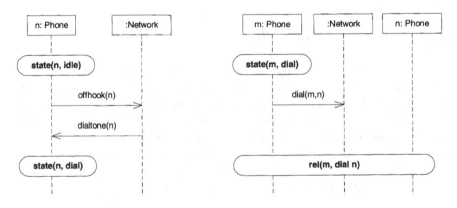

Figure 15-1. Call Setup Protocols (1)

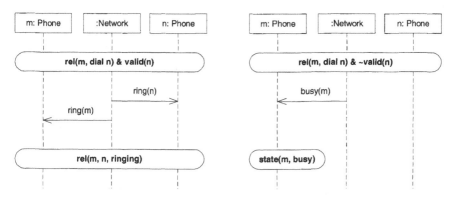

Figure 15-2. Call Setup Protocols (2)

Scenarios are MSC diagrams formally generated from basic protocols by means of consistent parallel and sequential compositions, inserting control conditions, annotations, and expressions.[53] The generation of a scenario starts from arbitrary states such that all preconditions of the initial protocols are valid and continues such that preconditions of each protocol in the scenario logically follow from the postconditions of previous protocols and the properties of the current state. Figure 15-3 shows a scenario that can be generated from the basic protocols depicted in Figure 15-1 and Figure 15-2. For all scenarios, the following condition must hold: if its preconditions are valid at some moment of time, then the corresponding basic protocol can be executed and its postconditions will be valid after the execution of the protocol. The composition of basic protocols into scenarios must be consistent in that if a protocol follows another protocol in the scenario, then the preconditions of that protocol must be consequences of the post-conditions of the preceding protocol.

Independent diagrams are MSC diagrams without annotations; they are not constructed from basic protocols. Instead, they are used to define the set of traces (tests), possibly augmented by temporal specifications. The only way to describe the change of state variables for independent diagrams are local actions with predefined semantics (assignment statements or non-deterministic change of values).

---

[53] Since basic protocols can be parameterized by instances, copies of the same basic protocol may involve different instances of a scenario at different locations.

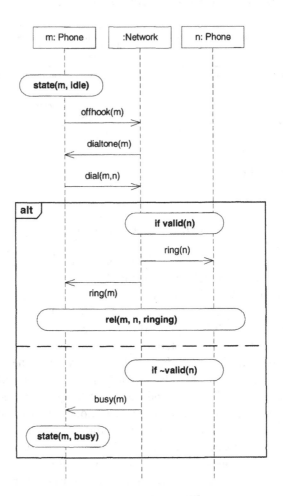

Figure 15-3. Call Setup Scenario

1.2   MSC Pathologies

A number of studies have highlighted traps that users can fall into when writing MSC-based specifications (see [8-12]).

For example, an MSC contains a race condition when an explicit arrival order is specified between two messages sent to a common instance but originating from independent instances, as illustrated in Figure 15-4. We refer to such problems as *pathologies*; characteristically such problem MSC conform to the semantics of the MSC language, but nonetheless would generate errors in an implementation, if implementable at all. We have developed tools to identify such pathologies as a check to be employed by engineers drafting MSC specifications.

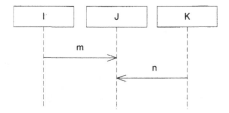

Figure 15-4. Race condition.

Currently, we identify several categories of pathologies including:
–   race conditions,
–   non-local choice,
–   non-local ordering,
–   false underspecification.
Some of these pathologies can be mitigated depending on architectural information, for example, by the underlying communication channel. For example, consider Figure 15-5 in which no race will occur if the message transit time is constant, or if the messages are buffered using a FIFO queue. Contrast this with Figure 15-4 where unless the sending of the two messages is somehow coordinated, say by prior communication, the channel behavior cannot remove the possibility of a race occurring.

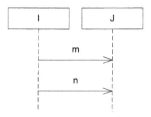

Figure 15-5. Race condition that can be mitigated by channel properties.

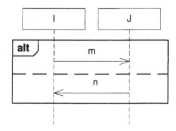

Figure 15-6. Non-local choice.

Figure 15-6 illustrates a non-local choice, in which either instance *I* is to send message *m*, and instance *J* does not therefore send message *n*, or instance *J* sends its message and instance *I* does not send a message. As for race conditions, it is sometimes possible to mitigate the problem, either through previous co-ordination or through the use of exclusive guards on the two choices, and our tools can distinguish pathologies that can be mitigated from those that are not.

Non-local ordering is a similar property to non-local choice except that it involves a *deus ex machina* to force an unsignalled ordering of events on different instances. An MSC general ordering arrow used to connect otherwise unordered events on different instances is an example of a non-local ordering.

False underspecification occurs where events apparently unordered within a co-region are in fact ordered via a path of signals that originates and terminates within the co-region.

2. FEATURE ANALYSIS

We have developed a tool for deductively verifying requirements and specifications for software systems expressed in terms of MSC diagrams.[54] Extensions of Z.120 with time expressions, imperative constructs, and logical annotations are used to capture specifications. Our tool provides automatic checking of the time consistency of MSC diagrams, of the consistency and completeness of underlying basic protocols, of the correct use of basic protocols for building scenarios, and of the annotation consistency of a scenario using deductive theorem proving techniques. The result of analysis is presented in the form of MSC diagrams annotated by comments: comments contain information about traces adjusting the

---

[54] The main verification component is the *Checking Machine*, which uses the *Action Language Simulator* for analyzing the processes defined by MSC diagrams. It formulates the statements to be proven for computing transitions in a model represented as a labeled transition system, checking annotations, and solving constraints. These statements are sent to the *Proving Machine* that organizes the search procedure; the Proving Machine in turn makes use of various solvers and returns values of variables determined by the solvers if it succeeded.

These components are implemented building on the foundation of the algebraic programming environment APS [13]. This environment is an open system in that it is comprised of generic components which can be used to adjust the system to different application domains, for example, by adding domain-specific prover or solver algorithms. Action Language Simulator and Proving Machine [14] implement the theory of interaction of agents and environments [15, 16]. This theory is also used for the development of an operational semantics of extended MSC.

incorrect or unexpected behavior of an MSC or places where inconsistency appears.

2.1 Consistency and Completeness of Protocols

Properties to be verified can be proven, can fail to be proven, or can be refuted. In the case of failure to prove a property, the trace or traces terminating in a state where an annotation cannot be proven or refuted, or where a time constraint is inconsistent with the event ordering of the trace are generated. The following properties can be verified automatically.

Transition consistency of basic protocols. The behavior of a system defined by basic protocols is characterized by the scenarios it generates. When generating a scenario, at each step an applicable basic protocol must be selected. A basic protocol is applicable at a state if all its preconditions are true in that state, given the values of its state variables. In order to construct a deterministic system, the selection of a protocol must depend only on the initial event, i.e., the message or local action that can be performed when a protocol starts. Therefore, each time when some protocol can be applied and there is at least one initial event defined, there must be exactly one applicable protocol.

A sufficient condition for establishing the transition consistency of basic protocols is the following: if the preconditions of two basic protocols are intersected, that is, if the negation of their conjunction cannot be proven or can be refuted, then the processes defined by these protocols as well as their postconditions must be equivalent, provided there exists a common initial event (weak consistency) or a common trace (strong consistency). To prove transition consistency, all pairs of basic protocols are considered and for each pair the consistency condition (the negation of the conjunction of all preconditions) is generated and a proof attempt is initiated. If the proof succeeds (for all symbolic values of state variables and parameters), the pair of protocols is consistent and these two protocols cannot be applied at the same time. Otherwise (not proven or refuted), the protocols and the induced processes are checked for equivalence. Equivalent processes generate the same traces and have provably equivalent postconditions.

Note that this condition is sufficient but not necessary, as it is possible that the intersection of a set of preconditions cannot be refuted but there are no reachable states that validate this intersection.

Completeness of basic protocols. This property implies that at any moment in time, there must be at least one basic protocol that can be used to continue the scenario at this point unless the scenario has terminated. A sufficient condition for completeness is for the disjunction of all preconditions of all basic protocols to be valid, for a given initial event.

Actually, this condition is too strong and can be weakened if an admissibility condition is given for a set of protocols. By admissibility condition we refer to a precondition that is implied by a particular event occurring.[55] In this case, the disjunction of the preconditions of protocols in this set must be valid if the conjunction of admissibility conditions for this set is valid.

Annotation consistency of scenarios. Each diagram obtained from a scenario by substitution of referenced diagrams and selecting paths for alternatives, loops, and parallel compositions must belong to the set of basic protocols generating this scenario. In addition, all annotations must be valid at corresponding states in any admissible basic protocol. If a scenario can be decomposed into a set of basic protocols, it is annotation consistent.

To check for annotation consistency, we use symbolic simulation of MSC diagrams. We start from initial conditions, determine which of the basic protocols can be applied by checking preconditions, match events found in the diagram against expected events according to the basic protocols generating the diagram, and obtain the conditions at the end of each protocol executed concurrently with others. Each time annotations are encountered, they are verified to be consequences from the conditions that currently hold at that state. The current conditions characterizing the internal state of a diagram may be insufficient for the selection of a basic protocol even if the set of basic protocols is transition consistent. In this case, the alternatives will be determined by control conditions. In the case of loops, annotations can be used as loop invariants. If the invariant of a loop is proven, the loop needs to be symbolically evaluated only once.

Time consistency. Each MSC diagram defines some partial order on the set of events which can occur during its execution. This ordering must be consistent with time specifications, which must not violate the partial order of MSC without those time specifications.

Time consistency is verified by symbolic simulation of a diagram. The state variables are time variables corresponding to the moments of time at which events happen. Verifying constraints on the time variables is reduced to solving a system of linear equalities and inequalities over the reals. A special prover and solver have been used to implement a method for determining time consistency.

2.2   Example Verification

In order to verify specifications of system requirements to following input is considered:

---

[55] For example, a phone can only go off hook if it had been on hook before.

- MSC diagrams in the form of basic protocols capturing the system specifications,
- MSC diagrams annotated by logic and time specifications describing system scenarios, and
- information about the subject domain captured in axioms, definitions, supplementary equations, etc., which will be utilized by the proofs.

As example, we specified POTS (a basic call bearer service) extended by two supplementary services, Call Waiting (CW) and 3-way calling (3WAY) in 22 basic protocols. Figure 15-1 and Figure 15-2 show the call setup protocols for POTS, while Figure 15-7 and Figure 15-8 give the call teardown protocols for the two supplementary services.

To formalize basic protocols for this example, three predicates were introduced to characterize the states of a telephony system: $rel(m,n,x)$, $state(m,y)$, and $valid(m)$.[56] A set of axioms characterizing these predicates was formulated. Other axioms were discovered and added through unsuccessful attempts to prove consistency: When an inconsistency was found, it was analyzed to explain why given preconditions are not intersected, which yielded additional axioms that allowed the proof to succeed.

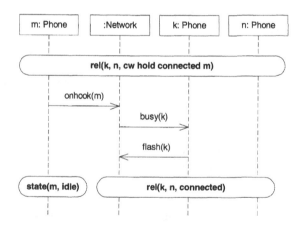

Figure15-7. CW teardown protocol.

---

[56] Here m and n are subscriber identifiers, x is a name of a relation that can join two terminals, and y is the state of a terminal. The predicate rel expresses that a certain relationship holds between two terminals, *state* describes the state of a terminal, and *valid* determines whether a dialed number identified an applicable terminal.

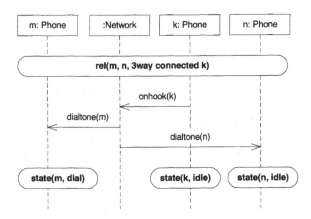

Figure 15-8. 3WAY teardown protocol.

Our tool then generated the consistency statements (there are more than 200 of them). Six of these statements cannot be proven or refuted, and point to inconsistencies due to the interaction between the supplementary services. These inconsistencies can only be removed by redesigning the specification.

An example of such inconsistency is the pair of protocols depicted in Figure 15-7 and Figure 15-8. The consistency condition that is obtained for these two protocols is

Forall(z, k' ,n' ,m'' ,n'')
(~(rel(k', n', cw hold connect z)) ∨ ~(rel(m'', n'',3way connected z)))

given the common initial event *onhook(z)*, where $z=m'$ in the CW case, and $z=k''$ in the 3WAY case, which cannot be proven. Note that if this situation were possible, the network could end up in a state where, upon receiving an *onhook* message, the network would not know how to respond, as the two services demand a different response (it would have to either send a *busy* message to phone k or a *dialtone* to phone k). To ascertain whether the failure to prove the consistency condition indeed points to an inconsistency in the specification, one has to prove that a state satisfying the negation of the consistency condition is reachable from the initial state. Such state indeed exists and our tool constructs a scenario leading to this state. With $k'=n''$, the scenario depicted in Figure 15-9 leads to a state in which the negation of the consistency condition holds.

Our system generates as a verdict a set of traces showing the reachability of the state to be proven. For inconsistencies based on time annotations, the verdicts are annotated with recommendations for adjustments to specified intervals that would eliminate the demonstrated inconsistency.

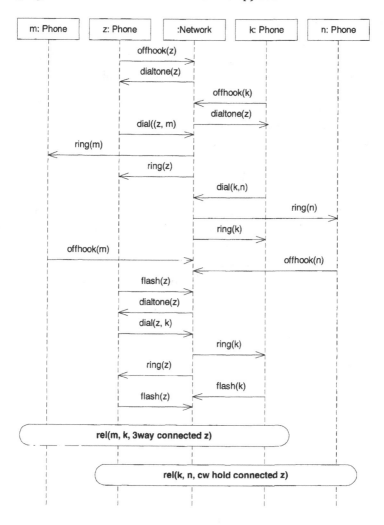

Figure 15-9. Error scenario

3. TEST CASE GENERATION

The aim of test generation is to extract from requirements MSC test sequences that can be used to verify that an implementation has the behavior specified by the MSC. Typically, the target of the tests is an implementation of several of the instances represented in the MSC. That is, the implementation is architected as a number of concurrent processes, each represented by one of the instances in the requirements MSC.

Given an MSC and a declaration of which instances constitute the implementation under test (IUT), test generation is about picking out the MSC events that are responsible for communicating with the IUT instance, and assembling tests from these that respect the partial order defined by the MSC. A test may have to cope with specified non-deterministic behavior of the IUT, and conversely, where non-deterministic behavior is admitted by the non-IUT instances, we generate separate tests for each possible behavior. In this way, a single MSC may generate many tests [17].

3.1   Semantic Model

We build a set of partial order graphs to represent the semantics of a single MSC, in which each node corresponds to an event in the source MSC. These graphs are used subsequently during test generation. It is the *alt* construct in MSC and branching in high-level MSC that requires a set of partial order graphs to represent completely the semantics of a single MSC.

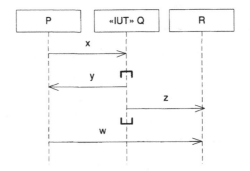

Figure 15-10. Simple MSC with IUT Q.

In the case of Figure 15-10, the semantics requires just the single partial order graph represented in Figure 15-11.

In addition to serving as the foundation of test case generation, the semantic model is also used for aiding the user in understanding the developed test cases. We have developed an off-line debugger for analyzing the IUT behavior. The debugger allows traversal of the specification in single-steps or continuously until breakpoints are reached. At each step, it is possible to observe variables, time labels, and message parameters.

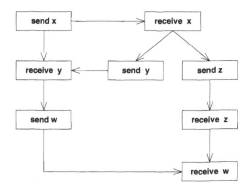

Figure 15-11. Semantic graph for MSC in Figure 15-10.

3.2   Test Generation

Our tools generate black box tests for the IUT, where the box is represented by a subset of MSC instances. Thus, any messaging or other events internal to IUT instances will not appear in the generated tests. The tests generated verify that the order of messaging across any IUT instance/non-IUT instance boundary is as specified by the MSC.

Tests are generated by first building the partial order graphs to represent the semantics of an MSC, and then reducing these to a set of graphs consisting only of those events that are to be in the final tests. Only messages that cross between an IUT instance and a non-IUT instance or vice-versa will appear in a test script. Thus, neither of the two events representing a message that is passed between two IUT instances, or between two non-IUT instances, will appear in a test script. Even though such internal events will not appear in the generated tests, they can impose an order on the test events that test generation algorithms have to take into account. Aside from messages, events such as non-IUT action boxes may also be retained in test scripts, for example, if they are used to compute values used to set the parameters of subsequent outgoing test messages.

These test graphs respect the partial ordering defined by the semantic graphs.

The set of tests is extracted from the test graphs. Each test has a tree form, in which the events are either MSC events, or are extra statements used in the course of a test, such as the setting of a test verdict, timer events used to supervise time constraints, or 'otherwise' statements to catch errant behavior. Apart from otherwise statements, branching in a test represents possible non-deterministic behavior of messages received from the IUT.

These abstract trees are the basis for the code generators. They contain enough information to generate the concrete test code without being specialized to the target test languages.

The nature of the test generated takes into account of how the test system is connected to the equipment under test. We offer two architectures: in one case, the test system is remotely connected to the IUT via communication channels that behave as in the complete deployed system. Alternatively, the test system is connected directly to the ports of the IUT, for which the tests have to simulate any latency effects that may be present in the channels, such as message overtaking.

The number and size of the test scripts that our tools produce can become extremely large even for modestly sized MSC, because all possible interleaving of events need to be expressed. In order to cut down the number of tests, options are provided that select a single ordering of events internal to a test script, notably action boxes, or reduce the size of test scripts by factoring out common subtrees into test steps.

3.3   Test Strategies

We support three strategies that generate tests to be executed as a single process, each potentially generating different test cases. The different test strategies revolve around how the tests deal with non-deterministic behavior in messages received from the IUT, resulting either from branching constructs in the MSC, such as in-line alternatives, or from unordered messages, arising from co-regions, or natural concurrency between different instances.

– Trace Testing: in which each trace of test events through an MSC is created as a separate test script.
– Branch Testing: in which each test represents a separate path through an MSC that contains branching such as in-line alternatives. A path may contain many traces. There may be multiple tests generated to cover each MSC path. Each test here is distinguished by sending the same messages to the IUT in a fixed order whilst accommodating messages received from the IUT in any order.
– Completion Testing: in which each test continues as long as the IUT behaves correctly, no matter which branches of an alternative it goes down (where the choice is made by the IUT). The messages sent by a test script will be dependent upon how the IUT behaves at execution time, but will be fixed within the branch taken.

Under the branch testing strategy each test is formed by combining into a single script all those test traces that differ only in the order that receive messages occur (see Figure 15-12). Thus, the order of all non-receive events (sends, actions, etc.) will be the same on all paths through a single script. This also means that traces containing events from different operands of an alternative cannot be combined, so that a test caters for just one choice of each alternative in the source MSC.

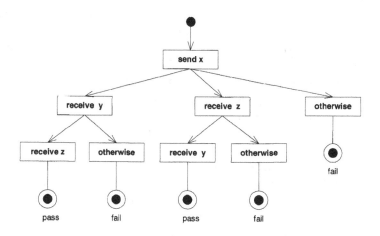

Figure 15-12. Single test for MSC of Figure 15-10.

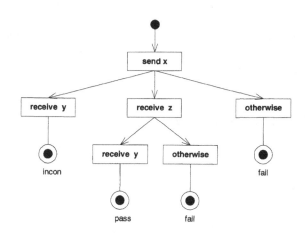

Figure 15-13. One of two trace tests for Figure 15-10.

If the test depicted in Figure 15-12 passes upon execution, then we can say that the IUT behaved as specified, but we cannot say in which order the messages *y* and *z* were received. There are occasions where knowing which order occurred is important to ensure that all possible scenarios are eventually tested. The single test could be split into two tests, each covering just one possible ordering of the messages *y* and *z*.

To avoid false failures, the trace testing strategy requires a third kind of verdict–inconclusive, which is used to terminate a test when the IUT behaves correctly according to its specification, but is not the scenario covered by the test in question (see Figure 15-13).

Under Completion Testing, tests produced by Branch Testing are combined into single scripts where the IUT is free to choose which branches are taken. That is, if the IUT is free to initiate events from more than one branch, then the test script will respond accordingly. Test execution will continue to completion as long as the IUT behaves correctly.

On the sequential model, conformance tests are generated from an MSC where each test is executed as a single process. We have also incorporated concurrent test script generation, where the implementation under test can be interrogated by a collection of parallel test components (PTC), each running their own test script independently. The PTC can be autonomous processes running over a distributed system and can synchronize their behavior by dedicated communication channels carrying coordinating messages.

A concurrent test script can be considered as a set of ordinary test scripts, one per PTC, except that they may send and receive messages to or from other scripts in the set as well as the IUT; the final verdict is computed automatically from the individual verdicts by a master test component. Generating concurrent test scripts from an MSC may require new messages in the scripts, which are used to synchronize the actions between PTC as it communicates with the IUT.

4.   END-TO-END V&V

The tools discussed in Section 2 prove correctness of the implementation (i.e., they verify the implementation). However, we still need to run tests in order to validate the system (to demonstrate that it really performs as expected).

Places of incorrectness are inconsistencies that have been proven. When inconsistencies are detected, counter-examples in the form of an MSC trace are generated, which need to be studied by the user in order to correct the specification. For this trace, test cases can be generated and the trace can be examined in the test debugger (see section 3.1).

In the process of proving, additional constraints (usually in the form of expressions with equalities and inequalities) may be provided by the user. These constraints are accumulated and are used to create filters for application inputs. Due to these filters, the proving process is performed only in the areas governed by these constraints.

As discussed above, we may not succeed in proving correctness of the complete system, in which case we need to perform residual testing of the unverified portions. However, validating a verified system requires far fewer test cases than direct testing of the complete application.

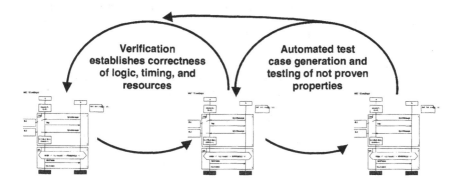

Figure 15-14. Interaction between verification and validation steps.

As a result of verification, we obtain a verdict, which indicates the areas for residual testing. This verdict is in the form of an MSC which may be submitted to our test case generation tool or (after corrections to the system) resubmitted to the verification tools. The user selects the parameter values for test generation against the unverified parts of the specification in order to validate the system through residual testing. Residual testing will again deliver a verdict, in the form of an MSC. If validation did not succeed, then this verdict shows a trace that is a counter-example for the expected behavior. This trace may be corrected manually and then resubmitted for verification.

By leveraging verification before testing, we can provide test coverage based on the functional areas of the application, rather than examining the complete state space of all possible test cases. We have also observed that the obtained test coverage is more effective in detecting defects, as while redundant tests are avoided, tests for obscure scenarios are generated, which might not otherwise be foreseen by a developer preparing tests manually.

REFERENCES

[1] International Telecommunications Union, *Method for the Characterization of Telecommunication Services supported by an ISDN and Network Capabilities of an ISDN*, Recommendation I.130, 1988.

[2] T. Weigert and R. Reed, "Specifying Telecommunications Systems with UML", this volume, Chapter 14.

[3] International Telecommunications Union, *SDL Combined with UML*, Recommendation Z.109, 1999.

[4] J. Godskesen, "A Compositional Operational Semantics for Basic SDL", *Proc. of the 5th SDL Forum*, North-Holland, Amsterdam, 1991.

[5] J. Tsai and T. Weigert, "A logic-based requirements language for the specification and analysis of real-time systems", *Proc. 2nd Conf. Object-Oriented Real-Time Dependable Systems*, Laguna Beach, 1996, pp. 8–16.

[6] International Telecommunications Union, *Message Sequence Charts (MSC)*, Recommendation Z.120, 1999.

[7] A.A. Letichevsky, J.V. Kapitonova, V.P.Kotlyarov, A.A.Letichevsky Jr, and V.A.Volkov, Semantics of timed MSC language, *Cybernetics and System Analyses*, 4, 2002.

[8] L. Helouet. "Some Pathological Message Sequence Charts, and How to Detect Them", *Proc. 10th SDL Forum*, Lecture Notes in Computer Science 2078, Springer, 2001, pp. 348-364.

[9] G. Holzmann. "Formal Methods for Early Fault Detection", in *Proc. Formal Techniques for Real-Time and Fault Tolerant Systems*, Lecture Notes in Computer Science 1135, Springer, 1995, pp. 40-54.

[10] G. Robert, F. Khendek, and P. Grogono, "Deriving an SDL specification with a given architecture from a set of MSC", *Proc. of the 8th SDL Forum*, Elsevier/North Holland, 1997, pp. 197-212.

[11] R. Alur, G. Holzmann, and D. Peled, "An Analyzer for Message Sequence Charts", *Software - Concepts and Tools*, 17, 1996, pp. 70-77.

[12] G. Holzmann, "Early Fault Detection Tools", *Software - Concepts and Tools*, 17, 1996, pp. 63-69.

[13] J.V. Kapitonova, A.A. Letichevsky, and S.V. Konozenko, "Computations in APS", *Theoretical Computer Science*, 119, 1993, pp. 145-171.

[14] A.A. Letichevsky, J.V. Kapitonova, A.B. Godlevsky, and V.A. Volkov, "Evidence Algorithm and its extension", in *Proc. Intl. Workshop on Logic and Complexity in Computer Science*, Creteil, 2001, pp. 159-167.

[15] A.A. Letichevsky and D. Gilbert, "A Model for Interaction of Agents and Environments", in D. Bert, C. Choppy, and P. Moses (Eds.), *Recent Trends in Algebraic Development Techniques*, Lecture Notes in Computer Science 1827, Springer, 1999, pp. 311-328.

[16] A.A. Letichevsky and D. Gilbert, "A general theory of action languages", *Cybernetics and System Analyses*, 1, 1998, 16-36.

[17] P. Baker, P. Bristow, C. Jervis, D. King, and B. Mitchell, "Automatic Generation of Conformance Tests From Message Sequence Charts", *Proc. of 3rd SAM Workshop*, Aberystwyth, to appear in Lecture Notes in Computer Science, Springer, 2003.

Chapter 16

Software Performance Engineering

Connie U. Smith[1] and Lloyd G. Williams[2]

[1]*Performance Engineering Services, PO Box 2640, Santa Fe, NM 87504, www.perfeng.com*
[2]*Software Engineering Research, 264 Ridgeview Lane, Boulder, CO 80302, (303) 938-9847*

Abstract: Performance is critical to the success of today's software systems. However, many software products fail to meet their performance objectives when they are initially constructed. Fixing these problems is costly and causes schedule delays, cost overruns, lost productivity, damaged customer relations, missed market windows, lost revenues, and a host of other difficulties. This chapter presents *software performance engineering* (SPE), a systematic, quantitative approach to constructing software systems that meet performance objectives. SPE begins early in the software development process to model the performance of the proposed architecture and high-level design. The models help to identify potential performance problems when they can be fixed quickly and economically.

Key words: performance, software performance engineering, architecture

1. INTRODUCTION

While the functionality delivered by a software application is obviously important, it is not the only concern. Over its lifetime, the cost of a software product is determined more by how well it achieves its objectives for quality attributes such as performance, reliability/availability or maintainability, than by its functionality.

This chapter focuses on developing software systems that meet performance objectives. Performance is the degree to which a software system or component meets its objectives for timeliness. Thus, performance is any characteristic of a software product that you could, in principle, measure by sitting at the computer with a stopwatch in your hand.

There are two important dimensions to software performance: *responsiveness* and *scalability*. *Responsiveness* is the ability of a system to

343

L. Lavagno, G. Martin and B. Selic (eds.), UML for Real, 343-365.
© 2003 *Kluwer Academic Publishers.*

meet its objectives for response time or throughput. In real-time systems, responsiveness is a measure of how fast the system responds to an event, or the number of events that can be processed in a given time. *Scalability* is the ability of a system to continue to meet its response time or throughput objectives as the demand for the software functions increases. Scalability is an increasingly important aspect of today's software systems.

Performance is critical to the success of today's software systems. However, many software products fail to meet their performance objectives when they are initially constructed. Fixing these problems is costly and causes schedule delays, cost overruns, lost productivity, damaged customer relations, missed market windows, lost revenues, and a host of other difficulties. In extreme cases, it may not be possible to fix performance problems without extensive redesign and re-implementation. In those cases, the project either becomes an infinite sink for time and money, or it is, mercifully, canceled.

Performance cannot be retrofitted; it must be designed into software from the beginning. The "make it run, make it run right, make it run fast" approach is dangerous. Recent interest in software architectures has underscored the importance of architecture in achieving software quality objectives, including performance. While decisions made at every phase of the development process are important, architectural decisions have the greatest impact on quality attributes such as modifiability, reusability, reliability, and performance. As Clements and Northrup note [1]:

> "Whether or not a system will be able to exhibit its desired (or required) quality attributes is largely determined by the time the architecture is chosen."

Our experience is that performance problems are most often due to inappropriate architectural choices rather than inefficient coding. By the time the architecture is fixed, it may be too late to achieve adequate performance by tuning. While a good architecture cannot guarantee attainment of performance objectives, a poor architecture can prevent their achievement.

This chapter presents an overview of *software performance engineering* (SPE), a systematic, quantitative approach to constructing software systems that meet performanced objectives. SPE prescribes principles for creating responsive software, the data required for evaluation, procedures for obtaining performance specifications, and guidelines for the types of evaluation to be conducted at each development stage. It incorporates models for representing and predicting performance as well as a set of analysis methods [2]. Use of the UML for deriving SPE models is discussed in [3].

Because of the importance of architecture in determining performance, SPE takes an architectural perspective. The principles and techniques of

SPE form the basis for PASA^SM, a method for performance assessment of software architectures [4]. PASA was developed from experience in conducting performance assessments of multiple software architectures in several application domains including web-based systems, financial applications, and real-time systems. It uses the principles and techniques described in this chapter to determine whether an architecture is capable of supporting its performance objectives. When a problem is found, PASA also identifies strategies for reducing or eliminating those risks.

The PASA process consists of ten steps [4]. They are based on the SPE modeling process described below. The method may be applied to new development to uncover potential problems when they are easier and less expensive to fix. It may also be used when upgrading legacy systems to decide whether to continue to commit resources to the current architecture or migrate to a new one. And it may be used on existing systems with poor performance that require speedy correction.

The next section describes the SPE model-based approach. The SPE modeling process is then illustrated with a case study.

2. OVERVIEW OF SOFTWARE PERFORMANCE ENGINEERING

SPE is a model-based approach that uses deliberately simple models of software processing with the goal of using the simplest possible model that identifies problems with the system architecture, design, or implementation plans. These models are easily constructed and solved to provide feedback on whether the proposed software is likely to meet performance goals. As the software process proceeds, the models are refined to more closely represent the performance of the emerging software.

The precision of the model results depends on the quality of the estimates of resource requirements. Because these are difficult to estimate for software architectures, SPE uses adaptive strategies, such as upper- and lower-bounds estimates and best- and worst-case analysis to manage uncertainty. For example, when there is high uncertainty about resource requirements, analysts use estimates of the upper and lower bounds of these quantities. Using these estimates, analysts produce predictions of the best-case and worst-case performance. If the predicted best-case performance is unsatisfactory, they seek feasible alternatives. If the worst-case prediction is satisfactory, they proceed to the next step of the development process. If the

---

^SM PASA and Performance Assessment of Software Architectures Method are service marks of Software Engineering Research and Performance Engineering Services.

results are somewhere in between, analyses identify critical components whose resource estimates have the greatest effect and focus on obtaining more precise data for them. A variety of techniques can provide more precision, including: further refining the architecture and constructing more detailed models or constructing performance prototypes and measuring resource requirements for key components.

Two types of models provide information for architecture assessment: the *software execution model* and the *system execution model*. The software execution model is derived from UML models of the software. It represents key aspects of the software execution behavior. It is constructed using execution graphs [3] to represent workload scenarios. Nodes represent functional components of the software; arcs represent control flow. The graphs are hierarchical with the lowest level containing complete information on estimated resource requirements.

Solving the software execution model provides a static analysis of the mean, best- and worst-case response times. It characterizes the resource requirements of the proposed software alone, in the absence of other workloads, multiple users or delays due to contention for resources. If the predicted performance in the absence of these additional performance-determining factors is unsatisfactory, then there is no need to construct more sophisticated models. Software execution models are generally sufficient to identify performance problems due to poor architectural decisions.

If the software execution model indicates that there are no problems, analysts proceed to construct and solve the system execution model. This model is a dynamic model that characterizes the software performance in the presence of factors, such as other workloads or multiple users, which could cause contention for resources. The results obtained by solving the software execution model provide input parameters for the system execution model. Solving the system execution model provides the following additional information:

- refinement and clarification of the performance requirements
- more precise metrics that account for resource contention
- sensitivity of performance metrics to variations in workload composition
- identification of bottleneck resources
- comparative data on options for improving performance via: workload changes, software changes, hardware upgrades, and various combinations of each
- scalability of the architecture and design: the effect of future growth on performance
- identification of critical parts of the design
- assistance in designing performance tests
- effect of new software on service level objectives of other systems

The system execution model represents the key computer resources as a network of queues. Queues represent components of the environment that provide some processing service, such as processors or network elements. Environment specifications provide device parameters (such as CPU size and processing speed). Workload parameters and service requests for the proposed software come from the resource requirements computed by solving the software execution model. The results of solving the system execution model identify potential bottleneck devices and correlate system execution model results with software components.

If the model results indicate that the performance is likely to be satisfactory, developers proceed. If not, the model results provide a quantitative basis for reviewing the proposed architecture and evaluating alternatives. Feasible alternatives can be evaluated based on their cost-effectiveness. If no feasible, cost-effective alternative exists, performance goals may need to be revised to reflect this reality.

3.   THE SPE MODELING PROCESS

The SPE modeling process focuses on the system's use cases and the scenarios that describe them. In a use-case-driven process such as the Unified Process [5,6], use cases are defined as part of requirements definition (or earlier) and are refined throughout the design process. From a development perspective, use cases and their scenarios provide a means of understanding and documenting the system's requirements, architecture, and design. From a performance perspective, use cases allow you to identify the *workloads* that are significant from a performance point of view, that is, the collections of requests made by the users of the system. The scenarios allow you to derive the processing steps involved in each workload.

The SPE process includes the following steps. The activity diagram in Figure 16-1 captures the overall process.

1. Assess performance risk: Assessing the performance risk at the outset of the project tells you how much effort to put into SPE activities. If the project is similar to others that you have built before, is not critical to your mission or economic survival, and has minimal computer and network usage, then the SPE effort can be minimal. If not, then a more significant SPE effort is needed.

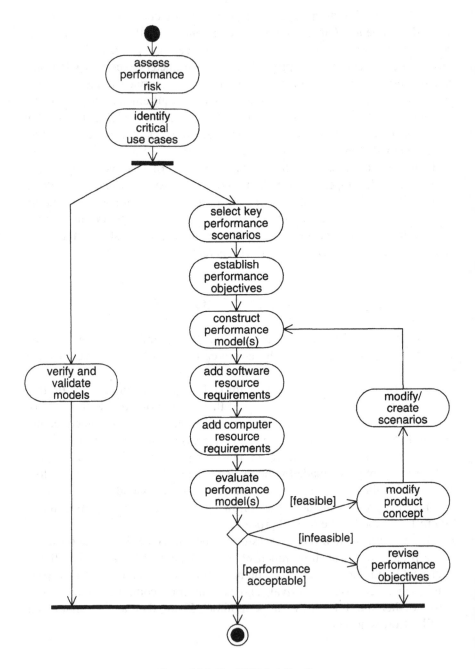

Figure 16-1. The SPE Modeling Process

2. Identify *critical use cases*: The critical use cases are those that are important to the operation of the system, or that are important to responsiveness as seen by the user. The selection of critical use cases is also risk driven. You look for use cases where there is a risk that, if performance goals are not met, the system will fail or be less than successful.

   Typically, the critical use cases are only a subset of the use cases that are identified during object-oriented analysis. In the UML, use cases are represented by use case diagrams.

3. *Select key performance scenarios*: It is unlikely that all of the scenarios for each critical use case will be important from a performance perspective. For each critical use case, the key performance scenarios are those that are executed frequently, or those that are critical to the perceived performance of the system. Each performance scenario corresponds to a workload. We represent scenarios by using sequence diagrams augmented with some useful extensions.

4. *Establish performance objectives*: You should identify and define *performance objectives* and *workload intensities* for each scenario selected in step 2. Performance objectives specify the quantitative criteria for evaluating the performance characteristics of the system under development. These objectives may be expressed in three primary ways by response time, throughput, or constraints on resource usage. For information systems, response time is typically described from a user perspective, that is, the number of seconds required to respond to a user request. For real-time systems, response time is the amount of time required to respond to a given external event. Throughput requirements are specified as the number of transactions or events to be processed per unit of time.

   Workload intensities specify the level of usage for the scenario. They are specified as an arrival rate (e.g., number of sensor readings per second) or number of concurrent users.

   Repeat steps 5 through 8 until there are no outstanding performance problems.

5. *Construct performance models*: We use execution graphs to represent software processing steps in the performance model. The sequence-diagram representations of the key performance scenarios are translated to execution graphs.

6. *Determine software resource requirements:* The processing steps in an execution graph are typically described in terms of the software resources that they use. Software resource requirements capture computational needs that are meaningful from a software perspective. For example, we

might specify the number of messages sent or the number of database accesses required in a processing step.

You base estimates of the amount of processing required for each step in the execution graph on the operation specifications for each object involved. This information is part of the class definition in the class diagram. When done early in the development process, these may be simple best- and worst-case estimates. Later, as each class is elaborated, the estimates become more precise.

7. *Add computer resource requirements:* Computer resource requirements map the software resource requirements from step 6 onto the amount of service they require from key devices in the execution environment. Computer resource requirements depend on the environment in which the software executes. Information about the environment is obtained from the UML deployment diagram and other documentation. An example of a computer resource requirement would be the number of CPU instructions and disk I/Os required for a database access.

Steps 6 and 7 could be combined, and the amount of service required from key devices estimated directly from the operation specifications for the steps in the scenario. However, this is more difficult than estimating software resources in software-oriented terms and then mapping them onto the execution environment. In addition, this separation makes it easier to explore different execution environments in "what if" studies.

8. *Evaluate the models:* Solving the execution graph characterizes the resource requirements of the proposed software alone. If this solution indicates that there are no problems, you can proceed to solve the system execution model. This characterizes the software's performance in the presence of factors that could cause contention for resources, such as other workloads or multiple users.

If the model solution indicates that there are problems, there are two alternatives:

–   *Modify the product concept:* Modifying the product concept involves looking for feasible, cost-effective alternatives for satisfying this use case instance. If one is found, we modify the scenario(s) or create new ones and solve the model again to evaluate the effect of the changes on performance.

–   *Revise performance objectives:* If no feasible, cost-effective alternative exists, then we modify the performance goals to reflect this new reality.

It may seem unfair to revise the performance objectives if you can't meet them (if you can't hit the target, redefine the target). It is not wrong if you do it at the outset of the project. Then all of the stakeholders in the system can decide if the new goals are acceptable. On the other hand, if you get to the end of the project, find that you didn't meet your goals, and *then* revise the objectives—*that's* wrong.

9. *Verify and validate the models*: Model verification and validation are ongoing activities that proceed in parallel with the construction and evaluation of the models. Model verification is aimed at determining whether the model predictions are an accurate reflection of the software's performance. It answers the question, "Are we building the model right?" For example, are the resource requirements that we have estimated reasonable?

Model validation is concerned with determining whether the model accurately reflects the execution characteristics of the software. It answers the question [7], "Are we building the right model?" We want to ensure that the model faithfully represents the evolving system. Any model will only contain what we think to include. Therefore, it is particularly important to detect any model omissions as soon as possible.

Both verification and validation require measurement. In cases where performance is critical, it may be necessary to identify critical components, implement or prototype them early in the development process, and measure their performance characteristics. The model solutions help identify which components are critical.

These steps describe the SPE process for one phase of the development cycle, and the steps repeat throughout the development process. At each phase, you refine the performance models based on your increased knowledge of details in the design. You may also revise analysis objectives to reflect the concerns that exist for that phase.

4.   CASE STUDY

To illustrate the process of modeling and evaluating the performance of a real-time system, we will use an example based on a telephony switch. This is not a hard real-time system, but it does have some important performance objectives that are driven primarily by economic considerations: a telephony system should be able to handle as many calls per hour as possible.

The case study is based on information in [8] and our own experience. It is not intended to be representative of any existing system. Some aspects of the call processing have been simplified so that we may focus on the basic performance issues and modeling techniques.

4.1   Overview

When a subscriber places a call, the local switch (the one that is connected to the caller's telephone) must perform a number of actions to set up and connect the call, and, when the call is completed, it must be cleared. For simplicity, we'll focus on the simplest type of call, often referred to as POTS (plain, ordinary telephone service). Figure 16-2 schematically illustrates the connection between the calling and called telephones. Note that switches A and B may be connected directly, or they may be connected by a route through the public switched telephone network (PSTN). It is also possible that the calling and called telephones are connected to the same local switch.

Figure 16-2. Telephony Network

The following sections illustrate the application of the SPE process to this case study.

4.1.1   Assess Performance Risk (Step 1)

Performance is very important, however, the construction of telephony software is well understood. This project will be the first time that this development organization has used object-oriented technology. Thus, because this technology is unfamiliar, we rate the performance risk as high. As a result, the SPE effort will be substantial, perhaps as much as 10% of the overall project budget.

4.1.2   Identify Critical Use Cases (Step 2)

Since we're limiting ourselves to POTS calls, the only use cases are PlaceACall and ReceiveACall. In placing or receiving a call, the local switch interacts directly with only one other switch in the PSTN. There may, however, be several intermediary switches involved between the caller and the receiver of the call.

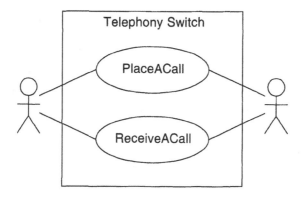

Figure 16-3. POTS Use Case Diagram

4.1.3 Select Key Performance Scenarios (Step 3)

Figure 16-4 shows the sequence of events required to complete a call for a customer. For simplicity, we show only two switches in the PSTN. The rectangle labeled loop is an iterator and the rounded rectangle is a reference to another sequence diagram. These extensions to the UML sequence diagram notation are taken from the MSC standard [9]. For more details on these extensions, see [3].

The sequence of events is as follows:

1. The caller picks up the telephone handset, generating an offHook event to the switch. The switch responds by applying a dial tone to the telephone.

2. The caller then dials a number of digits. The number of digits dialed may depend on the type of call (local versus long distance).

3. The switch analyzes the dialed digits, determines which outgoing trunk to use, and transmits a connect message to the next switch. This message "seizes" or reserves the connection until the call is completed.

4. The destination switch applies a ring signal to the called telephone, and sends an alerting message back to the originating switch which, in turn, applies a ringback tone to the calling telephone.

5. When the called subscriber answers, the destination switch sends an answer message to the calling switch, which completes the connection to the caller's telephone. The call then proceeds until one of the parties hangs up.

6. When one of the parties hangs up, an onHook message is transmitted to his/her local switch. That switch then sends a release message to the other switch.

7. When the other party hangs up, a clear message is returned.

Our task is to provide the software that manages the processing of a call for an individual switch.[57]

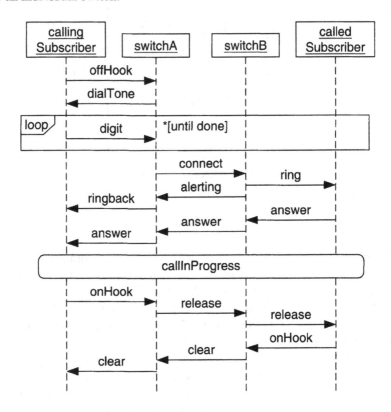

Figure 16-4. Call Sequence Diagram

4.1.4   Establish Performance Objectives (Step 4)

We'll assume that a performance walkthrough has determined that a module should be able to set up three originating calls per second, and handle their setup within 0.5 second.

---

[57] The sequence diagram in Figure 16-4 shows one scenario from the PlaceACall use case. There are several other scenarios belonging to this use case. For example, some calls receive a busy signal, some are unanswered, sometimes the caller hangs up before the call can be answered, and so on. For this example, we focus on the scenario described by Figure 16-4. Later, we'll discuss how to include these other possibilities.

4.1.5   Construct Performance Models (Step 5)

To construct the performance models, we need to know the details of the processing that is performed during the execution of the scenario in Figure 16-4. We begin with an overview of the architecture and design of the switch.

A telephony switch serves a number of lines for subscriber telephones and trunks, over which calls can be made to, or arrive from, other switches. To make it possible to easily field switches of different capacities, or upgrade an existing switch to handle more lines, it has been decided that the switch will be composed of a number of module processors. Each module processor serves a fixed number of lines or trunks. To increase the capacity of a particular switch, we simply add more module processors, up to the maximum capacity of the switch.

When a subscriber places a call, it is handled by the module processor that is connected to the user's telephone (the *calling* module processor). The calling module processor sets up the call and determines a path through the switch to a module processor (the *called* module processor) connected to the required outgoing line or trunk. The outgoing line may be attached to the called party's telephone, or it may be connected via an outgoing trunk to another switch in the PSTN.

Each module also has a line/trunk interface. This interface provides analog-to-digital and digital-to-analog conversion for analog telephone lines, as well as capabilities for communication with other switches via trunks. The line/trunk interface also provides a path for communication with other modules within the same switch.

With this architecture, each call is handled by two module processors within each switch: a calling module processor and a called module processor. Each module needs objects to manage its view of the call.

To accommodate the two views of a call, we use two active classes: an OriginatingCall and a TerminatingCall, as shown in Figure16-5.[58] For each call, there is an instance of OriginatingCall in the calling module processor, and an instance of TerminatingCall in the called module processor. Each instance of OriginatingCall and TerminatingCall has a DigitAnalyzer object to analyze the dialed digits, and a (shared) Path object to establish and maintain the connection. These are passive objects that execute on the thread of control belonging to their respective call objects.

---

[58] The active classes are indicated using the usual stereotype of a thick-bordered rectangle.

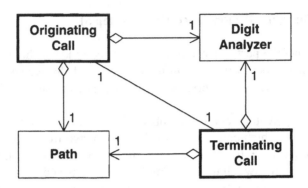

Figure 16-5. Class Diagram

When a subscriber goes "off hook," an OriginatingCall object is created to handle the call. The OriginatingCall object, in turn, creates instances of DigitAnalyzer and Path as needed. (The Path object maintains the physical connection through the switch—it does not need to interact with other objects.) The refined sequence diagram for call origination is shown in Figure 16-6. There is a similar refined sequence diagram for call termination which is not shown here.

The software model for call origination is straightforward; there is no looping or branching. The only issue in constructing this model is how to handle the time between when the call is connected and when one of the parties hangs up. We could estimate an average call duration, and include it as a delay corresponding to the callInProgress step in the sequence diagram. This is awkward, however, and the long delay will hide more interesting aspects of the model solution.

It is much simpler to divide this scenario into two parts: one for initiating the call, and one for ending the call. Thus, we create a separate performance scenario for originating a call and for a hang-up. The hang-up scenario would have the same intensity (arrival rate) as call origination, because every call that is begun must also be ended.

We actually have four performance scenarios for each module processor: call origination (for calls that originate in that module); call termination (for calls that terminate in that module), calling-party hang-up (for when the calling party hangs up first), and called-party hang-up (for when the called party hangs up first).

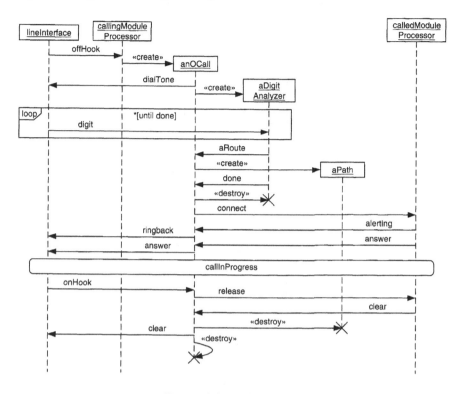

Figure 16-6. Call Origination

Figure 16-7 shows the execution graph for call origination. Most of the nodes in this execution graph are expanded nodes that aggregate several steps in the sequence diagram of Figure16-6. This graph shows the major steps in call origination.

Figure 16-8 shows the execution graph corresponding to the calling party ending the call.

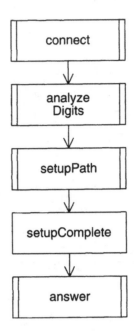

Figure 16-7. Call Origination Execution Graph

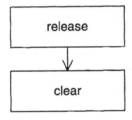

Figure 16-8. Calling-Party Hang-Up Execution Graph

4.1.6   Determine Software Resource Requirements (Step 6)

The types of software resources will differ depending on the type of application and the operating environment. The types of software resources that are important for the telephony switch are:
- CPU—the number CPU instructions (in thousands) executed for each step in the scenario
- Line I/F—the number of visits to the line interface for each step in the scenario

We specify requirements for each of these resources for each processing step in the execution graph. Figure 16-9 and Figure 16-10 show the expansion of the first two nodes in the call origination execution graph of Figure 16-7. The figures also show the resource requirements for each node. Again, these resource requirements are reasonable for this type of system, but are not representative of any particular telephony switch. Details for other nodes are omitted to save space.

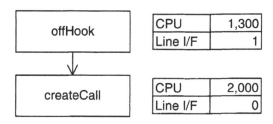

Figure 16-9. Expansion of connect node

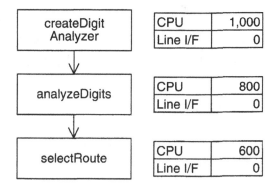

Figure 16-10. Expansion of analyzeDigits node

4.1.7   Add Computer Resource Requirements (Step 7)

We must also specify the *computer resource requirements* for each software resource request. The values specified for computer resource requirements connect the values for software resource requirements to device usage in the target environment. The computer resource requirements also specify characteristics of the operating environment, such as the types of processors/devices, how many of each, their speed, and so on.

Table 16-1 is known as an overhead matrix; it contains the computer resource requirements for the telephony switch. There are two devices of interest: the CPU and the line interface. CPU requirements are specified in units of K instructions.

Table 16-1. Overhead Matrix

Devices	CPU	Line I/F
Quantity	1	1
Service Units	K Instr.	Visits

CPU	1	
Line I/F	100	1

Service Time	.000015	.005

Several processing steps require sending or receiving one or more messages via the line interface. We could explicitly model the sending or receiving of each message. However, that level of detail complicates the model and adds nothing to our understanding of the software's performance. Instead, we include the line interface as overhead, and specify the number of visits to the line interface to send or receive a message for each processing step. Each visit to the line interface requires 100K CPU instructions and a 5 ms. delay to enqueue or dequeue a message and perform the associated processing.

4.1.8   Evaluate the Models (Step 8)

The arrival rate for the call origination scenario is 3 calls per second. For each originating call in one module, there must be a corresponding terminating call in some other module. Thus, on average, each module must also handle three termination calls per second.

To derive intensities for the hang-up scenarios, we'll assume that the probability of the calling party hanging up first is the same as the probability of the called party hanging up first. Then, the arrival rates for these scenarios are the same and, to keep a steady-state rate of calls, they must each also be 3 calls per second. Table 16-2 summarizes the workload intensities for the four scenarios.

Table 16-2. Workload Intensities

Scenario	Intensity
Call Origination	3 calls/sec
Call Termination	3 calls/sec
Calling Party Hang-Up	3 calls/sec
Called Party Hang-Up	3 calls/sec

For this example, we focus on the call origination scenario. We'll follow the simple-model strategy and begin with the software execution model. This will tell us whether we can meet the goal of 3 calls per second in the best case—with no contention between scenarios. Figure 16-11 shows the solution for the software execution model (no contention) for this scenario. The overall response time is 0.2205 second. The time required to set up the call is 0.1955 second (0.2205 - 0.0250).[59]

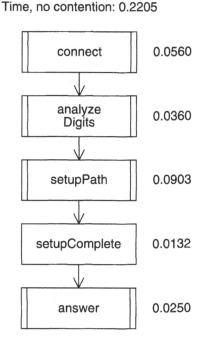

Time, no contention: 0.2205

connect	0.0560
analyze Digits	0.0360
setupPath	0.0903
setupComplete	0.0132
answer	0.0250

Figure 16-11. Software Execution Model Solution

The response time indicated by the software model is well within our goal of 0.5 second, so we proceed to solve the system model to determine the effects of contention for this one scenario. The system model solution indicates a residence time of 0.3739 second for call setup. This is still within

---

[59] The time to set up a call does not correspond directly to the end-to-end time for the execution graph of Figure16-7. Call setup does not include the processing that occurs after the called party has answered (the last node in the graph). Thus, the time to set up the call is taken to be the time from when the user goes "off hook" until the setupComplete step is done (the first four nodes in Figure 16-7).

our required time limit. Table 16-3 shows the residence time, time for call setup, and CPU utilization for each of the four scenarios.

Table 16-3. Contention Results for Individual Scenarios with Object Creation

Scenario	Residence Time	Setup Time	CPU Utilization
Call Origination	0.4156 sec	0.3739 sec	0.53
Call Termination	0.2326 sec	0.2143 sec	0.38
Hang-Up (Called Party)	0.0492 sec		0.12
Hang-Up (Caller)	0.0661 sec		0.14

We now proceed to the next level of complexity in our modeling, constructing and solving the system execution model for all four scenarios. The solution to this model will show the effects of contention among the four scenarios for system resources. The solution indicates a residence time of 16.31 seconds for call setup. This is clearly well over our design goal of 0.5 second.

The reason for this high number can be found by examining the CPU utilization. With all four scenarios executing on the same processor, the CPU utilization is 1.00—the CPU is saturated. In fact, if you add the utilizations for the individual scenarios in Table 16-3, you find that they total more than 1.00!

The formula for residence time at a device is:

$$RT = S/(1 - U)$$

Where S is the service time and U is the utilization.

As the CPU utilization gets closer to 1, the residence time goes to infinity. Our result of more than 16 seconds is an indication that the denominator in this formula is approaching zero.

To meet our design goal, we must reduce the CPU utilization. While no single scenario exceeds the limits, the combined demand on the CPU is enough to put us over the limit.

If we pre-allocate a block of call objects instead of creating them dynamically, we can save this unnecessary overhead. This is an example of "recycling" objects—one of the recommended refactorings of the Excessive Dynamic Allocation antipattern [3]. Each call object is used over and over again, rather than creating a new one for each offHook event.

When this change is made, the software model result for call origination becomes 0.1280 second (call setup only), and the contention solution for this scenario is 0.1726 second. Table 16-4 shows the residence time, time for call setup, and CPU utilization for each of the four scenarios without dynamic object creation.

Table 16-4. Contention Results for Individual Scenarios without Object Creation

Scenario	Residence Time	Setup Time	CPU Utilization
Call Origination	0.2048 sec	0.1726 sec	0.32
Call Termination	0.1243 sec	0.1087 sec	0.22
Hangup (Called Party)	0.0224 sec		0.05
Hangup (Caller)	0.0376 sec		0.08

Solving the system execution model with all four revised scenarios shows a residence time for call origination of 0.3143 second, with an overall CPU utilization of 0.68, which is within our performance objective.

We have been following the simple-model strategy [3]; at each step building the simplest possible model that will uncover any problems. We have modeled call processing assuming that all calls are actually completed. As we noted earlier, this is not the actual case. In fact, some calls receive a busy signal, some are unanswered, sometimes the caller hangs-up before the call can be answered, and so on. At this point, we might go back and include these other possibilities. We could then construct scenarios for these additional possibilities, and use either probabilities or arrival rates to reflect the percent of time that they occur.

We'll leave the construction and solution of these additional models as an exercise for the reader.[60]

4.1.9   Verify and Validate the Models (Step 9)

We need to confirm that the performance scenarios that we selected to model are critical to performance, and confirm the correctness of the workload intensity specifications, the software resource specifications, the computer resource specifications, and all other values that are input into the model. We also need to make sure that there are no large processing requirements that are omitted from the model. To do this, we will conduct measurement experiments on the operating environment, prototypes, and analogous or legacy systems early in the modeling process. We will measure evolving code as soon as viable. SPE suggests using early models to identify components critical to performance, and implementing them first. Measuring

---

[60] Motivated readers will find this example in [3]. It is possible to obtain the models from www.perfeng.com for further study using the methods explained in the book.

them and updating the model estimates with measured values increases precision in key areas early.

5.   SUMMARY

Architectural decisions are among the earliest made in a software development project. They are also among the most costly to fix if, when the software is completed, the architecture is found to be inappropriate for meeting performance objectives. Thus, it is important to be able to assess the impact of architectural decisions on performance at the time that they are made. The SPE process focuses on the system's use cases and the scenarios that describe them. This focus allows you to identify the workloads that are most significant to the software's performance, and to focus your efforts where they will do the most good.

SPE begins early in the software development process to model the performance of the proposed architecture and high-level design. The models help to identify potential performance problems when they can be fixed quickly and economically.

Performance modeling begins with the software execution model. You identify the use cases that are critical from a performance perspective, select the key scenarios for these use cases, and establish performance objectives for each scenario. To construct the software execution model, you translate the sequence diagram representing a key scenario to an execution graph. This establishes the processing flow for the model. Then, you add software and computer resource requirements and solve the model.

If the software execution model solution indicates that there are no performance problems, you can proceed to construct and solve the system model to see if adding the effects of contention reveals any problems. If the software execution model indicates that there are problems, you should deal with these before going any further. If there are feasible, cost-effective alternatives, you can model these to see if they meet the performance goals. If there are no feasible, cost-effective alternatives, you will need to modify your performance objectives, or perhaps reconsider the viability of the project.

To be effective, the SPE steps described in this chapter should be an integral part of the way in which you approach software development. SPE can easily be incorporated into your software process by defining the milestones and deliverables that are appropriate to your organization, the project, and the level of SPE effort required.

The quantitative techniques described in this chapter form the core of the SPE process. SPE is more than models and measurements, however. Other aspects of SPE focus on creating software that has good performance characteristics, as well as on identifying and correcting problems when they arise. They include [3]:

- Applying *performance principles* to create architectures and designs with the appropriate performance characteristics for your application
- Applying *performance patterns* to solve common problems
- Identifying *performance antipatterns* (common performance problems) and refactoring them to improve performance
- Using *late life cycle techniques* to ensure that the implementation meets performance objectives

By applying these techniques, you will be able to cost-effectively build performance into your software and avoid performance failures.

The SPE principles and techniques also form the basis for PASA^{SM}, a method for the performance assessment of software architectures. This method may be applied to new development to uncover potential problems when they are easier and less expensive to fix. It may also be used when upgrading legacy systems to decide whether to continue to commit resources to the current architecture or migrate to a new one. And it may be used on existing systems with poor performance that requires speedy correction. The topics not included here are explained in [3].

REFERENCES

[1] P. C. Clements and L. M. Northrup, "Software Architecture: An Executive Overview," Technical Report No. CMU/SEI-96-TR-003, Carnegie Mellon University, Pittsburgh, PA, February, 1996.

[2] C. U. Smith, *Performance Engineering of Software Systems*, Reading, MA, Addison-Wesley, 1990.

[3] C. U. Smith and L. G. Williams, *Performance Solutions: A Practical Guide to Creating Responsive, Scalable Software*, Boston, MA, Addison-Wesley, 2002.

[4] L. G. Williams and C. U. Smith, "PASA^{SM}: A Method for the Performance Assessment of Software Architectures," *Proceedings of the Third International Workshop on Software and Performance (WOSP2002)*, Rome, Italy, July, 2002, pp. 179-189.

[5] P. Kruchten, *The Rational Unified Process: An Introduction*, Reading, MA, Addison-Wesley, 1999.

[6] I. Jacobson, G. Booch, and J. Rumbaugh, *The Unified Software Development Process*, Reading, MA, Addison-Wesley, 1999.

[7] B. W. Boehm, "Verifying and Validating Software Requirements and Design Specifications," *IEEE Software*, vol. 1, no. 1, pp. 75-88, 1984.

[8] M. Schwartz, *Telecommunications Networks: Protocols, Modeling and Analysis*, Reading, MA, Addison-Wesley, 1988.

[9] ITU, "Criteria for the Use and Applicability of Formal Description Techniques, Message Sequence Chart (MSC)," International Telecommunication Union, 1996.

Index